terra australis 55

Terra Australis reports the results of archaeological and related research within the south and east of Asia, though mainly Australia, New Guinea and island Melanesia — lands that remained terra australis incognita to generations of prehistorians. Its subject is the settlement of the diverse environments in this isolated quarter of the globe by peoples who have maintained their discrete and traditional ways of life into the recent recorded or remembered past and at times into the observable present.

List of volumes in Terra Australis

terra australis 55

Histories of Australian Rock Art Research

Edited by Paul S.C. Taçon, Sally K. May,
Ursula K. Frederick and Jo McDonald

Australian
National
University

ANU PRESS

Australian
National
University

ANU PRESS

Published by ANU Press
The Australian National University
Canberra ACT 2600, Australia
Email: anupress@anu.edu.au

Available to download for free at press.anu.edu.au

ISBN (print): 9781760465353
ISBN (online): 9781760465360

WorldCat (print): 1341901099
WorldCat (online): 1341901071

DOI: 10.22459/TA55.2022

Terra Australis Editorial Board: Sue O'Connor, Sally Brockwell, Ursula Frederick, Tristen Jones and Mathieu Leclerc
Series Editor: Sue O'Connor

Cover design and layout by ANU Press. Cover photograph by Paul S.C. Taçon with permission of Injalak Traditional
Owner Julie Narndal.

This book is published under the aegis of the Terra Australis Editorial Committee of the ANU Press.

Contents

List of figures

List of tables

1

Introduction

Paul S.C. Taçon, Sally K. May, Ursula K. Frederick, Jo McDonald and Mary Blyth

In every field of research, there comes a time when its early practitioners are viewed as founding members and their actions become the subject of critical reflection. Now is that time for the study of Australian rock art. This complex history of research is imbued with unique personalities, international influences, politically charged debates and shifting relationships within and across established disciplines, such as archaeology. This is why we convened the Histories of Australian Rock Art Research Symposium at Griffith University's Gold Coast campus in December 2019. This symposium brought together people from across Australia to reflect on unique events, ideas and trajectories in the history of the study of Australian rock art (Table 1.1). With almost 30 presentations over two days, we had a full program representing the contemporary diversity of rock art research in Australia. This volume grew out of that symposium.

Figure 1.1: Histories of Australian Rock Art Research Symposium participants, Gold Coast campus, Griffith University, December 2019.
Source: Photograph by Emily Miller.

Table 1.1: List of speakers at the December 2019 Histories of Australian Rock Art Research Symposium, Griffith University, Gold Coast campus.

LeeAnne Bear	Wanjina Wunggurr Wilinggin Traditional Owner and Wilinggin Aboriginal Corporation
Mary Blyth	Miniaga Clan, Northern Territory
Liam Brady	Flinders University of South Australia
Emerald Brewer	Kombumerri Traditional Custodian, Welcome to Country
Adam Brumm	Griffith University
Patrick Churnside	Murujuga Aboriginal Corporation
Annie Clarke	University of Sydney
Noelene Cole	James Cook University
Victor Cooper	Ayal Aboriginal Tours, Kakadu
Tootsie Daniel	Murujuga Aboriginal Corporation
Robin Dann	Wanjina Wunggurr Wilinggin Traditional Owner, Wunggurr Rangers and Wilinggin Aboriginal Corporation
Iain Davidson	University of New England
Max Dillon	Kombumerri Traditional Custodian, Welcome to Country
Josephine Flood	Independent researcher
Ursula Frederick	University of Canberra
Joakim Goldhahn	University of Western Australia
Jake Goodes	Parks Victoria
Robert 'Ben' Gunn	Monash University
Sam Harper	University of Western Australia
Doug Hobbs	Archaeo Cultural Heritage
Jillian Huntley	Griffith University
Andrea Jalandoni	Griffith University
Iain G. Johnston	Australian Institute of Aboriginal and Torres Strait Island Studies
Tristen Jones	Australian National University
Richard Kuba	Frobenius Institute
Jeffrey Lee	Parks Australia (Kakadu)
Susan Lowish	University of Melbourne
Jo McDonald	University of Western Australia
Melissa Marshall	University of Notre Dame Broome
Kadeem May	Parks Australia (Kakadu)
Sally K. May	Griffith University
David Milroy	Budadee Aboriginal Corporation
Mark Moore	University of New England
Ken Mulvaney	Rio Tinto
Alfred Nayinggul	Njanjma Aboriginal Corporation
Lloyd Nulgit	Wanjina Wunggurr Wilinggin Traditional Owner and Wilinggin Aboriginal Corporation
Gabrielle O'Loughlin	Parks Australia (Kakadu)
Sven Ouzman	University of Western Australia
Folau Penaia	Worrora Traditional Owner, Dambimangari Aboriginal Corporation
Martin Porr	University of Western Australia
Mariah Reed	Murujuga Aboriginal Corporation
June Ross	University of New England
Benjamin Smith	University of Western Australia
Claire Smith	Flinders University of South Australia
Mike Smith	National Museum of Australia
Matthew Spriggs	Australian National University
Paul S.C. Taçon	Griffith University
Leah Umbagai	Worrora Traditional Owner, Dambimangari Aboriginal Corporation
Kelly Wiltshire	Australian Institute of Aboriginal and Torres Strait Island Studies

Source: Authors' summary.

Rock art may have been made soon after the arrival of people in Australia, as much as 65,000 years ago, given that vast quantities of used pieces of ochre have been recovered from the lowest levels of the archaeological deposits dating to this time at Madjedbebe (e.g. Clarkson et al. 2017). However, rock art is notoriously difficult to date, and most images across all parts of Australia do not have direct dates. Despite this, relative chronologies have been worked out across the continent, showing that rock art in Australia has a long history with lengthy sequences. In some parts of northern Australia, those long sequences can be shown to go back to the late Pleistocene (e.g. Finch et al. 2020, 2021), include a diversity of Holocene styles (e.g. McDonald 2017; Taçon et al. 2020), and hold contemporary Indigenous significance (e.g. Taçon 2019).

Rock art was remarked upon as soon as colonial settlers arrived in Australia from Europe in the late 1700s (e.g. Phillip 1789), and it fascinated early explorers such as Matthew Flinders (1814:188–189; Chapters 3 and 11, this volume) and Ludwig Leichhardt (1846:3; Chapter 11, this volume) in parts of the Northern Territory, George Grey (1841:175; 201–202; Chapter 10, this volume) in the Kimberley of Western Australia, and many others. However, the first British exploration parties to enter Central Australia from 1845 did not notice or remark upon rock art, with Ernest Giles (1889) the first to describe rock art for this region in 1872 (Chapter 8, this volume). In the late 1800s and early 1900s, anthropologists such as Robert H. Mathews (1894), Alfred C. Haddon (see Brady 2007 for Haddon's 1888 and 1898 recordings), W. Baldwin Spencer (1914; and see Gunn 2000), Norman Tindale (1925–26), A.P. Elkin (1930), James R.B. Love (1930), Daniel S. Davidson (1936) and Phyllis M. Kaberry (1939) were remarking on and studying rock art, along with professional surveyors and 'gentleman scholars' (such as W.D. Campbell and Lawrence Hargrave, see Frederick 2020).

Eventually, an archaeology of rock art developed with roots in the 1940s and driven by Fred McCarthy (Chapter 2, this volume). Our cover photo pays homage to this as the group of animated Northern Running Figures (also known as Mountford figures) was first photographed on the 1948 American–Australian Scientific Expedition to Arnhem Land that McCarthy was a key part of. In 1953, it was used by UNESCO on the cover of a travelling exhibition booklet on Australian Aboriginal culture (UNESCO 1953) and on or in related products (e.g. see UNESCO 1954:PL. VII and Chapter 11, this volume).

Through the 1960s and 1970s, contemporary formal Australian rock art research had its genesis in the work of John Clegg, Lesley Maynard at the University of Sydney (Chapter 4) and Andrée Rosenfeld at The Australian National University, Canberra (Chapter 5), along with other European-trained archaeologists such as like Michel Lorblanchet and Peter Ucko (e.g. see Lorblanchet et al. 2018; Ucko 1977). The arrival in Australia of Andrée Rosenfeld, with her experience of the European Upper Palaeolithic (Ucko and Rosenfeld 1967), and Patricia Vinnicombe with research in southern Africa (Vinnicombe 1976), brought new insights and dimensions to the study of Australian rock art (Chapter 4). The importance of the Form in Indigenous Art Symposium (Ucko 1977) as a catalyst for new research directions drawing on a number of international areas of practice is highlighted by several chapters (e.g. Chapters 4 and 9). However, many other people from various parts of the world were also making or soon would make advances in the recording, analysis and understanding of Australian rock art (e.g. see Chapters 9 and 11), including non-academics (such as George Chaloupka, Chapter 11; Percy Trezise, Chapter 13; Graeme Walsh, Chapter 10) and some artists (Chapters 6 and 13). Journalists, such as Colin Simpson (1951), filmmakers such as Kim McKenzie (2006) and other media professionals have also actively promoted Australian rock art research since the late 1940s but especially since the 1990s (Taçon 2001:552–554, 2012).

In this volume, the first attempt to detail a suite of Australian rock art research histories (but also see Taçon 2001:531–534 for a summary; Morwood and Smith 1994 for the period 1974–1994), we explore the work of hundreds of people, from Australia and many other parts of the world. We begin by focusing on some of the individuals who helped shape the early history of Australian rock art research, even though their contributions may be little known (Chapter 3). There are many others who might have been included in this early period of developing rock art research, such as Bob Edwards (presented at the symposium and published in Smith et al. 2021). However, most key individuals are mentioned in subsequent chapters that take a regionally focused approach (e.g. George Chaloupka in Chapter 11, Josephine Flood and Percy Trezise in Chapter 13, Grahame Walsh in Chapter 10), as are some of the organisations that have promoted Australian rock art research (see especially Chapter 4). The work of Robert Bednarik in the Pilbara region is acknowledged in Chapter 9, while his promotion of Australian and world rock art research through the launch of the journal *Rock Art Research* has been discussed elsewhere (e.g. Morwood and Smith 1994:25; Reddy 2007; Taçon 2001:532).

Indigenous Australians were also instrumental in the study of their rock art heritage, with many generations working alongside non-Indigenous researchers to document this key part of their living cultures (e.g. Taçon 2001:546–552). Increasingly, this vital contribution is acknowledged but there are, no doubt, many Indigenous rock art research collaborators historically that have not been publicly credited, just as many Indigenous guides, co-researchers and knowledge-keepers have only recently been recognised in the scholarly literature. Across Arnhem Land, Aboriginal people have been engaged in rock art research as much as non-Aboriginal people (Chapter 11, this volume), often playing an active role in locating, interpreting and recording rock art (e.g. McCarthy and Kulpidja, see Chapter 2, this volume). The collaboration of Aboriginal people with researchers has been a key, ongoing feature of rock art research in the Laura/Quinkan region of Cape York Peninsula since the 1960s (Chapter 13). Collaboration (or not) is the focus of the last paper of this volume. In Chapter 14, rock art research by Australian-affiliated researchers in Southeast Asia and Micronesia is explored in terms of how they collaborated with local researchers and communities. This rock art research is a logical extension of recent rock art research findings and interests in Australia, especially northern Australia, and some of Australia's leading rock art scholars continue to conduct research both in Australia and beyond to the north.

The Gold Coast symposium emphasised a diversity of views and approaches to not only the study of Australian and nearby rock art but also the contextualisation and interpretation of its history. In terms of how rock art should be studied in the future, it was stressed that the involvement and ownership of relevant Indigenous communities is paramount. Rock art should be studied with respect – for the rock art itself, the cultures that produced it, the contemporary, descendant Indigenous communities associated with it and for whom it is often part of living culture, and the land where rock art remains and about which important stories are held for contemporary communities.

In the symposium there were a number of Aboriginal participants (e.g. Chapters 7 and 12) and audience members from across Australia and some of their sentiments are expressed by Mary Blyth in the closing remarks of this preface and introduction. As is pointed out in Chapter 11, with over 31 years of experience, Mary has been involved with rock art research and researchers in western Arnhem Land more than any other First Nations person. For the symposium, she chose an interview-style presentation, some of which is captured below, setting the scene for the chapters that follow.

Closing remarks by Miniaga Traditional Owner Mary Blyth (questions by Paul S.C. Taçon)

1. What first got you interested in rock art?

I became a ranger so that I could look after Country. Listening to the Elders telling stories and being shown amazing Country with rock art, I became interested in the way it was told as a story and recorded in this way.

2. What were some of the biggest challenges you faced managing rock art?

The way I see it is women weren't really considered to have a role in managing rock art as they weren't painters, they were generally the weavers and more domestic. When working at Parks [Australia] it was usually the men going out working in teams to do the recording and maintenance of rock art sites. In the early days, women weren't invited as much or given the opportunity to go. Another issue was getting the resources needed to work with knowledgeable Elders who can pass on the stories of the art.

3. What were some of the rock art–related highlights of your long career?

Having the opportunity to get out in the escarpment to places I would never have had the opportunity to go and view the art. It was always hard work but being on Country was fun and rewarding.

4. What message do you have for rock art researchers today?

They should continue to do the right thing by Traditional Owners and, when the Traditional Owners want it, record everything you can so that we have this information to pass on to the future generations. Work closely with Traditional Owners, Parks, Aboriginal Organisations, to teach new skills to Bininj men and women and to help to record stories of paintings and giving local people the skills to manage and teach future generations the importance of research and keeping our culture alive.

5. What are some of the problems communities have had with past rock art research? How can we make sure it doesn't happen again?

In the past some researchers have taken the information they recorded with them and have not given it back to the local people or local organisations such as Parks. Some didn't even work with Traditional Owners but were doing it their own way. There has also been a lot of miscommunication between researchers and Traditional Owners. Researchers need to understand that English is not a first language for many people and they need to explain their work more clearly.

Researchers also need to have clear direction from Traditional Owners about what they and their communities want to be researched and how the work should be done. A written MoU [Memorandum of Understanding] that all parties agree to would be best. Work together!

6. What would you like to see happen in the future for the rock art of western Arnhem Land and Australia more generally?

It's important to keep monitoring the condition of the art and if and where necessary intervene and manage to prevent loss of pigments and further damage to the site.

7. Based on your long history and experience with rock art, rock art managers and rock art researchers, are there any last insights you would you like to share with us? Where to from here?

It is important to acknowledge and reflect upon those people past and present who have contributed to Rock Art Research. There have been good and bad experiences for communities, and we need to talk about these. But a lot of great work has been done by one and all over many years. My message to researchers is to listen to Bininj, support local communities with their work, and continue working together to capture 'our living culture and keep it alive' for future generations.

Figure 1.2: Mary Blyth with Paul S.C. Taçon, Ursula K. Frederick, Sally K. May and Jo McDonald, December 2019.
Source: Photograph by Annie Clarke.

Acknowledgements

We are indebted to the Australian Research Council (FL160100123), Griffith University and Australia ICOMOS (International Council on Monuments and Sites) for supporting the 2019 Histories of Australian Rock Art Research Symposium and this volume. Two anonymous referees are thanked for comments that substantially improved all chapters of this volume. Injalak Traditional Owner Julie Narndal is thanked for permission to use the cover photo. We are also very grateful to the many, many First Nations individuals and communities we have worked with while undertaking rock art research the past few decades. Without them none of this would have been possible.

References

Brady, L. 2007. A different look: Comparative rock-art recording from the Torres Strait using computer enhancement techniques. *Australian Aboriginal Studies* 2007(1):98–115.

Clarkson, C., Z. Jacobs, B. Marwick, R. Fullagar, L. Wallis, M. Smith, R.G. Roberts, E. Hayes, K. Lowe, X. Carah, S.A. Florin, J. McNeil, D. Cox, L.J. Arnold, Q. Hua, J. Huntley, H.E.A. Brand, T. Manne, A. Fairbairn, J. Shulmeister, L. Lyle, M. Salinas, M. Page, K. Connell, G. Park, K. Norman, T. Murphy and C. Pardoe 2017. Human occupation of northern Australia by 65,000 years ago. *Nature* 547:306–310. doi.org/10.1038/nature22968.

Davidson, S.D. 1936. *Aboriginal Australian and Tasmanian rock carvings and paintings*. Memoirs of the American Philosophical Society, Philadelphia.

Elkin, A.P. 1930. Rock-paintings of north-west Australia. *Oceania* 1(3):257–279. doi. org/10.1002/j.1834-4461.1930.tb01649.x.

Finch, D., A. Gleadow, J. Hergt, V. Levchenko, P. Heaney, P. Veth, S. Harper, S. Ouzman, C. Myers and H. Green 2020. 12,000-Year-old Aboriginal rock art from the Kimberley region, Western Australia. *Science Advances* 6, eaay3922. doi.org/10.1126/sciadv.aay3922.

Finch, D., A. Gleadow, J. Hergt, P. Heaney, H. Green, C. Myers, P. Veth, S. Ouzman and V. Levchenko 2021. Ages for Australia's oldest rock paintings. *Nature Human Behaviour* 5:310–318. doi.org/10.1038/s41562-020-01041-0.

Flinders, M. 1814. *A voyage to Terra Australis*. Volume 2. G. and W. Nicol, London.

Frederick, U.K. 2020. Flights of fancy: The production, reception and implications of Lawrence Hargrave's magic lantern lecture 'Lope de Vega'. In M. Jolly and E. DeCourcy (eds), *The magic lantern at Work: Witnessing, persuading, experiencing and connecting*, pp. 120–137. Routledge, London. doi.org/10.4324/9780429317576-8.

Giles, E. 1889. *Australia twice traversed: The romance of exploration, being a narrative compiled from the journals of five exploring expeditions into and through Central South Australia, and Western Australia, from 1872 to 1876* [Facsimile edition 1964]. Libraries Board of South Australia, Adelaide.

Grey, G. 1841. *Journals of two expeditions of discovery in north-west and Western Australia during the years 1837, 38 and 39*. T. and W. Boone, London.

Gunn, R.G. 2000. Spencer and Gillen's contribution to Australian rock art studies. *Rock Art Research* 17(1):56–74.

Kaberry, P.M. 1939. *Aboriginal women, sacred and profane*. George Routledge and Sons Ltd, London.

Leichhardt, L. 1846. Dr Leichardt's lectures (Lecture II). Delivered at School of Arts, on Tuesday, August 25. *The Sydney Morning Herald*, Thursday 27 August 1846.

Lorblanchet, M., G. Ward and K. Mulvaney 2018. *Archaeology and petroglyphs of Dampier (Western Australia) as archaeological investigation of Skew Valley and Gum Tree Valley*. Technical Reports of the Australian Museum, Online, Number 27. doi.org/10.3853/j.1835-4211.27.2018.1684.

Love, J.R.B. 1930. Rock paintings of the Worora and their mythological interpretation. *Journal of the Royal Society of Western Australia* 16:1–24.

Mathews, R.H. 1894. Aboriginal rock paintings and carvings in New South Wales. *Proceedings of the Royal Society of Victoria* 7:143–156.

McDonald, J. 2017. Discontinuities in arid zone rock art: Graphic indicators for changing social complexity across space and through time. *Journal of Anthropological Archaeology* 46:53–67. doi.org/10.1016/j.jaa.2016.08.005.

McKenzie, K. 2006. *Fragments of the owl's egg* [film]. Warddeken Productions, 38 min.

Morwood, M. and C. Smith 1994. Rock art research in Australia 1974–1994. *Australian Archaeology* 39:19–38. doi.org/10.1080/03122417.1994.11681525.

Phillip, A. 1789. *The voyage of Governor Phillip to Botany Bay: with contributions from other officers of the First Fleet and observations on affairs of the time by Lord Auckland*. John Stockdale, London.

Reddy, P.C. (ed.) 2007. *Exploring the mind of ancient man: Festschrift to Robert G. Bednarik*. Research India Press, New Delhi.

Simpson, C. 1951. *Adam in ochre: Inside Aboriginal Australia*. Angus and Robertson, Sydney.

Smith, M.A., J. Ross, and D. Kimber 2021. Robert Edwards and the history of Australian rock art research. *Historical Records of Australian Science* 32(1):41–51. doi.org/10.1071/HR20011.

Spencer, W. Baldwin 1914. *The native tribes of the Northern Territory of Australia*. Macmillan, London.

Taçon, P.S.C. 2001. Australia. In D. Whitley (ed.), *Handbook of rock art research*, pp. 530–575. Altamira Press, Walnut Creek, California.

Taçon, P.S.C. 2012. Presenting rock-art through digital film: Recent Australian examples. In B. Smith, K. Helskog and D. Morris (eds), *Working with rock art*, pp. 214–222. Wits University Press, Johannesburg.

Taçon, P.S.C. 2019. Connecting to the Ancestors: Why rock art is important for Indigenous Australians and their well-being. *Rock Art Research* 36(1):5–14.

Taçon, P.S.C., S.K. May, R. Lamilami, F. McKeague, I. Johnston, A. Jalandoni, D. Wesley, I. Domingo, L. Brady, D. Wright, and J. Goldhahn 2020. Maliwawa Figures – A previously undescribed Arnhem Land rock art style. *Australian Archaeology* 86(3):208–225. doi.org/10.1080/03122417.2020.1818361.

Tindale, N.B. 1925–26. Natives of Groote Eylandt and of the West Coast of the Gulf of Carpentaria, Parts 1 and 2. *Records of the South Australian Museum* 111(1 and 2):61–134.

Ucko, P. (ed.) 1977. *Form in Indigenous art: Schematisation in the art of Aboriginal Australia and prehistoric Europe*. Australian Institute of Aboriginal Studies, Canberra.

Ucko, P. and A. Rosenfeld 1967. *Paleolithic cave art*. Weidenfeld and Nicolson, London.

UNESCO (ed.) 1953. *Australian Aboriginal culture: An exhibition arranged by the Australian National Committee for UNESCO*. A.H. Pettifer, Govt. Printer, Sydney.

UNESCO (ed.) 1954. *Australia: Aboriginal paintings – Arnhem Land*. The New York Graphic Society, Milan.

Vinnicombe, P. 1976. *People of the Eland: Rock paintings of the Drakensberg Bushmen as a reflection of their life and thought*. University of Natal Press, Pietermaritzburg.

Part A: Early pioneers and perspectives

2

Style and substance: McCarthy versus Mountford and the emergence of an archaeology of rock art 1948–1960

Anne Clarke, Sally K. May, Ursula K. Frederick
and Iain G. Johnston

Introduction

The Australian rock art research community is no stranger to epic battles between individuals with differing viewpoints on rock art. These disputes are not a new phenomenon, as this paper outlines. It is rare, however, for these arguments to reflect major shifts in the nature of rock art research and, more broadly, archaeological research. In this paper we present the story of two individuals – Frederick 'Fred' McCarthy and Charles 'Monty' Mountford – whose rock art research and ongoing debates and disputes over methodologies and interpretive frameworks represent a foundational turning point in the history of Australian rock art research. Spanning the 1940s to the 1960s, their documentation of rock art during the 1948 American–Australian Scientific Expedition to Arnhem Land and their subsequent arguments reflect both antiquarianism and innovation (Figure 2.1). Importantly, these debates reflect an attempt to introduce scholarly standards and recognisable archaeological methods into rock art research in Australia as well as early struggles to link the evidence from archaeological excavations and recordings of rock art.

The feud: An introduction

> The claims made by Mountford are completely unfounded and incorrect, they are in fact downright unscientific. They demonstrate either a lack of understanding of the true value of records of superimposition in cave paintings, or a deliberate refusal to do so. (McCarthy to Evans, 18 January 1956)

This passage from a letter written in 1956 by a clearly exasperated Fred McCarthy to John Evans, the director of the Australian Museum, some eight years after the conclusion of the American–Australian Scientific Expedition to Arnhem Land (hereafter referred to as the Expedition) is fairly typical of the tenor of much of the correspondence written by members of the Expedition, both to each other and to their institutions (see below and Jones 2011:48–49, 52). Penned in the midst of a period of dispute over the authorship and order of volumes for the Expedition records, it cuts straight to the heart of the conflict over the methodologies and analytical frameworks employed in the recording of rock art during fieldwork in 1948, characterised here as a matter of substance versus style.

Figure 2.1: 'Group photograph of the members of the 1948 American–Australian Scientific Expedition to Arnhem Land, taken on Groote Eylandt.'

'From left to right, back row: Ray Specht, Brian Billington, Robert Miller, John Bray, Keith Cordon. Middle row: Kelvin Hodges, Margaret McArthur, Charles Mountford, Frank Setzler, Bert Deignan, Bessie Mountford. Front row: Frederick McCarthy, Peter Bassett-Smith, Harrison Howell (Hal) Walker, David Johnson. Not shown: Bill Harney, Reg Hollow'.

Source: Mountford-Sheard Collection, State Library of South Australia, PRG 1218/34/2847.

Mountford and McCarthy with a cameo by Norman Tindale

The scholarly and professional lives of Charles Pearcy Mountford (1890–1976), Frederick David McCarthy (1905–1997) and Norman Barnett Tindale (1900–1993) were entangled in ways that, although unexpected on first encounter, are perhaps not so surprising on deeper reflection. All three men were born around the turn of the twentieth century, their lives and careers encompassed by the late nineteenth and early twentieth-century traditions of antiquarian curiosity and the museological imperative of universal description and classification, culminating in the mid-to-late twentieth-century transition to more scientific methods of inquiry and analysis. In the first half of the twentieth century, the three men were among a handful of museum professionals, academics and independent scholars engaged in the study of Australian Indigenous cultures (Spriggs 2020). Although our research focuses on the deep and bitter feud between Mountford and McCarthy over the documentation, analysis and interpretation of Australian Aboriginal rock art, the imposing figure of Norman Tindale looms in the backstory to this historical altercation.

Tindale was colleague and adversary alike to both Mountford and McCarthy. Mountford wrote his first paper with Tindale in the *Transactions of the Royal Society of South Australia* for 1926, describing rock engravings at Morowie, South Australia (Tindale and Mountford 1926). In 1934 Tindale, accompanied by Mountford, excavated Kongarati Cave on the south coast of South Australia (Tindale and Mountford 1936), and in 1935 they both went on the expedition for the University of Adelaide Board of Anthropological Research to the Warburton Ranges in Western Australia. Mountford was employed as the photographer and to record Aboriginal art, while Tindale was leader and ethnologist (Tindale 1936). Tindale and McCarthy engaged in a decades-long tussle over their interpretations of the stratigraphic and stone tool sequences documented in excavations at Tartanga and Devon Downs, both excavated by Tindale (Hale and Tindale 1930; Tindale 1957), and Lapstone Creek excavated by McCarthy (e.g. 1948, 1958). In 1958 McCarthy took full aim at Tindale's 1957 attempt at a synthesis of a cultural sequence for south-eastern Australia. He believed Tindale's findings were 'premature and untenable', noting: 'For these reasons, the paper cannot be let go unchallenged, and I have tried, in this review to present an unbiased and impersonal criticism of the archaeological problems involved' (McCarthy 1958:177). Interestingly, Tindale's first substantive fieldwork in 1921 was on Groote Eylandt (Tindale 1925–26a, 1925–26b), coincidentally the first field location on the American–Australian Scientific Expedition to Arnhem Land and the setting where the initial 'terms of engagement' between Mountford and McCarthy over rock art came into sharp definition.

The feud: Authorship, rivalry, deceit and disputed ownership

Reflections on the history of the 1948 Expedition have been well published, firstly by Sally K. May in her 2009 book *Collecting cultures: Myth, politics, and collaboration in the 1948 Arnhem Land Expedition* and secondly via the various papers published in the 2011 edited volume, *Exploring the legacy of the 1948 Arnhem Land Expedition* (Thomas and Neale 2011). From February to November 1948, 17 researchers from an array of disciplines worked at base camps in Arnhem Land as part of a National Geographic Society and Australian Government–sponsored research expedition. While it might seem that scientific research was the key motivator for the expedition, in fact, politics and promoting collaboration with the USA was the reason it took place – while the Americans were funded via the National Geographic Society of America, the Australian contingent was funded by the Commonwealth Government and the Australian Broadcasting Commission (Simpson 1951; see also Jones 2011:49). The key base camps were Groote Eylandt, Yirrkala and Oenpelli. Under the overall leadership of Mountford, the team investigated the people, animals and environment of Arnhem Land and acquired substantial collections for both the Australian and Smithsonian museums. Official findings from their research were published in four volumes (Mountford 1956; Specht and Mountford 1958; Mountford 1960; Specht 1964) and featured in two popular *National Geographic* articles (Mountford 1949; Walker 1949; see also Simpson 1951).

Philip Jones (2011), in a delightfully engaging account of the politics and personality clashes that characterised the Expedition, sets out and contextualises how the conflicts between Mountford and the other Expedition members simmered away even before the team had assembled in Darwin in March 1948. The conflicts began in earnest at Umbakumba on Groote Eylandt, where the first

Expedition base camp was located. People actively chafed at Mountford's leadership style and personality, both in the field and, in the following years, as the expedition reports were prepared for publication. This extract from a letter sent to McCarthy by the American archaeologist Frank Setzler hints at these issues:

> I'm sure we never realized the type of individual nor the uncanny methods such a person would use to promote his own ego. After all, you were the only one of the Australian group that he could not completely dominate. (Setzler to McCarthy, 26 June 1957)

An extract from an earlier 1951 letter by McCarthy was more direct in outlining aspects of the field-based conflicts. More than 70 years later, it is still possible to hear the somewhat dismissive tone accompanying McCarthy's description of Mountford's field of study as 'art and legends':

> The insinuation that I intruded upon Mr. Mountford's field of study of art and legends can be answered simply by stating that whatever I did was with his permission as leader of the Expedition. (McCarthy to Walkom, c. 1951)

McCarthy was very clear in his own mind as to the reasons for Mountford's hostility towards him. In another blunt letter to the Australian Museum director, McCarthy (to Evans, October 1957) summarises what he considers to be the main reasons:

> There are several reasons for Mountford's hostility, as follows:
>
> 1. My refusal to grant him co-authorship of several papers (cave paintings of Chasm Id. To be separated from my main cave painting paper in the Expedition reports, and of two other papers published in our records) because I had done all of the work and he was not entitled in any way to joint authorship.
>
> 2. My analysis of Oenpelli cave painting sequences which he had failed to detect – he was extremely jealous of the work I did on cave paintings during the Expedition and has been critical of its results ever since.
>
> 3. The taking over from him of the Expedition's collection of bark paintings, after the late Professor Nadel had asked me for information about this collection and other material held by Mountford from the Expedition. It should be recorded here that there are several hundreds of wood carvings, sacred objects, etc., illustrated in vol. 1 of the Expedition Records by Mountford that were concealed by him during the course of the Expedition, and were not submitted for the sharing of the anthropological collection between the Australian Museum, U.S. National Museum, and the Commonwealth Government, although Mountford insisted as leader in taking his share of all other specimens. The Commonwealth Government took possession of the bark paintings held by Mountford but I do not know whether it also secured the wood carvings, sacred objects, etc. held by him.

As we can see from this letter, issues of authorship, methodology, access to collected materials for analysis, plus the incendiary accusations of deceitful practices over the institutional distribution of objects collected during the Expedition were all part of McCarthy's ongoing feud with Mountford.

Chasm Island

During the Expedition, it was a very small island, Chasm Island, located off the north coast of Groote Eylandt, that became the fulcrum for these disputes. Mountford had demanded joint publication of the data but McCarthy refused point blank to comply (McCarthy to Evans, October 1957) with the result that both men wrote about the rock art of Chasm Island in separate volumes.

The Expedition had landed on Groote Eylandt in early April 1948, when a series of mishaps with the delivery of food supplies and equipment meant that the Expedition members spent far longer – some 17 weeks – on Groote Eylandt than originally planned. In early July, in the week before finally departing for Yirrkala on the north-east Arnhem Land coast, a group, including Mountford and McCarthy, spent a few days exploring Chasm Island. It was on Chasm Island that the differences in methodology and analytical framing came to the fore and continued to reverberate long after the Expedition members packed up their notebooks and sample jars. Ongoing disputes over authorship and the order of volumes affected not only the Australian members of the Expedition but also the Americans, creating difficulties for the contributing institutions, as can be seen in a longer extract from Frank Setzler's letter to McCarthy.

> Unfortunately, he created a spell over Dr. Wetmore, who thinks he can do no wrong; moreover, N.G.S. does not want to interfere in another country's affairs. In this connection, Dr. and Mrs. Gilbert Grosvenor, the originators of the N.G.S., now retired, are planning a trip to Australia this fall. Perhaps you and the new director of your museum can urge the publication of vol. II. (Setzler to McCarthy, 26 June 1957)

Mountford's own single authored Expedition volume on Aboriginal art was the first to be published in 1956, with volume 3 on the botany and ecology of Arnhem Land published next in 1958 (Specht and Mountford 1958), and volume 2 on Arnhem Land anthropology and nutrition, including chapters on rock art and archaeology by McCarthy and McCarthy and Setzler, only appearing in 1960 (Mountford 1960). The following are examples of correspondence documenting the disputes over the Expedition Records.

> Might I suggest that it be pointed out to Mr. Mountford that a difficult situation has arisen in respect to the fact that he, as editor of the reports, is writing on the Chasm Island cave paintings according to his letter of 11th January, whilst I have described the paintings in a large number of sites on this island in a detailed and comparative systematic study. In these circumstances I do not feel disposed to submit my manuscript because it would place the editor in an invidious position. (McCarthy to Walkom, 8 June 1951)

> I am sorry to say that, due to my refusal to accept some very poor work from McCarthy, and his attempt to use political pressure, vol. II will follow Ray Specht's work Vol. III. (Mountford to unknown, 16 March 1957)

> It is obvious that Mountford's statement to the US National Museum about my 'very poor work' is for the purpose of discrediting me as his excuse for changing the order of publication of volumes II and III of the expedition reports. (McCarthy to Evans, 10 July 1957)

> The assertion that I 'have attempted to use political pressure' is a deliberate fabrication. The whole of the correspondence about the publication of papers has been conducted officially by Mountford, and not as it should be between author and editor. In this correspondence he has consistently exceeded his editorial rights by using every possible opportunity to disparage my work. (McCarthy to Evans, 10 July 1957)

> The reasons for the change in the order of publication of the volumes are certainly not those given to the US National Museum by Mountford. I feel he should be reproved by the Department of News and Information, which is handling the Expedition reports, and request to withdraw the remarks in his unwarranted attack upon me. (McCarthy to Evans, 10 July 1957)

> There has been a lot of acrimonious correspondence with Mr. Mountford over the Arnhem Land reports, but it is quite unjust that Mountford in this fashion should write about McCarthy's work, and certainly he has never attempted to use political pressure in any way at all. The reasons for Mountford's disparaging remarks are well-known to me and do him no credit. (Evans to Kellogg, 15 August 1957)

The published chapters and their accompanying images of rock art encapsulate the differences between the way that the two men approached both documentation and interpretation.

> Whilst there McCarthy made complete records of some of the painted caves on the western side [of Chasm Island], noting the relationship of the designs to each other, their superimpositions and their colours. My interest, on the other hand, was in the study of the art forms themselves. (Mountford 1956:102)

On Chasm Island, Mountford surveyed rock-shelters on the eastern and north-western sides, focusing on what he called 'predominant figures'. He only illustrates and discusses individual motifs – those he considered to be the singular and the exceptional, all identified without any clearly articulated criteria. There are no maps of the sites he documented, nor, indeed, an indication of how many he visited. His comments about the rock art are descriptive and assertive, for example: 'A is some lizard-like creature'. Mountford's cherry-picking approach to recording rock art leaves us with pages of decontextualised rock art drawings and lists of 'interpretations'. There are no clear methods and he shows no interest in recording context, spatial relationships, superimpositioning, media or techniques of production. He also formed the opinion in his conclusion that 'Groote Eylandt art is the simplest in the Arnhem Land area' (Mountford 1956:104).

Four years later, in the opening paragraph of his chapter on the 'Cave Paintings of Groote Eylandt and Chasm Island', McCarthy goes for the proverbial jugular, taking a large swipe at Mountford's primitivist and particularistic approach to the cave paintings:

> Most of the literature on Australian cave paintings deals with a selection of the outstanding figures in a particular site. In the few papers where all of the figures are described they are usually arranged conveniently for illustration so that their position in relationship to one another is not apparent. One result of the publication of such inadequate descriptions of sites from all over the continent, viewed from the comparative and chronological approaches, is that only incomplete data are available to the archaeologists, even though in some instances, the description satisfies the social anthropologist or the student of primitive art. (McCarthy 1960:297)

He goes on to outline his approach to the systematic and analytical study of rock art, noting in particular the importance of superimpositioning to understanding the chronology of styles and colours on Groote Eylandt:

> In the present study a systematic analytical method was adopted with the aim of overcoming some of these deficiencies, and of revealing the fundamental characteristics of the cave art on Groote Eylandt and Chasm Island; further, with the purpose of providing a complete record of the art represented in the groups recorded. (McCarthy 1960:297)

McCarthy provides a location map and a detailed description of each of the 27 sites he recorded, and the published drawings show the motifs in their spatial relationships. McCarthy used a grid system to record and contextualise his recordings (Clarke and Frederick 2011). His analysis focused on some basic statistics and includes a comparative analysis of the different sites, concluding with a schema of styles and a chronological sequence based on colour and superimpositions. In a final riposte to Mountford, McCarthy (1960:390) noted: 'The artistic merit of the paintings of Chasm Island and Groote Eylandt is equal to that elsewhere in Australia where representative, naturalistic painting occurs'.

Oenpelli (Gunbalanya)

By the time the Expedition reached its final base camp, tensions were boiling over (see May 2009:90–93). The differences in approaches to rock art recording were unchanged and neither Mountford nor McCarthy were in any mood to resolve their differences. Mountford dedicated his limited research time to acquiring bark paintings and visiting and photographing rock art sites near the Oenpelli settlement.

> The cave paintings of Oenpelli are more skilfully executed and more varied in design than in any other part of Arnhem Land; in fact, they are the most numerous and beautiful series of cave paintings that we know of in Australia. (Mountford 1956:109)

During the seven weeks they were camped at Oenpelli, Mountford documented paintings (Figure 2.2) on Injalak Hill, Arguluk Hill, and around Red Lily Lagoon (Inagurdurwil) as well as collecting bark paintings (Mountford 1956:109). On a later visit he added other areas to his study, including Ubirr and Cannon Hill in what is now Kakadu National Park. It is important to note that Mountford and his team were not welcomed by the Oenpelli missionaries and, as such, they were forced to work mainly with people from outside of the region, especially people from the Liverpool River region (Mountford 1956:111; May 2009:187).

Figure 2.2: An example of Mountford's 'polychrome X-ray art' from Injalak Hill.
Source: Photograph by Sally K. May.

As with Chasm Island, Mountford's methodology for recording rock art was far from systematic. He simply selected paintings of interest to him, photographed and/or sketched them and noted some basic characteristics (such as colours used). He argued for two basic periods/types of rock art at Oenpelli:

> They are (a) polychrome X-ray paintings of animals, birds, reptiles and fish, but seldom of human beings, in which both the external and internal details are indicated, many having been painted within the memory of living man; and (b) single-line drawings which, the aborigines claim, are not the work of their kind, but of a fairy people called the *Mimi*.

The polychrome X-ray art. Although aboriginal art, or for that matter any art, is visual, the X-ray art is, in addition, intellectual. The aboriginal artist of Oenpelli not only paints what he sees but also what he knows is there but cannot see: the skeleton, heart, lungs, stomach, intestines and other organs of the body …

The monochrome Mimi art. On the other hand, the *Mimi* artists had a feeling for composition and movement which the X-ray artists lacked. Their main subject was man in action, running, fighting and throwing spears. (Mountford 1956:112)

Mountford says little of superimposition, simply noting that:

Although there has been extensive over-painting in some of the galleries of the X-ray paintings, this characteristic was not often seen in the *Mimi* drawings. Groups of Mimi drawings, some containing as many as thirty figures, appear to have been complete compositions, conceived and carried out by one artist. (Mountford 1956:112)

Mountford's analysis is based upon his selection of key images from a site rather than looking at them in context – a key point of difference with McCarthy. He presents his results as individual motifs or scenes redrawn and then discussed individually in text. His interpretation is based on his own insights, mixed with ethnographic information drawn from previous research and occasionally from his own ethnographic research, though who he obtained this information from is not generally recorded.

Mountford's interpretation is clearly lacking in ethnographic detail and depth. For example, one painting depicting the widely known story of Yingarna, is simply described as a '*Mimi* woman with many carrying-bags suspended from her shoulders' (Mountford 1956:136; Figure 2.3). He attributes this interpretation to his informants, who he suggests could either not be bothered explaining the actual story of the painting, or did not want to share it with him. On occasion he compares the paintings with others elsewhere in Australia or even overseas. Mimi figures are, for example, compared with 'similar figures in Europe and Africa' (Mountford 1956:112) or, specifically, with the 'prehistoric Levantine art of eastern Spain, and in the Bushman art of South Africa' (Mountford 1956:260).

Figure 2.3: Yingarna, Injalak Hill.
Source: Photograph by Sally K. May.

Figure 2.4: Photograph of the adult and baby birds referred to by McCarthy in his field diaries, Injalak Hill.

Source: Photograph by Sally K. May.

While much has been written about Mountford's aims and expectations relating to the study of art during the 1948 Expedition, less is known of McCarthy's role. As such, we focus here on McCarthy at Oenpelli and present new information relating to his rock art recordings and his arguments with the Expedition leader.

On first arrival at Oenpelli, McCarthy ventured to the other side of the billabong to climb Injalak Hill (he refers to it as Billabong Hill in his diary). He noted:

> I walked over to the cave paintings and saw some remarkable art far too complex to record by the grid technique. Figures are superimposed one over the other and all the x-ray ones are covered in fine line polychrome decoration. Some are from single colour silhouettes in red, yellow and white, others have a thick outline around another solid colour. Some of the most fascinating figures comprise a bird feeding two open-mouthed young ones on a branch, all in black, women and men in beautiful line work on a plane with Bushman art, and many other extraordinary subjects. They will best be recorded with colour-film. They are painted in numerous shelters & protected surfaces & there appear to be a succession of techniques as on Groote & Chasm Is. (McCarthy, Diary 5, 17 September 1948; Figure 2.4)

It was clear, however, that Mountford did not appreciate McCarthy's interest in rock art. Presumably unable to continue with his rock art studies, McCarthy turned his attention to helping Frank Setzler with archaeological excavations (Figure 2.5). While excavating, McCarthy occasionally noted the presence of rock art in a number of the shelters, but offered little description or interpretation. For example, during excavations of a site on Injalak Hill, he noted: 'There are some red paintings on these walls chiefly solid red but some old and faded X-Ray figures' (McCarthy, Diary 5, 4 October 1948).

Figure 2.5: Frederick McCarthy and Frank Setzler excavating Site 1 on Injalak Hill in 1948.
Source: Photograph from the Frank M. Setzler Collection, National Library of Australia, nla.obj-142216040.

McCarthy's other focus was plotting his escape from the main Expedition camp. He began campaigning to accompany Margaret MacArthur to 'Gamada' (Fish Creek). While MacArthur would focus on diet and nutrition, McCarthy would make notes on Aboriginal life and take photos for 'groups & murals' (McCarthy, Diary 5, 4 October 1948). Of course, Mountford pushed back against this bid for independence and put multiple obstacles in the way: 'I think he will do everything he can to sabotage this trip' (McCarthy, Diary 5, c. 25 September 1948). Mountford insisted that MacArthur and McCarthy could not be alone at Gamada and that they have a chaperone with them – the job eventually fell to transport officer John Bray. The resulting MacArthur and McCarthy research paper from this trip became arguably one of the most important research outcomes from the Expedition (Altman 2011; McCarthy and MacArthur 1960). Away from the politics of the Oenpelli expedition camp, McCarthy (Diary 5, c. 22 October 1948) declared: 'It was a most successful camp … & a very happy one'.

In the days before the final Expedition base camp packed up ready to return to Darwin, McCarthy spent a 'hot & strenuous' day photographing rock art on 'gallery hill (Injaluk)' (McCarthy, Diary 5, 27 October 1948) and at Red Lily Lagoon (McCarthy, Diary 5, 4 November 1948). It is interesting to note that in his official Oenpelli diaries McCarthy barely mentions Aboriginal people by name. Yet, in his rough sketch books he does mention individuals and includes brief descriptions of those in camp with him at Gamada. Reading his official diaries gives the impression that he was very much alone in many of his explorations, though sometimes in company with Setzler, Harney or MacArthur. While the Gamada expedition suggested he had an anthropological interest in local culture, he notably lacked the opportunity to engage with local people. Did he ask anyone about the rock art? There is some evidence that he did during a one-day trip to Red Lily Lagoon. McCarthy noted the existence of a number of rock paintings –

men and women in 'various action poses', 'a delightful wallaby' and more. He also wrote about a large human figure said to be about 15 ft: 'It is said to be a female but strongly resembles the <u>wandjina</u> of the Kimberley in style' (McCarthy, Diary 5, 3 October 1948). We can only assume that a local Aboriginal person had informed him the figure was female, but there is no mention of companions on this day trip. Likewise, during a trip to Red Lily Lagoon with Margaret MacArthur, he noted a type of rock painting known as *mimi* featuring 'beautiful action postures of dancing, fighting, etc.'. Importantly, he stated, ' … they are supposed to be the rock spirits but the natives know nothing about their origin' (McCarthy, Diary 5, 4 November 1948). This statement suggests he tried to talk to local people about the rock art but they were unwilling to share cultural knowledge with him.

McCarthy's interest in the superimposition of styles as an archaeological approach is seen in his examination of western Arnhem Land rock art, and in later publications (e.g. McCarthy 1979:35–37). For example, he wrote:

> We made copious notes on the superimpositioning of styles for comparison with the Groote & Chasm paintings. We didn't finish till 5pm & then walked into camp, arriving at 7pm, after a long & weary day. (McCarthy, Diary 5, 4 November 1948)

On his final days in camp, McCarthy continued to visit nearby rock art sites including 'Gallery Hill' (Injalak Hill) where he made further notes on 'superimpositioning' (McCarthy, Diary 5, 5 November 1948). He was also hastily trying to collect any 'ethnographic' artefacts from the Aboriginal camp. While successfully acquiring some spears and baskets, his attempts to acquire sacred objects was unsuccessful: 'I got another batch of specimens from the chap where they had muraian stones (painted), feathered string etc for a forthcoming ceremony & would not part with them' (McCarthy, Diary 5, 9 November 1948).

At the end of the Expedition, the National Geographic Society photographer and journalist Howell Walker asked McCarthy what he considered the most significant contribution to anthropology made by the Arnhem Land Expedition. His answer is telling. He highlights the archaeological research undertaken as well as the collection of string figures from Yirrkala. He also takes the time to address Mountford's study of Aboriginal art:

> In regard to the study of aboriginal art made by mr. C.P. mountford I would point out that, in my opinion it is not the most significant contribution for two reasons. Firstly, the paintings on bark from Groote Eylandt were obtained with a lack of understanding of the true relationship of the painting to the legend; the method used by mr. mountford produces a large series of paintings of figures of animals, etc. and not as should have been collated, a series of paintings depicting the legendary story. Secondly, mr. and mrs. BBrndt [Berndt] had already … more detailed and prolonged work in the same field as mr. Mountford at Yirrkala and Oenpelli. (McCarthy to Walker November 1948 in McCarthy Diary 5)

While he is specifically discussing the bark painting collection, it is interesting to note the contradiction in McCarthy's preferred methodologies. While he suggests the bark paintings should have been collected and studied in their ethnographic context, his criticism of Mountford's rock art recording methodology focuses only on the lack of scientific vigour. Rock art was archaeological work, bark paintings were anthropology …

During the publicity tour, plans for publication of the findings from the Expedition emerged as a point of contention, and again provide interesting insights into McCarthy's attitude to art research.

> Monty was in a frightful anger & attacked me … asserting that I had no right to publish a comparison of art styles in the cave ptgs [paintings] nor any of the four bark painting (which formed part of my research). He also wanted to be a co-author on the Chasm Id [Island] paintings. I rejected all his requests, on the grounds that I had done the research &

had the right to publish it. He raised the old 'Artifact' argument but I pointed out that I was interested in the art chiefly from the archaeological sequence & techniques point of view. He claimed the sole right to publish papers on art, & was very bitter. Setzler was astounded at his outburst & told me to hold my ground, which I fully intend to do. (McCarthy, Diary 5, November 1948)

Discussion

> Charles P. Mountford we did not know
> You'd test black magic on this show.
> You've proved it on boats, so do refrain
> From any research on the Aeroplane
> (McCarthy, Diary 5, part of a song written at Oenpelli during the Expedition)

We can perhaps trace some of the underlying reasons for the feud beyond the 1948 Expedition, back to the training, personalities and intellectual inclinations of both men. Kate Kahn and John Mulvaney have commented alike on McCarthy's unassuming personality, Mulvaney noting that 'Fred McCarthy is a humble and modest man' (Mulvaney 1993:23) and Kahn stating that 'He has not sought kudos by becoming a personality on television or radio' (Kahn 1993:4). In contrast, as Philip Jones has written about Mountford on the 1948 Expedition in a paper called 'Inside Mountford's tent: Paint, politics and paperwork' (Jones 2011:34): 'Indeed, Mountford's bluff demeanour and his utter lack of pretension better match the careers he transcended – those of the farmer, the tram conductor and the telegraph technician'.

When Fred McCarthy began his career at the Australian Museum at the age of 14, he was appointed to the position of library clerk, becoming embedded in the world of order and cataloguing that pertains to the life of a librarian. Some 10 years later, in 1930, he joined the Department of Birds and Reptiles, adding taxonomy to his kitbag of skills and training. In 1932 he became the assistant curator of ethnology and then curator following the death of William Thorpe in the same year. Mountford on the other hand started out life in farming and trades, developing over time an interest and skills in photography and filmmaking (Lamshed 1972). Here we can see a little something of the genesis to their different approaches – McCarthy, trained in the systematics of cataloguing and classification, is drawn to the detail, the context and the taxonomic relationships between the paintings. Mountford, on the other hand, has a photographer's sensibility, his eye drawn to the singular and the exceptional, to the exemplary motifs that are representative of a corpus, all brought into sharp focus by the lens and framed by the dimensions of the photograph.

It is evident, we think, that the basic methodological and analytical frameworks laid down by McCarthy went a long way towards creating the foundations of contemporary rock art research in Australia. His insistence on the systematic recording of sites with a close reading of media, technique, spatial relationships, colour and superimpositioning is not so far from the field recordings carried out today. Where, of course, contemporary conceptual frameworks depart from McCarthy are the advances in chronology, regional variation and the application of scientific techniques of the analysis of pigments, rock surfaces and the like. Mountford's work is far less applicable today, although he professed an interest in style and the ethnography of art – glossed as 'myths' and 'legends' in the language of the day – his work was fast surpassed by a new generation of anthropologists of art such as Nancy Munn, Howard Morphy and Fred Myers, and his work is rendered now, perhaps a little unfairly, as a curio, emblematic of its time. Philip Jones (2011:34) reads Mountford more generously:

Indeed in later life, Mountford was characterised more than once as a bumbling, opportunistic amateur with a tin ear, hardly capable of making sense of the rich anthropological data he gathered. Yet, with all their defects, Mountford's *Nomads of the Australian Desert* (1976) and *Art, Myth and Symbolism* (1956) are works of substance and scholarship, and his extraordinary career as a discoverer and promoter of Aboriginal art is overdue for reassessment.

Perhaps this is, in the end, the lesson to be learned from the archives and records of the 1948 American–Australian Scientific Expedition to Arnhem Land, that despite the feuding and bitter arguments, an extraordinary group of men and women carried out foundational research for a whole range of disciplines – archaeology, anthropology, botany, ecology and biology.

References

Altman, J. 2011. From Kunnanj, Fish Creek, to Mumeka, Mann River: Hunter-gatherer tradition and transformation in Western Arnhem Land, 1948–2009. In M. Thomas and M. Neale (eds), *Exploring the legacy of the 1948 Arnhem Land Expedition*, pp. 113–134. Canberra: ANU Press. doi.org/10.22459/ELALE.06.2011.06.

Clarke, A., and U.K. Frederick 2011. Making a sea change: Rock art, archaeology and the enduring legacy of Frederick McCarthy's research on Groote Eylandt. In M. Thomas and M. Neale (eds), *Exploring the legacy of the 1948 Arnhem Land Expedition*, pp. 135–155. Canberra: ANU Press. doi.org/10.22459/ELALE.06.2011.07.

Evans, J.W. to Kellogg, 15 August 1957. Australian Museum Archives: series 235, Central Correspondence Files 1949-1969; G70/513 (Arnhem Land Expedition).

Hale, H.M. and N.B. Tindale 1930. Notes on some human remains in the Lower Murray Valley, South Australia. *Records of the South Australian Museum* 4(2):145–218.

Jones, P. 2011. Inside Mountford's tent: Paint, politics and paperwork. In M. Thomas and M. Neale (eds), *Exploring the legacy of the 1948 Arnhem Land Expedition*, pp. 33–54. ANU Press, Canberra. doi.org/10.22459/ELALE.06.2011.02.

Khan, K. 1993. Frederick David McCarthy: An appreciation. *Records of the Australian Museum, Supplement* 17:1–5. doi.org/10.3853/j.0812-7387.17.1993.54.

Lamshed, M. 1972. *Monty: A biography of C.P. Mountford*. Rigby, Adelaide.

May, S.K. 2009. *Collecting cultures: Myth, politics, and collaboration in the 1948 Arnhem Land Expedition*. Rowman Altamira.

McCarthy, F. 1948. The Lapstone Creek Excavation: Two culture periods revealed in Eastern New South Wales. *Records of the Australian Museum* 22:1–34. doi.org/10.3853/j.0067-1975.22.1948.587.

McCarthy, F. Diary 5, 1948. AIATSIS Library: American–Australian Scientific Expedition to Arnhem Land, MS3513 Box 22, Item 269, Canberra.

McCarthy, F. to A.B. Walkom, c. 1951 (found in association with papers from July 1951 and in response to Mountford's letter dated 27 July 1951). Australian Museum Archives: series 10, Correspondence 1927–1956, 22/1948 (Arnhem Land Expedition).

McCarthy, F. to A.B. Walkom, 8 June 1951. Australian Museum Archives: series 10, Correspondence 1927–1956, 22/1948 (Arnhem Land Expedition).

McCarthy, F. to J.W. Evans, 18 January 1956. Australian Museum Archives: series 235, Central Correspondence Files 1949–1969, G70/513 (Arnhem Land Expedition).

McCarthy, F. to J.W. Evans, 10 July 1957. Australian Museum Archives: series 235, Central Correspondence Files 1949–1969, G70/513 (Arnhem Land Expedition).

McCarthy, F. to J.W. Evans, October 1957. Australian Museum Archives: series 235, Central Correspondence Files 1949–1969, G70/513 (Arnhem Land Expedition).

McCarthy, F. 1958. Culture succession in South Eastern Australia. *Mankind* 5:177–190. doi.org/ 10.1111/j.1835-9310.1958.tb00305.x.

McCarthy, F.D. 1960. The cave paintings of Groote Eylandt and Chasm Island. In C.P. Mountford (ed.), *Records of the American–Australian Scientific Expedition to Arnhem Land. Volume 2: Anthropology and nutrition*, pp. 297–414 Melbourne University Press, Melbourne.

McCarthy, F.D. 1979. *Australian Aboriginal rock art.* 4th edition. The Australian Museum, Sydney.

McCarthy, F.D. and M. McArthur 1960. The food quest and the time factor in Aboriginal economic life. In C.P. Mountford (ed.), *Records of the American-Australian Scientific Expedition to Arnhem Land 1948. Volume 2: Anthropology and nutrition*, pp. 145–194. Melbourne University Press, Melbourne.

Mountford, C.P. 1949. Exploring Stone Age Arnhem Land. *National Geographic* 96(6):745–782.

Mountford, C.P. (ed.) 1956. *Records of the American-Australian Scientific Expedition to Arnhem Land. Volume 1: Art, myth and symbolism.* Melbourne University Press, Melbourne.

Mountford, C.P. to unknown person at the United States National Museum, 16 March 1957, quoted in Setzler, F. to F. McCarthy, 26 June 1957. Australian Museum Archives: series 235, Central Correspondence Files 1949–1969, G70/513 (Arnhem Land Expedition).

Mountford, C.P. (ed.) 1960. *Records of the American–Australian Scientific Expedition to Arnhem Land. Volume 2: Anthropology and nutrition.* Melbourne University Press, Melbourne.

Mulvaney, D.J. 1993. Sesqui-centenary to bicentenary: Reflections of a museologist. *Records of the Australian Museum* 17: 17–24. doi.org/10.3853/j.0812-7387.17.1993.56.

Setzler, F. to F. McCarthy, 26 June 1957. Australian Museum Archives: series 235, Central Correspondence Files 1949–1969, G70/513 (Arnhem Land Expedition).

Simpson, C. 1951. *Adam in ochre: Inside Aboriginal Australia.* Angus and Robertson, Sydney.

Specht, R.L. 1964. *Records of the American–Australian Expedition into Arnhem Land. Volume 4: Zoology.* Melbourne University Press, Melbourne.

Specht, R.L. and C.P. Mountford 1958. *Records of the American–Australian Expedition into Arnhem Land. Volume 3: Botany and plant ecology.* Melbourne University Press, Melbourne.

Spriggs, M. 2020. Everything you've been told about the history of Australian archaeology is wrong! *Bulletin of the History of Archaeology* 30(1):1–16. doi.org/10.5334/bha-626.

Thomas, M. and M. Neale (eds) 2011. *Exploring the legacy of the 1948 Arnhem Land Expedition.* ANU Press, Canberra. doi.org/10.22459/ELALE.06.2011.

Tindale, N.B. 1925–26a. Natives of Groote Eylandt and of the West Coast of the Gulf of Carpentaria, pt. I. *Records of the South Australian Museum* 3(1):61–102.

Tindale, N.B. 1925–26b. Natives of Groote Eylandt and of the West Coast of the Gulf of Carpentaria, pt. II. *Records of the South Australian Museum* 3(2):103–134.

Tindale, N.B. 1935. General report on the anthropological expedition to the Warburton Range, Western Australia, July-September, 1935. *Oceania* 6(4):481–485. doi.org/10.1002/j.1834-4461.1936. tb00207.x.

Tindale, N.B. 1957. Culture succession in South Eastern Australia from late Pleistocene to the Present. *Records of the South Australian Museum* 13(1):1–49.

Tindale, N.B. and C.P. Mountford 1926. Native markings on rocks at Morowie, South Australia. *Transactions of the Royal Society of South Australia* 50:156–159.

Tindale, N.B. and C.P. Mountford 1936. Results of the excavation of Kongarati Cave near Second Valley, South Australia. *Records of the South Australian Museum* 5(4):487–502.

Walker, H. 1949. Cruise to Stone Age Arnhem Land. *National Geographic* 96(3):417–430.

3

Shades of red: Peter Worsley's rock art research on Groote Eylandt

Ursula K. Frederick and Anne Clarke

Introduction

The Groote Eylandt archipelago is unique within Australia, by having one of the longest trajectories of rock art recording. Commencing in 1803 when paintings at Chasm Island were noted by Matthew Flinders and sketched by William Westall, a sustained program of research began in earnest in the early twentieth century. Largely comprising the work of anthropologists and archaeologists, along with the observations of keen-eyed amateurs, this history reveals a rich vein of approaches, analytical methods, theories and techniques. From Norman Tindale in the 1920s to George Chaloupka in the 1980s, each researcher brought something of themselves and their own agenda just as they grappled with the opportunities and constraints characteristic of their time and purpose. Hence, this twentieth-century history of rock art research on Groote Eylandt conveys a range of questions and interpretive frameworks, which we propose collectively reflect the glow of a Golden Age of rock art research in the archipelago.

The term 'Golden Age' was first used in the context of Groote Eylandt by the anthropologist Peter Worsley, whose doctoral dissertation and subsequent publication 'Early Asian contacts with Australia' (Worsley 1955a) presents his study of the history and kinship system of Groote Eylandt. Worsley referred to the Golden Age as a remembered period of contact between Groote Eylandters and Makassan outsiders, a past that we argue has historically influenced both the production and the perception of Groote Eylandt rock art. A little-known fact about Worsley's time on Groote Eylandt is the effort he made to document, characterise and synthesise the rock art made by Anindilyakwa-speaking people. In this paper we draw attention to Worsley's work and, in doing so, bring to light one of the largely unknown histories of Australian rock art research.

Peter Worsley (1924–2013) started his academic career as a social anthropologist, undertaking his doctoral research at the newly founded Research School of Social Sciences, The Australian National University (ANU). His field studies were based at Umbakumba on Groote Eylandt between 1952 and 1953. Like fellow anthropologist Frederick Rose, Worsley joined the Communist Party during his undergraduate studies at Cambridge University in the early 1940s. This decision affected his subsequent academic career, as he was prevented from undertaking postgraduate field research in Africa by the British Secret Services (Worsley 2008:52–78) and later when he returned to the UK after completing his PhD (Worsley 2008:125–126). This prompted his move from social anthropology into sociology, first at Hull University in 1956 and then in 1964 at the University of Manchester (Worsley 2008:113–148). He noted in his autobiography that in moving into sociology he found himself increasingly distanced from social anthropology and was unable to complete a planned book on Groote Eylandt kinship (2008:135). He is best known internationally for his book *The trumpet shall sound: A study of 'cargo' cults in Melanesia*, published in 1957.

An anti-colonial in the antipodes

Peter Worsley initially studied English at Cambridge University, where at the age of 18 he 'went into the arms of the Communist Party' (Worsley and Thomas 2010–11:Session 3, 00:01:09). After having his undergraduate studies interrupted by active military service in World War II, he returned to the university and changed to anthropology. Through his wartime army experience, Worsley developed an abiding interest in Africa, learned Swahili and, after completing his degree, 'wanted to go back to Africa badly' (Worsley and Thomas 2010–11:Session 4, 27:33). In the following years, Worsley spent time working in Tanzania where he strengthened his interest in language and indigenous knowledges, all the while under the surveillance of the UK Security Service MI5. At that time, with the rise of the Cold War and McCarthyism taking hold, Western governments were suspicious of Marxism, anti-colonial ideas and anyone with affiliations to the Communist Party. As a result, Worsley's early hopes of a research post in Africa were dashed, as he explains:

> I was very actively involved in the anti-colonial movement. Well that was all to my undoing. They blocked me going to Africa. I could see, so Max [Gluckman] said, 'that's the end of the road, why don't, well you better go to Australia'. (Worsley et al. 1989:0:46:05)

Despite these initial setbacks, ANU had just been established and Worsley was awarded a research scholarship to pursue anthropology. He and his wife Sheila headed to Australia originally intending to undertake fieldwork in the Central Highlands of New Guinea, at that time an Australian-administered territory. Once in Canberra, Worsley made new connections on campus and through local Communist Party meetings, most notably the meteorologist-turned-anthropologist Frederick Rose, who had worked on the Qantas flying boat base at Port Langdon on Groote Eylandt.

In preparation for his research trip to New Guinea Worsley read the Russian works of Soviet anthropologists working in the area, while also maintaining his activity within the Communist Party. This confluence of interests stood out in an era of Red Scare politics and, on the eve of his departure for fieldwork, the Australian authorities denied Worsley a visa for New Guinea. Worsley had come to the attention of the Australian Security Intelligence Organisation (ASIO) and was considered 'a dangerous red'; his academic pathways had narrowed again.

> These were bad times, doing anthropology under McCarthy … What happened with McCarthy in the U.S. happened everywhere in the 1950's. It was awful and we thought they were going to arrest all the Communists. I buried my C.P. [Communist Party] literature in the garden. (Worsley et al. 1989:00:50:51)

Worsley feared that his academic career was in ruins 'because you couldn't become an anthropologist without doing fieldwork of course, it's the end …' (Worsley et al. 1989:59.07). But soon after his New Guinea plans were scuppered, Frederick Rose 'solved my life problem for me', Worsley recalled (Worsley and Thomas 2010–11:Session 5, 01:05:00).

Figure 3.1: Peter and Sheila get their photograph taken on Groote Eylandt.
Source: Pitt Rivers Museum 2009.10.33.

Fortunately, the same communist sympathies and associations that had been negatively perceived by the British and Australian authorities also worked positively to realign Worsley's research trajectory: 'Freddy Rose, he said "look why don't you go and study the Australian Aborigines" ... He said "go to Groote Eylandt where I was"'(Worsley et al. 1989:0:03:00). Following this suggestion, Worsley sought the assistance of Professor A.P. Elkin of the University of Sydney to arrange access to the mission settlement at Angurugu, run by the Church Missionary Society (CMS). Elkin was a highly influential scholar of Aboriginal studies and a man of the cloth (Wise 1985). The ANU chair of anthropology at the time, Professor S.F. Nadel, also wrote to Elkin supporting Worsley's plan to work on Groote Eylandt, suggesting he would abandon 'Marxist phantasies' (Nadel to Elkin 1952, cited in Gray 2015). On Nadel's part, this was to both resolve the impasse over Worsley's future, and in respect of an 'unofficial agreement that the ANU would leave Aboriginal Australia to Sydney' (Gray 2015:37). Regardless of Elkin's influence, however, CMS permission was refused due to Worsley's communist affinities (Worsley 1982) and, once again, Fred Rose stepped in. In a letter of support to Fred Gray, then a designated 'Honorary Protector of Aboriginals' (Northern Territory), Rose wrote to ask if Worsley might be able to do fieldwork at the settlement Gray had established at Umbakumba, describing Worsley as a 'serious anthropologist' who would 'not cause any trouble and will be reliable ... do anthropology, not politics' (Worsley and Thomas 2010–11:Session 7, 37:40). Gray agreed to Rose's request, and by 1952 Peter and Sheila Worsley had arrived on Groote Eylandt to commence fieldwork (Figure 3.1).

Figure 3.2: Peter Worsley spearing fish in a billabong on Groote Eylandt 1953.

The Pitt Rivers Museum attributes the photograph to Sheila Worsley, however Peter Worsley notes in his 2008 autobiography that the photograph was taken by 12-year-old Groote Eylandt boy Nakinyapa.

Source: Pitt Rivers Museum 2009.10.208.

Despite initially not knowing what he would do there, Worsley chose to focus on kinship because 'it was an intellectual magnet'; Rose had generously shared his own field notebooks and kinship data as well as his 'matrix' approach to kinship research (Worsley and Thomas 2010–11:Session 8, 16:50). Worsley was talented with languages. He used his linguistic skills to not only study the Anindilyakwa language and kinship of Groote Eylandt, but also 'was interested in all dimensions of the life of these people, incredibly rich … a very very very complex culture' (Worsley et al. 1989). Although expected to reside with the Grays, Worsley spent his days with the 'Wanindiljaguawa' (Anindilyakwa), learning as much as he could of their language and kinship structure. As indicated in Figures 3.1 and 3.2, much of the time Peter Worsley:

> normally wore nagas, little loincloths just like the Aborigines did. Sheila wore a bra as well … Partly for comfort and partly to be identified with the Aborigines … It did help us equalise … I spent all my time of course with the Aborigines. They came every day. (Worsley and Thomas 2010–11:Session 7, 00:26–27:49)

It was through an immersion in the everyday lives of local people that Worsley came to accompany Anindilyakwa families on bush camping trips. He had not sought out rock art sites, specifically, but was taken to old peoples' camping places as part of the lived geography of Anindilyakwa Country. In order to better situate Worsley's approach and the embedded merits, motivations and meanings of his rock art studies, it is worth outlining the history of rock art research on Groote Eylandt prior to 1950.

A short history of rock art research on Groote Eylandt prior to 1950

The first known recordings of rock art in the Groote Eylandt archipelago were made by Matthew Flinders and William Westall in 1803, during Flinders's efforts to circumnavigate and map the coastline of Australia. Along with pencil sketches of the landscape, Westall (1803a, 1803b) produced two watercolours emulating rock art panels he saw on Chasm Island. Neither Westall nor Flinders made contact with Groote Eylandters; they had visited the rock art sites without the accompaniment (or possibly knowledge) of local people. Rather, their encounters with local culture were mediated through their impressions of the Groote Eylandt landscape and the pictures that had been made in rock-shelters by its Indigenous inhabitants.

It was not until some 120 years later that the art of Groote Eylandt began to be considered by researchers in earnest. The South Australian Museum anthropologist Norman Tindale accompanied the Reverend Perry on his voyage around the island in 1921 to identify a suitable site for the establishment of a CMS mission. Once a site was chosen on the Emerald River, Tindale spent many months undertaking excursions around Groote Eylandt, venturing both inland and around the coast. Tindale's efforts to record the rock art were undertaken in the context of a broader ethnographic survey documenting language, cultural practices, material culture, art and 'Malay' (Makassan) contact. His subsequent publication on Groote Eylandt's 'pictorial art' focused on the technical aspects of production, such as the types of pigments used, their possible sources and the methods used to make paint. He also commented on subject matter, proposing that 'the cave and hut paintings' were primarily related to hunting and fishing activities and that mythical beings and ceremonial figures were not depicted in art (Clarke and Frederick 2008; Tindale 1925–26).

The anthropologist Fred Rose came to a different conclusion after living at the Port Langdon flying boat base and the Shell Company fuel depot near Umbakumba, in 1938–1939 and 1941 (Munt 2011). In contrast to Tindale, Rose regarded Groote Eylandt paintings as aesthetic and magical, publishing his interpretations in a speculative paper on the rock art and a short note on the presence of totemic symbols in bark paintings (Rose 1942). Munt (2011:114) noted that Rose went to Groote Eylandt because he was interested in documenting an Aboriginal society in 'pristine' condition, which sets an interesting backdrop for his observations on the influence of Makassans on Groote Eylandt society.

A few years after Rose left Groote Eylandt, Frederick McCarthy undertook an extensive rock art recording program, during the 1948 American–Australian Scientific Expedition to Arnhem Land (McCarthy 1955, 1960; Clarke and Frederick 2011; Chapter 2, this volume). As one of the two archaeologists on the Expedition, McCarthy focused on recording 45 sites in three locations on Groote Eylandt – Junduruna, Angoroko (Angurugu) and Chasm Island. McCarthy's detailed, taxonomical approach to recording rock art was instrumental in establishing an archaeological approach to its analysis and interpretation (Clarke and Frederick 2008; Chapter 2, this volume). Establishing a relative chronology for Groote Eylandt rock art production was central to McCarthy's motivation, which effectively required a detailed and systematic approach to recording. McCarthy was not alone in his pursuit, relying on the assistance of local Groote Eylandt men, such as Kulpidja (Gulpidja), to locate and carry out a detailed mapping of motifs at specific sites, incorporating intra-site spatial and superimpositioning relationships. The notational system he used to place each motif within a gridded plane is carried over to his text, which resulted in a bare-bones yet comprehensive coverage of the rock art.

McCarthy's interest in Groote Eylandt rock art was shared by expedition leader Charles Mountford, although their approaches were very different (see Chapter 2, this volume). They had both gone to Chasm Island and visited several rock-shelters with paintings. Mountford's 'consuming passion', however, was collecting bark paintings and 'recording mythological details for bark paintings systematically' (Jones 2011:42, 49). On Groote Eylandt he applied his experience of the 'crayon drawing technique', often used by anthropologists at the time, to the making of bark paintings. The technique would:

> ask the men to make bark paintings for me, seldom suggesting subject. At the end of the day, the artists brought the work to my tent, related the associated myth, and explained the meanings of the designs. (Mountford cited in Jones 2011:45)

The result, according to Jones (2011:45), was an impressively 'detailed set of documentation of individual artworks', but Mountford seems not to have integrated or compared this corpus of collected information against the rock art he saw there. As Elkin noted in 1952, 'The reports [of the 1948 expedition] are in preparation' and, with a hint of derision against Mountford and his work, 'No experts in language, social organisation and religion accompanied this party' (Elkin 1952:291). Elkin's critical view of Mountford was shared by many Australian researchers at the time (May 2008), and may well have influenced Peter Worsley when he turned his attention to doing fieldwork in Australia.

The Worsleys went to Groote Eylandt in 1952, only four years after the 1948 Expedition. As very little had yet been written about Groote Eylandt in general, Worsley had limited extant literature to draw upon. While Worsley was well aware of the Expedition, the mainstay of material he had at his disposal was Norman Tindale's 1920s study and the invaluable work on kinship Fred Rose had already undertaken and shared with him. To complement and contextualise his Groote Eylandt research, Worsley looked into the broader literature of Arnhem Land for background and comparison, through the work of the Berndts, Elkin and his tutor W.E.H. Stanner, among others.

Going bush: Worsley's rock art 'discoveries'

As already noted, Peter Worsley's time on Groote Eylandt was dedicated to studying the kinship and social structure of the local society. He did not set out to undertake rock art research, but, like other anthropologists before and since (Rose 1942; Tindale 1925–26; Turner 1974), he became attuned to the presence of rock art in the context of working and living alongside Groote Eylandt people. Worsley was accompanied during his fieldwork by his wife Sheila, and together they stayed at the residence of Fred Gray, an English pearl and trepang trader who established the settlement of Umbakumba in 1938 (Dewar 1992; see also Figure 3.1). The two Anindilyakwa men with whom Worsley worked most closely were Kulpidja and Mini-Mini, both bark painters who had worked previously with non-Indigenous researchers such as McCarthy and Mountford. At times the Worsleys would also accompany Groote Eylandt families on camping excursions into the bush. They camped on the beach and in rock-shelters, for weeks at a time (Pitt Rivers images 2009.10.101; 2009.10.133). They often wore minimal clothing and relied on the rich natural resources of the Groote Eylandt landscape and local Indigenous knowledge to survive (Figure 3.2). It was during such 'walkabout trips', as Worsley described them, that he first encountered Groote Eylandt rock art.

Most of the rock art recordings took place during bush camping trips of 2–3 weeks' duration. In a field notebook entry for January 1953,[1] Worsley recorded his visit to 'rock-paintings' at Central Hill. One long word jumps out from the page: YINIMALAWALYAMADYA, the name

---

1   The date of Worsley's notebook entry is actually 9/10/53, but entries from January 1953 either side of this indicate the 0 was probably an accidental inclusion.

of the place where they were visiting. He keenly observed the excellent living conditions of the cave as 'roomy, water in rockholes round about' with a 'view right to Ayukuripa sea-inlet from nearby'. He noted the colours, the subject and frequency of the 'drawings' and their 'styles', as well as fairly general approximations of the size and positioning of some motifs 'near the entrance' of the shelter. He also draws attention to how natural circles in the roof were chosen for the placement of stingray (YIMADUWAYA) paintings and that 'Kids have written "Mr. Gray" in charcoal over two stencilled hands, no damage' (Worsley 1952–53:MS 1857/1 Item 4:28–32).

A few months later, in April 1953, the Worsleys joined a group of six Groote Eylandters as they set out from Umbakumba south to Talimbo (Dalumba) Bay in canoes. Their journey was described by Worsley in terms of landscape features and their Anindilyakwa place names, where they camped, what they ate and other activities that passed the time. It was during this trip that Worsley visited Marngkala Cave and made an extensive description of the setting and a 'quick census' of its rock art, the condition of the paintings and other observations about superimpositions. For the most part, he seems to have focused on counting the motifs, noting their subject and colour. He also spent time drawing a select number of motifs on the paper he had to hand (see Figure 3.3). A small number of black-and-white photographs were taken, including some of the rock art at Ayuwawa and Marngkala (e.g. Pitt Rivers Museum 2009.10.126).

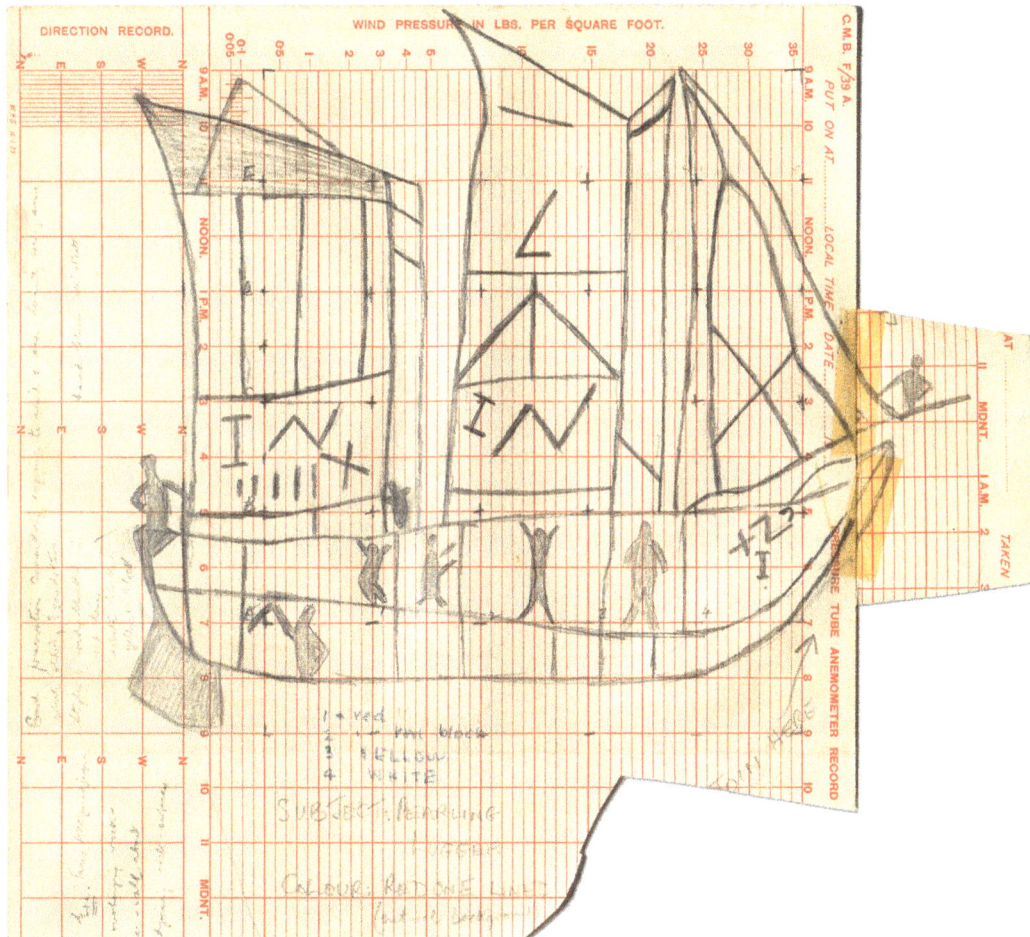

Figure 3.3: Detail of original pencil drawing of polychromatic rock art painting of 'Pearling Lugger' made by Peter Worsley during his fieldwork.

Source: Courtesy of Australian Institute of Aboriginal and Torres Strait Islander Studies (AIATSIS), Peter Worsley collection, Item MS1857/3/31.

Worsley's notes move between English and Anindilyakwa – suggesting that as he was recording he was actively learning and thinking in language. In the context of canoes, he wrote: 'ANJANDILYUPA predominate, only v. few MALAMUKA'. But rock art in the context of paintings of canoes is not all that Worsley wrote about – his notebooks reflect the rhythms of life, from daily activities, incidents and 'living habits' to important ritual occasions such as coffin-making. The singing of songs and the making of string figures are interspersed with observations on food gathering and preparation practices such as the cooking of turtle or shell-collecting. This may be seen to reflect Worsley's anthropological background and training, but it also has the effect of locating the rock art in the framework of everyday cultural life and Anindilyakwa Country. As well as describing in his notebook what he saw, Worsley also made drawings of particular motifs he identified in the rock art. He made these recordings on baking paper and barograph chart paper normally used for measuring atmospheric pressure. He used lead pencil, fountain pen and, occasionally, red and yellow coloured pencils (Worsley 1952–53:MS 1857/3).

Worsley's field notebooks from 1953 offer a direct insight into his initial encounter with Groote Eylandt rock art images and places. While his tone is more analytical than emotional, and descriptive than interpretive, there is nonetheless an inherent vitality to the way he directly recounts his experiences of 'discovering' rock art. Following fieldwork, the Worsleys returned to Canberra where Peter wrote up his doctoral dissertation and, after its examination, returned to England. Peter Worsley went on to write only a few papers based on his Groote Eylandt fieldwork (Worsley 1955a, 1955b) including one about rock art that was never published.

The unpublished manuscript

Sometime after his doctoral fieldwork Worsley wrote up his rock art observations in a paper titled 'Newly-discovered rock-paintings sites on Groote Eylandt, Northern Territory' (Worsley 1952–53:MS 1857/2 Item 24). He notes that he specially produced the article at the invitation of Charles Mountford for a proposed volume on Aboriginal art that was to be published by UNESCO (Worsley 2008). The paper was most likely written sometime around 1955/1956, following the Mountford-edited UNESCO publication (UNESCO 1954). At 49 typed pages, Worsley's unpublished rock art paper was a detailed account and reflects not only the results of his recordings, but also his thoughts about the place of rock art in contemporary Groote Eylandt Indigenous society. Some 30 years later, after his retirement from academia, Worsley deposited the manuscript, along with his notebooks and original rock art recordings, at the Australian Institute of Aboriginal Studies (later the Australian Institute of Aboriginal and Torres Strait Islander Studies, or AIATSIS), where it remains today (AIATSIS n.d.:3–4).

A series of factors may account for why Worsley's rock art study was never published. Worsley lay the blame on Charles Mountford. Reflecting on the situation, Worsley stated:

> material that I collected on the, the tracings of rock paintings at Central Hill … he [Mountford] asked me to write it up for the second volume of the records of the [1948] expedition, which I did. And he re-, refused to publish it because I'd been nasty to him in a review. And it remains unpublished to this day. So this very important site has never been described in public. And the only copy of that article is with AIATSIS Institute in Canberra. I don't have one. Plus the tracings themselves on kitchen paper. (Worsley and Thomas 2010–11:Session 7, 14:16)

Worsley's suspicions appear to be justified. By the time he probably completed the manuscript, Worsley had reviewed two publications on the Mountford-led *1948 American–Australian Scientific Expedition to Arnhem Land* (Mountford 1956; UNESCO 1954; Worsley 1955c; Worsley 1957).

Neither review praised Mountford. His critique of *The art, myth and symbolism of Arnhem Land* was particularly scathing and represents a barely veiled strike at Mountford's self-made status as an ethnographer:

> the book must stand as a monumental demonstration of the truth that Professor Fortes has emphasized: it is no longer possible for the amateur to make a serious contribution to anthropology. The errors, major and minor, are so numerous it would take a book of comparable size to correct them. (Worsley 1957:186)

Mountford's (1958) published right of reply suggests a bruised ego, which would not have been soothed by Worsley doubling-down on his comments in response (Worsley 1958). Recalling the fracas in 2011, Worsley explained to historian Martin Thomas: 'Well, he's no anthropologist, and I said so in my review. He then replied defending himself, and then I wrote an even more sarcastic one' (Worsley and Thomas 2010–11:Session 7, 14:16).

Presumably, Worsley had not foreseen the ramifications of his critique; it is unclear exactly when he realised that his paper would not be welcomed under Mountford's editorship. The 1948 Expedition's anthropology volume appeared in 1960, and by 1966 all four volumes of the 1948 Expedition had been published. What none of this quite explains, however, is why Worsley did not publish his paper elsewhere, prior to donating the manuscript and accompanying materials to AIATSIS 'where it is there for the record' (Worsley 2008:90).

Looking back, it may have been convenient for Worsley to attribute this reticence or failure to publish to personal grievances. After all, Mountford had many detractors in the Australian anthropology community (Chapman and Russell 2011; Jones 2011; see Chapter 2, this volume). But the circumstances are probably more complex. By the time Worsley lodged his manuscript with AIATSIS, he had permanently relocated to Britain, and shifted his disciplinary focus to sociology. In short, animosity may have been initially responsible for the paper not being published but Worsley's subsequent physical and social distance from Australia, changing research interests and personal academic pathway probably also eventually played a part. With the many obstacles and U-turns he had faced early in his academic career, Worsley may have sensed that his professional path might radically alter course once again. Commenting on his own efforts to understand Anindilyakwa and his time on Groote Eylandt, Worsley (2008:86–7) stated:

> I continued working … up to the very last day I was there. Next day, as the dinghy pulled away from the shore, I thought to myself 'I shall never use this language again'.

Perhaps this was prescience on Worsley's part, or perhaps it was pragmatism, because once he 'decided I would not continue to write about one area, as E-Pritchard had done on the Nuer, so I would not go on about Groote Eylandt' (Worsley et al. 1989:0.51). Shortly thereafter he went on to write *The trumpet shall sound*, the book for which he is renowned (Worsley 1957). As he presaged in 1954, he never returned to Groote Eylandt. The fact that his rock art study was never published remained a persistent lament, evidenced by its mention well into Worsley's later life (Worsley 2008:89–90; Worsley et al. 1989; Worsley and Thomas 2010–11).

Worsley's rock art recordings and writing

So, what *did* Worsley find, record and write about Groote Eylandt rock art? Does it matter that his paper remained out of sight? Have we missed anything in the intervening half-century? What might his insights on 'newly-discovered' paintings tell us now?

Worsley summarised his rock art 'discoveries' in the context of previous observations by Tindale, Rose and McCarthy listing 12 key rock art areas identified by them. He then goes on to describe in more detail the specific rock art sites he visited and recorded. His recordings comprise a 'census' of the rock art in each site (e.g. Figure 3.4). He lists the number of motifs by subject including their colour and 'style'. His spartan notational description may reflect an expedited field-recording process, but it is not dissimilar to the methods McCarthy applied on Groote Eylandt during the 1948 Expedition. Worsley, however, does not emphasise superimpositioning, spatial relationships, relative art sequence nor the exhaustive site plans that McCarthy undertook. However, Worsley does give attention to the primary colours of the paintings and, unlike most of his contemporaries, provides the Anindilyakwa name for the pigments used. He noted visible distinctions in the names and shades of red ochre, explaining that 'the names of colours are in fact the names of the rocks'. The 'common red' is called 'either *mawurura* or *agalenjgura*', referring to 'one of two naturally-occurring forms of the ochre … but the resulting colour is the same' (Worsley 1952–53:MS 1857/2, Item 24, p. 6). He also described a pinky-red colour called *jiniba*, and a recognisably distinct and rarely used 'striking pucy-red' called *jinibmura* or *jiniburamura*. As well as these named shades of red, along with black (*amanina*), yellow (*merunjwa*) and white (*dunjura*), Worsley (1952–53:MS 1857/2, Item 24, p. 7) noted: 'It must be admitted that other shades can be found. Various coloured rocks can be picked up which depart from the basic colours we have mentioned, but these are usually small local occurrences', by which he may be referring to the pebbles of laterite scattered across the grounds of the archipelago. Throughout this attention to colour, Worsley draws a number of conclusions about sequence, such as the white pigment being the most recent.

Figure 3.4: Left: Photograph of red ochre paintings on ceiling at Yinumaluwalumanja, 2019. Right: Detail of drawings made by Peter Worsley while visiting Yinumaluwalumanja in 1953.
Source: Left: Photograph by Ursula K. Frederick 2019; Right: Drawing by Peter Worsley, courtesy of AIATSIS, Peter Worsley collection, item MS1857/3/27.

Although the recorded motifs are presented as a 'census' of subjects, Worsley does not offer any analysis of the data, neither in terms of frequency at specific sites nor comparatively across the different areas of the Groote Eylandt landscape he visited. Nor does he discuss relationships between these subjects, compositionally or spatially. Compositionally, his recordings of the motifs float in open space rather than appearing in correct spatial relationship to one another. The size of individual motifs is hard to discern and their scale in relation to one another is not proportionate to their actual renderings on-site. Worsley isolated specific motifs for illustration and discussion, an approach that tends to preference specific paintings as exemplary, unique or special rather than emphasising patterns in the rock art assemblage or the more mundane motifs present. In general, Worsley does not explain the reasoning behind his selective recordings, which range from including fauna and anthropomorphs to objects and scenes such as of dancing and fishing activities. He did not draw motifs in superimposition relationships to each other, however on some recordings he makes notes about the sequence of colours. Nevertheless, as individual drawings, Worsley's renderings warrant praise for their verisimilitude and his effort to incorporate local Indigenous language identifications and associated cultural details.

We know from the documents lodged with the manuscript that the paper was to be illustrated with some of the photos he took on-site, as well as images prepared from drawings he had made in the field (AIATSIS n.d.:11). 'Cleaned up' for publication, the line drawings of rock art are devoid of the handwritten notations that enliven and enhance the originals. These sanitised figures remove Worsley's perspectives and render them as objective drawings that conform to the trope of scientific illustration. Nor do these prepared figures do justice to the clarity and detail that Worsley's meticulous efforts sought to capture as accurately by hand as possible. The motifs he selected for reproduction tell us something about the focus of Worsley's study, just as the original recordings tell us about what motifs particularly caught his attention. Surprisingly, few of them relate to the Central Hill rock-shelter he considered so very important. Instead, they represent an intriguing ensemble of predominately marine fauna and technology. The emphasis on boats (praus, a lugger) and fishing scenes gives some indication of his interest in the themes of culture contact, economy and social change.

Unlike the line drawings intended to accompany the paper, Worsley's original recordings are full of notations. The majority reveal his commitment to identifying subjects and applying the correct Anindilyakwa language term. There are additions of interpretation and, less commonly, his subjective opinion on the aesthetics of a particular motif and its execution: 'V. graceful – well curved' (Worsley 1952–53:MS 1857/3, Item 35). Occasionally he included a note or observation on the recordings that could only have been obtained through conversation with his Anindilyakwa colleagues. For example, 'Suggestion by … [N.] … – a turtle being cut up; white dots are eggs' (Worsley 1952–53:MS 1857/3, Item 37). Importantly, on some recordings there are indications that a known individual was the artist responsible for creating a particular painting (Worsley 1952–53:MS 1857/3, Item 33). For example, on his recording of another painting at Marnkgala, Worsley identifies the subject as an 'alligator' and lists the Anindilyakwa name of the man (then deceased) who had painted it (Worsley 1952–53:MS 1857/3, Item 36). Such revelations indicate the production of rock art in living memory. Other notations suggest a process of thinking or active conversation on the part of Worsley and his colleagues, like 'notes to self' for later recall and contemplation. On the recording of the Marngkala painting identified as a turtle, Worsley has written: 'Do white lines indicate points of plates?' Such questioning is indicative of the kinds of thinking processes and ideas that emerge from and through the immediacy of direct engagement with rock art and its studied and thoughtful recording. Worsley excised the evidence of the active nexus of seeing, thinking and discussing that occurred with his collaborators in the field.

Reflecting on Worsley's contribution to rock art research

As it stands in the early twenty-first century, unpublished and effectively unread, Worsley's rock art paper has had minimal to no impact or influence. It is difficult to gauge what impact it may have had were it to have been published as he had first intended, in the mid-twentieth century. Would it have altered our understanding of Groote Eylandt archaeology or social anthropology, or shaped the direction of subsequent rock art research in northern Australia? Since Worsley's time on Groote Eylandt, there have been several rock art recording efforts, continuing the long historical trajectory commenced by Westall and Flinders. These have resulted in several publications (e.g. Chaloupka 1996; Clarke and Frederick 2006; Turner 1973, 1974), but much material also remains relatively inaccessible, existing in the form of survey, conservation and impact assessment reports, raw field recordings and data, and reconnaissance and recording programs commissioned by the Anindilyakwa Land Council.

As far as we can determine from his field recordings, all of the rock art sites Worsley visited, even those he considered 'new', have been reported on by the archaeologists and rock art researchers who have worked on Groote Eylandt rock art since then. Chaloupka (1989), for example, makes mention of the same lugger that Worsley saw and drew in pencil on wind-pressure measurement paper (Figure 3.3). The Dalumba Bay area, being coastal, may be approached by sea, land or air, and sites such as Ayuwawa and Marngkala continue to be known and visited by Groote Eylandters and visitors today. In comparison, it is much more difficult to access the area of Central Hill that Worsley visited then. Seasonal flooding and regrowth of dense vegetation make road vehicle access difficult to maintain without regular visitation and cultural burning. Nonetheless, even the Central Hill rock art shelter that Worsley described as 'quite as magnificent as anything in the whole of Arnhem Land' (Worsley 2008:90) has been visited by non-Indigenous researchers, including the present authors. The site has been the subject of archaeological investigation and repatriation activities on two separate occasions, in 1996 and 2019, respectively (Clarke 2020; Frederick and Clarke 2020). And a photograph of a rock painting from the site was also reproduced in John Mulvaney's 1989 book *Encounters in place*, attributed to C. Macknight.

What stands out in Worsley's rock art study, as reflected in his fieldnotes and recordings, is that he consistently labelled the name of the place and the colour of pigments used in the rock art and integrates the Anindilyakwa names of both rock art subjects and Country. This is an important and unusual advance for its time, clearly associating and integrating the rock art imagery with the names of the Anindilyakwa people who made it and for whom this was Country. This perspective, which was no doubt influenced by the immediacy of Worsley's experiences and interactions on Groote Eylandt, and by his training as a social anthropologist, is less prominent in his typewritten manuscript than in his original notes and recordings. Indeed, the prepared paper, written sometime later, carries a tone of emotional and cultural distance and reads as a somewhat more clinical appraisal of rock art images.

While Worsley's rock art study is an achievement that went unrecognised, it is not wholly unproblematic. There are surprising aspects of the paper that go beyond rock art analysis, and delve into commentary, for example, when he suggested that some of the Groote Eylandt rock art might be removed and sent to the Australian Museum in Sydney:

> there seems to be a very good case for the removal of some of the finer paintings from the cave-walls, as has been done in South Africa and in parts of the Sydney-Hawkesbury region … there seems little reason for allowing these splendid paintings to weather away in their present locations … such removal would not deprive the aborigines of their cultural heritage, especially as the paintings exist in thousands, and the loss of a few examples would not greatly affect them. Compensation could be arranged and the contribution to wider appreciation of aboriginal life and culture would be a considerable one. (Worsley 1952–53:MS 1857/2, Item 24, pp. 5–6).

While perhaps not unusual for the times, against the backdrop of Worsley's deep intellect and enlightened anti-colonialism, such commentary is startling. This proposition suggests a lack of understanding or appreciation for Wanindiljaguawa rights, responsibilities and respect for Country and cultural heritage that seems out of character with Worsley's keen understanding of Groote Eylandt life and society. Yet it is an attitude not out of keeping with a broader 'salvage anthropology' ethos circulating in the first half of the twentieth century that often involved promoting reserves and removing art and other belongings, under the auspices of securing and sharing their future in the interests of humanity and the heritage of the world. It is outside the scope of this paper to consider how much this attitude persists, but needless to say, it is unlikely any informed and respectful researcher would make such a suggestion today.

No doubt the whole of Worsley's experience in the archipelago informed his doctoral thesis and influenced his writing. Nonetheless a lot of the detailed information and insights that he gathered during his fieldwork were not included in his thesis. It is curious that his thesis makes no real mention of rock art, particularly given its attention to Groote Eylandt social and cultural change, the effects and implications of cultural contact, and the dynamic perceptions of history he proposed.

Conclusion

The reasons why Worsley came to work on Groote Eylandt tell a fascinating story of post–World War II politics, academic hierarchies and patronage and the growth of new and expanding disciplines like anthropology, archaeology and rock art research. It also tells of the political influences that worked to shape research during the Cold War, and since. It demonstrates how personal, public and government politics and ideologies can wittingly and unwittingly impact research; how popularity, alliances, favours and fashions can dictate what appears in academic press, and what gets left out.

In this paper we go some way towards reinstating a position for Worsley in Groote Eylandt's Golden Age of rock art research, by discussing his findings, how they reflect his broader research interests and some of the reasons why this research was never published. In doing so, we recognise Worsley's enthusiasm in wanting to share his encounter with Groote Eylandt rock art with a broader audience. Our hope is that it not only brings to light one of the largely unknown chapters embedded in one of the longest histories of Australian rock art research but that it removes an enduring thorn in Worsley's side. By way of consolation, at last, something has been published from his study of Groote Eylandt rock art.

Acknowledgements

We would like to thank the Anindilyakwa Land Council for permission to reproduce the images of rock art from Groote Eylandt, the Pitt Rivers Museum, Oxford, for permission to reproduce photographs from the Peter Worsley collection and AIATSIS for permission to reproduce photographs of Peter Worsley's drawings held in their collection.

References

AIATSIS (Australian Institute of Aboriginal and Torres Strait Islander Studies) n.d. Finding Aid: MS 1857 Peter Worsley; fieldwork with Anindilyakwa people on Groote Eylandt, 1952–1953.

Chaloupka, G. 1989. Groote Eylandt archipelago rock art survey 1988. Unpublished report to Heritage Branch, Conservation Commission Northern Territory. Darwin.

Chaloupka, G. 1996. Praus in Marege: Makassan subjects in Aboriginal rock art of Arnhem Land, Northern Territory, Australia. *Anthropologie* 34:131–142.

Chapman, D. and S. Russell 2011. The responsibilities of leadership: The records of Charles P. Mountford. In M. Thomas and M. Neale (eds), *Exploring the legacy of the 1948 Arnhem Land Expedition*, pp. 253–269. ANU E Press, Canberra. doi.org/10.22459/elale.06.2011.13.

Clarke, A. 2020. Blueshifts and transformations. In U.K. Frederick, C. Florance and K. Hayne (eds), *Expanding the field: Encounters in archaeology and art*, pp. 12–15. Lucky U Press, Canberra.

Clarke, A. and U.K. Frederick 2006. Closing the distance: Interpreting cross-cultural engagements through Indigenous rock art. In I. Lilley (ed.), *Archaeology of Oceania, Australia and the Pacific Islands*, pp. 116–33. Blackwell, Oxford. doi.org/10.1002/9780470773475.ch6.

Clarke, A. and U.K. Frederick 2008. The mark of marvellous ideas: Groote Eylandt rock art and the performance of cross-cultural relations. In P. Veth, P. Sutton and M. Neale (eds), *Strangers on the shore: Early coastal contacts in Australia*, pp. 148–164. National Museum of Australia, Canberra.

Clarke, A. and U.K. Frederick 2011. Making a sea change: Rock art, archaeology and the enduring legacy of Frederick McCarthy's research on Groote Eylandt. In M. Thomas and M. Neale (eds), *Exploring the legacy of the 1948 Arnhem Land Expedition*, pp. 135–155. ANU E Press, Canberra. doi.org/10.22459/ELALE.06.2011.07.

Dewar, M. 1992. *The 'Black War' in Arnhem Land: Missionaries and the Yolngu 1908–1940*. North Australia Research Unit, The Australian National University, Darwin.

Elkin, A.P. 1952. Research in Arnhem Land, preliminary report. *Oceania* 22(4):290–298. doi.org/10.1002/j.1834-4461.1952.tb00184.x.

Frederick, U.K. and A. Clarke 2020. *The Groote Eylandt Repatriation Project photobook*. Lucky U Press, Canberra.

Gray, G. 2015. 'A great deal of mischief can be done': Peter Worsley, the Australian National University, the Cold War and academic freedom, 1952–1954. *Journal of the Royal Australian Historical Society* 101(1):25–44.

Jones, P. 2011. Inside Mountford's tent: Paint, politics and paperwork. In M. Thomas and M. Neale (eds), *Exploring the legacy of the 1948 Arnhem Land Expedition,* pp. 33–54. ANU E Press, Canberra. doi.org/10.22459/elale.06.2011.02.

May, S.K. 2008. The art of collecting: Charles Pearcy Mountford. In N. Peterson, L. Allen and L. Hamby (eds), *The makers and making of Indigenous Australian museum collections*, pp. 446–471. Melbourne University Press, Carlton, Victoria.

McCarthy, F.D. 1955. Notes on the cave paintings of Groote and Chasm Islands in the Gulf of Carpentaria. *Mankind* 5 (2):69–75. doi.org/10.1111/j.1835-9310.1955.tb01422.x.

McCarthy, F.D. 1960. The cave paintings of Groote Eylandt and Chasm Island. In C.P. Mountford (ed.), *Records of the American–Australian Scientific Expedition to Arnhem Land. Volume 2: Anthropology and nutrition,* pp. 297–414. Melbourne University Press, Melbourne.

Mountford, C.P. (ed.) 1956. *Records of the American–Australian Scientific Expedition to Arnhem Land. Volume 1: Art, myth and symbolism*. Melbourne University Press, Melbourne.

Mountford, C. 1958. The art, myth and symbolism of Arnhem Land. *Man* 58(Jan.):13.

Mulvaney, D.J. 1989. *Encounters in place: Outsiders and Aboriginal Australians, 1606–1985*. University of Queensland Press, St Lucia, Queensland.

Munt, V. 2011. Australian anthropology, ideology and political repression: The Cold War experience of Frederick G. G. Rose. *Anthropological Forum* 21(2):109–129. doi.org/10.1080/00664677.2011.582832.

Rose, F. 1942. Paintings of the Groote Eylandt Aborigines. *Oceania* 13:170–176. doi.org/10.1002/j.1834-4461.1942.tb00376.x.

Tindale, N.B. 1925–26. Natives of Groote Eylandt and of the West Coast of the Gulf of Carpentaria, Parts 1 and 2. *Records of the South Australian Museum* 111:61–134.

Turner, D. 1973. The rock art of Bickerton Island in comparative perspective. *Oceania* 43:286–325. doi.org/10.1002/j.1834-4461.1973.tb01225.x.

Turner, D. 1974. *Tradition and transformation: A study of the Groote Eylandt area Aborigines of Northern Australia*. Australian Aboriginal Studies No 53. Australian Institute of Aboriginal Studies, Canberra.

UNESCO 1954. *Australia: Aboriginal paintings, Arnhem Land*. New York Graphic Society, Greenwich, Connecticut.

Westall, W. 1803a. *Chasm Island, native cave painting*, watercolour painting, 26.7 x 36.6 cm. National Library of Australia: ID 585900.

Westall, W. 1803b. *Chasm Island, native cave painting*, watercolour painting, 26.7 x 37.2 cm. National Library of Australia: ID 2108209.

Wise, T. 1985. *The self made anthropologist: A life of A.P. Elkin*. Allen & Unwin, Sydney.

Worsley, P.M. 1952–53. Fieldwork on Groote Eylandt, 1952–1953. Australian Institute of Aboriginal and Torres Strait Islander Studies: MS 1857, Series 1, Series 2, Item 24; Series 3, Items 27–55. Canberra.

Worsley, P.M. 1955a. Early Asian contacts with Australia. *Past & Present* 7(Apr.):1–11. doi.org/10.1093/past/7.1.1.

Worsley, P.M. 1955b. The totemic system of the Wanindiljaugwa. *Man* 55(Apr.):57–58. doi.org/10.2307/2795208.

Worsley, P.M. 1955c. Australia: Aboriginal Paintings-Arnhem Land [Review]. *Man* 55(Sep.):142–143.

Worsley, P.M. 1957. Records of the American–Australian Expedition to Arnhem Land: Vol. I, art, myth and symbolism [Review]. *Man* 57(Dec.):186.

Worsley, P.M. 1958. Records of the American–Australian Expedition to Arnhem Land: Vol. I, art, myth and symbolism [Review]. *Man* 58(May):80.

Worsley, P.M. 1982. Letters. *RAIN* 53(Dec.):13.

Worsley, P.M. 2008. *An academic skating on thin ice*. Berghahn Books, New York, Oxford.

Worsley, P.M., A. Macfarlane and S. Harrison 1989. *Peter Worsley: A life*. Interview by Alan Macfarlane, filmed by Sarah Harrison, at his home on 25 February 1989, using a video 8 camera. Available at: www.alanmacfarlane.com/DO/filmshow/worsley1_fast.htm (accessed 21 January 2021).

Worsley, P.M. and M. Thomas 2010–11. Peter Worsley interviewed by Martin Thomas, 30–31 December 2010 and 3 January 2011. London. National Library of Australia: ORAL TRC 6279; nla.obj-2197 61211.

4

The Sydney School and the genesis of contemporary Australian rock art research

Jo McDonald

Introduction

Australian rock art research as a field of research has progressed through a series of phases, each with its own research aims, understandings and methods, and each dependent on the previous but also on the rise of archaeology as a discipline: the study of humans through their material remains. The earliest days of settler encounter/arrival/invasion in eastern Australia realised the endemic presence of Aboriginal rock art (Phillip 1789). But it was only in the 1800s that ethnographers began to document rock art as part of the long-term and widespread evidence for Aboriginal Australia's cultural practices (e.g. Mathews 1894, 1896). This was part of a worldwide trend of learned societies and museums increasing anthropological understandings of cultural groups across the world and making significant collections of their material culture (Pitt Rivers 1882). At first steeped in antiquarian interests that spoke of the West's own deep antiquity, the recording of people in place was encouraged by the learned societies of Great Britain and France, an 'ethnomania' (Thomas 2011:15) for increasingly vast audiences wanting to be informed by an 'indefatigable' collection of new and interesting facts (Thomas 2011:62). The accumulating curios and 'facts' in anthropological knowledge required arrangement into museum collections, which Hicks (2013) argues was central to the development of anthropology's four-field approach (see below). The early 1900s thus saw a continued enhancement of rock art documentation across the continent with the professionalisation of specialist academic fields by people with varying backgrounds: for example, the Frobenius expeditions to the Pilbara and Kimberley, D.S. Davidson and Fred McCarthy across much of the continent, and later Bob Edwards through Central Australia (see Smith et al. 2021).

Anthropology was first taught at the University of Sydney in 1925 (Conway and Philp 2008) but *prehistory* – as Australian Indigenous archaeology was then called – only became a discipline for study at Australian universities in the early 1960s. The first university teachers were Australians: John Mulvaney and Isabel McBryde, both Cambridge-trained. Mulvaney returned to teach in the Ancient History Department at the University of Melbourne in the mid-1950s where he had previously studied history as an undergraduate. During this time, he undertook several foundational deep excavations recognising the importance of stratigraphic sequences (Griffiths 2018; Mulvaney 2011; Murray and White 1981). Isabel McBryde was the first prehistory lecturer at the University of New England in 1960, the first (in 1966) to complete a PhD based on Australian fieldwork and the supervisor of the first prehistory Honours thesis (by Sharon Sullivan in 1964; Bowdler and Clune 2000:29). Meanwhile, she also undertook a foundational disciplinary approach, combining regional analyses, field archaeology and ethnohistory (Bowdler and Clune 2000; Moser 2007). Around this time (in 1961) Jack Golson first joined The Australian National University (ANU) as a Research Fellow in the School of Pacific Studies, and John Mulvaney was recruited to the ANU Faculties.[1] The University of Sydney only developed a full four-field approach in the early 1960s, when the Anthropology and Prehistory Department taught social anthropology, linguistics, prehistory and physical anthropology. Fuelled by a 'Cambridge in the Bush' pathway of training and influence (Murray and White 1981), this influx to the University of Sydney included archaeologists Richard Wright, Rhys Jones and John Clegg, and slightly later Roland Fletcher and J. Peter White – whose journey post-Cambridge included the University of California at Berkeley, where he adopted 'New Archaeology', advocating logical positivism modelled on scientific methods as the guiding research philosophy.

Rock art courses were taught in Australian universities after this Cambridge influx, first at the University of Sydney (with John Clegg from 1965) and then at ANU with the arrival of Andrée Rosenfeld in 1973. Isabel McBryde recorded rock art as part of her PhD research, but the University of New England (UNE) only offered a rock art course after Mike Morwood arrived in 1981 (Morwood 2002). Morwood, originally from New Zealand, undertook his PhD at ANU (supervised by John Mulvaney). Iain Davidson joined UNE in 1974, and initially taught religion and portable art, having 'done cave art at Cambridge which was dominated by Leroi-Gourhan with Ucko and Rosenfeld as a counter' (Iain Davidson, pers. comm., April 2021).

The early underpinnings of Australian rock art research flourished and included regional, landscape and contextual studies. Research interest shifted from 'art as an object' (Mulvaney 1969) to 'style' as a means of communication (Hodder 1978; Wobst 1977). European, and particularly French and Spanish Palaeolithic, rock art research at this time provided stimulus for early Australian rock art researchers (e.g. Laming-Emperaire 1962; Leroi-Gourhan 1968; Ucko and Rosenfeld 1967; although see comment by Maynard below). By the early 1980s, these were being adapted to an Australian flavour, founded on firm archaeological approaches to style and signalling behaviour, as a new generation of anglophone archaeological researchers working at the junction of social anthropology and social theory began to make their mark (Conkey 1980; Hodder 1978; Wobst 1977). These new research endeavours were fuelled by increasing resources to record rock art, and in the mid-1980s by a burgeoning group of anthropologists especially coming from ANU (for instance Howard Morphy and Luke Taylor) who undertook research in northern and central Australia, building on earlier anthropological approaches (such as Munn 1960; Myers 1976 and later 1991) and moulded by the growing recognition of Aboriginal ownership (Langford 1983) and ontologies (e.g. Mowaljarlai et al. 1988). The development of formal archaeological approaches to rock art and the mobilisation of myriad scientific techniques (e.g. Rosenfeld et al. 1981) has resulted in the realisation of rock art's potential to contribute to archaeological discourse. These developments in archaeology went on to inform approaches (beyond ethnographic analogy) used by anthropologists (led in this timeframe by scholars such as Margaret Clunies-Ross, Les Hiatt, Anthony Forge, Howard Morphy, Fred Myers and Bob Layton) and mobilised by early practitioners such as Ian Crawford in the Kimberley.

The Sydney School

'The Sydney School' has been used previously to describe a group of regionally based practitioners who represent a distinct praxis. The Sydney School of Architecture reacted against modernism and developed an ethos of organic residential designs that celebrated the natural environment

---

1   For more information, see: humanities.org.au/our-community/tribute-john-mulvaney.

(Jahn 1997). Similarly for linguists, although perhaps less well known, the functional linguistic perspective on genre analysis distinguishes the Sydney School of linguistics (Rose 2011). In this chapter I argue that a combination of factors, approaches and personalities created a Sydney School of rock art research, during a foundational phase in Australian rock art research as archaeology became a discipline (Moser 2007). The 1960s efflorescence of Cambridge-trained archaeologists at the University of Sydney created this platform. John Clegg was the first academic to teach rock art in Australia and to train a generation of researchers how to *do* rock art research. Lesley Maynard was the first Australian to write a rock art Honours (and then a Masters) dissertation, thereby providing both an archaeological approach and a chronological stylistic framework within which subsequent generations of rock art researchers practised. These two researchers (Figure 4.1) were responsible for driving one of the most significant paradigm shifts in Australia (Clegg 1971, 1977a, 1977b, 1978a, 1978b, 1981, 1987; McMah 1965; Maynard 1977, 1979), during a pivotal time when rock art became an archaeological subdiscipline. Both Maynard and Clegg worked on classification, typology, style and chronology – supported initially by Richard V.S. Wright's focus on multivariate statistical analyses and the development of computer programming at the University of Sydney (next by Ian Johnson, and later Andrew Wilson). Maynard's and Cleggs's distinctive approaches and joint outputs, inspired by each other's creativity and individuality, provide a dual legacy for an energetic generation of scholars – a new breed of Australian university students, inspired by Gough Whitlam's free education mandate and the concomitant recognition of Aboriginal land rights (Krishna 2014). Their approaches were genuinely archaeological, at a time where there was scepticism that rock art could play any role in understanding Australia's deep history (in part because of problems in dating it). Clegg railed against a comment by John Mulvaney (1969:173) that people studying rock art 'are amongst the workers whose memoirs will contribute basically to art appreciation'.[2] While ANU a decade later arguably trained more of the current rock art practitioners to PhD level in this same mould, the Sydney School was the key teaching and research group in the sixties and seventies responsible for the disciplinary shift from an antiquarian focus on cataloguing rock art as a relic of times past (e.g. D.S. Davidson, R.H. Mathews and to a lesser extent McCarthy), to a research framework that was theoretically informed and scientifically oriented. Maynard and Clegg had very different career trajectories, publication outputs and training roles, and I focus on these in this chapter.

Following the foundation of the Sydney School, from the mid-seventies to mid-nineties, there was an Australia-wide halcyon period. This was a time when the Australian Institute of Aboriginal and Torres Strait Islander Studies (AIATSIS), formerly the Australian Institute of Aboriginal Studies (AIAS), supported rock art and anthropological research projects across the continent (see below), providing the research funding and impetus for this early generation of Australian-trained rock art researchers to thrive. Many of Australia's contemporary rock art faculty members were trained at Australian universities (except for several South African, German and Swedish researchers now at the University of Western Australia, who trained at Cambridge, University of California Berkeley, Southampton and Umea universities; and Paul Taçon, who trained in Canada and at ANU). The intellectual groundings provided by the Sydney School in the sixties and seventies opened Australian archaeological career pathways that were missing in many other countries, notably the USA, where rock art was rarely taught at universities, and where rock art research was not considered to be mainstream by the majority of practitioners and was and continues to be often undertaken by avocationalists.

---

2   I note that by the early 1980s Mulvaney explicitly recognised the great importance of rock art, and acknowledged that it was an under-studied field in Australian archaeology, amending his earlier comment in later editions of *The Prehistory of Australia*.

Figure 4.1: John Clegg and Lesley Maynard at her Masters graduation ceremony in the University of Sydney Quad in 1976.

Source: Photograph provided by Lesley Maynard.

Lesley McMah/Maynard (1945–)

Australia's first Australian-born and university-trained rock art researcher was Lesley Maynard, who enrolled at Sydney University in 1962. She was then 16. She took subjects in anthropology in her first year of undergraduate studies while also studying English and history, intending initially to be a teacher. That same year, while attending a Sport and Recreation Camp at Commodore Heights (now in Ku-ring-gai Chase National Park), she saw her first rock engravings:

> Bushwalking to rock engravings was the main activity; we played games on Mundoes and Echidna because it was the only flat area. We bivouacked at America Bay; I first met Daramulan while carrying a big metal milk can. (Lesley Maynard, pers. comm., 2021)

Richard V.S. Wright and Rhys Jones who arrived at Sydney University in 1963 were her prehistory lecturers (Rhys Jones was also her tutor), Harry Oxley taught her 'very dense'[3] social anthropology, and Betty Meehan and Ian Glover were in her Honours cohort. John Clegg arrived to take up a teaching fellowship. Lesley remembers Richard announcing in a lecture that 'carbon dating showed that Aborigines had inhabited Australia for at least 7,000 years'. She completed her Honours dissertation (McMah 1965), one year after Sharon Sullivan's landmark Honours thesis at UNE (see above). Lesley's study of the Sydney Hawkesbury engravings (Figure 4.2) aimed 'to produce, first, a typology of the engravings, and second a spatial distribution of the traits, based on typology' (McMah 1965:7). This analysis indicated that 'there are definite patterns of distribution in both north–south and east–west planes; and, that the differences between one end of the range and the other may be ascribed to cultural causes – except those obviously resulting from the stimulus of different environments' (McMah 1965:75). She applied quantitative analysis to thousands of motifs, the data for which she harvested from previous records collected by W.D. Campbell, Fred McCarthy and Ian Sim (and see Griffiths 2018:188–189). It was early days for computers. I recollect my father telling of riding a pushbike from one end of the mainframe computer to the other, at this same time, when he worked in the Oak Ridge Nuclear Research Facility (Tennessee). To process this huge dataset, Lesley used computer punch cards to numerate her data, but then used knitting needles to sort the sites. I asked her why she did this, and she replied:

> The bloody punch cards were entirely Richard's idea = New Technology. Rhys suggested applying it to Sydney rock engravings. The amount of practical work was huge, punching characteristics around a card 8" ′ 5" (nonextant except in my thesis in National Library), thousands of figures – Campbell (original from Fisher), McCarthy, Sim, and a few etc. Then using a needle with a wooden handle (new technology) to sort the North–South matrix. One of the markers suggested I should have managed the East–West one as well – the one that shows the fish are near the sea (simple numbers). Billy Griffiths wrote that I was inspired by Leroi Gourhan and Andrée Rosenfeld but I didn't hear of them until years later. (Lesley Maynard, pers. comm., 2021).

---

3   All quotes from Lesley Maynard are from email correspondence with the author during the writing of this paper (between 2019 and 2021). Where I have used short passages, these are in unreferenced quotation marks; where I have extemporised Lesley's extravagant language, I indicate with an exclamation mark! – homage to John Clegg …

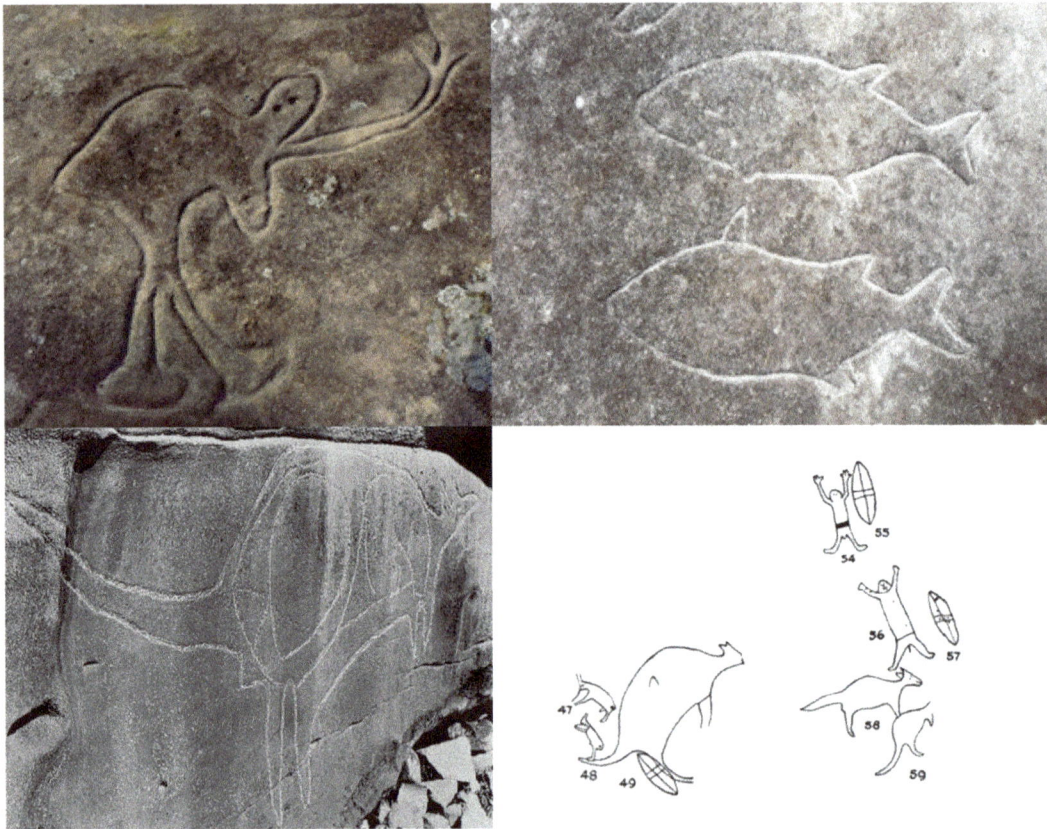

Figure 4.2: East–west differences in the Sydney Basin can be attributed to environmental factors (top), with a cultural style boundary at the Georges River – north of this boundary kangaroos are depicted with four legs; south with two legs in profile (McMah 1965).

Source: Photographs by Jo McDonald; figure from McCarthy 1967.

Lesley insists on it being recorded here that she was marked 62/100 for this 'first analytical study': (i.e. her thesis) although for their overall degrees, both she and Betty Meehan got 2/As (at that time Second Class, A division was 75–85 per cent). It has always been apocryphal at the University of Sydney that a 2/A Honours (contra a first-class Honours degree) did not mean the end of one's archaeological career: noting that Rhys Jones was famous for 'not having a first' for his Cambridge Masters thesis, completed during his first years at the University of Sydney (in 1966; Pollard 2014) – while this author (in 1982) received a final mark of 84.5! In 1966, Rhys left the University of Sydney (accompanied by his new partner, Betty Meehan; she recently returned from fieldwork in Maningrida with ex-husband Les Hiatt). Maynard replaced Jones as a University of Sydney teaching fellow: she was 21.

1n 1967, Maynard recorded the rock art of Koonalda Cave with Bob Edwards, while Richard Wright was re-excavating and analysing 'the Gallus site', as it was then known by some (this informal naming was also steeped in contemporary disputes on research, interpretation and publication of the site; Wright 1971). The radiocarbon samples from the excavation 'were sent by passing trucks to Canberra, "the local mail system". The telegram came back the same way with an Ice Age date' (Lesley Maynard, pers. comm., 2021). Bob Edwards proved to be highly influential for the budding rock art researcher that Maynard was. He was then curator of anthropology at the South Australian Museum and he had been recording rock art across the arid zone and the Northern Territory for over a decade (e.g. Edwards 1965). Maynard and Edwards's Koonalda Cave recordings included 'meticulous and well-written descriptive analysis … helped out by good drawings and excellent photographs' (Elkin 1973:162) of the site's Pleistocene finger flutings (Part II in Wright 1971). This focused a spotlight for Maynard on the potential of Australian rock art to be very old. Maynard and Edwards's contribution to the Koonalda Cave published edited volume concluded cautiously of a 'ritual' intent, but also described that the markings transcended the range 'from non-art to art' (Elkin 1973:163).

Lesley also discussed desert petroglyphs of Central Australia with Edwards: the style she would later name 'Panaramitee' (after the type site at Panaramitee Station). Edwards had already developed an extensive record of these arid zone sites (Smith et al. 2021:47–48) and had quantified large samples (1000+ motifs) as well as positing that this was an archaic Australian art form (Mountford and Edwards 1963; Edwards 1965; Rosenfeld 1991). As Lesley has said since then: 'should I have named it the "Edwardian?"'.

That same year, Maynard flew to Laura in Far North Queensland with Channel 7 (she was sent as a rock art expert by Richard Wright, who had completed his nearby excavation at Mushroom Rock) to comment on Percy Trezise's find – Giant Horse Gallery. All of her early experiences as a student and nascent researcher at the University of Sydney spoke of developing a strong sense of rock art research, in an archaeological context that was being developed concurrently by her colleagues. She also excavated, and for many years she held the earliest Pilbara Pleistocene occupation date for her work in Newman Rockshelter (Maynard 1980).[4] For over 30 years now, Newman Rockshelter's radiometric chronology has been central to archaeological discourse on the Pleistocene Aboriginal occupation of the Pilbara. Recent re-excavation of Newman Rockshelter (Slack et al. 2020) has refined the radiometric chronology using optically stimulated luminescence (OSL) ages – a technique not available until decades after her work – and confirmed an even longer occupation sequence (c. 45 and 40 kya; Slack et al. 2020:1).

In 1968, Maynard enrolled in her Masters degree at the University of Sydney. Richard Wright was again her supervisor 'in the Cambridge manner ~ set it up and leave it alone'. This was completed (Maynard 1976) just before John Clegg finished his own master's thesis, titled 'Mathesis pictures; Mathesis words', a cheeky play on words in the irreverent Clegg style (Clegg 1978a). Maynard published a long extract from her thesis (Maynard 1979), following presentations made in 1974 at both the AIAS Biennale and in Canada:

> In 1974 I was invited to a Symposium ~ The Art of Oceania ~ at McMaster Uni, Hamilton, Ontario, organised by Sidney Mead (never heard of him). I never found out who gave him my name, possibly after the Institute (AIAS) conference. Papers submitted months beforehand; on arrival we were issued with a thick volume of everyone's. I was teased about the length of mine ~ 56 pages including the never published pictures. Was I going to read it aloud? Not at all, I showed slides, Koonalda to Kakadu, and talked. Back in Oz I showed them to anyone who would sit still in the dark, thus my Tripartite Theory spread ahead of the publication. (Lesley Maynard, pers. comm., 2021)

Lesley's move to Western Australia was facilitated by the Whitlam (and then Fraser) Government's putting 'buckets of money into Aboriginal Affairs' (see below). A proliferation of funded activity increased rock art databases and anthropological knowledge about sites around the country. In 1975 Bruce Wright, to whom Lesley was later married, became the registrar of Aboriginal sites at the West Australian Department Aboriginal Sites (DAS), which later (in 1995) separated from the Western Australian Museum (WAM) and became the Aboriginal Affairs Department. He had already published his detailed Pilbara rock art opus (Wright 1968). Lesley was hired by the DAS to do 'stones and bones, maps and snaps'. At the same time three male anthropologists were hired to work in the Kimberley, Pilbara and Western Desert. The Pilbara anthropologist was Kingsley Palmer (e.g. Palmer 1975); the others were Charles Hamilton and Ken Liberman (Moya Smith, WAM, pers. comm., February 2022).

---

4   The Pilbara is in north-western Australia, where she initially recorded rock art with Bruce Wright.

Figure 4.3: Lesley excavating at Newman Rockshelter in 1976; and recording Pilbara rock art with Bruce Wright in 1978.

Source: Photographs provided by Lesley Maynard.

In 1978, Lesley began a PhD at ANU studying the well-known Pilbara engraved rock art province at Woodstock/Abydos – centred on the old pastoral station boundaries (Figure 4.3). She undertook a solitary three-week pilot study in October/November that year, when temperatures reached '44 degrees at the homestead and somewhat hotter standing on a bloody big rock'. Lesley recorded 1000+ motifs and 200 grinding patches during that field season. She used low-level colour air photography to find sites and focus her recording effort. In 1979, Kingsley Palmer went to a regional gathering of Aboriginal male Elders, known as a Pilbara Men's Meeting. At this he reported on various pieces of 'museum news' along with details of Lesley's research project. He reported to Lesley afterwards that the men's response to her project had been hostile – largely because of her gender. She said: 'Kingsley told me "They are afraid that you might find out something that they don't know themselves". To which I snarled "That's what archaeologists DO!!!"'. Soon afterwards, the Roebourne Aboriginal Association (an organisation representing the language groups on the coastal Pilbara) wrote to the Aboriginal Sites Department complaining about Lesley's research, a short news article appeared in the *West Australian* and Maynard's research permit was cancelled.

There was a lengthy period after this time in Western Australia when women were actively discouraged from working on rock art. Many felt this was because there had been a gendered divide in the information being collected by male anthropologists about sites, mythological narratives and the role of women in ceremony (e.g. Bell 2002). Certainly, the careers of Lesley, Pat Vinnicombe and Moya Smith – to some extent – were all affected by this.

> Years later I realised what I should have done when trouble started ~ tow a caravan to Roebourne and do my own bloody social anthropology. Taking women and kids to lovely picnic sites and showing them seed-grinding patches. (Lesley Maynard, pers. comm., 2021)

Maynard never completed her PhD. Leaving ANU, she became the regional archaeologist for the Northern Region of the New South Wales National Parks and Wildlife Service (NSW NPS): 'the most exciting, productive and happiest part of my career was helping Sharon (Sullivan) invent Cultural Resource Management in Oz'. In 1986, 'while driving at night [Lesley] had an overwhelming spiritual experience which kicked off a major manic episode'. This change in her mental health meant that she has rarely published again (cf. Maynard 1988).

> In 1999, in a manic phase, I couldn't stand the sight of my career relics ~ No More Bloody Archaeology! I packed up all my original manuscripts and photographs, [from] 1960's Anthropology lecture notes to *Egina* [a desert rock art province] research. [I] drove to Canberra, AIAS, where Kingsley Palmer was then Deputy Principal. Dumped my boxes on his office floor and conversed briefly. I didn't keep any copies, make a list or sign anything.

This material (in five boxes) is now held in the AIATSIS digital collection (MAR03/288), where it remains unprocessed (Lesley Maynard, pers. comm., 1 May 2021).

Lesley recalls that well-known local avocational rock art enthusiast and surveyor John Lough (see Rhodes 2018:159) was the only rock art recorder she worked with in Sydney, mostly after she joined the NSW NPWS in 1981, where John Lough was a frequent visitor 'usually at 5pm'. Lesley credits Lough with the invention of 'The Night-time Method … carbide lamps and chalk in the dark; he gloated over many details missed by Fred [McCarthy]. The following morning, he would use a chalked string to snap a grid over the engravings and drew them on squared paper' (Lesley Maynard, pers. comm., May 2021). I, too, remember going out to record rock art at Devil's Rock, Maroota, with John Lough at night (McDonald 1986) using carbide lamps and our 1980s 'innovation' – Dolphin torches – which were an improvement because of the better angle that could be achieved with the oblique light. Lough was indeed vainglorious about his improved accuracy over previous recorders: I was scolded for introducing over 100 errors into my Maroota (McDonald 1986) recording but praised for being much better than Fred (McCarthy) 'who had more than 1,280 errors' for the same large complex panel (John Lough, pers. comm., 1987). I remember being amused by the fact that the very accurate Lough, who still used imperial measurements 20 years after introduction of the metric system to Australia, used his shod foot (his shoe was exactly 12 inches long) for measuring purposes!

John K. Clegg (1935–2015)

John Clegg emigrated to Australia in 1961 with a Bachelor of Arts (Honours) and Certificate in Education (1959) and Fine Arts Honours (awarded in 1962) from the University of Cambridge, where his archaeological mentor was Charles McBurney. When he arrived in Australia he first tutored at the University of Queensland, and then in the mid-1960s became a part-time tutor at the University of Sydney while also enrolled at East Sydney Technical College studying drawing and sculpture. John's drawing skills were instrumental to his seeing and understanding the Sydney Basin's Aboriginal charcoal drawings. His interests in fine art led to his later focus on aesthetics with Thomas Heyd (e.g. Heyd and Clegg 2005). His focus on the cognitive processes that contribute to art's creation meant that he analysed rock art from a different perspective to his predecessors and many of his contemporaries. He undertook experimental work on Sydney's sandstone to determine likely timeframes required to produce the large engravings on the open horizontal platforms, a kind of 'experimental archaeology' akin to experimental research occurring elsewhere in the world especially in the 1970s and 1980s. His interest in the techniques and technologies of rock art production (materiality) influenced his analysis of rock art. He applied and developed several fieldwork approaches, which improved the accuracy of the recording process (night photography; tracing on polythene for later photography (Figure 4.4); use of a monopod [pre-drone] to get extra height/distance imagery for photogrammetry).

Figure 4.4: John Clegg tracing rock art on polythene at Little Devils Rock, Old Northern Road, 1972.

Source: Photograph taken and provided by Kate Sullivan.

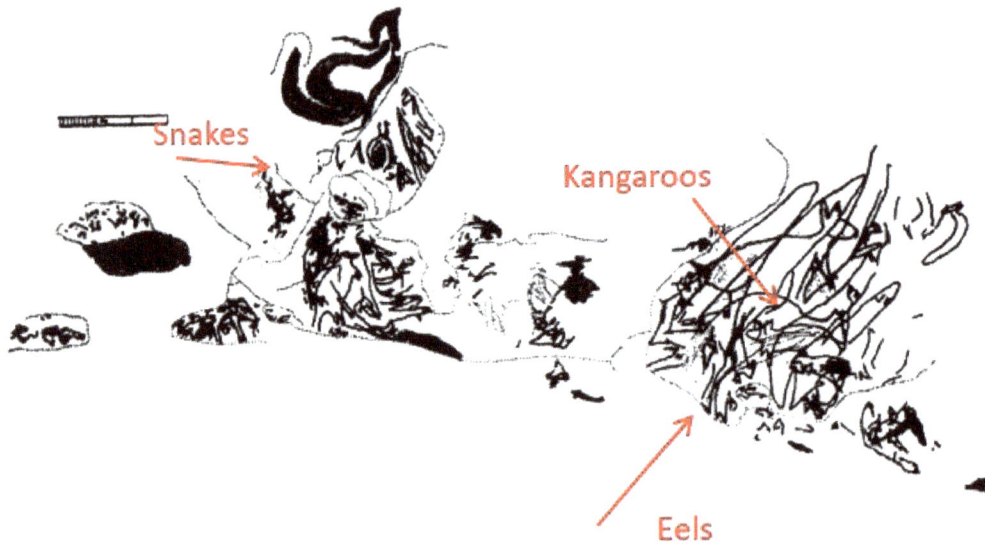

Figure 4.5: The Woronora rock-shelter assemblage where the placement of motifs was explored.

Source: From Clegg 1971, amended by author.

One of his first papers (Clegg 1971) explicitly aimed at contradicting John Mulvaney's views on (unsystematic) rock art research being 'art appreciation' (Mulvaney 1969:173). This early paper on a Woronora rock-shelter assemblage (in the south of the Sydney region) counteracted the prevailing view at the time that hunter-gatherer art was essentially random in its placement and intent (following Laming-Emperaire 1962; Leroi-Gourhan 1968). Most of the animal species depicted in the Woronora rock-shelter assemblage (snakes, bats, macropods, eels and fish) were positioned on the walls in what John described as 'their natural order': that is, according to their natural habitats (Figure 4.5). However, while 14 of the 21 animal motifs conformed to this expected landscape positioning, the snakes and eels did not. John quantified the relative sizes of these depictions (Table 4.1) and realised that the size ratios of the depicted animals was also patterned. The eels and snakes were depicted as extremely large creatures, while other species were generally life-size.

Table 4.1: A metaphysical approach to the study of Aboriginal rock paintings.

Motif	Natural	Woronora	Relative size
Eel	1.2	6	5
Snake	1.25	3.5	2.8
Wallaby	1.95	3.8	1.4
Fish	0.3	0.4	1.3
Bat	0.4	0.4	1
Tortoise	0.2	0.2	1

Note: Measurements in metres.
Source: Data from Clegg 1971:39.

Clegg used spirit animal ethnography to explain this result. Rainbow Serpents (Radcliffe-Brown 1930) could be in the sky as well as in water sources and on land; and in the Sydney region they are also sometimes depicted as huge eel-like creatures with tails (Sim 1969). Clegg's (1971) paper also confirmed schematic differences that McMah (1965) had identified for either side of the Georges River (a regional style boundary): with eels pointing downwards at Woronora (a rock-shelter south of the Georges River), compared to those depicted at Canoelands (a rock-shelter in the north of the region) oriented upwards. Clegg concluded that:

> a drawing is just as much an artefact as a Bondi point is, and as such, should be just as illuminating for prehistory … [and that] Archaeologists need to be educated to deploy a range of new techniques, rather than rejecting the great potential of rock art studies. (Clegg 1971:40)

While teaching at the University of Sydney, John completed his Anthropology and Prehistory Department Masters of Arts (Hons) dissertation (Clegg 1978a), for which he was awarded the University Medal. Richard Wright was his official supervisor, although this relationship was a tense one. According to Kate Sullivan (Clegg's spouse, and now widow, and a student at the University of Sydney in the early 1970s), John waited until Richard was away on leave to lodge his thesis. The two volumes of John's Masters' thesis were entitled 'MAthesis words' and 'MAthesis pictures'. Clegg loved the pun of the word 'mathesis' (i.e. meaning 'the measuring of things not normally measured') combined with the formal MA (Master of Arts) thesis title. The confusion that this caused in the Examination Office at the University of Sydney is legendary (as recounted by Chris Chippindale in 2015 at the memorial service for John held in MacLaren Hall).

John Clegg's research addressed a central question in much rock art research: how do we know what a painting/engraving is meant to depict? His scholarly work is perhaps best known for his insistence on the pointlessness of trying to construct emic meaning for motifs given the impossibility of securely ascertaining the motivation of the artists (see Clegg 1981, 1987). Clegg (1991) developed, and a few other scholars initially adopted, the typographic convention of an exclamation mark before their own categorisations of motifs to emphasise their view that the names allocated to motifs may not convey the same meaning as was intended by the artists, but rather simply signalled what a motif looked like to the researcher (e.g. !fish, !kangaroo). For some researchers, this was satisfactorily pronounced as a !Kung click (glottal stop) and represented an improvement on using double quotation marks to signal this same point. In due course, as rock art researchers and social anthropologists began to explicitly point out that motif names allocated by researchers were not necessarily meant to represent emic meanings, the use of the exclamation mark began to be dropped in line with the changing times and improved assumptions behind rock art recordings.

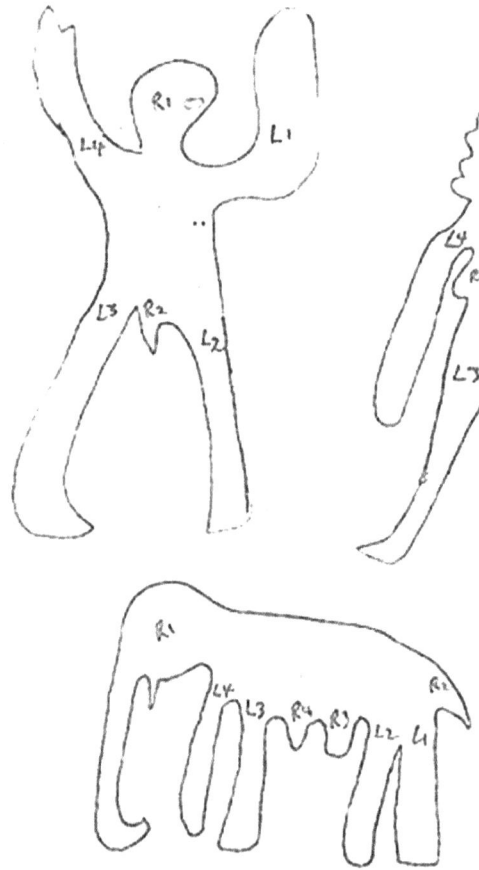

Figure 4.6: Knobs and blobs: A neutral geometric way to describe the shape of a motif.
Source: Clegg 1981:65.

John continued to wrestle with questions of meaning in his development of 'a geometry which would allow the description and definition of motif forms without the need of nouns' (Clegg 1981:60). 'Knobs (K) and blobs (B)' was in effect an early attempt at morphometric analysis: a four-legged dog with tail up and two ears would be B 2R (2 round attachment) 5L (long addendums); an ungendered anthropomorph with arms up and legs down would be B R 4L; an elephant B R1 R2 2L 2R 2L R3 L (Figure 4.6). While proving repeatable and therefore fully 'scientific', the lack of ultimate insight in these labels and a geometry that 'seems to maximize incomprehensibility' (Clegg 1986:60), meant that many of his students experimented with – but moved quickly past – this abstract coding towards John's objective approach.

Another early morphometric approach – which has retained relevance in the interpretation of different animal species depicted in rock art (De Koning 2014; Gunn et al. 2011; Jones et al. 2017; McDonald 1993; McDonald and Veth 2006), was John's early work on interpreting which striped mammals were thylacine depictions, as opposed to numbats, bandicoots, striped hare-wallabies, etc. (Clegg 1978b). His approach used zoological imagery and diagnostic attributes that he then applied to recorded striped animals from around northern Australia (Figure 4.7). He manually matched the imagery and scored motifs on their similarities and then tested this using a Chi-squared calculation (Clegg 1978b:24). Just over half of the striped mammals could be identified as thylacines based on this approach, with another six being classed as different kinds of striped animals. Three images were indistinguishable from multiple species, having shared characteristics (e.g. of numbat and/or thylacine). He concluded that this systematic approach was repeatable and allowed confidence in accepting the statement that 'thylacine designs are widely distributed … in western and central Arnhem Land rock painting sites' (Calaby and Lewis 1977:150), with crucial implications for better understanding the age of the rock art, given the known timing of the extinction of the thylacine in mainland Australia (Clegg 1978b:29).

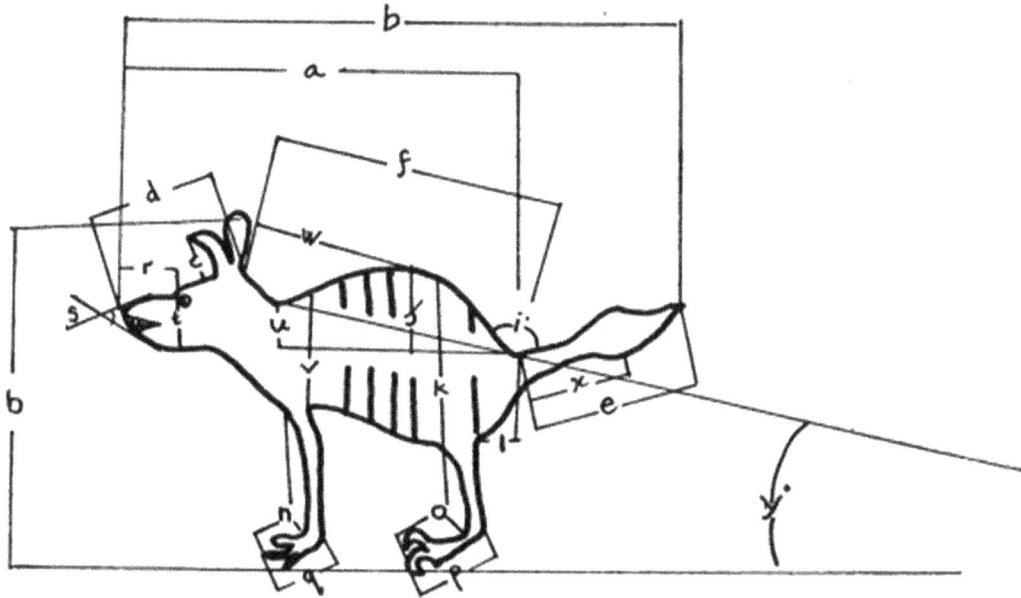

Figure 1—Measuring points

Figure 4.7: An early morphometric approach to striped animal depictions.
Source: Clegg 1978b: Figure 1.

Like Maynard, John was also fully engaged with the contextualisation of rock art through the excavation of associated archaeological deposits. One of his more eccentric collaborations was with Spike Milligan (and this also involved Lesley Maynard, by this time at NSW NPWS). Spike (who 'lived at Woy Woy, you know!' *The Goons*, 1965) had found a rock-shelter with midden and charcoal drawings and engravings (of a fish/echidna and a macropod) low on the sloping back wall – as well as several large whale engravings at nearby Daley's Point on the NSW central coast. Clegg excavated the shelter prior to the NSW NPWS constructing a metal grid to protect the art from vandals. The predominantly *Anadara granosa* (now *Tegillarca* spp.) shell midden was dated to the last millennium, and the shelter had a Mid-Holocene basal date (Clegg 1979:2; McDonald 2008:301).

Bull Cave, near the Georges River, was similarly excavated prior to the installation of a protective grid (by David Bell, archaeologist at NSW NPWS), and this lithic assemblage was later analysed by a University of Sydney Honours student (Miller 1983), who did not attempt to correlate the art with the occupation evidence. The pigment art at Bulls Cave includes several motifs among its complex assemblage of black and red drawings and white hand stencils interpreted as colonial-period contact motifs: large bulls executed in traditional drawing techniques. Clegg (1981) argued that these drawings depict the polled cattle that went missing from the early days of the British colony (in 1788; Tench 1789). The 'bull' motifs have no horns, unlike the 61 progeny of the escapees, which were eventually found by settlers in 1795 in (what is now) the Sydney suburb of Cowpastures. Clegg also argued for a 'developmental' or 'bitsa' schema whereby one of these (red) drawings is more bird-like than bull-like, while the other, black version, is more schematically 'correct'. The bulls' feet were obviously problematic for the Aboriginal artist (i.e. these drawings are not naturalistic) and Clegg argues that this is because these were unlike any native fauna known to the Aboriginal artists. Intriguingly, another cave with similar motifs has since been found in the north of the Sydney region, near Putty, by avid rock art recorder Ron Volmerhausen (Figure 4.8). While this does not discount the original European contact period interpretation (it is still hard to discern the feet on these paintings), it does suggest that these depictions could be a mythical bird-like being known to the Darkingung/Tharawal language speakers from the western parts of the Sydney region.

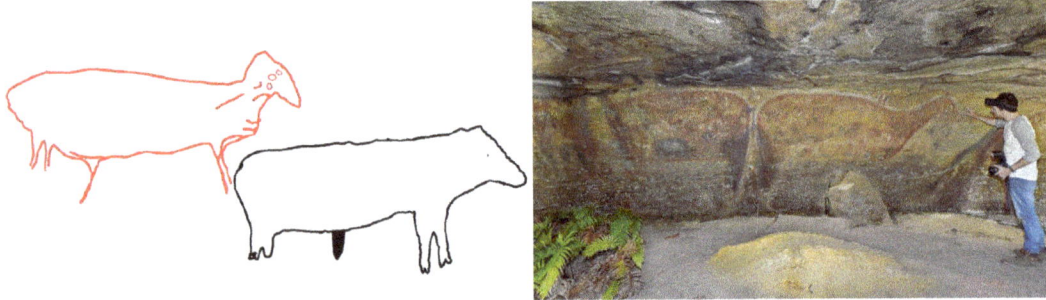

Figure 4.8: The Bull Cave Bulls (left) – and mythical creature of similar schemata found in Putty (right) – to the north of the Sydney Basin.
Source: Sketch by Jo McDonald from Clegg 1981; photograph by Ron Volmerhausen, used with permission.

Throughout his tenure at Sydney University, John Clegg inspired and trained a new generation of rock art scholars on how to look at and how to think about Aboriginal rock art (Smith and McDonald 2015). I remember doing a rock art unit in second year and another in third year, when his *Notes towards mathesis art* (1981) was freshly minted. This self-published textbook, with its incomparable typing and sketched figures (captioned in his distinctive handwriting, usually green in the original), included information from multiple projects undertaken in the classroom with his students over the preceding 10 years. I still refer to this book when I need inspiration for how to structure teaching about perception, schemas, classification, taxonomy and more.

John supervised 18 Honours theses (between 1981 and 2004), one Masters and three PhD dissertations (between 1999 and 2004) while at the University of Sydney (Table 4.2; White 1994). Of his Honours students, seven went on to complete PhD theses, and another three completed higher degrees in other fields. One, George Susino, was supervised by John for both his Honours and PhD dissertations. Almost without exception, every one of these graduates went on to participate fully in an archaeology/heritage/regulatory or management role. Several of his early students are now university lecturers and training current undergraduates and postgraduates (e.g. myself included, and Laurajane Smith), overseeing the regulation of state or federal legislation (e.g. Katherine Sale, Sam Higgs, Natalie Franklin), or running companies that employ large numbers of archaeologists (e.g. Richard Mackay, Matthew Kelleher).

In 1994, the University of Sydney awarded John a Long Service Medal and he remained an academic there until his retirement in 2001. Australian archaeology benefited from John's genuine individuality, his sharp wit and his acute observations. He was an intellectually formidable scholar for whom eccentricity, intellect and humour were intertwined.

Table 4.2: Honours, Masters and PhD students supervised by John Clegg.

Year	Student	Thesis title	Subsequent career
1981	Graf, Christina	What is primitive art?	?
1981	Konecny, Tania A.	What could it all mean – Conclusions on an enigmatic subject	Grad Certificate, Australian museum collections manager, registrar Historic Houses Trust
1982	McDonald, Josephine	On the write track	PhD (ANU), ARC Future Fellow, professor UWA
1982	Jones, Ann	A Saussurian analysis of Aboriginal bark paintings from east Arnhem Land and Groote Eylandt	Public servant
1983	Mackay, Richard	The use and abuse of ethnographic analogy from Australia in the study of rock art	MBA, director GML Heritage, Mackay Strategic
1983	Smith, Laurajane	What's in the size of a macropod? A study of variance in prehistoric pictures from the Mangrove Creek area	PhD (USyd), professor ANU
1984	Franklin, Natalie	Of !macropods and !men: An analysis of the Simple Figurative styles	PhD (La Trobe), regulator/consultant/researcher Qld
1988	Sefton, Caryll (MA)	Site and artefact patterns on the Woronora Plateau	Consultant
1989	Bell, M.	Least effort art: An investigation of the rock engravings in Wardaman Country, Victoria River District, Northern Territory	?
1989	Edgar, John	Stylish messages	Consultant
1991	Drew, Julie	Women & gender relations in Australian Aboriginal rock art	Consultant
1992	Sale, Katharine	Make 'em bright' – Aboriginal re-marking of rock art in past and present Australia	Commonwealth public servant, heritage regulation
1994	Wilson, Meredith	Shaping Pacific rock art	PhD (ANU), World Heritage List heritage adviser
1996	Susino, George	Fitting pictures and stories: A study of archaeology as a resource	PhD (USyd)
1997	Barry, Michael	I would sooner not call them Bradshaws	Private researcher
1998	Forsyth, Hannah	Classification. An examination of principals and methods	PhD (USyd), ARC DECRA, ACU
1999	James, Pamela	A pillar curiously engraven …: What is the Ruthwell Cross?	Art crime, museologist, University of Western Sydney
1999	Susino, George (PhD)	Microdebitage and the archaeology of rock art: An experimental approach	UoW, University of the Witwatersrand, private researcher
2002	Kelleher, Matthew (PhD)	Archaeology of sacred space: The spatial nature of religious behaviour in the Blue Mountains National Park Australia	Director, Nightingale Kelleher Pty Ltd
2003	Higgs, Samantha	Emu bums & second generation knobs: A taxonomic look at some Sydney Rock engravings	PhD (ANU), NSW regulator
2004	Black, Adam	YAPA-PUWAN KARUL the Mount Grenfall 'rocks with art', a significant physical, cultural, historical/political archaeological landscape	MA, PhD candidate, research officer at Gunditj Mirring Traditional Owners Corporation
2004	Jordan, Darran (PhD)	From semiotics to mapping: Semiotics, gaps, multivocality & theory clouds	Principal archaeologist, AECOM

Notes: ACU: Australian Catholic University; ANU: The Australian National University; ARC: Australian Research Council; DECRA: Discovery Early Career Researcher Award; USyd: University of Sydney; UoW: University of Wollongong; UWA: University of Western Australia.

Source: Author's summary.

Theory, practice and 'buckets of money'

While universities in Australia began to teach a new generation of rock art researchers, AIATSIS came to play an important role in the development of Australian rock art research, through several phases of focused funding of national rock art research and conservation programs. Fred McCarthy, the first AIAS principal (1964–1972), brought his long rock art career to the role (McCarthy 1967), as did his replacement Peter Ucko (AIAS principal 1972–1981; along with deputy Bob Edwards). Ucko is considered by many (e.g. Griffiths 2018; Morwood and Smith 1994; Ward 2011) to have been pivotal for the development of Australian rock art research. He championed Aboriginal peoples' rights to be recognised as the owners and managers of their own heritage, as well as providing the mechanisms to increase the discourse around rock art research and archaeological practice. Ucko's arrival in Australia was timely, with the Whitlam Government creating the Aboriginal Land Fund (in 1974) and the drafting of the *Aboriginal Lands Right Act* (1975), which significantly increased funding to Aboriginal Affairs and the capacity of AIAS for largesse in funding cycles.

During his tenure at AIAS, Ucko promoted a change in AIAS funding priorities, giving rock art a greater precedence in this grants scheme. He also encouraged several European rock art researchers (Michel Lorblanchet, Bob Layton) to come and work in Australia, and funded targeted anthropological and archaeological rock art research programs around the country. Rock art research by Lorblanchet and Layton, Andrée Rosenfeld (who worked with Percy Trezise in Laura), Ian Crawford (Kimberley) and Peter Sims (Tasmania) were all funded by AIAS. Bob Edwards, along with Warwick Dix (AIAS deputy principal after 1974), implemented the National Site Recording Program (NSRP, 1973–1979). The NSRP funded Indigenous cultural places research and protection and the employment of site recording staff, through Australian state and territory agencies. As with AIAS's general grants program, rock art recording became a central focus of this funded research, contextualised by other broader regional analyses also supported through this funding scheme (Ward 2011:8). Among the 20+ site recorders funded were rock art researchers Lesley Maynard and Bruce Wright (DAS/WAM), George Chaloupka and Darrell J. Lewis (Museum and Art Gallery of the Northern Territory), Grahame L. Walsh (Queensland NPWS) and Patricia Vinnicombe (first at NSW NPWS, later at DAS). A later AIATSIS program that prioritised rock art conservation was initiated in 1986 as the Rock Art Protection Program (Ward and Sullivan 1989). The Australian Heritage Commission was also fundamental in the recognition and conservation of rock art through their National Estates Grant Projects (e.g. Rosenfeld et al. 1981; Veth et al. 1993).

This national resourcing of research activities with a rock art focus was a much-needed injection of capital, but it would have had only short-term benefits had the training and financial support of rock art researchers not happened in tandem.

Style and classification – the 1974 AIAS Biennale Conference

The 'Schematisation in art' symposium was one of eight symposia held at the AIAS Biennale Conference that ran over 17 days in May–June 1974. This conference was highly influential in setting research agendas for Australian archaeology more generally, as well as fostering academic interest and consolidating theoretical approaches to the study of prehistoric art. *Form in Indigenous art* (Ucko 1977a) was one of eight ensuing volumes published from this marathon event.

Both John Clegg and Lesley Maynard participated in the 'Schematisation in art' symposium (which ran for three days). Both contributed to the volume that was published three years later (Ucko 1977a). When I asked Lesley about the significance of this conference and whether it and Peter Ucko had stimulated her into new ways of thinking about rock art, she snorted that Peter Ucko had been quite dismissive of Australian efforts to that point ('Australian Rock Art Studies? Excuse me while I laugh!', he had said), a remark that Lesley told me had definitely 'stimulated hers and John's opinions about Peter Ucko'!

While Ucko's personal views at the commencement of the symposium may have been dismissive of the colonial efforts of Australian rock art researchers until then, *Form in Indigenous art* was a landmark volume, clearly showing the strengths of a nascent Australian rock art research scene in 1974. The book contains 38 chapters, eight of which Ucko commissioned afterwards to include a range of aspects of Aboriginal art (sand sculptures, toas, bark paintings, bark dwellings) – 'a unique statement about the status and development of Aboriginal Studies at this particular period' (Ucko 1977b). In his preface to the volume – written three years after the conference – he says it 'was one of the most challenging editorial roles [he] had ever undertaken' (Ucko 1977b:4). The three sections he wrote, which include 'Opening Remarks' (Ucko 1977c) and an introduction (Ucko 1977d) – are deserving of an analytical chapter of their own!

The contributions by Maynard and Clegg at the symposium were foundational papers on style, schema, form and classification. Their papers are standout contributions on the archaeological approaches required to disentangle 'style' in an assemblage, as well as clearly defining the current state of Australian rock art pedagogy at the time. Papers by seasoned rock art researchers (Bruce Wright, Fred McCarthy, Ian Crawford, Warwick Dix, Eric Brandl, George Chaloupka, David Moore, Enzo Virili and others) revealed the depth and breadth of the national endeavour to this point, as well as marking the transition from a widespread, more antiquarian/art historical approach to an archaeological one.

Clegg's two contributions were chapters titled 'The meaning of schematisation' and 'A method of resolving problems that arise from style' (Clegg 1977a, 1977b). The first focused on defining and applying schematisation as it had been used in other fields of research (e.g. stone artefacts), to mobilise the concept for archaeological purposes. A schema was seen as a mental model and schematisation a reduction of a complex idea to a simple motif (Clegg 1977a:21). As described above, John was grappling with the dilemma of attributing original meaning:

> the trouble with most words when used for purely descriptive purposes is that they imply knowledge of the intention of the artist, or the process of making the art … 'Abstract' means derived from nature, 'stylise' infers conformation to a traditional norm, as does 'conventionalised'; 'poorly drawn' is a value judgement; 'symbolic' assumes some referent importance … information cannot be convincingly obtained if the original description of the artefact implies the answer. (Clegg 1977a:25)

His other paper in *Form in Indigenous art* dealt with classification and style, and here he defined four sets of causal factors that could be brought to play when trying to interpret 'style'. Clegg combined fine art approaches with archaeological methods applied to stone tool classifications (1977b:Table 1; Clegg 1977c) and argued that 'style' could be perceived as variation in an artefact/motif/regional art body caused by four factors (1977b:260):

- Function: the purposes (if any) for which the artefact was made and its uses.
- Medium: the physical materials of which an artefact is made, and the techniques used to create it.
- Culture: the social group to which (context within) the artificer belonged.
- Personality: the individuality of the artificer.

Here he deployed a multi-trait analysis to distinguish between the pigment rock art at Bare Hill (North Queensland) and six sites across the Sydney Basin and identified assemblage differences between the two geographically distinct regions in terms of motif compositions and proportions. He attempted to calculate (again, manually) a correlation matrix. While based on a small sample size, he concluded that his approach had great potential for identifying regional stylist patterning and confirmed that the Woronora site south of Sydney was stylistically distinct from those sites in northern Sydney, as McMah (Maynard) had demonstrated a decade earlier (McMah 1965). This early theorising and methodological approach to Australian rock art research is now standard archaeological practice, with a focus on regional, landscape and contextual studies.

While Clegg's work was focusing attention on methodological and theoretical quandaries yet to be overcome, Maynard's 'Classification and terminology in Australian rock art' outlined the approach she was deploying in her MA thesis (Maynard 1976, 1979). In this paper, published in *Form in Indigenous art*, she redefined how motifs and traits should be used in relation to Australian rock art styles, observing that 'styles' were 'clusters' of particular characteristics repeatedly manifested among figures (Maynard 1977:402). Maynard deconstructed McCarthy's (1967) nomenclature and methodologies. She identified why his separation of pigment and engraved art was problematic (i.e. his terminology 'ignored a common artistic intention' with an absence of 'consistent hierarchy of concepts' (1977:389)). She proposed a new terminology as an alternative to McCarthy's 'personal set of terms he has evolved during his long study of Australian rock art' (1977:390). She identified and defined five levels of descriptive process, which on combination could describe any rock art motif: technique, form, motif, size and character.

The influence of the Sydney School on current research

Lesley Maynard's 1965 Sydney Basin rock art research 'was a landmark' (Clegg 1983:88), and not only because it was the first rock art research by an Australian-trained rock art researcher at an Australian university. Her thesis found that:

> pictures as artefact-types may be defined with sufficient rigour to carry out the work; that patterns in the distribution of pictures may be discovered without any need to identify the subject of a depiction; … that those patterns may be explained by interpretation in relation to ethnography and geography. (Clegg 1983:88)

Research done decades later (Clegg 1983; McDonald 2008; Officer 1984) confirmed the major style boundary she identified at the Georges River (for both rock art media), and that these patterns are complex, with the rock art needing to be contextualised in a broader archaeological record.

John Clegg also wrote that, during the 1974 'Art in Oceania Symposium', Lesley Maynard 'made sense for the first time of the overall art history of the continent' (Clegg 1983:89) when she said:

> There are, within the whole corpus of Australian rock art, three major identifiable styles which can, at this stage of our knowledge of the material, be placed in a relative sequence. It is not very meaningful to call these units 'phases'. I have called the three major units, in the order in which I believe them to have been used in Australia, Panaramitee style, Simple Figurative styles, and Complex Figurative styles. (Maynard 1979:91–92, in Clegg 1983:89)

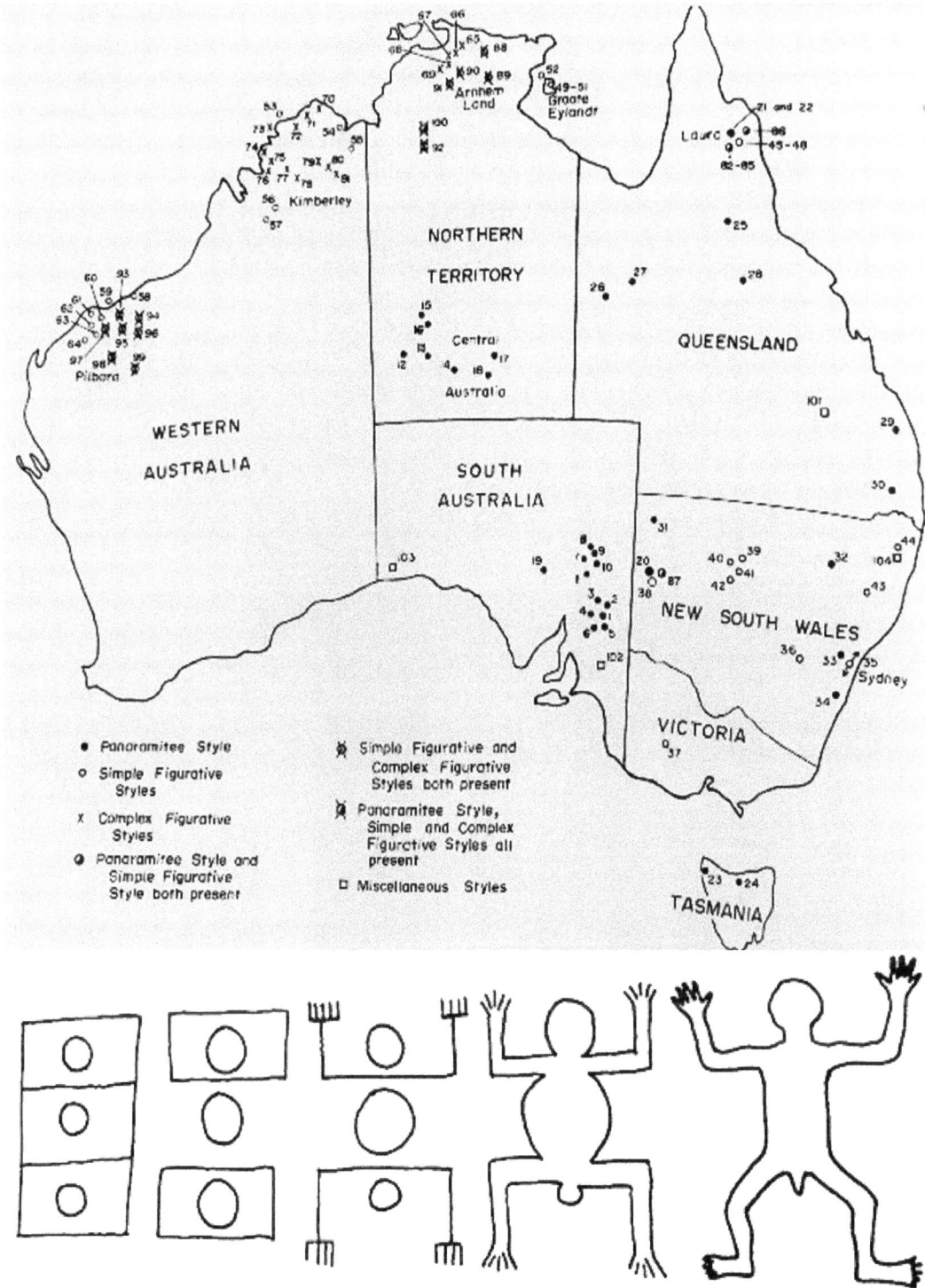

Figure 4.9: The pan-continental sequence (from Maynard 1979:Figure 4.1), and the transitional sequence from nonfigurative to figurative.

Source: Maynard 1977: Figure 1.

At the University of Sydney, Maynard's three-part pan-Australian art style sequence (Figure 4.8) set the rock art research agenda for decades to come, as well as more broadly among many (but not all) researchers (see, for instance, the 1988 debate in *Rock Art Research* 5(1)). No one has successfully attempted a pan-continental model since then (see Bednarik 1988), but detailed regional studies have proliferated, such as for Arnhem Land, the Kimberley, Murujuga, the

Pilbara and the Western Desert (e.g. Jones et al. 2017; McDonald 2017; McDonald and Veth 2013; Mulvaney 2015; Veth et al. 2018). Some of these regional sequences confirm aspects of Maynard's tripartite scheme (e.g. the earliest arid zone style is comprised of geometrics and tracks across many parts of the continent (McDonald and Veth 2010)). However, each and every one of these regional sequences contradict the scheme as a pan-Australian evolutionary model of art production from nonfigurative, to simple and then more complex figurative motifs (Figure 4.9). There is no evidence that style production (or perception) becomes more complex through time (see Rosenfeld 2000). Within regions defined as one or another of Maynard's original definitions (e.g. the Simple Figurative styles), significant internal variability has demonstrated the complexity of peoples' signalling behaviour at the site, local catchment and regional scale (Franklin 2007; McDonald and Harper 2016). In parts of the Western Desert, for instance, there is a parallel use of geometric and figurative forms in all style phases after the earliest abraded grooves and/ or cupules and then Panaramitee-like engraved phases (McDonald 2017, 2021; McDonald and Veth 2013). In other deep-time engraved sequences (such as at Murujuga), there is no clear 'progression' from track/geometric to figurative forms, and some of the most complex geometric and human forms are arguably Pleistocene in age, to be replaced by Simple Figurative styles in more recent times (McDonald 2015; Mulvaney 2015). Similarly, in the Kimberley, the Complex Figurative Gwion motifs have recently been dated to the Last Glacial Maximum (Finch et al. 2020), and a Simple Figurative Irregular Infill macropod has been dated to older than the Gwion style (Finch et al. 2021), while the Simple Figurative Wanjina styles have been dated to the past 4000 years (Harper et al. 2019). In Central Australia there is stylistic continuity through deep time and into the contemporary past (Ross and Davidson 2006).

The appointment of academic positions dedicated to rock art studies was crucial to the development of rock art as a subdiscipline in Australia. The international revolutions known as the new archaeology (e.g. Sabloff et al. 1987) in the USA and analytical archaeology (Clarke 1978) in the UK and post-processualism influenced Australian practitioners, but also resulted in the strong local development of archaeological thought and methods, and rock art has contributed significantly to these. Australian rock art research also has developed a strong collaborative component with Aboriginal and Torres Strait Islander Traditional Owners of rock art estates, moving beyond the ethnographic analogy 'trap' bemoaned by early practitioners worldwide. One of my earliest memories of Sydney rock art was a field trip organised by John that included University of Sydney undergraduates and Aboriginal trainees from Tranby College (in Glebe, Sydney); while similarly the 1982 Sturt's Meadows Australian Research Council (ARC) Linkage Project fieldwork (Clegg 1987) involved site visits from Aboriginal community members then based in Wilcannia and Broken Hill in western NSW. This was the first time I met Badger Bates, Baakandji Traditional Owner for Sturts Meadows (Bates 1993) and now a Traditional Owner well known to all Australian practitioners, who has participated in collaborative work with many in the Australian archaeological discipline for decades and is currently leading community activism countering water theft from the Darling River (*Baarka*) in western NSW (Ellis et al. 2021).

The Sydney School was at the forefront of this training revolution, and there was a proliferation at the University of Sydney in the 1980s of archaeological Honours theses with a rock art focus (see Table 4.2). This and the concurrent, and slightly later, rock art teaching and training programs at (especially) ANU in Canberra and UNE in NSW created the current generation of active Australian rock art researchers. My own research trajectory involved undergraduate training at the University of Sydney (with John Clegg), a PhD at ANU (supervised by Andrée Rosenfeld, Anthony Forge and Isabel McBryde), followed by decades as a cultural heritage practitioner before moving to my current role at as director of the Centre for Rock Art Research + Management (CRAR+M) at the University of Western Australia (UWA), where I teach undergraduates and supervise Honours, Masters and PhD candidates, as well as undertaking large

ARC-funded Linkage and Fellowship projects. Based on this I have commenced a 'genealogy' of rock art researchers that shows the spheres of connections between the University of Sydney, ANU and UWA (Figure 4.10). This does not represent the entire Australian rock art research network but is intended to demonstrate how that initial influence of the Sydney School has permeated the rock art field today. This diagram is a force-directed network visualisation plotted using the visNetwork package in R (Almende et al. 2019). Similar 'genealogical' influences and connections should also be made to show the interconnectedness of other key researchers, and their interdisciplinary influences, at UNE, Flinders, Monash and more recently Griffith's rock art centre, the Place, Evolution and Rock Art Heritage Unit (PERAHU), to reveal this entire entangled network of influences and effects.

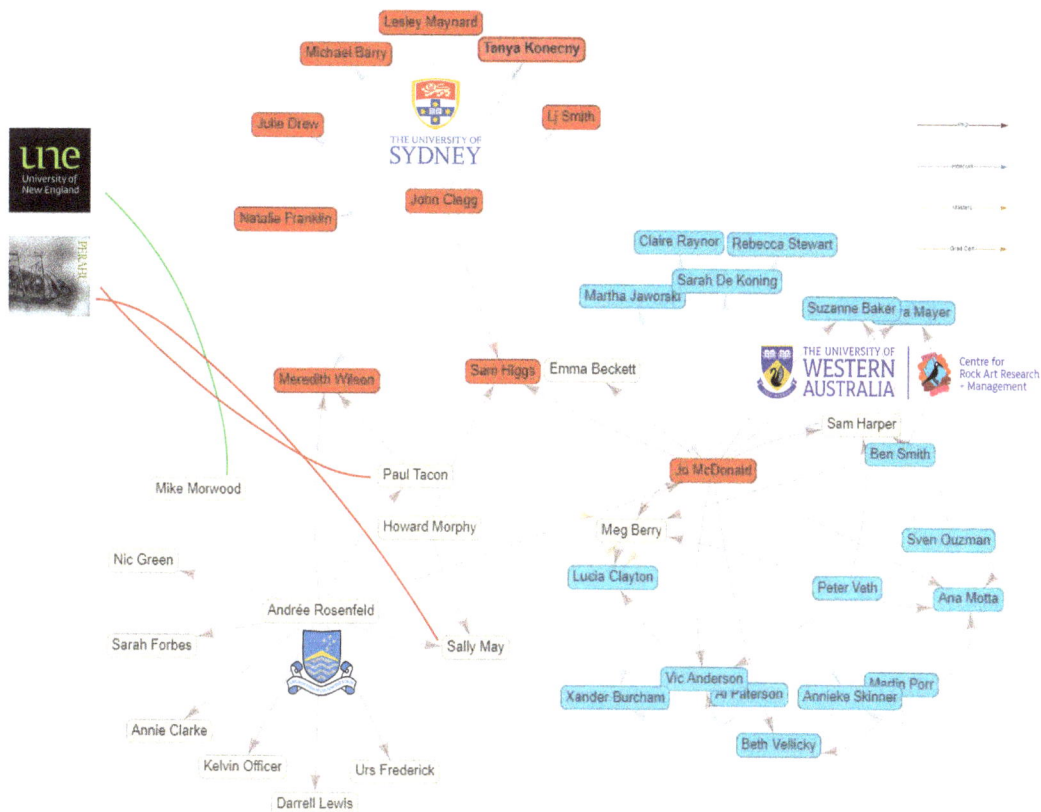

Figure 4.10: The Sydney School's influence on rock art research (including ANU and UWA): The start of a rock art research network map.

Researchers are colour-coded by first Australian institution where they studied rock art (University of Sydney in red, ANU in gold, UWA in blue). Solid lines represent thesis supervision, dashed lines represent colleagues.
Source: Jo McDonald.

At the turn of the millennium there was a degree of pessimism about the future of Australian rock art research among some commentators (McDonald 2004), with the retirement of key rock art academics (Rosenfeld, Clegg, Morwood and Davidson – sequentially) and their respective teaching departments realigning their research focuses. In 2004, only two rock art researchers were employed full-time: Paul Taçon at the Australian Museum and Bruno David at Monash University (and Bruno points out that he was employed through postdocs and fellowships for 23 years before he had a tenured position (Bruno David, pers. comm., 2022)). A decline in tertiary education funding (Wallis 2020) was accompanied by a decline in institutional resourcing (e.g. the closing of the Australian Heritage Commission in 2004 and loss of National Estate Grant Programme grants, and reduction in scale and scope of AIATSIS grants including the elimination of dedicated rock art research funding).

The last decade, however, has seen a major upswing in rock art research funding, largely through ARC funding accompanied by philanthropic and industry support. We are again in an exciting period of rock art research efflorescence. Rock art today is a viable subdiscipline of Australian archaeology with a vibrant research profile and more trained rock art specialists than ever before (McDonald 2020). Advances in digital technologies and archaeological sciences, and the important recognition of Indigenous knowledge means that interdisciplinary rock art research that contextualises rock art in its broader sociocultural context has again placed Australia at the forefront of international formal and informed research.

There are currently two recognised Rock Art Research Centres in Australia. PERAHU at Griffith University is directed by Paul Taçon (recently completing an ARC Laureate Fellowship), with Sally K. May, Jillian Huntley and Andrea Jalandoni as specialist staff funded by Taçon's laureate program, and Huntley now an ARC Discovery Early Career Research Award (DECRA) Fellow and May now an ARC Future Fellow at Adelaide, as well as Maxime Aubert (ARC Future Fellow) with large Linkage projects (led by Lynley Wallis and Adam Brumm) on the rock art of Cape York Peninsula in Far North Queensland and into Southeast Asia.

CRAR+M at UWA, directed by the author,[5] has two endowed chairs (Jo McDonald and Joakim Goldhahn) and several internationally recognised rock art and cognate scholars (Sven Ouzman, Alistair Paterson, Martin Porr, Benjamin Smith and Peter Veth). Current CRAR+M ARC projects include documenting rock art in the Kimberley, trialling innovative dating methods for Murujuga's engraved art, and exploring intergenerational knowledge transfer and long-distance social connections through rock art and Dreaming cosmologies.[6] There are also vibrant impactful rock art research projects being run out of Monash's Indigenous Studies Centre (led by Bruno David and his French collaborators, especially Jean-Jacques Delannoy), and Flinders University also continues to build research capacity with rock art researchers Claire Smith and Amy Roberts and ARC recipients Liam Brady (Future Fellow) and Daryl Wesley (DECRA). All these individuals and institutions are actively mentoring Honours, postgraduate and early career researchers specialising in rock art. The future of Australian rock art research is promising.

Conclusion

This paper has discussed ontological and methodological innovations evident in the early works of Lesley Maynard and John Clegg. Both drove a significant paradigm shift in Australia during a pivotal time when the international archaeological discipline was in a state of flux, and rock art research first began to be professionally recognised as an archaeological subdiscipline. Their work and the 'Sydney School' in which they delved and from which they trained their students, who in turn trained others, overturned antiquarian and art historical approaches and contributed significantly to the formation of a systematic archaeological approach to Australian rock art research, such as is now practised widely across Australia. Maynard and Clegg's approach(es) were genuinely archaeological, at a time when there was doubt that rock art could play any role in understanding Australia's deep history. The Sydney School was largely responsible for the shift from an antiquarian focus on collecting and cataloguing rock art as a relic of times past, at a time when there was scepticism about the ability of rock art research as an effective archaeological practice for the understanding of human behaviour. Practitioners from the Sydney School, directly and indirectly, have continued to develop research frameworks that are theoretically informed and scientifically oriented. Maynard and Clegg had very different archaeological callings, publication outputs and training roles. Their personalities, eccentricities

---

5   For more information on the centre, see: www.crarm.uwa.edu.au.

6   Further information on the centre's research can be found here: www.crarm.uwa.edu.au/research.

and professional lives, and their own career trajectories at the University of Sydney, at a time of considerable political change as well as intellectual upheaval, shaped both of their futures and the platform for future research endeavours. Lesley Maynard's faltering research career can be attributed in part to the political climate of the times that resulted in the rightful assertions by Aboriginal people as to how they wanted their heritage to be studied. It can also be attributed to a tension that has persisted between anthropological and archaeological approaches in some parts of Australia, particularly in the north-west of the country, with anthropologists often exerting an interdisciplinary gatekeeper role (also experienced by other archaeologists in the Kimberley). This has really only been resolved since Native Title legal practice has accepted the dual narratives provided by anthropological and archaeological evidence, and the burgeoning of heritage compliance work in places like the Pilbara that has resulted in a deep-time history of great pride to Aboriginal custodians (see the Juukan Gorge heritage disaster debate; and various submissions to the Senate Inquiry into the destruction of 46,000-year-old caves in the Pilbara region of Western Australia[7]).

Australian archaeological practice in 2022 is very different from that which was taught by researchers from 'Cambridge in the Bush' in the 1960s and 1970s, signalling that Australia is now a very different country post–Land Rights and Native Title. Both Maynard and Clegg's parallel efforts to redefine an Australian approach to classification, typology, style and chronology, and their joint outputs – no doubt inspired by each other's creativity, eccentricities and individuality – provided both a platform for future research directions and a training ground for Australian rock art archaeologists and their contemporary practices.

Acknowledgements

I want to thank Lesley Maynard and Kate Sullivan for providing details included here that would have been impossible to know without their input. I wish I had thought to have similar conversations with John Clegg when we were both younger. The photos provided in this paper have been provided by Kate and Lesley (as indicated) and are reproduced with their permissions. I thank Patrick Morrison (CRAR+M) for wrangling my 'spheres of connection' illustration, and Bruno David for thoughtful comments on the original manuscript.

References

Almende B.V., B. Thieurmel and T. Robert 2019. visNetwork: Network visualization using 'vis.js' library. R package version 2.0.9. CRAN.R-project.org/package=visNetwork.

Bates, B. 1993. Mootwingee National Park: A case study. *Historic Environment* 10(2/3):63–66.

Bednarik, R.G. 1988. Comment on F.D. McCarthy's rock art sequences: A matter of clarification. *Rock Art Research* 5(1):35–38.

Bell, D. 2002. *Daughters of the Dreaming*. Spinifex Press, Geelong.

Bowdler, S. and G. Clune 2000. That shadowy band: The role of women in the development of Australian archaeology. *Australian Archaeology* 50(1):27–35. doi.org/10.1080/03122417.2000.11681663.

Calaby, J.H. and D. Lewis 1977. The Tasmanian Devil in Arnhem Land rock art. *Mankind* 11(3):4–17.

---

7   See submissions to the Senate Inquiry at: www.aph.gov.au/Parliamentary_Business/Committees/Joint/Former_Committees/ Northern_Australia/CavesatJuukanGorge/Submissions.

Chippindale, C. 2015. Remembering John. Eulogy read at John Clegg's memorial Service, MacLaren Hall, University of Sydney. 15 May 2015.

Clarke, D.L. 1978. *Analytical archaeology*. Columbia University Press.

Clegg, J.K. 1971. A ?'metaphysical' approach to the study of Aboriginal rock painting. *Mankind* 8:37–41. doi.org/10.1111/j.1835-9310.1971.tb01440.x.

Clegg, J. 1977a. The meaning of schematisation. In P. Ucko (ed.), *Form in Indigenous art: Schematisation in the art of Aboriginal Australia and prehistoric Europe*, pp. 21–27. Australian Institute of Aboriginal Studies, Canberra.

Clegg, J.K. 1977b. A method of resolving problems which arise from style in art. In P. Ucko (ed.), *Form in Indigenous art: Schematisation in the art of Aboriginal Australia and prehistoric Europe*, pp. 260–276. Australian Institute of Aboriginal Studies, Canberra.

Clegg, J. 1977c. The four dimensions of artefactual variation. In R.V.S. Wright (ed.), *Stone tools as cultural markers – Change, evolution and complexity*, pp. 60–66. Australian Institute of Aboriginal Studies, Canberra.

Clegg, J.K. 1978a. Mathesis pictures; Mathesis words. Unpublished MA thesis, University of Sydney.

Clegg, J. 1978b. Pictures of striped animals: Which ones are Thylacines? *Archaeology and Physical Anthropology in Oceania* 13(1):19–29.

Clegg, J.K. 1979. Milligan's: The state at 1:xii:79. Unpublished manuscript. Copy held on file NSW National Parks and Wildlife Service.

Clegg, J.K. 1981. *Notes towards mathesis art*. Clegg Calendars, Balmain.

Clegg, J.K. 1983. From the study of Aboriginal art to the archaeology of prehistoric pictures. *Australian Archaeology* 16(1):87–91. doi.org/10.1080/03122417.1983.12092884.

Clegg, J.K. 1987. Style and tradition at Sturt's Meadows. *World Archaeology* 19(2):236–255. doi.org/10.1080/00438243.1987.9980037.

Clegg, J. 1991. !Pictures and pictures of … In P. Bahn and A. Rosenfeld (eds), *Rock art and prehistory*, pp. 109–111. Oxbow monograph 10. Oxbow, Oxford.

Conkey, M.W. 1980. The identification of hunter-gatherer aggregation sites – The case of Altamira. *Current Anthropology* 21(5):609–630. doi.org/10.1086/202540.

Conway, R. and J. Philp 2008. People, power, politics: The first generation of anthropologists at the University of Sydney. Catalogue for Macleay Museum exhibition, the University of Sydney. Available at: www.sydney.edu.au/museums/collections_search/imu/request.php?request=Multimedia&method=fetch&key=153804 (accessed 3 April 2022).

De Koning, S. 2014. Thatharruga: A stylistic analysis of turtle engravings on the Dampier Archipelago. Unpublished BA(Hons) thesis, University of Western Australia.

Edwards, R. 1965. Rock engravings and Aboriginal occupation at Nackara Springs in the north-east of South Australia. *Records of the South Australian Museum* 15:9–29.

Elkin, A.P. 1973. Archaeology of Koonalda Cave – A review article. *Archaeology and Physical Anthropology in Oceania* 8(2):162–166.

Ellis, I., W.B. Bates, S. Martin, G. McCrabb, J. Koehn, P. Heath and D. Hardman 2021. How fish kills affected traditional (Baakandji) and non-traditional communities on the Lower Darling–Baaka River. *Marine and Freshwater Research* 73(2):259–268. doi.org/10.1071/MF20376.

Finch, D., A. Gleadow, J. Hergt, V.A. Levchenko, P. Heaney, P. Veth, S. Harper, S. Ouzman, C. Myers and H. Green 2020. 12,000-year-old Aboriginal rock art from the Kimberley region, Western Australia. *Science Advances* 6(6):eaay3922. doi.org/10.1126/sciadv.aay3922.

Finch, D., A. Gleadow, J. Hergt, P. Heaney, H. Green, C. Myers, P. Veth, S. Harper, S. Ouzman and V.A. Levchenko 2021. Ages for Australia's oldest rock paintings. *Nature Human Behaviour* 5:310–318. doi.org/10.1038/s41562-020-01041-0.

Franklin, N. 2007. Discontinuous Dreaming networks: Analyses of variability in Australian pre-historic petroglyphs. *Rock Art Research* 24(1):79–103.

Griffiths, B. 2018. *Deep time Dreaming: Uncovering ancient Australia*. Black Inc, Carlton.

Gunn, R.G., L. Douglas and R. Whear 2011. What bird is that? Identifying a probable painting of *Genyornis newtoni* in Western Arnhem Land. *Australian Archaeology* 73:1–12. doi.org/10.1080/0312 2417.2011.11961918.

Harper, S., P. Veth and S. Ouzman 2019. Kimberley rock art. In C. Smith (ed.), *Encyclopaedia of global archaeology*, pp. 1–16. Springer International Publishing, Cham. doi.org/10.1007/978-3-319-51726-1_3449-1.

Heyd, T. and J.K. Clegg (eds) 2005. *Aesthetics and rock art*. Ashgate, Aldershot.

Hicks, D. 2013. Four-field anthropology: Charter myths and time warps from St. Louis to Oxford. *Current Anthropology* 54(6):753–763. doi.org/10.1086/673385.

Hodder, I.R. 1978. *The maintenance of group identities in the Baringo district, West Kenya. Social Organisation and Settlement*. British Archaeological Reports, International Series 47. British Archaeological Reports, Oxford.

Jahn, G. 1997. *Sydney architecture*. The Watermark Press, Sydney.

Jones, T., V.A. Levchenko, P.L. King, U. Troitzsch, D. Wesley, A. Williams and A. Nayingull 2017. Radiocarbon age constraints for a Pleistocene–Holocene transition rock art style: The Northern Running Figures of the East Alligator River region, western Arnhem Land, Australia. *Journal of Archaeological Science: Reports* 11:80–89. doi.org/10.1016/j.jasrep.2016.11.016.

Krishna, Y. 2014. Courting Blakness: Recalibrating knowledge in the Sandstone University. *Hecate's Australian Women's Book Review* 26(1/2):32.

Laming-Emperaire, A. 1962. *La signification de l'art rupestre paléolithique: méthodes et applications*. A. and J. Picard, Paris.

Langford, R.F. 1983. Our heritage – Your playground. *Australian Archaeology* 16:1–6. doi.org/10.1080/03122417.1983.12092875.

Leroi-Gourhan, A. 1968. *The art of prehistoric man in western Europe*. Thames and Hudson, London.

Mathews, R.H. 1894. Aboriginal rock paintings and carvings in New South Wales. *Proceedings of the Royal Society of Victoria* 7:143–156.

Mathews, R.H. 1896. Australian ground and tree drawings. *American Anthropologist* 9(2):33–49. doi.org/10.1525/aa.1896.9.2.02a00010.

Maynard, L. 1976. An archaeological approach to the study of Australian rock art. Unpublished MA thesis, Department of Anthropology and Prehistory, University of Sydney, Sydney.

Maynard, L. 1977. Classification and terminology in Australian rock art. In P.J. Ucko (ed.), *Form in Indigenous art: Schematisation in the art of Aboriginal Australia and prehistoric Europe*, pp. 385–402. Australian Institute of Aboriginal Studies, Canberra.

Maynard, L. 1979. The archaeology of Australian Aboriginal art. In S.M. Mead (ed.), *Exploring the visual art of Oceania*, pp. 83–110. University Press of Hawai'i, Honolulu.

Maynard, L. 1980. A Pleistocene date from an occupation deposit in the Pilbara region, Western Australia. *Australian Archaeology* 10(3):3–8. doi.org/10.1080/03122417.1980.12092747.

Maynard, L. 1988. Comment on F.D. McCarthy's rock art sequences: A matter of clarification. *Rock Art Research* 5(1):31–33.

McCarthy, F.D. 1967. *Australian Aboriginal rock art*. 3rd edition. Australian Museum, Sydney.

McDonald, J. 1986. Maroota historic site archaeological survey, Parts 1 and 2. Unpublished Report to National Parks and Wildlife Service NSW. Funded by grant from Aboriginal Arts Board.

McDonald, J. 1993. The depiction of species in macropod track engravings at an Aboriginal art site in western New South Wales. *Records of the Australian Museum, Supplement* 17:105–116. doi.org/10.3853/j.0812-7387.17.1993.62.

McDonald, J. 2004. Australia: Rock art capital of the world. In T. Murray (ed.), *Archaeology from Australia*, pp. 96–108. Australian Scholarly Publishing, Melbourne.

McDonald, J. 2008. *Dreamtime superhighway: Sydney Basin rock art and prehistoric information exchange*. ANU E Press, Canberra. doi.org/10.22459/DS.08.2008.

McDonald, J. 2015. I must go down to the seas again: Or, what happens when the sea comes to you? *Murujuga* rock art as an environmental indicator for Australia's north-west. *Quaternary International* 385:124–135. doi.org/10.1016/j.quaint.2014.10.056.

McDonald, J. 2017. Discontinuities in arid zone rock art: Graphic indicators for changing social complexity across space and through time. *Journal of Anthropological Archaeology* 46:53–67. doi.org/10.1016/j.jaa.2016.08.005.

McDonald, J. 2020. 'Disrupting paradise': Changing pedagogy, practice and specialisations into a collaborative venture to ensure Australian archaeology has a future. *Australian Archaeology* 49(3):1–3. doi.org/10.1080/03122417.2020.1834187.

McDonald, J. 2021. Desert rock art: Social geography at the local scale. In J. Magne and M.S. Arntzen (eds), *Perspectives on difference in rock art – The ALTA conference III proceedings in honour of Knut Helskog*, pp. 1–23. Equinox Publishing, ALTA, Norway.

McDonald, J. and S. Harper 2016. Identity signalling in shields: How coastal hunter-gatherers use rock art and material culture in arid and temperate Australia. *Australian Archaeology* 82(2):123–138. doi.org/10.1080/03122417.2016.1186345.

McDonald, J.J. and P. Veth 2006. A study of the distribution of rock art and stone structures on the Dampier Archipelago. Jo McDonald Cultural Heritage Management Pty Ltd. Unpublished report prepared for Heritage Division, Department of Environment and Heritage, Canberra.

McDonald, J. and P. Veth 2010. Pleistocene rock art. A colonising repertoire for Australia's earliest inhabitants. *Préhistoire, art et sociétés: Bulletin de la Société Préhistorique de l'Ariège* 65:172–173.

McDonald, J. and P. Veth 2013. Rock art in arid landscapes: Pilbara and Western Desert petroglyphs. *Australian Archaeology* 77(December):66–81. doi.org/10.1080/03122417.2013.11681980.

McMah, L. 1965. A quantitative analysis of the Aboriginal rock carvings in the district of Sydney and the Hawkesbury River.Unpublished BA(Hons) Thesis, Prehistory and Anthropology Department. University of Sydney, Sydney.

Miller, R. 1983. Archaeological evidence from Bull Cave, near Minto. Unpublished BA(Hons) thesis, Prehistory and Anthropology Department, University of Sydney, Sydney.

Morwood, M.J. 2002. *Visions from the past: The archaeology of Australian Aboriginal art.* Allen & Unwin, Sydney.

Morwood, M.J. and C.E. Smith 1994. Rock art research in Australia 1974–1994. *Australian Archaeology* 39:19–38. doi.org/10.1080/03122417.1994.11681525.

Moser, S. 2007. On disciplinary culture: Archaeology as fieldwork and its gendered associations. *Journal of Anthropological Method and Theory* 14:235–263. doi.org/10.1007/s10816-007-9033-5.

Mountford, C.P. and R. Edwards 1963. Rock engravings of Panaramitee Station, north-eastern South Australia. *Transactions of the Royal Society of South Australia* 86:131–146.

Mowaljarlai, D., P. Vinnicombe, G.K. Ward and C. Chippindale 1988. Repainting of images on rock in Australia and the maintenance of Aboriginal culture. *Antiquity* 62(237):690–696. doi.org/10.1017/S0003598X00075086.

Mulvaney, D.J. 1969. *The prehistory of Australia.* Thames and Hudson, London.

Mulvaney, D.J. 2011. *Digging up the past.* UNSW Press, Sydney.

Mulvaney, K. 2015. *Murujuga Marni: Rock art of the macropod hunters and mollusc harvesters.* UWA Press, Perth.

Munn, N.D. 1960. Walbiri graphic art and sand drawing: A study in the iconography of a Central Australian culture. Unpublished PhD thesis, The Australian National University, Canberra.

Murray, T. and J.P. White 1981. Cambridge in the bush? Archaeology in Australia and New Guinea. *World Archaeology* 13(2):255–263. doi.org/10.1080/00438243.1981.9979829.

Myers, F. 1976. To have and to hold: A study of permanence in Pintupi Social Life. Unpublished PhD thesis, Bryn Mawr College, Bryn Mawr.

Myers, F. 1991. Representing culture: The production of discourse(s) for Aboriginal acrylic paintings. *Cultural Anthropology* 6(1):26–62. doi.org/10.1525/can.1991.6.1.02a00020.

Officer, K. 1984. From Tuggerah to Dharawal. Unpublished BA(Hons) thesis, The Australian National University, Canberra.

Palmer, K. 1975. Petroglyphs and associated Aboriginal sites in the north-west of Western Australia. *Archaeology & Physical Anthropology in Oceania* 10(2):152–160.

Phillip, A. 1789. *The voyage of Governor Phillip to Botany Bay: With contributions from other officers of the First Fleet and observations on affairs of the time by Lord Auckland.* John Stockdale, London.

Pitt-Rivers, A.H.L.F. 1882. Anniversary address to the Anthropological Institute of Great Britain and Ireland. *Journal of the Anthropological Institute of Great Britain and Ireland* 11:487–509. doi.org/10.2307/2841783.

Pollard, K. 2014. Jones, Rhys Maengwyn. In C. Smith (ed.), *Encyclopedia of global archaeology,* pp. 4215–4218. Springer, New York. doi.org/10.1007/978-1-4419-0465-2_2386.

Radcliffe-Brown, A.R. 1930. The Rainbow Serpent myth in south-eastern Australia. *Oceania* 1:242–247. doi.org/10.1002/j.1834-4461.1930.tb01653.x.

Rhodes, J. 2018. *Cage of ghosts.* National Library of Australia, Canberra.

Rose, D. 2011. Genre in the Sydney School. In J. Gee and M. Handford (eds), *The Routledge handbook of discourse analysis,* pp. 209–225. Routledge, London.

Rosenfeld, A. 1991. Panaramitee: Dead or alive? In P. Bahn and A. Rosenfeld (eds), *Rock art and prehistory: Papers presented to symposium G of the AURA Congress, Darwin 1988,* Volume 10, pp. 136–144. Oxbow, Oxford.

Rosenfeld, A. 2000. Meanings in chronology: 'Direct dating' and style. In G.K. Ward and C. Tuniz (eds), *Advances in dating Australian rock-markings: Papers from the First Australian rock-picture dating workshop*, pp. 55–58. Occasional AURA Publication No. 10. Australian Rock Art Research Association, Melbourne.

Rosenfeld, A., D. Horton and J. Winter 1981. *Early man in North Queensland: Art and archaeology in the Laura area.* Terra Australis 7. Department of Prehistory, Research School of Pacific and Asian Studies, The Australian National University, Canberra.

Ross, J. and I. Davidson 2006. Rock art and ritual: An archaeological analysis of rock art in arid central Australia. *Journal of Archaeological Method and Theory* 13(4):304–340. doi.org/10.1007/s10816-006-9021-1.

Sabloff, J.A., L.R. Binford and P.A. McAnany 1987. Understanding the archaeological record. *Antiquity* 61(232):203–209. doi.org/10.1017/S0003598X00052005.

Sim, I.M. 1969. A gallery of cave art in the Macdonald River district New South Wales. *Archaeology & Physical Anthropology in Oceania* 4(2):144–179.

Slack, M.J., B. Law and L. Gliganic 2020. The early occupation of the Eastern Pilbara revisited: New radiometric chronologies and archaeological results from Newman Rockshelter and Newman Orebody XXIX. *Quaternary Science Reviews* 236:106240. doi.org/10.1016/j.quascirev.2020.106240.

Smith, C. and J. McDonald 2015. John Kay Clegg 11th January 1935–11th March 2015: Appreciation. *Antiquity.* Available at: journal.antiquity.ac.uk/tributes/clegg/ (accessed 3 April 2022).

Smith, M.A., J. Ross and D. Kimber 2021. Robert Edwards and the history of Australian rock art research. *Historical Records of Australian Science* 32(1):41–51. doi.org/10.1071/HR20011.

Sullivan, S. 1964. The Aborigines of the Richmond – Tweed. Unpublished BA(Hons) thesis, University of New England, Armidale.

Tench, W. 1789 (reprinted 1962). *Sydney's first four years: Being a reprint of A narrative of the expedition to Botany Bay and A complete account of the settlement at Port Jackson.* Angus and Robertson in association with the Royal Australian Historical Society.

Thomas, M. 2011. *The many worlds of R.H. Mathews: In search of an Australian anthropologist.* Allen and Unwin, Crows Nest, Australia.

Ucko, P.J. (ed.) 1977a. *Form in indigenous art: Schematisation in the art of Aboriginal Australia and prehistoric Europe.* Australian Institute of Aboriginal Studies, Canberra.

Ucko, P.J. 1977b. Preface. In P.J. Ucko (ed.), *Form in indigenous art: Schematisation in the art of Aboriginal Australia and prehistoric Europe*, pp. 1–4. Australian Institute of Aboriginal Studies, Canberra.

Ucko, P.J. 1977c. Opening remarks. In P.J. Ucko (ed.), *Form in indigenous art: Schematisation in the art of Aboriginal Australia and prehistoric Europe*, pp. 7–10. Australian Institute of Aboriginal Studies, Canberra.

Ucko, P.J. 1977d. Introduction. In P.J. Ucko (ed.), *Form in indigenous art: Schematisation in the art of Aboriginal Australia and prehistoric Europe*, pp. 11–18. Australian Institute of Aboriginal Studies, Canberra.

Ucko, P. and A. Rosenfeld 1967. *Paleolithic cave art.* World University Library, London.

Veth, P., E. Bradshaw, T. Gara, N. Hall, P. Haydock and P. Kendrick 1993. *Burrup Peninsula Aboriginal Heritage Project: National Estate Grant Project*. Department of Conservation and Land Management, Perth.

Veth, P., C. Myers, P. Heaney and S. Ouzman 2018. Plants before farming: The deep history of plant-use and representation in the rock art of Australia's Kimberley region. *Quaternary International* 489:26–45. doi.org/10.1016/j.quaint.2016.08.036.

Wallis, L.A. 2020. Disrupting paradise: Has Australian archaeology lost its way? *Australian Archaeology* 86(3):284–294. doi.org/10.1080/03122417.2020.1834181.

Ward, G.K. 2011. The role of AIATSIS in research and protection of Australian rock art. *Rock Art Research* 28(1):7–16.

Ward, G.K. and S. Sullivan 1989. The Australian Institute of Aboriginal Studies' rock art preservation program. *Rock Art Research* 6:54–62.

White, J.P. 1994. Theses about prehistoric archaeology and associated disciplines in Australia, 1975–1993. *Archaeology in Oceania* 29(2):95–106. doi.org/10.1002/arco.1994.29.2.95.

Wobst, H.M. 1977. Stylistic behaviour and information exchange. In C.E. Cleland (ed.), *For the director: Research essays in honour of JB Griffen*, pp. 317–342. Museum of Anthropology, University of Michigan, Ann Arbor.

Wright, B.J. 1968. *Rock art of the Pilbara region, north-west Australia*. Australian Institute of Aboriginal Studies, Canberra.

Wright, R.V.S. 1971. *Archaeology of the Gallus site, Koonalda Cave*. Australian Institute of Aboriginal Studies, Canberra.

5

Women in Australian rock art research: The legacies of Andrée Rosenfeld and Patricia Vinnicombe

Sven Ouzman and Claire Smith

Introduction

Australian rock art research, management and advocacy have enjoyed significant shaping by female practitioners. The strong and enduring female participation and shaping of rock art research is a noteworthy feature in an otherwise historically androcentric archaeology, at least in the northern hemisphere in erstwhile colonial centres (cf. Fredengren 2018; Hays-Gilpin 2000). Significantly, as one moves away from Europe, female participation and shaping of archaeology in general, and rock art research in particular, is a hallmark of disciplinary development. Indeed, in the last decades this trend is marked (e.g. Mate and Ulm 2016, 2021; Ulm et al. 2013). We examine the lives and contributions of two remarkable rock art researchers – Andrée Rosenfeld and Patricia Vinnicombe. Both scholars were extremely good at what they did – though their expertise and opportunities differed. Their work offers insights into how today's rock art research developed, and where rock art research may go in the future.

Archaeology and gender

In its early development, archaeology, at first in its guise as antiquarianism and like most Western scholarship, was predominantly an androcentric pursuit, beginning with wealthy eighteenth-century European amateurs before evolving into a structured scientific enquiry in the early 1900s (cf. Bolger 2013; Fagan 2018:122–127, 261–265). Awareness of gender as a research pursuit was late in being recognised (e.g. Conkey and Spector 1984), as was the case also of many academic disciplines, though it is now integrated into much – but not all – research. Awareness of gender bias in research is still a matter of concern (Fredengren 2018), together with the wider issue of the under-recognition of BIPOC (Black, Indigenous and people of colour) and other subaltern and subjugated voices (e.g. Franklin et al. 2020), especially in Australia. Encouragingly, archaeology and related fields of enquiry have undergone a marked feminisation in this millennium, though in Australia and South Africa this arguably began in the last decades of the previous millennium. This is evident in a more self-conscious positioning of perspectives, eschewing a single authoritative narrative and embracing a greater concern with social factors such as race and class (see Conkey and Gero 1997). It is notable that gender as either research pursuit or area of bias recognition seems to have subsided, at least in comparison with levels of activism in the 1980s–2000s. Australia largely mirrors this trend, and of the approximately 1000 archaeologists currently working here, more than 55 per cent are female,[1] though a 36 per cent gap in wages between females and males persists (Mate and Ulm 2021), and there are still significant gender-based challenges (Smith and Burke 2006). The earlier male-dominated history masks a small but persistent and influential group of female scholars in the development of archaeology globally and in Australia (see Allen 2019; Bowdler and Clune 2000; Du Cros 1993; Macfarlane et al. 2005). Women have always contributed to archaeological knowledge, though an under-researched question is how gender influences knowledge production (but see Cullen et al. 2019; Engelstad 2007).

Rock art research and gender in Australia and southern Africa

For many years rock art research operated at the fringes of mainstream archaeology due to an inability to date or excavate it, which relegated rock art largely to an illustrative and peripheral form of material culture studied by avocationalists (Chaloupka 1993; Walsh 1994). In the early days, dedicated male practitioners tended to be 'heroic blokes' such as Harold Coates, George Chaloupka, Percy Trezise and Graham Walsh in Australia and Burchard Brentjes, Cran Cooke, Neil Lee and Herbert Woodhouse in southern Africa. However, there were many significant female researchers. In Australia, Phyllis Kaberry recorded women creating rock art in the Kimberley (Kaberry 1939:398) while numerous women, including Ursula McConnel, Olive Pink, Nancy Munn and Ellen Murray-Prior, were involved in learning directly from Aboriginal communities, though without a clear focus on rock art (see Marcus 1993; Smith 1991). In southern Africa, people like Dorothea Bleek and Lucy Lloyd – the latter being the first woman to receive a PhD in South Africa – were active in the early twentieth century (Skotnes 2007). They were followed by people such as Maria Wilman – first female museum director in South Africa – the McGuffie sisters, Helen Tongue, Joan Simpson, Patricia Vinnicombe, Jeanette Deacon, Anne Solomon and many others (see Mitchell 2002:Chapter 8). Rock art research in Australia started later, in the mid-to-late twentieth century, but had equally influential and numerous researchers such as Noelene Cole, Phyllis Kaberry, Lesley Maynard, Andrée Rosenfeld, Josephine Flood, Patricia Vinnicombe and many others (Bowdler and Clune 2000; Griffith 2018:48–49, 157–158, 268–269). Similarly, even large male-led expeditions were frequently shaped and furthered by their female members. For example, the Frobenius expeditions to southern Africa (1928–1930) and northern Australia (1938) consisted mostly of female copyists and researchers such as Agnes Schultz and Gerta Kleist (Porr and Doohan 2017), who did the bulk of the work and who had their own interactions with Indigenous women in the areas they were working.

By the 1970s, Australian archaeology was becoming more scientific, partly through the use of processualism and human behavioural ecology, combined with the need to 'document' sites and artefacts. Isabel McBryde, who had been appointed to a lectureship in prehistory and ancient history at the University of New England in 1960, the first titled position of its kind in Australia, became the first female head of an archaeology department, at The Australian National University (ANU; Macfarlane et al. 2005). In a parallel development, more female practitioners, such as Sharon Sullivan, Betty Meehan and subsequently Josephine Flood, were appointed to senior government positions at the Australian Heritage Commission. Concurrently, rock art started to be recognised by Australian archaeologists as both an artefact and a legitimate field of research (Griffith 2018:177–179; Morwood and Smith 1994). The increasing professionalisation of rock art studies in Australia led to an increase in the pace and calibre of research, and also to a greater emphasis on quantitative work by researchers – as seen in Lesley Maynard (1976, 1977) and John Clegg's (1979) studies of rock art in the 1960s and 1970s – as was being used

---

1   We acknowledge a female–male binary is not always useful as humans have multiple gendered and other identities, but we retain it for historical purposes and because few researchers, especially historically, publicly self-identified in non-binary ways.

in the United Kingdom and United States (see Chapter 4, this volume). The arrival of Peter Ucko in Australia in 1972 to take up the position of principal of the Australian Institute of Aboriginal Studies was a turning point. Supported by his partner and rock art specialist in her own right, Andrée Rosenfeld, he was primarily responsible for the 1974 'Schematisation in art' symposium, which was highly influential in the development of Australian rock art research and, among eight volumes, produced *Form in Indigenous art* (Ucko 1977). In addition, he promoted a change in the Australian Institute of Aboriginal Studies' funding priorities, so rock art was given greater precedence than it had previously, and he encouraged other European researchers with a commitment to rock art studies, such as Robert Layton and Michel Lorblanchet, to come to Australia. These key moments and interventions eventually led to Australia becoming a world leader in rock art research and, more recently, Indigenous engagement. Another legacy has been that rock art research continues to have high levels of female participation. It is an opportune time, as archaeology in general, and rock art research in particular, reach maturity to consider this history of research in more detail, to better understand the challenges and opportunities faced by early female contributors and the legacies they left to us today.

In this chapter, we discuss the legacy of two key, highly influential researchers in Australian rock art – Andrée Rosenfeld and Patricia Vinnicombe. We identify each scholar's key areas of impact and assess how their ideas were received at the time they were published. Finally, we consider their long-term impact upon archaeological knowledge production, both in Australia and globally. While their individual contributions are distinct, they have much in common. Almost identically contemporaneous, neither was Australia-born and neither chose archaeology as their first choice of study, yet both had influential intellectual careers on two continents, ending their careers in Australia (cf. Lewis-Williams 2009; Mountain 2014).

Andrée Jean Rosenfeld (1934–2008)

Early life and education

Andrée Rosenfeld was born in Liege, Belgium in 1934. Her mother, Dr Yvonne Rosenfeld, was one of the first women in Europe to obtain a PhD in physics (McBryde 2008:58). Her father, Professor Léon Rosenfeld, was a world-renowned physicist and founder of the journal *Nuclear Physics*. When the Nazis invaded Holland in 1940, he secretly gave seminars to Jewish students in his home and supervised young Jewish scholars, including Abraham Pais, the American physicist and biographer of Alfred Einstein (Smith 2009:83). The languages that Andrée Rosenfeld mastered over her lifetime included French, Dutch, Danish, German and Spanish. In an obituary for his colleague, George E. Brown wrote that Léon Rosenfeld:

> had a thorough knowledge of many languages and a few years ago was still able to write in Latin to his daughter Andrée to punish her because she had written to her mother in English rather than in French, which was the home language. (Brown 1974:iv)

The household was upper middle class, middle-century European – cultured, ordered, understated. Andrée Rosenfeld carried these qualities with her all her life.

In 1947, the Rosenfeld family moved to Manchester in England. Andrée Rosenfeld and her brother Jean followed their father into science. Andrée enrolled in a Master of Science at University College London, and later upgraded to a PhD. Her thesis topic was the sedimentology of cave deposits from sites in Devon, England. In 1960, she graduated with a PhD in environmental archaeology from the Institute of Archaeology, London, under the supervision of Professor Frederick Zeuner (McBryde 2008:58). She worked as his assistant until 1964, when she was appointed as a curator at the British Museum in London (Mountain 2014:6380).

Career in Europe

While in London, Andrée Rosenfeld gave guest lectures for the Department of Anthropology, University College London. She was an accomplished teacher who mentored young scholars who later became leaders in the anthropology and archaeology of art, including Howard Morphy and Robert Layton. In collaboration with her partner Peter Ucko, Andrée Rosenfeld undertook experiments in archaeological and ethnographic science:

> We experimented with the cutting properties of stone tools; and cooking the meat thus butchered both by pot-boiling with hot stones (the results were lukewarm and undercooked) and somewhat more successfully in an earth oven. Andrée devised a series of experiments in which we measured the heat at the centre of the fires to discover something about the fracturing properties of different types of stones. The purpose and the results of the experiments have faded with time but the raw materials of antiquity proved highly explosive! (Morphy and Mulvaney 1999:93)

Andrée Rosenfeld and Peter Ucko were a major force in the establishment of material culture studies at the Institute of Archaeology and, later in Rosenfeld's own right, at ANU. While based in Britain, Andrée Rosenfeld undertook extensive visits to rock art sites in Europe and also travelled to Nigeria to work with Ekpo Eyo, a former student at the Institute of Archaeology, where she undertook an analysis of microlithic industries from the Rop Rock Shelter (Rosenfeld 1972).

Andrée Rosenfeld's international reputation in archaeology was established through two books. Her first, *The inorganic raw materials of antiquity* (Rosenfeld 1965), was a groundbreaking exploration of the sourcing and transportation of raw materials to chart the trade in turquoise, tin and lapis lazuli between Egypt and western Asia. Her second book, *Palaeolithic cave art* (Ucko and Rosenfeld 1967), deconstructed popular interpretations of rock art (e.g. art for art's sake; sympathetic magic; totemism) and offered a sophisticated methodological rethinking of how to analyse Upper Palaeolithic cave art. This work analysed both parietal (art on fixed rock surfaces) and portable art, arguing that both religious and secular themes were at play. This work received critical acclaim:

> Ucko and Rosenfeld have produced a valuable introduction to the study of Paleolithic art whose modest format and price belie its importance. They survey the Paleolithic epoch, canvass the mural art, offer a compact and brilliant review of the interpretative traditions, and conclude with a critical analysis of interpretations. Nowhere, on any level of erudition or seriousness of purpose, will one find as sensitive and clear-headed a discussion of methodology as in this book. (Levine 1968:151)

In a separate review, Movius (1968:808) stated: 'They are certainly to be congratulated for having produced what is undoubtedly the most scholarly and provocative book on the subject that has been published to date'. Not only was this work influential at the time, its legacy is lasting, as evidenced by being cited by over 400 subsequent works. This work shifted research focus from entrenched concerns with pattern recognition to consideration of the ways in which style might encode social information and towards the problem of pattern generation.

Career in Australia

Andrée Rosenfeld moved to Australia in 1972 with her partner Peter Ucko, and in 1973 she accepted a post at the newly established Department of Archaeology and Anthropology at ANU, where she remained until her retirement in 1997. She taught courses on the archaeology of art, material culture and the prehistory of Australia (Mountain 2014:6381). Rosenfeld established rock art research at the ANU and actively promoted it as a serious field of research in Australia.

She applied the analytical skills she developed to analyse European Upper Palaeolithic cave art and integrated ethnographic dimensions into the study of rock art. For example, she was a weaver herself and hosted an Iban weaver as a scholar in residence at ANU.

While based at ANU, Andrée initiated projects that were critical to the development of archaeology and rock art research in Australia. For example, she was one of the first archaeologists in Australia to attempt to understand relationships between rock art and excavated archaeological deposits by undertaking pioneering excavations at Early Man rock-shelter near Laura in Cape York Peninsula (Rosenfeld 1975; Figure 5.1). This project produced the first firm demonstration of Pleistocene age for Aboriginal rock art in the form of engravings covered by archaeological deposits dated to ~13,000 BP, although the excavation's uncovering of broken engraved items was also significant (Rosenfeld et al. 1981). Rosenfeld, influenced by work at La Mouthe in France, was very much attuned to the importance of buried art for both dating and understanding the contexts of the art. Furthermore, by relating stylistic differences in the rock art to changes in the distribution of ochre in the excavations, Rosenfeld presented a convincing case for significant technical and stylistic changes in the art around 4000 BP. Her work informed a broader program of rock art research where, by the 1980s, detailed information had begun to be published on the frequency of rock art motifs and design conventions, their diversity and character, for many parts of Australia. In many cases, extensive site recording programs led to more specialist work on rock art chronology and excavation of associated cultural deposits. For example, the rock art recordings undertaken by Percy Trezise over the 30 years since the 1960s in south-east Cape York Peninsula provided a platform for Rosenfeld et al. (1981) and later rock art researchers across the broader region (e.g. Cole 1988; David 1992; Flood 1987; Flood and Horsfall 1986; Morwood and Hobbs 1994).

Figure 5.1: Andrée Rosenfeld at Early Man Rockshelter, Cape York Peninsula, 1974.
Source: Darrell Lewis.

This early relative and stylistic dating work, begun before Rosenfeld's work in the Laura district but refined and expanded to include minimal radiocarbon ages for the art by Rosenfeld, established a solid and systematic foundation for the subsequent and, at times, spectacular developments in the scientific dating of rock art (David et al. 2013; Finch et al. 2021). More than anything else, the difficulty in dating rock art had been a major impediment to its acceptance as useful archaeological data, and to the taking of its practitioners as serious contributors to archaeological research. The invention of radiocarbon dating in the late 1940s allowed dates to be produced for materials associated with rock art in various ways (e.g. as minimum or maximum (statistical) age calculations), such as when engraved fragments of rock art were found in archaeological excavations (e.g. Mulvaney 1975:289; Rosenfeld et al. 1981). In the late 1980s through the 1990s, developments in accelerator mass spectrometry (AMS) radiocarbon dating enabled the 'direct' dating of rock art by directly dating the materials that paintings were made of (items in 'paint pots', as sometimes called in Europe), and by dating carbon-bearing mineral or biogenic coatings that had accumulated (sometimes in stratigraphically differentiated micro-strata) above or below engravings (e.g. Dragovich 1984; Watchman 1987). Spurred by a torrid debate regarding the relative utility of stylistic chronologies versus direct radiocarbon dating of engraved rock art in the Cóa Valley, Portugal (see Bednarik 1995a, 1995b; Watchman 1995, 1996; Zilhão 1995a, 1995b), Andrée Rosenfeld once again took on the role of impartial reviewer of competing theoretical perspectives and methodological approaches. Her review paper argued that the conflict between the two dating methods demanded an evaluation of the advantages and the limitations of both:

> While the advent of radiocarbon methods constitutes a methodological breakthrough, it does not follow necessarily that stylistic methods should be discarded in favour of 'scientific' direct dating. Rather, archaeologists need to face the problems inherent in the uses of both radiocarbon and stylistic methods more determinedly and critically, and to move beyond simple correlations that do not address the complexities of each approach. This needs to be done at the levels of theory, method and interpretation. (Rosenfeld and Smith 1997:409)

In parallel with her scholarly work, Andrée Rosenfeld also contributed to early developments in the conservation and management of rock art sites. Coinciding with her arrival in Australia, in the mid-1970s and early 1980s heritage institutions became increasingly concerned with conservation issues, including those relating to rock art (Rosenfeld et al. 1984). Under the auspices of Australia's Joint Academies' Committee on the Protection of Prehistoric Places, a symposium on rock art recording, management and conservation was held in Sydney in 1980. A year later, a smaller meeting was held in Canberra, formulating proposals for directions and priorities in rock art conservation (Rosenfeld et al. 1984; Hall 1999:163). One proposal was to commission a review of the present state of knowledge on rock art conservation applicable to Australian conditions. This study, undertaken through the Australian Heritage Commission, resulted in the book *Rock art conservation in Australia* (Rosenfeld 1985), which laid the groundwork for the development of rock art conservation as a serious field of endeavour in Australia. This book was an important step that drew together all existing research and experimental data. The book was designed for heritage professionals in state agencies and National Parks services as well as others concerned with, but not necessarily working in, the field of rock art conservation. Since then, a new generation of researchers have continued to build on Andrée Rosenfeld's foundational work on rock art conservation in Australia, a lead that emanated from what could be called the 'ANU school' of rock art research led by Andrée (e.g. Hall 1999; Marshall and Taçon 2014.)

In this same spirit, Andrée Rosenfeld was one of the many supporters of the establishment of the Australian Rock Art Research Association (AURA). She and Paul Bahn co-convened a symposium on rock art and prehistory at the first AURA Congress in Darwin in 1988, and this seeded the establishment of the International Federation of Rock Art Organisations (IFRAO). Among the publications that emerged from this congress was Bahn and Rosenfeld's (1991) *Rock art and prehistory* that questioned established concepts and proposed new ones (Huchet 1992:87). Immediately following her retirement, AURA acknowledged Andrée Rosenfeld's contribution to rock art at a 1998 symposium in Canberra. The resulting festschrift took the form of a special issue of *Archaeology in Oceania* (Frederick and Wilson 1999).

While Andrée Rosenfeld was 'an archaeological scientist before the term had been invented, using scientific knowledge and methods in the solution of archaeological problems' (Morphy and Mulvaney 1999:93), her work traversed and connected the sciences and humanities, something that she was herself passionate about doing, and doing sharply. She also was a key proponent of the importance of social archaeology and the humanity underpinning rock art, a social anthropological dimension that also came to deeply underpin the ANU school of rock art research. Much of Andrée Rosenfeld's research focused on a detailed and systematic analysis of style. A deeper understanding of this topic was pursued by many of her students. One outstanding example, sometimes overlooked, is Kelvin Officer's doctoral research (1991). He developed a system of graphic motif analysis that crossed the artificial boundary between figurative and nonfigurative that Rosenfeld (1992:236) argued was a fundamental problem in Australian rock art research since Maynard's key works of the 1970s (including her broad tripartite division of Australian rock art, which came to significantly influence some, but not all, Australian rock art researchers). Officer (1991) argued for the very different nature of cultural information embodied in those analyses based on motif (subject matter) and those based on the grammar of graphic constructions (topics also influential in Western European rock art research, and that had come to deeply influence Andrée's own rock art training). Andrée Rosenfeld's analysis of rock art in terms of territoriality and corporate landowning groups (influential topics at the more socially oriented 'Department of Archaeology and Anthropology' in the ANU School of General Studies, where Andrée was based), combined with minimum Pleistocene dates associated with rock art in her Early Man excavations, and later evidence for regionalisation of rock art systems, provided important evidence for major developments in Aboriginal land use and the emergence of corporate landowning groups:

> It is not until the terminal Pleistocene, however, that symbolic activity can be shown to be regularly focussed on places fixed in the landscape rather than between individuals, who are presumably mobile within the landscape … In view of the co-existence of corporate and individual gestural systems up to the recent past, it is probable that the integration of corporate territoriality was an addition to the earlier ideational system, not its replacement. However, there seems to be a shift in focus from the mediation of power relationships expressed essentially at the individualised level to its expression in corporate relations to territory. (Rosenfeld 1999:32)

Legacy

Andrée Rosenfeld's legacy can be divided into two parts: (1) her theoretical and methodological contributions to the discipline, including systematic analysis of rock art, the combining of excavation with details of on-wall rock art, and the systematic application of social anthropological insights to rock art, all through influential case studies and synthetic analyses; and (2) the impacts that her students (and *their* students) have had on rock art research, arguably at least in part through her promotion and mentoring of precise, accurate, reflective and systematic research. Her ability to balance the scientific and the conceptual allowed her contributions to rock art research to range from dating and conservation to deep theoretical conceptualisations of the meaningfulness and social roles of rock art. For example, Rosenfeld's (1992) article on then-recent developments in Australian rock art research (see also Rosenfeld 1993), contributed to archaeologists understanding that 'meaning', which lies at the core of social anthropology as a disciplinary practice, requires understanding of the social and ontological contexts of cultural practice, rather than being singular and frozen in time (Rosenfeld 1992:232). Using style as an analytical tool, her research focused on identifying archaeological signatures of social contexts of rock art production (e.g. Rosenfeld 1997, 1999). Paul Taçon characterised her approach in the following terms:

> Rosenfeld, in many of her publications, has actively pursued certain forms of meaning. However, she has not done this in an ad hoc or subjective way. Instead, her approach is to first gain a thorough understanding of the nature of a rock-art's structure, form, subject matter and 'style', to explore the best use of ethnography or analogy, to see how chronology and dating can assist with understanding and finally to tease out different levels of meaning from the data. It is only in this way that we can begin to more critically examine and more fully understand ancient imagery with any form of confidence. (Taçon 1999:95)

Andrée Rosenfeld was an accomplished teacher who supervised and mentored a plethora of young scholars, many of whom became leaders in the anthropology and archaeology of art. At ANU her students included Ian Coates, Bruno David, Sarah Forbes, Ursula Frederick, Nicholas Hall, Darrell Lewis, Jo McDonald, Mahirta, Kelvin Officer and Paul Taçon. This training has produced lasting legacies. For example, in 2021, Professor Jo McDonald is the director of the Centre for Rock Art Research + Management at the University of Western Australia. McDonald holds the Rio Tinto Chair in Rock Art Studies, funded by Rio Tinto's Conservation Agreement with the Commonwealth for the Dampier Archipelago National Heritage Listed Place, and UNESCO World Heritage Site nominee – the first such nomination for an Australian rock art site (McDonald 2021). This conservation agreement also established the Patricia Vinnicombe Scholarship, with Ken Mulvaney being the inaugural recipient. Andrée Rosenfeld also supervised the doctoral research of Professor Paul Taçon, who is chair in rock art research and professor of anthropology and archaeology at Griffith University. Taçon holds a prestigious Australian Research Council Laureate Fellowship (Taçon 2021) and is director of Griffith University's Place, Evolution and Rock Art Heritage Unit. The legacy of Andrée Rosenfeld's influence can be found in the people she mentored and the colleagues with whom she conducted fieldwork, including Julie Dibden, Howard Morphy, Mike Morwood, June Ross and Claire Smith. She undertook extensive fieldwork in Central Australia with Mike Smith and Winifred Mumford (Rosenfeld and Mumford 1996; Rosenfeld and Smith 2002). The legacies of these researchers is also at least in part the legacy of Andrée Rosenfeld.

Andrée Rosenfeld's scholarship is recognised internationally. She held fellowships at the Getty Institute in Los Angeles in 1988 and at Oxford University in 1989 (McBryde 2008:60). She was elected as a Fellow of the Australian Academy of the Humanities. A portrait of Andrée Rosenfeld by Robin Wallace-Crabbe and Diane Fogwell is held in the collections of the National Gallery of Australia (Figure 5.2). In a more subtle, less easily quantifiable way, Andrée's influence on scholars young and old was also marked by her many unassuming but deeply impactful ways of respectful two-way discussions, sitting quietly with scholars in extended discussions about cutting edge research directions, away from the 'maddening crowd', leaving her colleagues looking forward to their next opportunity to meet. A feature of Andrée's mentoring was this kind of one-on-one discussion, never boisterous but deeply intellectually impactful. Rosenfeld's work transcended the divide between the humanities and sciences. At the celebration of her life in Canberra on 6 March 2009, her friend and colleague, Mike Smith, mentioned that she had described rock art research as a field with 'a lunatic core and a sane fringe' (Smith 2009). Rosenfeld's steadying influence on the archaeological study of art, and her application of scientific rigour to this study produced level heads and substantive outcomes for rock art research, both nationally and internationally.

Figure 5.2: Portrait of Andrée Rosenfeld by Robin Wallace-Crabbe and Diane Fogwell.

Source: National Gallery of Australia, courtesy Robin Wallace-Crabbe and Diane Fogwell.

Patricia Joan Vinnicombe (1932–2003)

Early life and education

A contemporary of Rosenfeld, Patricia 'Pat' Vinnicombe had a very different life and career trajectory but was equally influential. She was born in 1932 on the electricity-less farm 'West Ilsley' in rural Mount Currie, adjacent to the uKhahlamba-Drakensberg Park where her pioneering work would later take place. Rock art formed part of her daily life (Ward 2003:223), as did 'speaking the Zulu click-language of her playmates' and her brother John (Buxton 1977:169). In high school she made rock art tracing and copying a hobby, and this would later develop into the substantive archive of southern African San ('Bushman')[2] rock art copies curated at the

2   We reject any pejorative connotations the terms 'San' or 'Bushman' may have, recognising both terms are exonyms.

University of the Witwatersrand's African Digital Rock Art Archive (African Digital Rock Art Archive 2021). Her diligence at school led to her studying at the University of Witwatersrand and qualifying as an occupational therapist in 1954 (Deacon 2003:223). Her studies also brought her into contact with Australian-born Raymond Dart and Philip Tobias (Hallam 2003), and she focused again on rock art. Even during an interlude in London where she worked as a therapist she was able to exhibit her rock art copies at the Imperial Institute (Deacon 2003:223). Sylvia Hallam noted that when Patricia Vinnicombe met the renowned French rock art researcher, Abbé Breuil, he told her: 'You just go ahead and do the job. It doesn't matter how you do it. Nobody knows more than you do. Develop new ideas, new techniques' (Hallam 2003:48). As Hallam pointed out, she did. Together with subsequent analytical work where she divided each painted motif into attributes, her reputation as a skilled thinker and copyist led to an invitation in 1958 by South Africa's Human Sciences Research Council (the equivalent of the Australian Research Council) to conduct a more methodical survey of Drakensberg rock art under the aegis of archaeologist B.D. 'Berry' (Barend) Malan (Ward 2003:80). In 1961 she met and married Cambridge-trained Patrick Carter, an archaeologist active in excavations in Lesotho and based at the Natal Museum where Patricia was then conducting her archival and rock art research. Her career would from there be distributed across Africa (South Africa, Ethiopia, Ghana and Tanzania) and Australia (New South Wales and Western Australia).

Career in Africa

Patricia Vinnicombe was able to enter southern African male-dominated archaeology through rock art. Viewed as more artist than archaeologist – and, more specifically, as a rock art researcher – by most of her male peers, she was able to use her skills at copying to better understand and interpret San rock art, which at that time was thought to be a simple record of everyday life (Lewis-Williams 2009:17). Her meticulous field tracings and subsequent copies came to number 868 sheets of tracings with nearly 8478 individual painted motifs that she produced over 40 years, constituting a national treasure (Deacon 2003:224). Vinnicombe realised that rock art research was, indeed, a 'Cinderella' endeavour in southern African archaeology (cf. Deacon 1993), largely because it was perceived as data-poor and seldom interrogated in terms of specific attributes. Her work with Berry Malan developed one of the first computer punch-card systems for categorising rock art image attributes (Vinnicombe 1967a; Lewis-Williams 2009:26). This helped integrate rock art and excavation-centric archaeology as well as influencing the development of fellow rock art researchers David Lewis-Williams, Harald Pager, Dora and Gerhard Fock, and Lucas Smits. Vinnicombe not only challenged deficient and simplistic interpretations of rock art but also proposed viable alternatives. She wrote at a time when the major accepted motivations for the creation of rock art in southern Africa were 'sympathetic magic', whereby an image was drawn with the hope of effecting a successful hunting outcome (Brentjes 1969), or 'art for art's sake', which assumed that, given sufficient leisure time, art was executed for the pleasure of the artist and beholder (Willcox 1963:84), created purely for its aesthetic qualities (Cooke 1969:50). In two separate, mutually reinforcing review essays of several books published in the 1960s, Vinnicombe (1972a, 1972b) produced a devastating critique of such Eurocentric interpretations. Drawing on observations by Ucko and Rosenfeld (1967:130) concerning the Abbé Breuil's interpretations of Upper Palaeolithic rock art, she powerfully deconstructed attributed motivations of rock art as sympathetic magic:

> … paintings of predators may be engendered through fear or through a desire to emulate, because they are undesirable food competitors or desirable food providers; they may be badly drawn or altogether avoided because they were not desired as food, or because they were regarded as an embodiment of evil. In short, sympathetic magic may be the basis for all of the art, some of the art, or none of the art. (Vinnicombe 1972b:128)

Figure 5.3: Patricia Vinnicombe tracing uKhahlamba-Drakensberg rock art.

Source: Rock Art Research Institute: University of the Witwatersrand.

Together with her field skills and technical virtuosity (Figure 5.3) came an analytical adeptness that produced a series of groundbreaking papers in southern African rock art research (Vinnicombe 1960, 1967a, 1967b, 1972a, 1972b, 1975). The key to these interpretations was the relative frequencies of different animal species in rock art and in excavated deposits. Eland, in particular, were found to occur in around 43 per cent of rock art motifs while smaller antelopes, the faunal remains of which were much more dominant than eland in archaeological deposits, comprised only 18 per cent of the rock art images (Vinnicombe 1976). This mismatch between iconography and faunal remains strongly suggested that animal species were depicted not for their economic value, but because of how they were woven into religious and social practices; an approach also followed by Laming-Emperaire and Leroi-Gourhan, but without the benefit of relevant ethnography. Vinnicombe argued that the 'ritual importance attached to various animals may be reflected in the numerical emphasis on the animals selected for portrayal: the less important they were ritually, the less frequently they may appear in the art' (Vinnicombe 1972a:199). Vinnicombe did not eschew the economic, but embraced the role that innovation had in generating new ritual and technological advances in hunting techniques, both in Africa and elsewhere:

New technologies instigate social changes which are in turn reflected in ritual, and so the whole cycle of life is structured by inter-related factors. In attempting to solve the eternal problem of man in relation to this cycle, the stone-age artist selected items for portrayal which symbolized his interpretation of life. By creating a feeling of cohesion and security in the face of uncertainty, by expressing and ordering social relations, man sought to maintain the necessary balance between himself and his environment that was fundamental to survival. This, I suggest, is the framework within which we should assess the products of his artistic creativity. (Vinnicombe 1975:202)

These ideas led Patricia Vinnicombe to her enduringly influential book, *People of the eland: Rock paintings of the Drakensberg Bushmen as a reflection of their life and thought* (Vinnicombe 1976). Supported by spectacular illustrations based on Vinnicombe's meticulous tracings of the rock art, this book broke new methodological and theoretical ground in rock art research in southern Africa and internationally in two ways. First, it drew on nineteenth-century ethnographic and historical accounts of San people to interpret rock art in emic terms, relating to rituals and belief systems in addition to economics. In doing so, Vinnicombe extended the idea put forward by Levi-Strauss (1966) that some animals were depicted because they were 'good to think' rather than because they were of economic importance. Her work parallels that of Laming-Emperaire and Leroi-Gourhan but while generally informed by them, diverges markedly in seeking to match up relevant San ethnography as a 'test' of the schema, whereas the French approach largely eschewed ethnography in favour of structuralist findings per se. Vinnicombe's approach paved the way for later researchers, such as David Lewis-Williams, Janette Deacon, Thomas Dowson, David Morris, Anne Solomon, Edward Eastwood and Catelijne Cnoops, Sven Ouzman, Geoffrey Blundell, Jeremy Hollmann, Lara Mallen, Ghilraen Laue, Dawn Green and many others (cf. Mitchell and Smith 2009) to delve deeply into San belief systems to interpret the rock art. The second way in which Vinnicombe's research was groundbreaking was in the use of statistical methods to compare the frequencies of depictions of species in rock art and their occurrence in the local environment. This was a major step in the acceptance of rock art as a useful form of archaeological data and prompted other southern African researchers to apply statistical analyses to rock art (e.g. Davidson 1999).

In 1977, the University of Cambridge awarded Patricia Vinnicombe a doctorate for this work, and *People of the eland*, recently reprinted with a companion volume (Mitchell and Smith 2009), remains a standard and much-cited reference work and model in southern African rock art research and beyond.

Patricia Vinnicombe was not taken up into the museum or university sectors despite her qualifications and will, but began a peripatetic career with then-husband, Patrick Carter, moving to central and East Africa to work on archaeology, rock art and heritage, including the excavation of sites that would have been flooded by the Aswan High Dam project (Deacon 2003:224). For many years, her work was largely tethered to her husband's employment. However, after their divorce, her career trajectory changed and what followed was 25 years of work, especially in Australian Aboriginal cultural heritage and advocacy.

Career in Australia

Patricia Vinnicombe emigrated to Australia with her son Gavin, seeking to make a new start after her divorce from archaeologist Patrick Carter who had taken up a post as assistant curator at the Archaeology and Anthropology Museum at the University of Cambridge (Chapman 2005:68). In 1978, she took up a contract position with the New South Wales (NSW) National Parks and Wildlife Service to work as a project archaeologist on the large North Hawkesbury Project to salvage archaeological sites prior to inundation by a large dam (Veth 2003:49), while also working for the Australian Institute of Aboriginal Studies in Canberra. This was the first large-scale regional commercial archaeological project in NSW, if not in Australia (Ward 2003:82). Vinnicombe's ability to mesh multiple sources of evidence – archaeological, ethnographic and documentary – reached perhaps its greatest expression in this project. In a short time, she produced a voluminous 740-page, two-volume report (Vinnicombe 1981) that is still used as a template for similar work, especially in NSW. This work challenged and extended her skills to include the recording and analysis of engravings on sandstone pavements as well as paintings, drawings and stencils (Deacon 2003:225). Vinnicombe brought to bear her technical and analytical skills to introduce new and more meticulous forms of recording for both rock art and archaeological deposits, in the process introducing to Australian archaeological nomenclature the PAD (Potential Archaeological Deposit), to designate sites with excavation potential, enabling decision-making on research strategies across a wide landscape (see Veth 2003:49).

Vinnicombe's NSW work prepared her for more rock art–focused work in Western Australia. Some of the first rock art recording programs in Australia were initiated as impact assessments, such as occurred in the Pilbara in response to industrialisation of the Burrup Peninsula. In 1980, Vinnicombe took up what was to be her final job at the Department of Aboriginal Sites at the Western Australian Museum. She was also drawn to the Kimberley in Australia's north-west both for its rock art and because it had a living Aboriginal rock art tradition and living Dreaming cosmology – in contrast to her putting together San lives from archival mentions and fragments. Here she could talk to people about their rock art past and present. This immediacy and also the stark reversal from South Africa – with its Indigenous majority – confirmed to her that research is only one part of a larger process of reconciliation for which advocacy for heritage as a human right was a logical extension (Vinnicombe 2001). As part of this conviction, Vinnicombe became committed to the rights of Aboriginal peoples and Torres Strait Islanders to manage their own cultural heritage and to facilitating Indigenous voices. At the 1988 Congress of the Australian Rock Art Research Association in Darwin, she memorably and powerfully co-presented two papers with Aboriginal Elder David Mowaljarlai, of the Mowanjum community near Derby in Western Australia. One paper was on the significance of rock paintings in the north-western Kimberley (Vinnicombe and Mowaljarlai 1995; also Vinnicombe 1992), and the other was as part of a symposium on retouching rock art that was initiated as a result of the controversial Gibb River repainting project (Mowaljarlai et al. 1988).

While based in Western Australia, Patricia Vinnicombe developed close relationships with female Aboriginal artists from Turkey Creek and facilitated wider understandings of their views on art and land. Her close friends included the late artist Queenie McKenzie, of, and for, whom Vinnicombe wrote a moving tribute that provides deep insights into the artist's relationship to country:

> 'Yarlka, this white mountain, this my spirit place. My mother, old Dinah, she found white porcupine la swag la Yarlka. That porcupine [echidna] was me. That white stone from that hill, they break him up for spear. Good spear, that one.' (Queenie McKenzie, tape 1994) … Queenie was therefore focused on a locality from which she never moved, a landscape that she knew intimately: 'Every rock, every hill, every water, I know that place backwards and forwards, up and down, inside out. It's my country and I got names for every place.' It was this singularly close relationship with her country, that prompted Queenie to take up painting. (Vinnicombe 2000)

In her work on Aboriginal sites at the Western Australian Museum, Patricia Vinnicombe became known as a fair, empathetic and fierce worker for Aboriginal heritage and rock art. Her tenure coincided with one of Australia's major rock art crises – the industrial development of the Burrup Peninsula, Western Australia (Vinnicombe 1987). It was this advocacy work, informed by scientific research and by taking seriously Aboriginal knowledge and perspectives, that rounded out Patricia Vinnicombe's career (see Vinnicombe 1992). She synthesised her understanding of Australian rock art research combining emic and etic views (Vinnicombe 1995). She retired in the same year as Andrée Rosenfeld, 1997. Like Rosenfeld, she remained active in research and advocacy. This work started immediately upon her formal retirement, with a 1997 Australian Institute of Aboriginal and Torres Strait Islander Studies (AIATSIS) grant to study Bardi ceremonial and dance artefacts (Deacon 2003:225). In 2000, Patricia Vinnicombe returned to South Africa as a visiting research fellow at the Rock Art Research Institute of the University of the Witwatersrand (Veth 2003:49) to work on ensuring that her legacy of tracings was digitally preserved and accessible (Vinnicombe 2001), completing the circle of her career on two continents.

Legacy

Patricia Vinnicombe's legacy lies both within and beyond academia and rock art research. Her early life and career are instructive of how closed academia often was to women and how determined and skilled women needed to be, even just to be admitted to the fringes of institutionally supported rock art work, often having to deal with an ascribed status as the partner of an archaeologist. Rock art research offered a different pathway, one that combined technical skill with the ability to think creatively, using ethnographic insights to justify the then-radical notion that San rock art was symbolic, spiritual and meaningful. Patricia Vinnicombe pioneered a new way of tracing and copying rock art through acetate sheets copied in the field to produce exact dimensions of motifs and their relationship to each other and the rock face. These acetate sheets were then used to make colour-correct 'redrawings' of the rock art, replacing many of the sketched or black-and-white copies that were then the norm, with the notable exception of Harald Pager's work. The information she recorded in the field was entered into a database using a punch-card system, and later lucidly and accessibly written and published in works that both specialist and lay audiences could understand and enjoy. Her ability not just to adapt rock art recording techniques to surveys and excavation-centric archaeology, but to integrate rock art and excavation, remain models of work.

Most of the completed redrawings of Vinnicombe's tracings are in the Rock Art Collections at the KwaZulu-Natal Museum and University of the Witwatersrand (Mitchell and Smith 2009) and accessible to everyone via the African Digital Rock Art Archive. The lasting value of Vinnicombe's research on southern African rock art is attested by the reprinting of *People of the eland* in 2009, with an accompanying volume that explored Vinnicombe's legacy and functions as a belated festschrift: *The eland's people: New perspectives in the rock art of the Maloti-Drakensberg Bushmen. Essays in memory of Patricia Vinnicombe* (Mitchell and Smith 2009). Alan Barnard's (2010) review of *People of the eland* highlights the enduring impact of Vinnicombe's work:

> The book not only brought an extraordinary and dynamic body of art to the attention of a global audience, but also helped to lay the foundations for a new generation of research into the meaning of prehistoric art. *People of the Eland* aimed to gain an insider's view of the rock art using San understandings of the world. While following this approach, it quickly became clear to Vinnicombe that the art was very far from simple depictions of daily life as had once seemed likely, but instead reflected the most deeply held San beliefs and symbols. This approach and this understanding has now become the standard for all those working with San rock art. *People of the Eland* remains a seminal work, the impact of which cannot be underestimated. (Barnard 2010:63)

Patricia Vinnicombe's life – and perhaps more pertinently her death – are lessons in why archaeology matters, especially as regards using archaeology to establish meanings of art to local Indigenous people. Towards the end of March 2003, Patricia Vinnicombe and her colleague, Warren Fish, completed some fieldwork on the Burrup Peninsula, north of Dampier and Karratha in northern Western Australia. This was followed by a meeting with resource-extraction developers:

A meeting in the area with the developers regarding the possible damage to the art by industrial emissions followed the fieldwork. Pat did not feel very well and at the end of the meeting left the room. Shortly afterwards she was found dead in the bathroom. Pat could not have arranged a better end: in a place that she loved and doing what she enjoyed – fighting heritage issues. (Ward 2003:82)

While much of Vinnicombe's work on the Burrup remains unseen – field trips, reports on sites, advocacy, meetings, building relationships, outreach activities and the like – it helped shape the past two decades' efflorescence of research and heritage management at Murujuga. The area that Vinnicombe was fighting to protect is now on the UNESCO tentative list for World Heritage Site status – the first such recognition of a rock art precinct in Australia (McDonald 2018).

Like Andrée Rosenfeld, Patricia Vinnicombe was internationally recognised and respected, and she brought that initial recognition to Australia. In the early 1970s, a research fellowship at Clare Hall, University of Cambridge, allowed Vinnicombe the time to develop her ideas more fully (see Vinnicombe 1972b). Later, a grant from Oxford University's Swan Fund helped her to employ a research assistant, Justine Olofsson, of the University of Witwatersrand's Rock Art Research Unit, to work up some of the remaining tracings that she had made 40–50 years previously (Ward 2003:81).

Discussion

Australian rock art research owes a debt to all of the people who have contributed to increasing the available data and to improving methods and ideas, and especially to female and other marginalised researchers, who had to carve a space to work both empirically and empathetically. Andrée Rosenfeld and Patricia Vinnicombe were pioneers in rock art research, not only in Australia but also internationally. Their work spanned three continents: Africa, Europe and Australia. As individuals they had tremendous impact on rock art research. Their work was associated with the use of new methods, theories and ideas. Though working largely independently, their work melded archaeological and anthropological practice and theory and this has profoundly influenced today's rock art research in Australia in a fascinating regional and national mosaic. Working in different contexts and using different approaches (e.g. Rosenfeld published more and so has an easier-to-quantify influence, while Vinnicombe worked behind the scenes more, though she paved the way for the post-2000s influx of researchers from southern Africa to Australia), both investigated the possibility that rock art was created as part of 'elaborate, religiously sanctioned relationships between people and place' (Rosenfeld and Smith 2002:103). Both researchers drew upon using established 'practice-based' methods, such as tracing and drawing, for analytical and interpretative purposes and both were committed to 'the judicious use of ethnographic parallels … to narrow down the field of plausible explanation even if patent demonstration is out of the question' (Vinnicombe 1972b:130–131).

Finally, some comments on gender and opportunity. When assessing the legacies of Andrée Rosenfeld and Patricia Vinnicombe it is important to understand the contexts and confines within which they were working. While Rosenfeld's work in Australia was solidly based in a university environment, Vinnicombe's contact with the academy was more ephemeral and was largely undertaken as part of consultancies and a museum position. As Morwood and Smith (1994) point out, the appointment of researchers with a commitment to rock art research at Australian universities, museums and other institutions during the 1970s and 1980s was crucial in the development of Australian rock art studies. Such appointments were a necessary precursor to the establishment of rock art studies as a viable subdiscipline within archaeology. These appointments were the means by which this field of study was made available to students, providing a pathway for graduates to pursue rock art research and management studies in their own right rather than via other disciplines or as an adjunct of excavation-centric work. Andrée Rosenfeld was fortunate. She moved to Australia in 1972 at a time that a new Department of Archaeology was being established at ANU. Arriving a few years later, in 1978, Patricia Vinnicombe faced a situation in which four positions in rock art research had been filled (Andrée Rosenfeld at ANU; John Clegg at the University of Sydney; and Mike Morwood and Iain Davidson at the University of New England). There would not be new university posts for rock art researchers until the late 1990s and early 2000s, with the appointments of Noelene Cole at James Cook University, Jo McDonald, firstly at ANU and then at the University of Western Australia, Paul Taçon at Griffith University, and Claire Smith at Flinders University and, later, Bruno David at Monash University. At AIATSIS, a sole post in rock art was established in the 1980s and was held by Graeme Ward. There is no question that Patricia Vinnicombe's capabilities as a rock art researcher in Australia were constrained by not having the resources and student base of a university. As Lesley Maynard put it, for a slightly earlier time, 'in early 1966 I was sweeping up the cold ashes of my undergraduate anthropology and contemplating with dread a year at Teachers College' (pers. comm. to Sven Ouzman, October 2020; see Chapter 4, by McDonald, this volume). Faced by such constraints, Patricia Vinnicombe pursued her scholarly pursuits in Australia via consultancies and, finally, a position at the Western Australia Museum. She used her opportunities judiciously and produced groundbreaking research.

Rock art researchers today owe a debt of gratitude to both Andrée Rosenfeld and Patricia Vinnicombe. Their lives and careers allow us to better understand rock art's disciplinary growth. In future, we can anticipate a pleasing diversity of practitioners, but they will still face challenges such as in making technological advances in research socially meaningful, in ensuring greater Indigenous leadership of research, and in making rock art – a national treasure in most countries – known and appreciated by the many publics we serve.

Acknowledgements

We thank the organisers of the 'Histories of Australian Rock Art Research' conference, 2019, for the invitation to write this paper. We thank the very thorough reviewers, whose comments have improved this paper and further illuminated our understanding of Australian rock art research.

References

African Digital Rock Art Archive 2021. *Vinnicombe collection*. Available at: sarada.co.za/#/library/vinni combe/collections/PJV.

Allen, H. 2019. The first university positions in prehistoric archaeology in New Zealand and Australia. *Bulletin of the History of Archaeology* 29(1):1–12. doi.org/10.5334/bha-606.

Bahn, P. and A. Rosenfeld (eds) 1991. *Rock art and prehistory: Papers presented to Symposium G of the AURA Congress, Darwin 1988*. Oxbow Books, Oxford.

Barnard, A. 2010. Review of Patricia Vinnicombe *People of the eland: Rock paintings of the Drakensberg Bushmen as a reflection of their life and thought*. *Africa* 80(4):663–664. doi.org/10.3366/afr.2010.0407.

Bednarik, R. 1995a. The Cóa petroglyphs: An obituary to the stylistic dating of Palaeolithic rock-art. *Antiquity* 69(266):877–883. doi.org/10.1017/S0003598X00082430.

Bednarik, R. 1995b. The age of the Cóa valley petroglyphs in Portugal. *Rock Art Research* 12(2):86–103.

Bolger, D. (ed.) 2013. *A companion to gender prehistory*. Wiley-Blackwell, Malden. doi.org/10.1002/9781118294291.

Bowdler, S. and G. Clune 2000. That shadowy band: The role of women in the development of Australian archaeology. *Australian Archaeology* 50(1):27–35. doi.org/10.1080/03122417.2000.11681663.

Brentjes, B. 1969. *African rock art*. Dent, London.

Brown, G.E. 1974. Leon Rosenfeld. *Nuclear Physics B* 83(1):i–viii. doi.org/10.1016/0550-3213(74)90068-6.

Buxton, D. 1977. Patricia Vinnicombe: *People of the eland*. *Antiquity* 51(202):169–170. doi.org/10.1017/S0003598X00071659.

Chaloupka, G. 1993. *Journey in time*. Reed, Chatswood, NSW.

Chapman, G. 2005. Patrick Lea Carter. *Downing College Association Newsletter and College Record 2005*:66–70. www.dow.cam.ac.uk/sites/default/files/associationnewsletter_2005_web.pdf (accessed 16 June 2021).

Clegg, J. 1979. Science, theory and Australian prehistoric art. *Mankind* 12:42–50. doi.org/10.1111/j.1835-9310.1979.tb00676.x.

Cole, N. 1988. The rock art of Jowalbinna (Laura). Unpublished BA(Hons) thesis, James Cook University of North Queensland.

Conkey, M.W. and J.M. Gero 1997. Programme to practice: Gender and feminism in archaeology. *Annual Review of Anthropology* 26:411–437. doi.org/10.1146/annurev.anthro.26.1.411.

Conkey, M.W. and J. Spector 1984. Archaeology and the study of gender. *Advances in Archaeological Method and Theory* 7:1–38. doi.org/10.1016/B978-0-12-003107-8.50006-2.

Cooke, C.K. 1969. *Rock art of southern Africa*. Books of Africa, Cape Town.

Cullen, P., M.M. Ferree and M. Verloo 2019. Introduction to special issue: Gender, knowledge production and knowledge work. *Gender Work and Organization* 25:765–771. doi.org/10.1111/gwao.12329.

David, B. 1992. An AMS date for North Queensland rock art. *Rock Art Research* 9:139–41.

David, B., J.-M. Geneste, F. Petchey, J.-J. Delannoy, B. Barker and M. Eccleston 2013. How old are Australia's pictographs? A review of rock art dating. *Journal of Archaeological Science* 40(1):3–10. doi.org/10.1016/j.jas.2012.08.019.

Davidson, I. 1999. Symbols by nature: Animal frequencies in the Upper Palaeolithic of Western Europe and the nature of symbolic representation. *Archaeology in Oceania* 34(3):121–131. doi.org/10.1002/j.1834-4453.1999.tb00442.x.

Deacon, J. 1993. The Cinderella metaphor: The maturing of archaeology as a profession in South Africa. *South African Archaeological Bulletin* 48:77–81. doi.org/10.2307/3888945.

Deacon, J. 2003. Remembrance: Dr Patricia Joan Vinnicombe, 1932–2003. *African Archaeological Review* 20(4):223–226. doi.org/10.1023/B:AARR.0000005678.67177.8b.

Dragovich, D. 1984. Desert varnish as an age indicator tor Aboriginal rock engravings: A review of problems and prospects. *Archaeology in Oceania* 19(2):48–56. doi.org/10.1002/j.1834-4453.1984.tb00079.x.

Du Cros, H. 1993. Female skeletons in the closet: A historical look at women in Australian archaeology. In H. Du Cros and L. Smith (eds), *Women in archaeology: A feminist critique*, pp. 239–244. Occasional Papers in Prehistory 23. Department of Prehistory, The Australian National University, Canberra.

Engelstad, E. 2007. Much more than gender. *Journal of Archaeological Method and Theory* 14:217–234. doi.org/10.1007/s10816-007-9035-3.

Fagan, B. 2018. *A little history of archaeology*. Yale University Press, New Haven.

Finch, D., A. Gleadow, J. Hergt, P. Heaney, H. Green, C. Myers, P. Veth, S. Harper, S. Ouzman and V.A. Levchenko 2021. Ages for Australia's oldest rock paintings. *Nature Human Behaviour* 5:310–318. doi.org/10.1038/s41562-020-01041-0.

Flood, J. 1987. Rock art of the Koolburra Plateau, North Queensland. *Rock Art Research* 4:91–120.

Flood, J. and N. Horsfall 1986. Excavation of Green Ant and Echidna shelters. *Queensland Archaeological Research* 3:4–64. doi.org/10.25120/qar.3.1986.181.

Franklin, M., J.P. Dunnavant, A.O. Flewellen and A. Odewale 2020. The future is now: Archaeology and the eradication of anti-Blackness. *International Journal of Historical Archaeology* 24:753–766. doi.org/10.1007/s10761-020-00577-1.

Fredengren, C. 2018. Archaeological posthumanities: Feminist re-invention of humanities, science and material pasts. In R. Braidotti and C. Åsberg (eds), *Reinventing the humanities*, pp. 129–140. Springer, New York. doi.org/10.1007/978-3-319-62140-1_11.

Frederick, U. and M. Wilson 1999. Introduction. *Archaeology in Oceania* 34(3):91–92. doi.org/10.1002/j.1834-4453.1999.tb00437.x.

Griffith, B. 2018. *Deep time Dreaming: Uncovering ancient Australia*. Black Inc., Carlton.

Hall, N. 1999. Building blocks and stepping stones: Some key foundations in the development of rock art conservation in Australia. *Archaeology in Oceania* 34(3):161–170. doi.org/10.1002/j.1834-4453.1999.tb00445.x.

Hallam, S.J. 2003. Pat Vinnicombe. *Australian Archaeology* 56:48–40. doi.org/10.1080/03122417.2003.11681751.

Hays-Gilpin, K. 2000. Feminist scholarship in Archaeology. *Annals of the American Academy of Political and Social Science* 571:89–106. doi.org/10.1177/000271620057100107.

Huchet, B. 1992. Rock art and prehistory. *Archaeology in Oceania* 27(2):87. doi.org/10.1002/j.1834-4453.1992.tb00288.x.

Kaberry, P.M. 1939. *Aboriginal woman: Sacred and profane*. George Routledge, London.

Levine, M. 1968. Reinterpretation of the earliest art. *Science* 161:150–152. doi.org/10.1126/science.161.3837.150.

Lévi-Strauss, C. 1966. *The savage mind*. University of Chicago Press, Chicago.

Lewis-Williams, J.D. 2009. Patricia Vinnicombe: A memoir. In P. Mitchell and B.W. Smith (eds), *The eland's people: New perspectives in the rock art of the Maloti-Drakensberg Bushmen. Essays in memory of Patricia Vinnicombe*, pp. 13–28. Witwatersrand University Press, Johannesburg.

Macfarlane, I., M.-J. Mountain and R. Paton 2005. *Many exchanges. Archaeology, history, community and the work of Isabel McBryde*. Aboriginal History Monograph 11. Aboriginal History Inc., Canberra.

Marcus, J. 1993. *First in their field: Women and Australian anthropology*. Melbourne University Press, Melbourne.

Marshall, M. and P.S.C. Taçon 2014. Past and present, traditional and scientific: The conservation and management of rock-art sites in Australia. In T. Darvill and A.P.B. Fernandes (eds), *Open-air rock-art conservation and management: State of the art and future perspectives*, pp. 214–28. Routledge, London.

Mate, G. and S. Ulm 2016. Another snapshot for the album: A decade of Australian Archaeology in Profile survey data. *Australian Archaeology* 82(2):168–183. doi.org/10.1080/03122417.2016.1213032.

Mate, G. and S. Ulm 2021. Working in archaeology in a changing world: Australian archaeology at the beginning of the COVID-19 pandemic. *Australian Archaeology* 87(3):229–250. doi.org/10.1080/031 22417.2021.1986651.

Maynard, L. 1976. An archaeological approach to the study of Australian rock art. Unpublished MA thesis, University of Sydney.

Maynard, L. 1977. Classification and terminology in Australian rock art. In P.J. Ucko (ed.) *Form in Indigenous art,* pp. 387–402. Australian Institute of Aboriginal Studies, Canberra.

McBryde, I. 2008. Andrée Jean Rosenfeld (1934–2008). *Australian Academy of Humanities Proceedings* 33:56–63.

McDonald, J. 2018. Murujuga (Dampier Archipelago) and the journey towards world heritage recognition. *Australian Archaeology* 84(2):1–3. doi.org/10.1080/03122417.2018.1534347.

McDonald, J. 2021. Jo McDonald [profile]. *University of Western Australia.* Available at: research-repository.uwa.edu.au/en/persons/jo-mcdonald (accessed 16 June 2021).

Mitchell, P. 2002. *The archaeology of Southern Africa.* Cambridge University Press, Cambridge.

Mitchell, P. and B. Smith (eds) 2009. *The eland's people: New perspectives in the rock art of the Maloti-Drakensberg Bushmen. Essays in memory of Patricia Vinnicombe.* Witwatersrand University Press, Johannesburg.

Morphy, H. and J. Mulvaney 1999. Andrée Rosenfeld: An appreciation. *Archaeology in Oceania* 34(3):93–94. doi.org/10.1002/j.1834-4453.1999.tb00439.x.

Morwood, M.J. and D. Hobbs 1994. *Quinkan prehistory: The archaeology of Aboriginal art in S.E. Cape York Peninsula.* Tempus 3. Anthropology Museum, University of Queensland, Brisbane.

Morwood, M. and C. Smith 1994. Rock art research in Australia 1974–94. *Australian Archaeology* 39:19–38. doi.org/10.1080/03122417.1994.11681525.

Mountain, M.J. 2014. Rosenfeld, Andrée. In C. Smith (ed.), *Encyclopedia of global archaeology,* pp. 6380–6382. Springer, New York. doi.org/10.1007/978-1-4419-0465-2_2153.

Movius, H.L. Jr 1968. *Palaeolithic cave art. American Anthropologist* 70:808–809. doi.org/10.1525/aa.1968.70.4.02a00560.

Mowaljarlai, D., P. Vinnicombe, G.K. Ward and C. Chippindale 1988. Repainting images on rock in Australia and the maintenance of Aboriginal culture. *Antiquity* 62(237):690–696. doi.org/10.1017/S0003598X00075086.

Mulvaney, D.J. 1975. *The prehistory of Australia.* Penguin Books, Harmondsworth.

Officer, K. 1991. *South East region rock art conservation project: An evaluation of the significance, conservation and management requirements of twenty Aboriginal rock art sites (including two major site complexes) within the NPWS NSW Southeast Region.* Volumes 1 and 2. Report to NSW National Parks & Wildlife Service.

Porr, M. and K. Doohan 2017. From pessimism to collaboration: The German Frobenius-Expedition (1938–1939) to Australia and the representation of Kimberley art and rock art. *Journal of Pacific Archaeology* 8(1):88–99.

Rosenfeld, A. 1965. *The inorganic raw materials of antiquity.* Weidenfeld and Nicolson, London.

Rosenfeld, A. 1972. Four papers on the Rop Rock Shelter, Nigeria. *West African Journal of Archaeology* 2:17–28.

Rosenfeld, A. 1975. The early man sites: Laura, 1974. *Australian Institute of Aboriginal Studies Newsletter* 3:37–40.

Rosenfeld, A. 1985. *Rock art conservation in Australia*. Special Australian Heritage Publication No. 2. Australian Government Publishing Service, Canberra.

Rosenfeld, A. 1992. Recent developments in Australian rock art studies. In R. Crowley and I. Crowley (eds), *Lojjineur, Aegean Bronze Age iconography: Shaping a methodology*, pp. 231–238. University of Liege, Liege.

Rosenfeld, A. 1993. A review of evidence for the emergence of rock art in Australia. In M.A. Smith, M. Spriggs and B. Fankhauser (eds), *Sahul in review: Pleistocene archaeology in Australia, New Guinea and Island Melanesia*, pp. 71–80. Occasional Papers in Prehistory, No. 24. Department of Prehistory, Research School of Pacific Studies, The Australian National University, Canberra.

Rosenfeld, A. 1997. Archaeological signatures of the social context of rock art production. In M. Conkey, O. Soffer, D. Stratman and N. Jablonski (eds), *Beyond art: Pleistocene image and symbol*, pp. 289–300. Memoirs of the California Academy of Sciences 23. University of California Press, Berkeley.

Rosenfeld, A. 1999. Rock art and rock markings. *Australian Archaeology* 49(1):28–33. doi.org/10.1080/03122417.1999.11681653.

Rosenfeld, A. and W. Mumford 1996. The Thuiparta rock engravings at Erowalle, Wallace Rock Hole, James Range, Northern Territory. In S. Ulm, I. Lilley and A. Ross (eds), *Australian Archaeology '95: Annual Conference*, pp. 247–255. Tempus 6. Anthropology Museum, University of Queensland, St Lucia.

Rosenfeld, A. and C. Smith 1997. Recent developments in radiocarbon and stylistic methods of dating rock art. *Antiquity* 72(272):405–11. doi.org/10.1017/S0003598X00085008.

Rosenfeld, A. and M.A. Smith 2002. Rock-art and the history of Puritjarra Rock Shelter, Cleland Hills, Central Australia. *Proceedings of the Prehistoric Society* 68:103–124. doi.org/10.1017/S0079497X00001468.

Rosenfeld, A., D. Horton and J. Winter 1981. *Early man in North Queensland*. Terra Australis 6. Department of Prehistory, Research School of Pacific Studies, The Australian National University, Canberra.

Rosenfeld, A., J. Golson, W. Ambrose and P. Hughes 1984. Report of a meeting on rock art conservation. *Rock Art Research* 1:54–59.

Skotnes, P. 2007. *Claim to the country: The archive of Lucy & Wilhelm Bleek*. Jacana, Johannesburg and Cape Town.

Smith, C. 1991. Female artists: The unrecognized factor in sacred rock art production. In P. Bahn and A. Rosenfeld (eds), *Rock art and prehistory. Papers presented to Symposium G of the AURA Congress, Darwin 1988*, pp. 45–52. Oxbow, Oxford.

Smith, C. 2009. Andrée Jean Rosenfeld (1934–2008). *Australian Archaeology* 68(1):83–84. doi.org/10.1080/03122417.2009.11681894.

Smith, C. and H. Burke 2006. Glass ceilings, glass parasols and Australian academic archaeology. *Australian Archaeology* 62:13–25. doi.org/10.1080/03122417.2006.11681826.

Taçon, P.S.C. 1999. Andrée Rosenfeld and the archaeology of rock-art. *Archaeology in Oceania* 34(3):95–102. doi.org/10.1002/j.1834-4453.1999.tb00440.x.

Taçon, P.S.C. 2021. Paul Taçon (profile). *Griffith University*. Available at: experts.griffith.edu.au/18923-paul-tacon (accessed 16 June 2021).

Ucko, P. (ed.) 1977. *Form in Indigenous art*. Australian Institute of Aboriginal Studies, Canberra.

Ucko, P. and A. Rosenfeld 1967. *Palaeolithic cave art*. Weidenfeld and Nicolson, London.

Ulm, S., G. Mate, C. Dalley and S. Nichols 2013. A working profile: The changing face of professional archaeology in Australia. *Australian Archaeology* 76:3443. doi.org/10.1080/03122417.2013.11681963.

Veth, P. 2003. Patricia Vinnicombe. *Australian Archaeology* 56:49–50. doi.org/10.1080/03122417.2003.11681751.

Vinnicombe, P. 1960. The recording of rock paintings in the upper reaches of the Umkomaas, Umzimkulu and Umzimvubu Rivers. *South African Journal of Science* 56(1):11–14. doi.org/10520/AJA00382353_708.

Vinnicombe, P. 1967a. Rock-painting analysis. *The South African Archaeological Bulletin* 22(88):129–141. doi.org/10.2307/3888475.

Vinnicombe, P. 1967b. The recording of rock-paintings: An interim report. *South African Journal of Science* 63:282–284. doi.org/10520/AJA00382353_8751.

Vinnicombe, P. 1972a. Myth, motive, and selection in southern African rock art. *Africa* 42(3):192–204. doi.org/10.2307/1159159.

Vinnicombe, P. 1972b. Motivation in African rock art. *Antiquity* 46(182):124–133. doi.org/10.1017/S0003598X00053382.

Vinnicombe, P. 1975. The ritual significance of eland (*Taurotragus oryx*) in the rock art of southern Africa. In E. Anati (ed.), *Les religions de la Préhistoire*, pp. 379–400. Centro Camuno di Studi Preistorici, Capo di Ponti.

Vinnicombe, P. 1976. *People of the eland: Rock paintings of the Drakensberg Bushmen as a reflection of their life and thought*. University of Natal Press, Pietermaritzburg.

Vinnicombe, P. 1981. Predilection and prediction: A study of Aboriginal sites in the Gosford-Wyong Region. Unpublished report for North Hawkesbury Project.

Vinnicombe, P. 1987. Dampier archaeological project. Woodside Offshore Petroleum Pty Ltd.

Vinnicombe, P. 1992. Kimberley ideology and the maintenance of sites. In G.K. Ward (ed.), *Retouch: Maintenance and conservation of Aboriginal rock imagery*, pp. 10–11. Occasional AURA Publication No. 5. Australian Rock Art Research Association, Melbourne.

Vinnicombe, P. 1995. Perspectives and traditions in Australian rock art research. In K. Helskog and B. Olsen (ed.), *Perceiving rock art: Social and political perspectives*, pp. 87–103. The Institute for Comparative Research in Human Culture, Oslo.

Vinnicombe, P. 2000. Queenie McKenzie. Tribute. *Artlink*. www.artlink.com.au/articles/1389/queenie-mckenzie/ (accessed 16 June 2021).

Vinnicombe, P. 2001. Forty-odd years down the track. *The Digging Stick* 18(2):1–2.

Vinnicombe, P. and D. Mowaljarlai 1995. That rock is a cloud: Concepts associated with rock images in the Kimberley region of Australia. In K. Helskog and B. Olsen (eds), *Perceiving rock art: Social and political perspectives. ACRA: The Alta Conference on Rock Art*, pp. 228–246. Novus Forlag, Oslo.

Walsh, G. 1994. *Bradshaws: Ancient rock paintings of north-west Australia*. Bradshaw Foundation, Geneva.

Ward, V. 2003. Obituaries: Patricia Vinnicombe (1932–2003). *The Natal Society Foundation* 20(33):80–82.

Watchman, A. 1987. Preliminary determinations of the age and composition of mineral salts on rock art surfaces in the Kakadu National Park. In W. Ambrose and J. Mummery (eds), *Archaeometry: Further Australasian studies*, pp. 36–42. The Australian National University, Canberra.

Watchman, A. 1995. Historic antiquity for the Foz Cóa rock engravings, Portugal. *WAC News* 3(2):iii–iv.

Watchman, A. 1996. A review of the theory and assumptions in the AMS dating of the Foz Cóa petroglyphs, Portugal. *Rock Art Research* 13(1):21–30.

Willcox, A.R. 1963. *The rock art of South Africa*. Nelson, London.

Zilhão 1995a. The age of the Cóa valley (Portugal) rock-art: Validation of archaeological dating to the Palaeolithic and refutation of scientific dating to historic or proto-historic times. *Antiquity* 69(266):883–901. doi.org/10.1017/S0003598X00082442.

Zilhão 1995b. A refutation of the direct dating of the stylistically Palaeolithic petroglyphs of the Cóa valley to recent times. *WAC News* 3(2):v–vii.

6

Australian artists as rock art researchers: Percy Leason's theories on cave art

Susan Lowish

Introduction

This chapter sheds light on non-Indigenous Australian artists who research rock art, while acknowledging Indigenous peoples' prior, intimate and familial engagements with and connections to their rock art (see Goldhahn et al. 2021; Harding et al. 2017; May et al. 2019; May et al. 2021; Taçon 2019). There are many well-known non-Indigenous Australian artists who have been inspired by Aboriginal rock art (see Frederick 2016, 2019; McDonald 2019; Scott 2019). Margaret Preston's travels to sites in western Arnhem Land in 1940 had a profound effect on her artistic practice; her observation of rock art and experimentation with natural pigments could be seen as practice-led research, but due to her eclectic range of interests, wide-ranging subject matter and short-term interest, she cannot rightly be called a rock art researcher. On the other hand, the Australian tonal realist Percy Alexander Leason (1889–1959) maintained a lifelong research interest in rock art. He made copies of paintings and caves near Glenisla (Glen Isla) for the National Museum of Victoria's 1929 exhibition of Aboriginal art. Subsequent visits to the Cave of the Serpent at Mount Langi Ghiran and to rock paintings in the Mootwingee range, New South Wales, set Leason on a path of research and to produce several publications outlining his ideas.

This chapter reveals some of Leason's contributions to rock art research in Australia, alongside his sketches, paintings and models, which illustrate his internationally recognised theories on western European cave art (Leason 1939, 1956). The example of Leason points to the existence of a much greater interest in rock art by Australian artists than has previously been documented. So great is this interest that arguably a new narrative of modern and contemporary Australian art could be written based entirely on artistic engagements with rock art. This narrative could include the great creative interest in ancient and contemporary (or near-contemporary) rock art by non-Indigenous present-day artists (e.g. Castillo Deball et al. 2019; McGill 2019; Mircan et al. 2015) and builds upon decades of collaborative projects between Traditional Owners, who are often also artists, and archaeologists, who sometimes are. It could also sit alongside and in dialogue with expressions of the much longer, deeper and continuing connection that Indigenous peoples have to their rock art throughout Australia (e.g. Mowaljarlai 1992; Neidjie 1985; Ngarjno et al. 2000; Taçon 2019).

A brief look through the archives of state, national and international galleries reveals that there are a great many famous, twentieth-century, non-Indigenous artists who have explicitly engaged with rock art in Australia as well as overseas. Australian examples include Russell Drysdale, Sidney Nolan, John Olsen, Clifton Pugh, Brett Whiteley and Fred Williams, to name a few.

Their engagements with rock art ranges from the fanciful to the matter of fact. Nolan imagined the shipwrecked Eliza Fraser to be transformed into rock art on K'gari, the traditional land of the Butchulla people, using acetate paint on hardboard, in a work at the Tate Gallery entitled *In the cave* (1957) (see Frederick 2016; McNiven et al. 1998). Drysdale used a camera to capture *No title (Bird tracks, Aboriginal Rock Art, Gallery Hill, Western Australia, Friday 17th October 1958)*, one of many colour transparencies of rock art in the National Gallery of Victoria's collection (see Boddington 1987). Master printmaker Grahame King's series of works on paper from the early 1980s reflects a less prosaic and more poetic sensibility towards rock art. He used highly sophisticated lithographic techniques, up to five stones in different colours, to produce his 'fleeting impressions of ancient Aboriginal markings' (Zimmer 2005:115), the layered effect being like a calligraphic landscape in *At Nowangi, Arnhem Land* (1984), National Gallery of Australia. Rock art has clearly made an impact on these artists.

Further back in the history of European Australian art, rock art was acknowledged and admired by the French Communard Lucien Henry who was exiled to Australia in 1879 (see Henry and Stephen 2001). A leaf from his major work, an unpublished book on Australian decorative art, shows a finely detailed plan for a dado (lower part of a wall) with the central panel covered in figures drawn most likely from the Basin site in Ku-ring-gai Chase National Park.[1] Belonging to the Garrigal people of the Guringai Nation, this site features some of the finest examples of rock engravings in the region (see Stanbury and Clegg 1990). Henry was inspired to copy these engravings and surround them with images of birds, both hunting snakes and being attacked by sharks, and of three Aboriginal men holding waddies (clubs) looking on from above. While research into this artist is ongoing, the remainder of this chapter focuses on Preston and Leason.

Margaret Preston

One of Australia's most loved artists, Margaret Preston was a driving force for modern art from the 1920s to her death in 1963. Best known for her paintings and prints of landscapes and flowers, she championed a distinctly Australian style that she developed from many sources locally and abroad. Preston's interests in Aboriginal art and her use of it in the development of her own practice has long been acknowledged and more recently critiqued (Edwards et al. 2005; Nicholls 2000). Famously, Preston wrote:

> In wishing to rid myself of the mannerisms of a country other than my own I have gone to the art of a people who had never seen or known anything different from themselves … These are the Australian aboriginals, and it is only from the art of such people in any land that a national art can spring. (Preston 1925:unpaginated)

This oft-quoted conviction reveals her general intentions but obscures the specific impact that rock art later had on her work.

It is widely reported that Preston's first experience of rock art was at Berowra, located in the Hornsby Shire, north of Sydney, where she lived in the 1930s (Butler 2005; Edwards et al. 2005; Grant 2017). There are hundreds of rock art sites recorded in Hornsby, around the suburb of Berowra, in addition to the neighbouring Berowra Valley National Park and Ku-ring-gai Chase (see Dibden 2019; Jo McDonald 2008). These include engravings and charcoal motifs in sandstone formations such as rock-shelters and pavements. Senior Curator of Australian Prints and Drawings at the National Gallery of Australia Roger Butler has noted that Preston visited Japan in the early 1930s, and the 'influence of Japanese art, with its asymmetrical compositions is revealed in many of her works from these years' (Butler 2005:paragraph 13). It is more difficult to see the influence of the Berowra region's Aboriginal rock art on her work from this time.

---

1   The design can be viewed at the Powerhouse Museum: collection.maas.museum/object/324601.

Figure 6.1 (left): Margaret Preston (Australia; England; France, b. 1875, d. 1963), *Banksia* **1938, oil on canvas, 53.2 × 42.6 cm.**

Source: Art Gallery of New South Wales, Gift of Society of Artists Sydney Ure Smith Memorial 1950. © Margaret Preston/Copyright Agency, 2021.

Figure 6.2 (right): Margaret Preston, *The brown pot* **1940, oil on canvas, 51 × 45.8 cm.**

Source: Art Gallery of New South Wales, Purchased 1942. © Margaret Preston/Copyright Agency, 2021.

I would argue, rather, that it was the experience of her 1940 trip to the Kakadu region and Arnhem Land, and Gunbalanya (Oenpelli) and Injalak Hill in particular, that had the most immediate and profound impact on Preston's art. A comparison of her painting style and technique in the treatment of a vase of *Banksia* cones in various stages of flowering, rendered in oil on canvas in two different artworks, one made slightly before her visit to Arnhem Land (Figure 6.1), and one made directly after climbing Injalak Hill (Figure 6.2), is revelatory. It is claimed that 'she reduced her palette to earth colours and surrounded simplified forms with black lines, based on her study of Aboriginal art' (Seivl 1988:paragraph 11). This change in her artwork is clear to see in these two examples. It is as though her whole way of seeing was affected by her contact with rock art.

The impact on Preston of seeing Aboriginal rock art was far greater than shifting her palette from pink, green and grey to yellow, brown and red. Immediately upon her return to Sydney, Preston wrote up her experience of visiting the main gallery on Injalak Hill and published it along with four photographs of these 'extraordinary aboriginal paintings on the roof of a rock shelter' in the top art industry journal, *Art in Australia* (Figure 6.3). In it she stated: 'there is a chance for Australia to have a national art … an art for Australia from Australians' (Preston 1940:63). In addition to that article with its accompanying set of photographs, Preston also produced many unique prints (monotypes) directly referencing recognisable rock art sequences, like *Aboriginal design* (1943) (Figure 6.4), printed in colour inks from one Masonite block onto soft cream Japanese paper (NGA 68.102); and *Fish* (1949), a colour stencil in gouache on pulpboard, now housed in the University of Melbourne Art Collection. These works drew their inspirations directly from the barramundi and long neck turtle that are still clearly represented in the rock art and kept alive in contemporary art created today by the local Bininj community of western Arnhem Land.

Figure 6.3 (left): Caption reads: 'Details of the aboriginal rock paintings which Margaret Preston discusses in her article'. Imagine this image in reverse.

Source: *Art and Australia*, 3rd series, no. 81, 1940:59.

Figure 6.4 (right): Margaret Preston, *Aboriginal design* 1943, woodcut, printed in colour inks, from one Masonite block, 38.4 × 39.6 cm (printed image), 43.1 × 45.4 cm (sheet).

Source: National Gallery of Australia, Canberra, 1968.102. Purchased 1968. © Margaret Preston/Copyright Agency, 2021.

According to Edwards et al. (2005) and Grant (2017), Preston brought ochres back from the Northern Territory and ground them to make her own pigments. She copied not only the techniques of dotting and cross-hatching that she had seen in Aboriginal rock art and bark painting but also their colours, and their specific and particular forms – and sometimes she did not vary them much at all from the Aboriginal works she was inspired by (compare Figures 6.3 and 6.4). This copying, appropriation and assimilation is not only symptomatic of colonialism but also of intensive artistic appreciation and experimentation. Preston was nothing if not rigorous in her efforts to encounter and absorb new styles, materials and processes. Preston travelled very widely, spending time in Europe, the Pacific, Asia, India, South America, the Middle East and Africa; she is said to have 'cultivated an interest in non-European art and culture' (AGNSW 2021:paragraph 5). Although it made a great impression, Australian Aboriginal rock art was just one of many sources upon which she drew.

For Preston, rock art was an inspiration but not an abiding passion. However, there is at least one Australian artist, who lived and worked around the same time as Preston, for whom the study of rock art (or cave art, more accurately) became a lifelong pursuit. In the following section, I suggest that through careful observation, astute vision, and creativity in research, a theory of European cave art was produced that may yet have relevance and importance to understanding rock art in Australia. In support of the claim that 'Exposure to Aboriginal art eventually led to his lifelong preoccupation with European prehistoric art' (Downer 1989:39), in the next section I argue that the dedication displayed by this artist constitutes a hitherto overlooked focus on rock art such that he deserves to be recognised as a rock art researcher. His importance to Australian art history will surely be enhanced as a result.

Percy Leason

Born on a remote western Victorian wheat farm in 1889, Percy Leason grew up in Kaniva in the Wimmera district and moved to Melbourne as a young man. He worked as an apprentice lithographer, attending evening art classes at the National Gallery School, where Preston in 1893 had spent four years training. In 1917, Leason moved to Sydney, meeting several artists including Lloyd Rees and Julian Ashton. He rapidly made a name for himself as a political cartoonist at

The Bulletin, where fellow artists George Lambert, William Dobell and several members of the Lindsay family were also employed. According to his biographer, Margot Tasca, Leason became part of a lively group that often gathered to discuss matters of the world, and it was through them that he became enthralled by H.G. Wells' *An outline of history* (1919–1920). It is further claimed by Tasca that this text inspired him 'to construct a chart of how Western art had evolved and this … would lead to lifelong studies of cave art' (Tasca 2016:51). Yet his interest in origins was there from an early age, as he would often scour the wheatfields of Kaniva for Aboriginal stone tools and evidence of past campfires (see Leason and Leason 1920–2010; Tasca 2016:90; and see also Griffiths 1996).

In 1924, Leason returned to Melbourne from Sydney to establish his career as an artist, while his black-and-white illustrations continued to appear frequently in the *Herald* newspaper, in *Melbourne Punch* and *Table Talk* magazines. Around this time, he was the highest-paid commercial artist in Australia (Leason 1999:23). Also around this time, he married, had kids, settled in Eltham (a leafy suburb at the north-eastern edge of Melbourne) and built a home and an art studio. He met Max Meldrum, an artist, teacher and leader of the Australian tonalist movement. They shared many similar views and theories of art, and together developed a 'constructive association' (Leason 1999:23). Tonalism, sometimes referred to as tonal realism, of which Meldrum was a leading exponent, builds form with paint by denoting areas of light and shade directly onto the canvas. Instinctive and reactive, rather than detailed and photographic, tonalist paintings are immediately identifiable by their soft-focus, 'misty' and atmospheric aesthetic (see Lock-Weir et al. 2008).

In 1934, Leason utilised this technique to paint a series of 31 portraits of Aboriginal people from the Lake Tyers Mission in Gippsland at the suggestion of Dr Donald F. Thomson, an anthropologist at the University of Melbourne whom he had met previously working at the *Herald* and who was also a close neighbour. These dark, tonal and sombre works were presented at the Athenaeum Gallery in August that year; it was Leason's first solo exhibition. The portraits demonstrated his understanding and control of the tonal technique, but a great critical row developed, and it was questioned whether the portraits were art or ethnographic studies (see Kleinert 1994 for detailed account and critique). Did they belong in the gallery or the museum? More recently, these portraits were reintroduced to the descendants of the sitters. 'We are happy to know that the portraits are still around. These faces and the names of those painted in the portraits live on in their descendants. Their families of today carry with them the generations before them' (Paton 1999:4). Currently, 22 of these paintings are in the La Trobe Pictures Collection at the State Library of Victoria, Melbourne; three more are with the Koorie Heritage Trust and one in a private collection. The location of five of the original artworks remains unknown.

But it is the 1929 exhibition, *Australian Aboriginal art,* held in the Print Room of the combined Public Library, Museums and National Gallery of Victoria, Melbourne, that was perhaps the most pivotal event for Leason in relation to his rock art research, and a quite remarkable showing by all accounts. In the months leading up to its opening, the exhibition was well promoted and supported by a number of articles in the press. Reading them en masse reveals the extent to which rock art dominated both the exhibition and the publicity leading up to it. For example, in the Adelaide *Advertiser,* the organisers state: 'Our mission was to examine the petroglyphs and paintings, and secure permanent records of them for the exhibition, subsequently to go to Museums' (Barrett 1929a:9). In the Melbourne *Herald*, the full scale and scope was revealed:

> The display of aboriginal art will include enlarged photos of remarkable rock paintings and engravings on the walls of caves in the Grampians, and plaster casts of the ancient rock drawings of Mootwingee, in western New South Wales. Examples will also be shown from the North and Central areas of the Continent and the Macdonnell Ranges. Another special feature of the exhibition will be a model of one of the strange red hand caves. The model will be 12 feet in length and will be moulded on a wooden frame. Reproductions from tracings in the caves will be painted on the model by Mr Percy Leason. (*Herald* 1929:23)

The dominance of rock art in the displays and publicity of this first and most important exhibition of Australian Aboriginal art is under-represented in exiting scholarship, as much of it has focused on critiquing the live displays or emphasising the exhibition's position in relation to the history of exhibitions of Aboriginal art (see Kleinert 2002; Lowish 2011; Vanni 2014). My investigations are yet to uncover the remains of the model cave, original plaster casts, tracings or indeed the enlarged photographs in the stores of the State Library of Victoria, Museums Victoria or the National Gallery of Victoria, but the search is ongoing. Further research is also needed into the preparation, planning and layout of this most auspicious event on the rock art exhibition timeline, as only a very few images have come to light (see Jones 1988).

Figure 6.5: Caption reads: 'Making tracings of rock paintings, Glen Isla Rock Shelter, Victoria Range, Victoria'. Percy Leason on the left.

Source: Barrett et al. *Australian Aboriginal art* (1929:39).

Charles Barrett (1929b and see Figure 6.5), one of the lead researchers and exhibition organisers, in an article for the *Portland Guardian*, wrote:

> A new aboriginal mystery cave, the Cave of the Red Hands, has been discovered in the Grampians. It contains age-old stencils or paintings – symbols sacred to the aborigines … No scientists had even heard of this cave and it is destined to become famous. It was a startling discovery. Until recently only one 'aboriginal art gallery' was known to exist in Victoria – at least by ethnologists. This is the rock shelter near Glen Isla, in the Victorian Range. It was discovered more than half a century ago. Our expedition was arranged with the object of examining this 'gallery' and obtaining tracings of the remarkable drawings on the rock wall, for a model to be shown at the exhibition of aboriginal art in July. (Barrett 1929b:1)

Barrett continued:

> Mystery veils the[m]. They are ceremonial and sacred in many cases, but we do not know their real meaning. Theories are plentiful, but none is convincing. So important to science are these rock drawings of the ranges that it is proposed to have them protected against vandalism. We washed from the Glen Isla, rock charcoal scribblings – the names and foolish comments of the thoughtless visitors and nonentities. The Government will be asked to provide funds that will enable us to shield the art of the aborigines in the Red Hand Cave and the Glen Isla shelter. The walls should be enclosed with strong wire-netting, as is done with similar relics of primitive man in other countries. (Barrett 1929b:1)

Barrett's emphasis on mystery throughout the article and in the title, 'Mystery cave in Grampians', would have most likely been part of a strategy intended to generate interest in the rapidly approaching exhibition. The absence of convincing ideas or knowledge as to the meaning(s) of the markings may also have piqued Leason's interest. The fact that Barrett and his team washed the site clean of graffiti in 1929 (and argued for the installation of protective fencing) demonstrates that the lack of respect for (and wilful vandalism of) rock art sites in this region has been continuous. It is ongoing, and this has long been recognised by some (see Gunn and Goodes in this volume). Leason further emphasised the need for protection in his promotional piece for the *Australian Aboriginal art* exhibition, published in *Table Talk*:

> if, beside serving the ends of students, it does create public interest and so lead perhaps to the preservation of painted rock shelters and rock carvings, it will have done all that those enthusiasts hoped it might. (Leason 1929:18)

As common at the time, the concern was for the art as a relic, not for its ongoing significance for the local Aboriginal communities.

In Leason's quite lengthy article, he acknowledged that the exhibition is one of considerable importance and that a 'great deal of work has gone to its organisation by Mr J. A. Kershaw, Mr Charles Barrett, Mr A. S. Kenyon and others', but he is otherwise disparaging of the art on display. Throughout the article, Leason makes detrimental comparisons to Rodin, and Raeburn, and writes of Aboriginal artists: 'seldom if ever did they achieve anything beyond the range of the clever child. Even at their best they were far behind the prehistoric Magdalenians of France and northern Spain; they had something to learn from the Bushmen of Africa and others' (Leason 1929:18). For him, as for other colonial commentators at the time (and since), it was the lack of realism and light and shade (tone) in the art that caused the most consternation:

> They were not sufficiently diligent explorers of optical truths. Thus, for all their vast quantity of pictures, they made no progress. They very frequently made fair outlines of animals, birds and fishes, but it was always a case of only a good beginning. (Leason 1929:54)

From a dyed-in-the-wool tonalist, this was to be expected, but not excused. Others, who wrote of the exhibition catalogue, were far less critical: 'This little book leaves one with a withering sense of shame over the crass way in which we have let aboriginal art perish almost unobserved' (*Argus* 1947:42).

A sustained investigation and critique of the systemic origins and individual instances of artistic biases and their application in the writing about Australian Aboriginal art has been mounted elsewhere (see Lowish 2009, 2011, 2015b, 2018), though the ongoing negative impacts of these value judgements should never be understated. For present purposes, the main point is the emergent emphasis in Leason's text placed on 'the prehistoric Magdalenians', whom he believed 'were beyond doubt the most diligent discoverers of optical reality'. He also noted: 'they did work that is little short of amazing, and the importance of which is not fully realised' (Leason 1929:18). He appears to have drawn heavily on a contemporary publication, *The art of the cave dweller* by the British art historian Gerard Baldwin Brown (1928), reproducing several drawings from its pages, and to have been captivated by its findings – a position not shared by contemporary reviewers who stated:

> either the professor is an extremely amiable gentleman who is very anxious that his pupils' mental exertions should be as small as possible, or else that these lectures must have been delivered to the first form of a public school. (Burlington Magazine 1929:107)

Brown's publication, whatever its shortcomings, is full of images captioned to accentuate live action: the 'Galloping reindeer, from St-Marcel' (1928:232); 'The "bellowing bison" from Altamira' (1928:227); and 'Two groups of ponies in movement from Limeuil' (1928:162). Leason reproduced these images in his 1929 review of the exhibition *Australian Aboriginal art* and several more times in the years following. Brown cites the noted French archaeologist Henri Breuil in relation to Aurignacian–Magdalenian art:

> its chief merit is the representation of life. The figures are not stuffed nor made up according to patterns, but alive and individual, possessed of character and mobility, and evince, Breuil has said, *un sentiment vraiment intense de la vie des animaux* [a really intense feeling of animal life]. (Brown 1928:147)

Thus, the stage was set for the debate at a meeting of the British Association for the Advancement of Science at Cambridge in August 1938, where Leason's paper 'A new view of the Western European group of Quaternary cave art' was presented.

Writing in the *Herald* in December 1946, Leason's long-time friend Donald Thomson called him 'a rebel who has already de-bunked accepted interpretations of cave art … and demonstrated that the "action" murals of European cavemen [illustrated in Brown] were of dead animals' (Thomson 1946:4). Again, citing Brown, and his claims made for the realistic movement depicted in cave art, Thomson goes on to outline the scientific method by which Leason exposed the falseness of the claims:

> Mr Leason scoured the countryside for months, photographing every dead animal he could find. Not a horse or cow or even a dog or cat that died at Eltham escaped his notice. Finally, he journeyed into Gippsland on a deer hunting expedition to see at first hand animals which had been killed in the chase. (Thomson 1946:4)

In Leason's 1939 paper he also recounts the time he spent up a ladder sketching a scene 'looking down on a domestic cat and a snake which had killed each other' (Leason 1939:58).

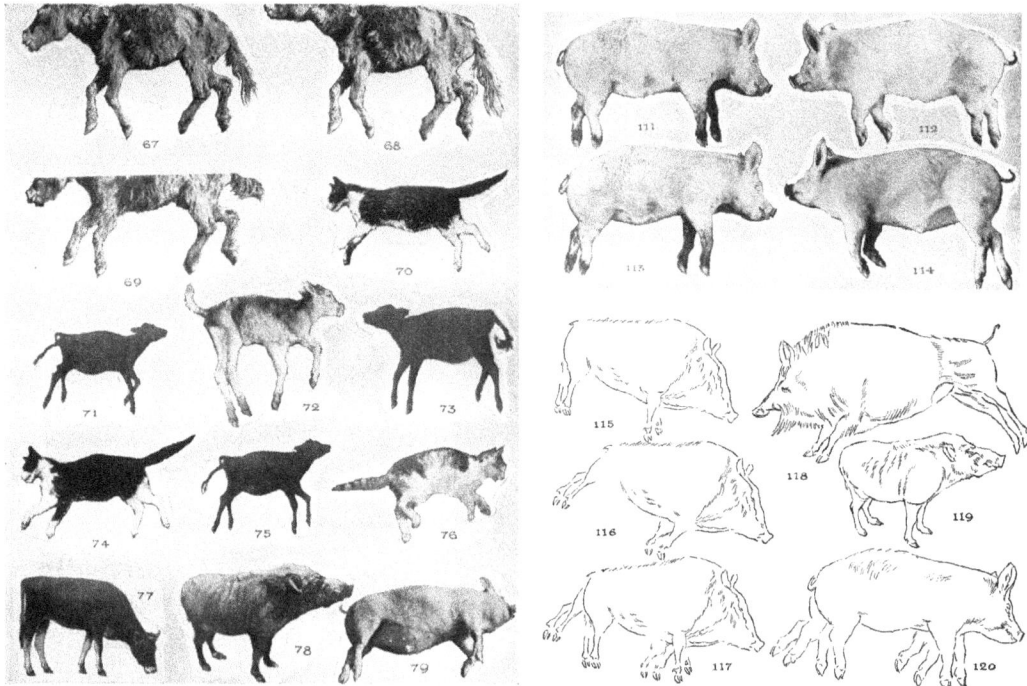

Figure 6.6 (left): Plate IV caption reads: 'Nos. 67–9, dead pony; nos. 70, 74, drowned domestic cat; nos. 71, 73, 75, drowned Jersey calf; no. 72 dead Jersey calf, as found; no. 76 dead domestic cat, as found; no. 77 Jersey heifer browsing; no. 78, wild boar's stance; no. 79, slaughtered pig'.
Source: Leason 1939.

Figure 6.6 (right): Plate V caption reads: 'Nos. 111–4, slaughtered pigs with legs in various positions; no. 115–6, Altamira boars showing alternative positions of legs; no. 117, combination of nos. 115–6; no. 118, Altamira boar; no. 119, living boar (tracing of no. 78); no. 120 combination of tracings of nos. 113–4'.
Source: Leason 1939.

Leason spent several years documenting dead animals in various stages of rigor mortis in his quest to demonstrate that the famous murals of the prehistoric caves of Europe, 'the "galloping wild boar" and the "bellowing bison" … featured in every textbook on prehistoric art and culture … were not action pictures, but still life studies' (Thomson 1946:4). His most convincing evidence appears when the stance of the live animal appears close to that of its dearly departed comrade. For example (Figure 6.6), compare illustration numbers 75 and 77 in the left-hand side with nos. 118 and 119 on the right. Leason's case is compelling, as the angle of the feet, the distribution of weight through the body, the angle of the shoulders and even the amount of belly shown differ markedly between the living and the dead. As he stated:

> It is not a question of whether the artists could or could not draw legs as well as they drew bodies and heads; there are enough instances to show that they could. (Leason 1939:51)

Leason devoted many hours over a great many years to his research and to developing his theory of visual reality based on objective criteria, posthumously published (see Leason and Leason 2019). A page from a draft of another of his unpublished books, titled *A brief history of painting*, reveals more of his creative thinking. He reimagines the art of Cro-Magnons (now thought of as Early Modern Humans, or early fully modern European *Homo sapiens*), with 'good paints and brushes' and utilising the techniques of building up areas of light and shade, as does a tonal realist painter (see Tasca 2016:94–95). His ideas 'did not find favour with the archaeologists and a hard fight followed' (Thomson 1946:4). A far more complex theoretical and political situation existed in archaeological circles than is possible to present here (see Conkey 2018). Perhaps

Leason's focus on artistic vision, creativity and imagination were at odds with those seeking the advancement of science through systematic and methodical investigation. Ironically, he firmly believed that art 'can and should be like science' (Leason and Leason 2019:5), a view that placed him out of step with much of the art world and the rise of modernism, which he saw as 'a threat to the very survival of Art' (Leason and Leason 2019:vii).

A late portrait of the artist (Figure 6.7), made possibly on the occasion he delivered a lecture on cave art in a tuxedo to the Salmagundi Club, Greenwich Village, New York, shows him standing in front of several sketches and beside several plaster models of prehistoric animals created from his earlier tracings and photographs to illustrate his 'Dead Animal' theory. This theory claimed that prehistoric artists could not have made their wonderfully accurate cave paintings of animals from living, moving specimens, but must have relied on static carcases, viewed from an elevated vantage point (see Leason 1939). Here, Leason's use of pictures-within-a-picture may have been a nod to the great Vermeer, who turned this technique into an art form in and of itself:

> a picture-within-a-picture that functions not as an embodiment of qualities opposed to those found in the principal action, but rather as a means of making clearer what one might call its notional essence. (Weber 1998:298)

Yet, in Leason's self-portrait we see no moralising message, no emblematic structure of the order of Vermeer. Leason's self-portrait reflects a man standing by his convictions, surrounded by the results of his research and fixing us with his gaze. His self-portrait seems to project perseverance, perception and steadfastness in his own beliefs.

Figure 6.7: Percy Leason, *Self-portrait with cave paintings* ca. 1956–1957, oil on canvas, 67.0 × 85.1 cm (sight), in frame 77.8 × 95.3 cm.

Source: Reproduced with permission, State Library of Victoria.

Figure 6.8: (left) Percy Leason, *Mammoth/Elephant* H32356; (right) Percy Leason, *The 'galloping' boar of Altamira* H32352, State Library of Victoria.

Source: Photograph by Susan Lowish, February 2020.

The State Library of Victoria not only has a large collection of Leason's paintings and cartoons, but also some rather spectacular cast bronze and plaster models of famous works of cave art, the figures he frequently reproduced in relation to his theory that they were direct studies of dead animals (Figure 6.8). The Pictures Collection contains photographs of what appear to be dioramas created by Leason that illustrate his theory, showing a man lying on a ledge drawing a dead bison lying below, along with some of his original sketches, and a small fragment of rock from Lascaux. In late 1957, Leason realised a lifelong dream to see the French cave art that he had only read about.

> Percy had been concerned that the cave artists may not have had a suitable height from which to look down while making their studies, but he discovered the Dordogne and Vézère River valleys were literally a mass of ledges. (Tasca 2016:230)

Leason's research into cave art was extensive and his learning about it was continuous, even if the recognition for his contribution to Australian art and culture did not reach the heights he had hoped. Through Thomson's advocacy, networks and connections, Leason's 'Dead Animal' theory was published in the *Journal of the Prehistoric Society of Great Britain* England in July 1939. Whether it was the outbreak of World War II shortly thereafter, or for some other reason relating to resistance among European academics, the immediate impact of Leason's theory has been difficult to trace. Concerned with the dwindling prospects of continued employment as a commercial artist, the rivalry in the Melbourne art scene and the impending world war, Leason left Australia. In 1938, he settled on Staten Island, New York, where he continued his work, painting, teaching, publishing and exhibiting, until his death in 1959. In the years just prior to his death he made models from his tracings of rock art (Figure 6.8) and photographed them. He even included them in his self-portrait (Figure 6.7). His biographer notes that, in 1958, 'His studies confirmed that his original theory was correct and as a result he published "Making Models in three dimensions from Quaternary Cave Pictures" in the Staten Island Institute's *Proceedings*' (Tasca 2016:232). This publication, along with the cave he constructed for the 1929 exhibition *Australian Aboriginal art*, remain hidden or lost in the archives, but it is hoped with more sustained sleuthing that they will eventually see the light of day.

Conclusion

Despite the strides that have been made towards understanding Australian Aboriginal art through the work of anthropologists and archaeologists, the story of Australian art as it currently exists in art history survey texts would lead us to believe that rock art (if it is mentioned at all) is little more than a first stop on a chronological tour (e.g. John McDonald 2008; Moore 1934; and for a critique see Lowish 2015a). However, it is clear from the examples of Preston and Leason that rock art has had great impact on some of Australia's best-known non-Indigenous artists, and on some who 'died poor and without adequate recognition' (Tasca 2016:234). In their recent work, 'On the possibility of another Australian art history', art historians Rex Butler and A.D.S. Donaldson write:

> Aboriginal art certainly forces us to re-read Australian art, although our real point is that it also disaggregates the category of Australian art; that, against all of the undoubtedly well-meaning efforts to write a history of Australian art that includes Aboriginal art, the real effect of Aboriginal art is to do away with the very possibility of a national art history. (Butler and Donaldson 2020:51)

Australia is comprised of many nations and Australian art has never been a unified category; much of its history has been based on exclusion (as argued by Lowish 2009, 2018 among many others). To my mind, the real effect of Aboriginal art is that it has helped to usher in the realisation that many histories of Australian art are possible and necessary. One of these histories can give just recognition to Australian Aboriginal rock art within a broader category of 'Australian art' (e.g. as with the chapter by Taçon (2011) in Anderson 2011), but other narratives are also possible. Preston, upon whom the impact of seeing rock art was so great that it transformed her vision, wrote: 'there is a chance for … an art for Australia from Australians' (Preston 1940:63). Now, there is a chance for an art history *for* Australian rock art from Indigenous and non-Indigenous perspectives. The example of Leason reminds us about a much greater interest in rock art by non-Indigenous Australian artists. A rock art–centred narrative of the whole of modern and contemporary Australian art could be written, combining Indigenous and non-Indigenous artistic engagements with rock art, with issues of appropriation (Huntley 2018) and 'inclusionism' (Savoy 2021) carefully navigated.

Australian art historians are only just beginning to articulate the complexity of relationships to rock art (see Frederick 2016, 2019; Gunn and Lowish 2019; Jorgensen 2019; Lynch 2019; McDonald 2019; Scott 2019). By reworking the grand narrative of 'Australian art' from one of chronology to one of engagement, performance and influence – one that maps encounters, meetings, networks and relationships, in addition to dates and times, and stylistic progression – the true extent and importance of rock art to Australia's art history can slowly be revealed. If the beginnings of Australian art can be anchored in the oldest rock art rather than the First Fleet (as per Allen 2021), and if these larger narratives also brought together and relayed ongoing artistic encounters with rock art by Indigenous and non-Indigenous artists alike, then the levels of familiarity with and respect for rock art and Country would continue to increase, as would their value beyond the price of iron ore, natural gas or marble benchtops.

Many researchers, curators and artists have long researched and deeply respected Aboriginal views of Aboriginal art, because Aboriginal knowledge holders have been teaching and passing on knowledge over and for many decades. It is important not to overlook that there are numerous accounts written and exhibitions curated that recognise the links in art and visual cultural practices over time within Aboriginal Australian art, as well as inspirations and collaborations between Indigenous and non-Indigenous artists, and others. By revealing more of the hidden history of Australian artists' research into rock art, the lengths to which they have gone in their research, positive contributions to the history of rock art in Australia can be further illuminated.

Acknowledgements

I would like to thank the editors for their patience, the referees for their comments, and the organisers and fellow interlocutors from the Histories of Australian Rock Art Research Symposium, Griffith University, Gold Coast, at which this paper was originally presented. The University of Melbourne provided funding to attend this event and to cover the costs of image permissions. I acknowledge the foundational work of Margot Tasca in researching the life of Percy Leason and thank Gerard Hayes, senior librarian Picture Collection, State Library of Victoria, for access to the archive and allowing me to include his hands in my photographs. I thank Max Leason for permission to reproduce his father's work and for responding to my correspondence before his recent passing. Condolences to his family. I thank Jane Brown, Visual Cultures Research Centre, for help with images, along with Eliza Williams (National Gallery of Australia), Jude from Image Requests (Art Gallery of NSW) and Glen Menzies (Copyright Agency). I acknowledge my Indigenous teachers, friends and family, and the many Indigenous people whose connection to their rock art makes them the key stakeholders and the priority when it comes to projects involving Indigenous art.

References

AGNSW 2021. Margaret Preston. Featured artist page. *Art Gallery of NSW.* Available at: artgallery.nsw. gov.au/collection/artists/preston-margaret/ (accessed 18 August 2021).

Allen, C. (ed.) 2021. *A companion to Australian art*. John Wiley & Sons, Hoboken, New Jersey.

Argus 1947. Aboriginal art. *Argus* (Melbourne), Saturday 8 November 1947:42.

Barrett, C. 1929a. Marvels of Mootwingee. *Advertiser* (Adelaide), Tuesday 2 April 1929:9.

Barrett, C. 1929b. Mystery caves in the Grampians. *Portland Guardian*, Monday 8 April 1929:1.

Barrett, C., A.S. Kenyon and Public Library, Museums and National Gallery (Victoria) 1929. *Australian Aboriginal art: Issued in connexion with the Exhibition of Australian Aboriginal Art, National Museum, Melbourne*. Published for the Trustees of the Public Library, Museums and National Gallery of Victoria by H.J. Green, Govt. Printer, Melbourne.

Boddington, J. 1987. *Drysdale, photographer*. National Gallery of Victoria, Melbourne.

Brown, G.B. 1928. *The art of the cave dweller: A study of the earliest artistic activities of man*. R.V. Coleman, New York.

Burlington Magazine 1929. Review of *The art of the cave dweller*, by G. B. Brown. *The Burlington Magazine for Connoisseurs* 54(311):107–108. www.jstor.org/stable/863870.

Butler, R. 2005. *Margaret Preston Australian printmaker 18 December 2004 – 25 April 2005*. Exhibition essay. Available at: nga.gov.au/exhibitions/margaret-preston/#Archive-essay (accessed 18 August 2021).

Butler, R. and A.D.S. Donaldson 2020. On the possibility of another Australian art history. In T. Bennett, D. Stevenson, F. Myers, and T. Winikoff (eds), *The Australian art field: Practices, policies, institutions*, pp. 44–55. Routledge, New York. doi.org/10.4324/9780429061479-6.

Castillo Deball, M., H. Mathews and M. Ratliff 2019. *Mariana Castillo Deball: Replaying life's tape*. Bon Dia Boa Tarde Boa Noite, Berlin.

Conkey, M. 2018. Interpretative frameworks and the study of the rock arts. In B. David and I. McNiven (eds), *The Oxford handbook of the archaeology and anthropology of rock art*, pp. 25–50. Oxford University Press, Oxford. doi.org/10.1093/oxfordhb/9780190607357.013.20.

Dibden, J. 2019. *Drawing in the land: Rock art in the Upper Nepean, Sydney Basin, New South Wales.* Terra Australis 49. ANU Press, Canberra. doi.org/10.22459/TA49.2018.

Downer, C. 1989. A prophecy unfulfilled: 'The last of the Victorian Aborigines' by Percy Leason. *La Trobe Journal* 11.43:39–40.

Edwards, D., R. Peel and D. Mimmocchi 2005. *Margaret Preston.* Art Gallery of New South Wales, Sydney.

Frederick, U. 2016. Marks and meeting grounds. In L. Brady and P. Taçon (eds), *Relating to rock art in the contemporary world: Navigating symbolism, meaning, and significance*, pp. 337–362. University Press of Colorado, Colorado. doi.org/10.5876/9781607324980.c014.

Frederick, U. 2019. Figure on a sandstone ground: Considering Brett Whiteley's rock art. *Australian and New Zealand Journal of Art* 19(2):168–188. doi.org/10.1080/14434318.2019.1681576.

Goldhahn, J., L. Biyalwanga, S. May, J. Blawgur, P. Taçon, J. Sullivan, I. Johnston and J. Lee 2021. 'Our dad's painting is hiding, in secret place': Reverberations of a rock art painting episode in Kakadu National Park, Australia. *Rock Art Research* 38(1):59–69.

Grant, K. 2017. Margaret Preston (1875–1963) *Kangaroos Feeding*, 1945. In *Important Fine Art + Indigenous Art, Melbourne, 29 November 2017* (exhibition). Available at: www.deutscherandhackett. com/auction/lot/kangaroos-feeding-1945 (accessed 18 August 2021).

Griffiths, T. 1996. *Hunters and collectors: The antiquarian imagination in Australia.* Cambridge University Press, New York.

Gunn, R. and S. Lowish 2019. Australian rock art in the expanded field: History, meaning, and contemporary context. *Australian and New Zealand Journal of Art* 19(2):139–141. doi.org/10.1080/ 14434318.2019.1701383.

Harding, D., H. Folkerts and A. Goddard 2017. *Dale Harding: Body of objects.* Griffith Artworks, Griffith University, Nathan, Queensland.

Henry, L. and A. Stephen 2001. *Visions of a republic: The work of Lucien Henry - Paris - Noumea - Sydney.* Powerhouse Publishing, Sydney.

Herald 1929. Aboriginal art exhibition: Fine collection expected. *Herald* (Melbourne), Wednesday 3 April 1929:23.

Huntley, J. 2018. Rock art, Egyptians and aliens: Rock art as colonial instrument – why recognising aboriginal authenticity matters. In D. Jordan and R. Bosco (eds), *Defining the fringe of contemporary Australian archaeology: Pyramidiots, paranoia and the paranormal*, pp. 47–64. Cambridge Scholars Publishing, Newcastle upon Tyne.

Jones, P. 1988. Perceptions of Aboriginal art: A history. In P. Sutton (ed.), *Dreamings: The art of Aboriginal Australia*, pp. 143–179. Viking, in association with The Asia Society Galleries, New York.

Jorgensen, D. 2019. Lucas Grogan and the eroticism of Aboriginal art. *Australian and New Zealand Journal of Art* 19(2):210–221. doi.org/10.1080/14434318.2019.1681578.

Kleinert, S. 1994. 'Jacky Jacky was a smart young fella': A study of art and Aboriginality in south east Australia 1900–1980. Unpublished PhD thesis, The Australian National University, Canberra.

Kleinert, S. 2002. On the identity politics of the 1929 Exhibition of Primitive Art in Melbourne. *Signatures* 5:1–39.

Leason, P. 1929. Current art shows. *Table Talk* (Melbourne), Thursday 18 July 1929:18.

Leason, P. 1939. A new view of the western European group of Quaternary cave art. *Proceedings of the Prehistoric Society* 5(1):51–60. doi.org/10.1017/s0079497x00020697.

Leason, P. 1956. Obvious facts of Quaternary cave art. *BMA Medical and Biological Illustration* 6(4):209–214.

Leason, P. 1999. *Recognition: Percy Leason's Aboriginal portraits*. National Portrait Gallery, Canberra.

Leason, P. and M. Leason 1920–2010. State Library Victoria: Papers of Percy Leason, MS 14453. Australian Manuscripts Collection. Melbourne.

Leason, P., and M. Leason 2019. *Visual reality: An analysis of the visual image in painting*. Australian Scholarly Publishing, North Melbourne.

Lock-Weir, T., M. Meldrum, P. Perry and Art Gallery of South Australia 2008. *Misty moderns: Australian tonalists 1915–1950*. Art Gallery of South Australia, Adelaide.

Lowish, S. 2009. Writing/righting a history of Australian Aboriginal art. *Humanities Research* 15(2):133–151. doi.org/10.22459/hr.xv.02.2009.09.

Lowish, S. 2011. Setting the scene: Early writing on Australian Aboriginal art. *Journal of Art Historiography* 4:1–12. Available at: arthistoriography.files.wordpress.com/2011/05/lowish-ed.pdf (accessed 21 August 2021).

Lowish, S. 2015a. Rock art and art history: Exploring disciplinary perspectives. *Rock Art Research* 32(1):63–74.

Lowish, S. 2015b. Evolutionists and Australian Aboriginal art: 1885–1915. *Journal of Art Historiography* 12(June):1–35. Available at: arthistoriography.files.wordpress.com/2015/06/lowish.pdf (accessed 21 August 2021).

Lowish, S. 2018. *Rethinking Australia's art history: The challenge of Aboriginal art*. Studies in Art Historiography. Routledge, New York. doi.org/10.4324/9781351049993.

Lynch, N. 2019. The Saint sequence, Cudtheringa (Castle Hill). *Australian and New Zealand Journal of Art* 19(2):222–235. doi.org/10.1080/14434318.2019.1681611.

May, S., J. Gumbuwa Maralngurra, I. Johnston, J. Goldhahn, J. Lee, G. O'Loughlin, K. May, C. Ngalbarndidj Nabobbob, M. Garde and P. Taçon 2019. 'This is my father's painting': A first-hand account of the creation of the most iconic rock art in Kakadu National Park. *Rock Art Research* 36(2):199–213.

May, S., L. Rademaker, J. Goldhahn, P. Taçon and J. Narndal Gumurdul 2021. Narlim's fingerprints: Aboriginal histories and rock art. *Journal of Australian Studies* 45(3):292–316. doi.org/10.1080/1444 3058.2021.1946709.

McDonald, H. 2019. In the landscape of extinction: The life of Murujuga's ancient rock art. *Australian and New Zealand Journal of Art* 19(2):236–252. doi.org/10.1080/14434318.2019.1681579.

McDonald, Jo 2008. *Dreamtime superhighway: Sydney Basin rock art and prehistoric information exchange*. Terra Australis 27. ANU E Press, Canberra. doi.org/10.22459/DS.08.2008.

McDonald, John 2008. *Art of Australia*. Pan Macmillan, Sydney.

McGill, C. 2019. Murujuga rock art: One artist's experience as a witness to the history, the contemporary and the politics. *Australian and New Zealand Journal of Art* 19(2):253–259. doi.org/10.1080/14434318. 2019.1675488.

McNiven, I., L. Russell and K. Schaffer (eds) 1998. *Constructions of colonialism: Perspectives on Eliza Fraser's shipwreck*. Leicester University Press, London and New York.

Mircan, M., V. van Gerven Oei and H. Ahmed 2015. *Allegory of the cave painting: A reader*. Mousse Publishing Milan, Italy.

Moore, W. 1934. *The story of Australian art: From the earliest known art of the continent to the art of to-day.* Angus & Robertson, Sydney.

Mowaljarlai, D. 1992. Ngarinyin perspective of repainting: Mowaljarlai's statement. In G.K. Ward (ed.), *Retouch: Maintenance and conservation of Aboriginal rock imagery*, pp. 8-9. Occasional AURA Publication 5. Archaeological Publications, Melbourne.

Neidjie, B., S. Davis and A. Fox 1985. *Kakadu Man: Bill Neidjie.* Mybrood Pty Ltd, NSW.

Ngarjno, Ungudman, Banggal and Nyawarra 2000. *Gwion Gwion: Secret and sacred pathways of the Ngarinyin Aboriginal People of Australia.* Könemann, Cologne.

Nicholls, C. 2000. *From appreciation to appropriation: Indigenous influences and images in Australian visual art.* Flinders University Art Museum, Adelaide.

Paton, D. 1999. A collaborative statement: Comments from some of the descendants of the portrait sitters. In P. Leason *Recognition: Percy Leason's Aboriginal portraits*, p. 4. National Portrait Gallery, Canberra.

Preston, M. 1925. The Indigenous art of Australia. *Art in Australia*, 3rd series, 11:unpaginated.

Preston, M. 1940. Paintings in Arnhem Land. *Art in Australia*, 3rd series, 81:58–63.

Savoy, D. 2021. Toward an inclusive art history. *World Art* 11(2):121–136. doi.org/10.1080/21500894. 2020.1838943.

Scott, S. 2019. 'A new kind of film': Performing Aboriginality in James Cant's *Wirritt Wirritt* (1957). *Australian and New Zealand Journal of Art* 19(2):189–209. doi.org/10.1080/14434318.2019.1681577.

Seivl, I. 1988. Preston, Margaret Rose (1875–1963). In the *Australian Dictionary of Biography*, National Centre of Biography, The Australian National University, Canberra. Available at: adb.anu.edu.au/ biography/preston-margaret-rose-8106 (accessed 3 February 2021).

Stanbury, P. and J. Clegg, with poems by D. Campbell 1990. *A field guide to Aboriginal rock engravings: With special reference to those around Sydney.* Sydney University Press, Sydney.

Taçon, P. 2011. Special places and images on rock: 50,000 years of Indigenous engagement with Australian landscapes. In J. Anderson (ed.), *Cambridge companion to Australian art*, pp. 11–21. Cambridge University Press, Melbourne.

Taçon, P. 2019. Connecting to the Ancestors: Why rock art is important for Indigenous Australians and their well-being. *Rock Art Research* 36(1):5–14.

Tasca, M. 2016. *Percy Leason: An artist's life.* Thames & Hudson Australia, Port Melbourne, Victoria.

Thomson, D. 1946. Man who debunked art of cavemen. *Herald* (Melbourne), Friday 13 December 1946:4.

Vanni, I. 2014. The archive and the contact zones: The story of Stan Loycurrie and Jack Noorywauka, performers at the 1929 Australian Aboriginal Art exhibition, Melbourne. *Journal of Australian Studies* 38(3):314–330. doi.org/10.1080/14443058.2014.921231.

Weber, G. 1998. Vermeer's use of the picture-within-a-picture: A new approach. *Studies in the History of Art* 55:294–307.

Zimmer, J. 2005. Grahame King: A Melbourne story. In S. Grishin (ed.), *The art of Grahame King*, pp. 89–143. Macmillan Art Publishing, South Yarra.

Part B: South-east coast to the far north-west

7

A short story of Gariwerd: The rock art management chapter

Robert G. Gunn and Jake R. Goodes

Introduction

Archaeologists have determined through archaeological excavations in the region that Aboriginal people have occupied Gariwerd (the Grampians Ranges in western Victoria) for at least 22,000 years (Bird and Frankel 2005). From Aboriginal perspectives, Gariwerd was made by Bunjil in the Dreaming, giving local Aboriginal peoples a charter that says 'we have always been here'. It is unknown when the first artist put paint to rock in Gariwerd but, on the basis of motif superimpositions and states of preservation, they started a process that continued for generations. This paper presents an outline of the story of Gariwerd's rock art, its recording, conservation and government management, and the increasing role of Aboriginal Traditional Owner groups in those endeavours.

Since its first recognition by non-Aboriginal Australians, academic attention to the rock art of Gariwerd has undergone a number of discrete phases. Each of these phases has added a new dimension of knowledge on the rock art repertoire and, hence, on the ongoing story of Gariwerd culture.

The Greater Gariwerd rock art region extends beyond the Grampians Ranges (Gariwerd) to include the immediate sandstone outliers of Burrunj (Black Range to the west of Gariwerd), Lil Lil (Red Rock), Punyole (Dundas Range), Dyurrite (Mt Arapiles), Mt Bepcha and Mt Talbot (Figure 7.1). These ranges and outcropping ridges are all composed of the same sandstone strata identified in the main Grampians Ranges (Cayley and Taylor 1997:10). These ranges and outcrops contain a wealth of rock art that together constitutes a broad rock art tradition that contrasts with rock art elsewhere in the State of Victoria (Gunn 1987a). A second Black Range, to the east of the Grampians Ranges, contains the site popularly known as 'Bunjil's shelter'. This eastern Black Range is composed of granite and is included within the Greater Gariwerd rock art region on the basis of a documented Aboriginal story connecting Bunjil's shelter and Gariwerd. The most recent rock art at Bunjil's shelter, and to which the story relates, is in a distinctly different art style to those styles present elsewhere in Greater Gariwerd, while the underlying art has direct parallel to one of the later styles within Gariwerd (see below).

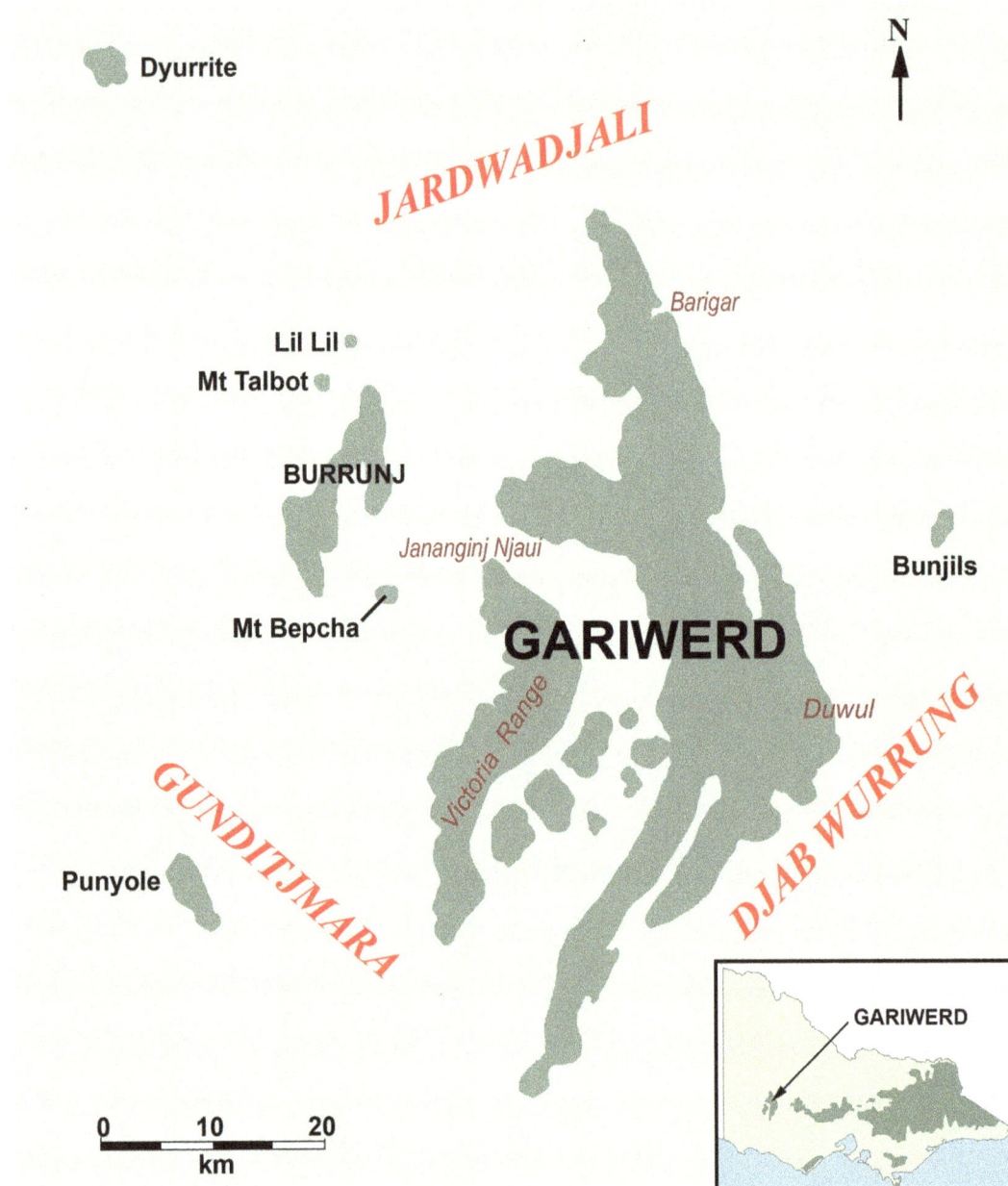

Figure 7.1: Location of Gariwerd and locations mentioned in the text.

Source: Map by Robert G. Gunn.

The Greater Gariwerd rock art region is within the lands of the Jardwadjali, Djabwurrung and Gunditjmara peoples (Figure 7.1), today represented by the Barengi Gadjin Land Council Aboriginal Corporation, based in the town of Horsham; Eastern Maar Aboriginal Corporation, based in Warrnambool; and Gunditj Mirring Traditional Owners Aboriginal Corporation, based in Heywood.

The Grampians Ranges of Gariwerd are a tightly grouped set of north–south trending quartzose sandstone ranges. The ranges rise steeply from the surrounding plains some 900 m below (Figure 7.2). The rainfall and temperature vary from warm and dry in the north (mean annual rainfall = 448 mm) to cool and wetter in the south (mean annual rainfall = 617 mm). The highest peak in Gariwerd, Duwul (Mt William), at 1167 m above sea level, has a mean annual rainfall of 1166 mm (BOM 2019). Duwul and the other high peaks receive seasonal snow falls every few years.

Figure 7.2: Central Gariwerd from the east.
Source: Photograph by R.G. Gunn.

Today, the vegetation across Gariwerd varies from swamp scrub-heathland in the broad valleys, to tall open forest with a dense scrubby understorey and alpine vegetation on the ranges varying with altitude and latitude (Day et al. 1984:40). In 1896, however, the Victoria Range consisted of 'rocky hills clad lightly with timber' and was grazed by both sheep and cattle (Mathew 1896:30). The present dense vegetation is thought to be largely the result of the removal of grazing and the cessation of earlier Aboriginal burning practices, as the early settlers ran sheep and could ride horses through much of the ranges (Wilkie 2020:68–76; Eric Barber pers. comm. 2019).

Background

In the beginning

The story of Gariwerd begins with the creation of the land by Bunjil, the creator-being of the Aboriginal peoples of south-eastern Australia (Howitt 1904:289–291). Features of the landscape were later modified by descendent Dreaming Beings, such as Tchingal the Emu who created the landmark features of Jananginj Njaui and Barigar (Figure 7.1). The rock-shelters that now house the rock art were created at the beginning of the Gariwerd story, during the Dreaming creation of the landscape. At this before-time era, Aboriginal peoples had the forms of birds and were capable of supernatural practices. At the era's end, the bird-people became human, but with the ability to return to their bird-states through appropriate achievements and rituals.

Aboriginal occupation

Aboriginal people have lived in and around Gariwerd from the beginning and continue to be an integral part of Gariwerd. Archaeological excavations have revealed that people have occupied the ranges of Gariwerd since at least 22,140±160 BP (no calibration possible; Bird and Frankel 2005:71). Elsewhere in Victoria, the oldest dated occupation is c. 32,000–26,600 calBP (Richards et al. 2007) but, given that older archaeological sites are known from every Australian state including Tasmania, and that the earliest dated archaeological site elsewhere in Australia dates to c. 65,000 years ago (Clarkson et al. 2017) – Madjedbebe in the Northern Territory – it is expected that further archaeological work will extend the period of human occupation in Victoria, including Gariwerd where (unexcavated and undated) sites are plentiful.

At some unknown time, Aboriginal people began using the rock-shelters of the region to produce pigment rock art. Initially this consisted of red stencils, paintings and prints, with a small number of yellow paintings (see below). Later, they produced a period dominated by dry pigment drawings in red or black. Most recently, white pigment was preferred for painting and drawing, and with the inclusion of a small number of abradings and scratchings into their repertoire (Gunn et al. 2019). The age and degree of overlap or separation of these phases is unknown. Also unknown is the extent to which the most recent art coincided with the impact of the colonial invasion.

Caroline Bird, then of La Trobe University, undertook an excavation of the Mt Talbot 1 rock-shelter, during the course of which art was identified on the shelter's rear wall (Bird 1986, 1995). She and her students later undertook the first extensive archaeological survey within Grampians National Park, concentrating on exposed sediment surfaces along roads and tracks rather than on the rock-shelters that had been the focus of all previous research (Bird 1989). Although many of the sites they recorded were single artefacts, the work clearly established that Aboriginal occupation extended throughout Gariwerd. Site types located included rock art but also scarred trees, stone quarries, large and small lithic scatters, and isolated artefacts.

During the 1990s and 2000s, a small number of rock art sites were recorded by rock climbers and bushwalkers, but the majority of archaeological information was derived from cultural heritage management plans relating to developments within the Grampians National Park or on adjoining Crown lands (e.g. Cekalovic 2000; Edmonds 1992; Gunn 1999; Gunn and Goodes 2020).

The colonial invasion

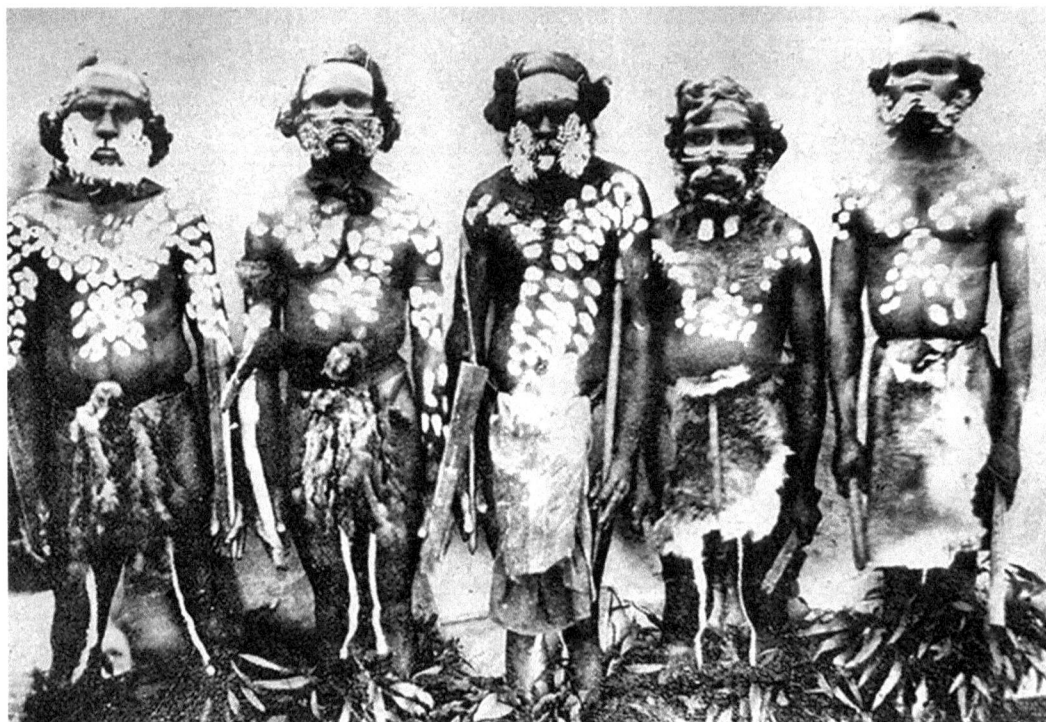

Figure 7.3: Mt Clay tribesmen painted up for Corroboree 1859.
Source: Photograph by Thomas Hannay.

The initial contact of Gariwerd Aboriginal people with Europeans began with the peaceful traversing of the area by Thomas Mitchell's expedition in 1836 (Mitchell 1839). From 1838, however, the subsequent invasion of the region by European settlers began, and with it the decimation and subjugation of local Aboriginal people (Clark 1990a, 1990b, 1995). No photographs of the Gariwerd people have survived from this time, but one of a group of Gunditjmara men from Mt Clay, to the south, shows them painted up for corroboree (Figure 7.3), with body patterns similar to those depicted on the image of Bunjil at Bunjil's shelter (see below). Although most of the physical fighting was over by 1848, the battle by Aboriginal people to gain recognition as Australian citizens had to wait for the 1967 Commonwealth Referendum; some sense of justice for the displacement came 26 years later with the *Native Title Act 1993* (Cth). No treaty with Aboriginal communities has yet been realised, but the formal participation of the Traditional Owner groups in the ongoing management of Gariwerd is forthcoming (Parks Victoria 2020).

Rock art recording

While numerous references were made to Aboriginal rock art around Sydney soon after the arrival of the British First Fleet in 1788 (e.g. Stockdale 1789), the first acknowledgement of Aboriginal rock art in Victoria was of that at the Billiminah shelter (now Billimina) by John Mathew in 1896, following its finding in 1865–1866 by local landholders Muirhead and Carter from nearby Glenisla Station (Figure 7.4). The existence of rock art in the Victoria Valley, in the centre of Gariwerd, had been earlier mentioned to the anthropologist E.M. Curr as a cavern 'the roof of which is covered in old Aboriginal paintings' (Curr 1886:96). This cavern site was most probably one of the three larger art shelters on the Victoria Range (Billimina, Manya or Jananginj Njaui).

Figure 7.4: Billimina rock-shelter (post-2013 fire).
Source: Photograph by Robert G. Gunn.

Mathew's illustration as published (Mathew 1896)

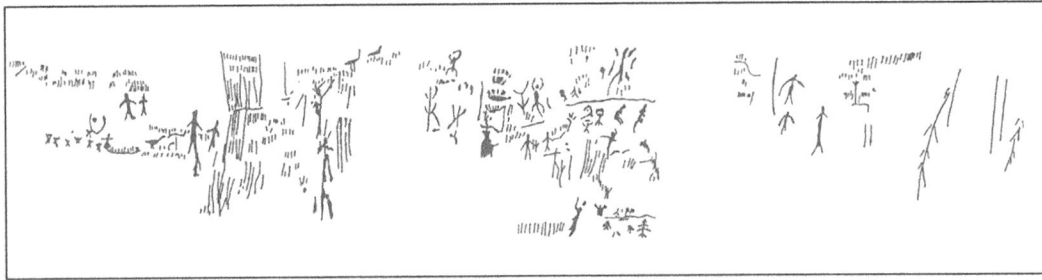

Mathew's original recording (from Massola 1973)

Figure 7.5: Mathew's drawing of the art at Billimina as published (above) and as originally drawn by him (below).

Source: Mathew 1896; Massola 1973a.

The large and well-decorated site of Billimina was first recorded by A. Ingham in 1894, but his sketchy record was not published until 1912 (Kenyon 1912:107–108). Mathew's brief publication of Billimina, while documenting the art, also offered an 'archaeological' and ethnological appraisal of the site. His observations included the size of the shelter floor, its absence of rubble, a possible banking on the south-western side, and its present use by sheep and cattle. He noted the size of the art panel (11.1 m long, with art extending from 0.9 m to 2.5 m above ground) and that the art consisted 'chiefly of numerous short upright strokes, a few slightly undulating lines drawn perpendicularly or horizontally, branches, foliage, and figures of animals' (Mathew 1896:30). Mathew also questioned unnamed Aboriginal Elders about the art, learning that the Elders had seen the paintings when they were young but were unable (or unwilling) to suggest who had painted them or when. One Elder suggested to him that the strokes might have been a 'record of time during which encampments had been continued at the place' (Mathew 1896:31). Mathew then gave his own subjective interpretation of 20 sets of motifs, and noted that some of the strokes were later additions as they overlay larger figures. His scale drawing of the site, excluding most of the strokes, was produced with difficulty due to the quantity of graffiti that covered the wall at that time. In a later publication (Kenyon 1912:108), Carter is quoted as saying that the practice of graffiti was begun by shearers from his station around 1875. Mathew's illustration was substantially rearranged for publication, greatly distorting the scale and visual impression of the panel (Figure 7.5), and causing a number of later general publications to misinterpret the nature of the art (e.g. Davidson 1936; see also Tugby and Tugby 1980).

While at the site, Mathew experimented with making pigment, and was told by Carter that the Aboriginal station hands gathered weathered red ochre from the neighbourhood and mixed it with possum fat for use as raddle for marking rams before they were joined with ewes, however, no source of good quality red ochre has yet been located within the Gariwerd region. Mathew also briefly made mention of a small number of images in a second site close by Billimina (now called 'GI-02'). As a final note, he compared the images at Billimina with those from the Kimberley and New South Wales, finding the Gariwerd art differed through the use of one colour (red) and infilled body cavities (Mathew 1896:33). By looking at a wide range of contexts for the art, rather than just the images, Mathew raised a higher bar for other recorders to follow.

An early allusion to another Gariwerd rock art site was a passing reference collected by geologist-turned-anthropologist A.W. Howitt (1904:291):

> One of the Mukjarawaint said that at one time there was a figure of Bunjil and his dog painted in a small cave behind a large boulder in the Black Range near Stawell, but I have not seen it, nor have I heard of anyone having seen it.

The Mukjarawaint (Jardwadjali) informant was John Connelly (Clark 2002). The location referenced caused a search for the illusive paintings, but most attention was given to looking in the Black Range (Burrunj) to the west of the Grampians, and not to the area also called Black Range on the eastern side of Gariwerd (Ian McCann, local naturalist, pers. comm., 1983). The discovery of Bunjil's shelter in the eastern Black Range had to wait until the 1950s (see below).

Mathew's high standard of recording for his time was not, however, followed by subsequent recorders until the 1970s. In 1929, two further rock art sites were recorded in the Grampians: Cave of Red Hands (now Manya) and Cave of Ghosts (now Ngamadjidj). Manya was recorded by C. Barrett (a newspaper reporter) when accompanying anthropologist A.S. Kenyon and artist P. Leason to undertake a tracing of the art at Billimina (Barrett 1929a). At the nearby town of Cavendish they heard of another art site that was well known to local residents: the 'Cave of Red Hands'. After a quick visit to the site, Barrett published a short article on the 'cave' in a Melbourne newspaper, along with a photograph of a set of hand stencils (Barrett 1929b). Kenyon also produced a similar summary report in his book *Australian Aboriginal art* (Kenyon 1929a). Later that same year, 1929, Kenyon reported on the Ngamadjidj shelter in a newspaper article, but provided only a cursory description of the art 'in this wild and rugged place' (Kenyon 1929b). Barrett, Kenyon and S.R. Mitchel, all members of the ethnological section of the Royal Society of Victoria, were also responsible for the construction of protective wire-mesh *grilles* (cages) at these three art sites in the mid-1930s (Clark 2002:456), the first such measures in Victoria (since replaced by more substantial structures).

In 1943, Barrett reported yet another art site, 'Brimgower Cave/Cave of Fishes' (now 'Larngibunja'). In contrast to his earlier reporting, this record included a more journalistic text and three photographs, although again little archaeological information was included (Barrett 1943).

The art at Billimina (Glenisla) was recorded with colour photographs and watercolour sketches in 1950 by historian Leonard Adams from Melbourne University (with the help of a young John Mulvaney), but apart from a description of the field trip, the results of the recording were never published or otherwise distributed (Adams 1952). In 1953, Donald Tugby, curator of anthropology at the National Museum of Victoria, rerecorded the art at Billimina and undertook an excavation of its deposits. He also excavated the deposits at the nearby Manya Shelter. Only a small section of Tugby's art recording was published (Tugby and Tugby 1980), and material from his Billimina excavation was not analysed until 1988 (Bird and Frankel 2005:41–42).

Substantial recording of Gariwerd rock art did not begin until the mid-1950s when members of the Field Naturalist Clubs of Stawell and Horsham reported finds to Aldo Massola, the curator of anthropology, 1954–1965, at the National Museum of Victoria (now Museums Victoria). Between 1956 and 1973, Massola published 16 papers in the *Victorian Naturalist* magazine that described 25 previously unreported rock art sites (Massola 1956a, 1956b, 1957, 1958, 1960a, 1960b, 1962, 1963, 1964a, 1964b, 1967, 1971a, 1971b, 1972, 1973a, 1973b) and a recording of the previously mentioned but not described Ngamadjidj site (Massola 1962). These reports were mostly brief accounts (1–2 pages) with a black-and-white photograph and, in some cases, a rough freehand rendition of selected motifs. These recordings are simple magazine reports rather than academic records (as is also Agar 1966). Massola also espoused a subjective interpretation for the art (e.g. Massola 1973b) but this was based purely on his assumption of one motif type as representing a lizard character, an interpretation that is no longer endorsed by the Aboriginal community or archaeologists. Despite the low standard of recording, Massola's papers did alert the public, the museum and the Forests Commission of Victoria, who then managed the Grampians State Forest, to the presence of rock art in the region. Massola is also recognised for the years he worked with Aboriginal people throughout Victoria, collecting 'myths' and documenting their significant places (e.g. Massola 1968, 1970, 1973c).

In early 1968, Alan West, later curator of anthropology at the Museum of Victoria, and archaeologist Dermot Casey (honorary ethnologist) undertook a test excavation of the Billimina floor deposits but failed to recognise any signs of occupation (Coutts and Lorblanchet 1982:5; see also Bird and Frankel 2005:42).

The 1960s and 1970s saw favourable changes in Australian public and political attitudes towards Aboriginal people, with amendments to the *Commonwealth Electoral Act 1962* granting Aboriginal people's rights to enrol to vote; however, recognition as Australian citizens had to wait for the 1967 Commonwealth Referendum. With these changes, Victoria, and other states, legislated to protect Aboriginal archaeology (then usually referred to as 'prehistory'). The *Archaeological and Aboriginal Relics Preservation Act 1972* (Vic) instituted the setting up of the Archaeological and Aboriginal Relics Office, which in 1975 became the Victoria Archaeological Survey (VAS), and began a program of public education (Coutts 1982a, 1982b). The latter instigated an archaeological site register, a series of detailed regional surveys, excavations and ethnohistoric studies (e.g. Coutts 1981; Coutts et al. 1976, 1978; Presland 1978). These recordings included the standardised documentation of the state's rock art (Gunn 1981, 1987d).

As part of their program, in 1974 VAS engaged the services of an experienced French rock art specialist, Michel Lorblanchet, to undertake the first comprehensive recording of Gariwerd's rock art (Coutts and Lorblanchet 1982); he also produced one of Australia's first rock art conservation reports (Lorblanchet 1975). Lorblanchet's tracings of the Billimina art panel (Figure 7.6) brought a new standard of recording to Australia, and 25 years after its publication it was still considered by Clark et al. (1999:29) to be 'one of the most definitive recordings in Australian rock art'. This evaluation still stands in 2021, even though Lorblanchet's published record was limited to black-and-white photographs and illustrations, and despite a number of very detailed recordings from elsewhere around Australia since.

Following Lorblanchet's recommendation, VAS replaced nine site *grilles* and began a range of conservation studies that included some of Australia's earliest studies of pigment analysis and shelter erosion. These Gariwerd studies paralleled similar movements elsewhere in Australia, where concerns for the preservation and presentation of rock art were taking priority over surveys (e.g. Gale and Jacobs 1987; Pearson 1978; Rosenfeld 1988). In Victoria, as well as *grille* replacements, these studies resulted in improved signage, boardwalks, silicone driplines, graffiti removal, terrestrial photogrammetry and the monitoring of rock deterioration (e.g. AUSLIG 1990; Gunn 1984; Kosinova Thorn 1988; McConnell 1981). While done with the tacit approval of the Aboriginal community, there was still little engagement of community members in either the decision-making process, training or in the undertaking of the tasks.

Figure 7.6: Section of Lorblanchet's 1975 detailed recording of the Billimina art panel.

Source: Courtesy of Michel Lorblanchet.

The recording of rock art continued during the early 1980s, supported by VAS but continuing to be undertaken from a purely archaeological perspective, involving little engagement with or input from Aboriginal community groups with ties to Gariwerd or other local Aboriginal people until the 1990s. These surveys for rock art sites developed a standard recording format with considerably more information than was required on the VAS site forms of the time. At this time, VAS also commissioned the detailed recording of a further 17 Victorian rock art sites, including 12 within Gariwerd (Gunn 1983a, 1983b, 1987b, 1987c) and detailed management plans for eight of the more visited rock art sites in Gariwerd (e.g. Clark 1991a, 1991b).

The period from the 1970s to the 1990s saw Aboriginal voices regarding directions of academic research into their own cultures begin to be increasingly heard throughout Australia (Wallace and Wallace 1977; Langford 1983; Ah Kit 1995).

Over the past 20 years there has been a significant increase in the quality of graphic documentation, description and interpretation for both research and management purposes in Victoria and throughout Australia: a quality that now surpasses the high standard set by Lorblanchet in 1974 (Coutts and Lorblanchet 1982). This is largely due to three significant developments:

- the acknowledgement of Aboriginal people as the rightful custodians of their own cultural heritage and the need to work with full permission, input and involvement of Traditional Owners

- the development of four new archaeological techniques: (1) digital photography that enabled rapid and extensive photography and immediate on-site viewing; (2) to be paired with digital enhancement, especially DStretch colour enhancement (Harman 2008, 2015; Gunn et al. 2010); (3) the Harris Matrix composer for rock art superimposition analysis (Harris and Gunn 2018); and (4) awareness of the Morellian method of recognising contemporaneous motifs (Gunn and Lowish 2017)

- the recognition by management of the need for a detailed record of the sites under their care and also of the need to give Aboriginal cultural sites a high priority for protection and management in a rapidly expanding visitor arena.

In 1992, VAS became Aboriginal Affairs Victoria (AAV), after which it became less directly involved in archaeological research, instead becoming primarily involved in supervision of the standards of pre-development archaeological surveys (now called 'cultural heritage management plans' or 'CHMPs') undertaken by private consultant archaeologists and Traditional Owner groups. In 2016, VAS/AAV changed its name again to become Aboriginal Victoria. The revised site recording system for the Victorian Aboriginal Heritage Register (VAHR), the state's formal site register, began to require a greater level of data collection for all cultural heritage sites, including rock art sites. The VAHR recording requirements continue to be periodically revised; however, they now require sub-metre GPS readings and mapping aids that necessitate specialist input. Detailed rock art recordings are now primarily the work of consultants acting for site managers.

Traditional Owner involvements

In 1984, the greater part of Gariwerd was transferred from the Forest Commission of Victoria (Grampians State Forest) to the Victorian National Parks Service as the Grampians National Park. One of the determining values for National Park status was recognition of the area's Aboriginal cultural values (Day et al. 1984), particularly its rock art. The change in administration also saw the need to involve local Aboriginal people in the park's management, and to this end the state government began a process that eventuated in the opening to the public of the Brambuk Cultural Centre in 1990. Brambuk, built by the state government for the park, was owned and operated by a joint body of representatives of each of the five Aboriginal communities who had associations to Country in the National Park. At the same time, there was a concerted effort to restore Aboriginal place names throughout the National Park and surrounding region (e.g. Gunn 1989; Clark and Harradine 1990), a movement supported by the publication of Ian Clark's authoritative reassessment of the distribution of the western Victorian Aboriginal languages and clans during the contact period (Clark 1990a).

While Aboriginal rock art and involvement had been tangentially mentioned in several books on the Grampians National Park (e.g. Calder 1987), in 1999 Aboriginal Affairs Victoria published the first book dedicated to Gariwerd Aboriginal heritage (Wettenhall 1999). At the same time, Brambuk began to sell a range of books on Aboriginal culture in south-east Australia, alongside mainstream books on the natural values of the National Park. Today, there are three groups that represent the Aboriginal Traditional Owner groups of the Gariwerd area: Barengi Gadjin Land Council Aboriginal Corporation, Eastern Maar Aboriginal Corporation and Gunditj Mirring Traditional Owners Aboriginal Corporation. Through these representative bodies, local Aboriginal people have an active engagement in management decisions and employment in works programs. The park, however, still remains to be formally committed as a jointly managed park.

Despite Parks Victoria running several trainee programs for Aboriginal people, most trainees did not remain in the Grampians National Park but moved on to higher positions in Parks Victoria or elsewhere. It was not until 2003 that Parks Victoria created a dedicated Aboriginal ranger position within the Grampians National Park, and in 2016 a rock art specialist position was created to oversee the management of all rock art sites within Crown Reserves across the state.

Discussion

The recording of Gariwerd rock art has been marked by a number of phases with different outcomes. Largely as a result of the different aims of the recorders, the recordings have not necessarily improved over time. Similarly, the reasons or driving force behind the recordings also varied (Figure 7.7), with casual recording by interested amateurs or professionals being paramount. These divisions are not exclusive, but indicate the prime driver in each period.

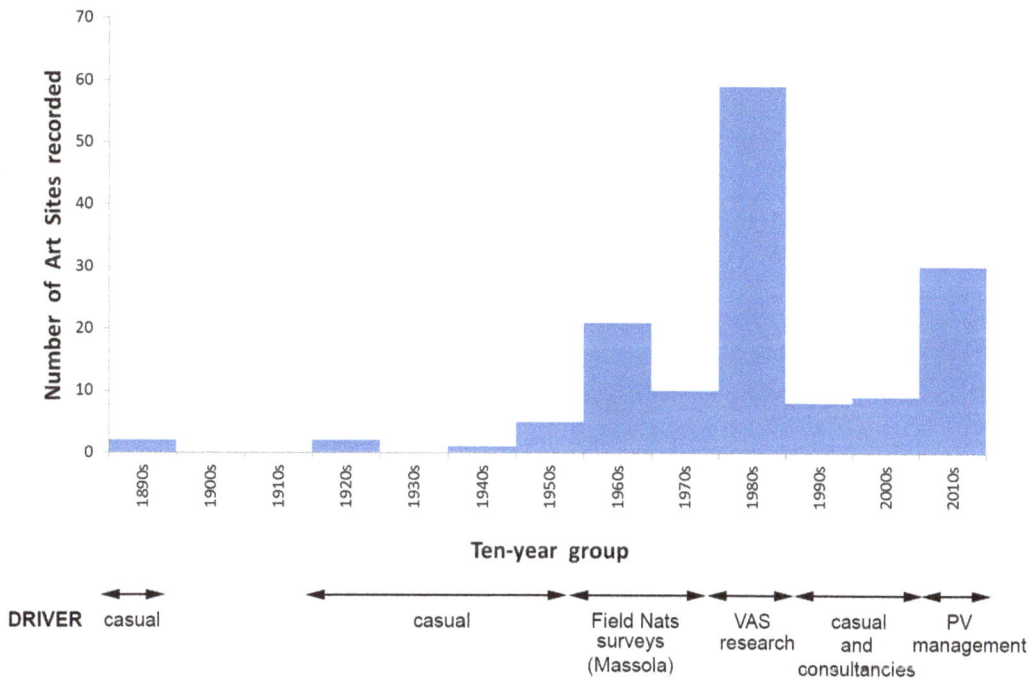

Figure 7.7: Drivers behind Victorian rock art recording.
Source: Photograph by Robert G. Gunn.

The peak period of recording was from 1979 to 1985 when VAS employed a consultant to rerecord known sites and to undertake surveys of adjacent areas, resulting in the recording of a further 58 rock art sites. The state of the art was then summarised and a preliminary analysis undertaken in an unpublished report (Gunn 1987a).

A second peak period of archaeological activity has been ongoing since 2014, resulting from post-fire assessments of the condition of the known rock art sites following three major bushfires that decimated 90 per cent of the Grampians National Park. In 2006, bushfires ravaged the central and southern areas of the park; in 2013, the Victoria Range in the west of the National Park; and in 2014, the northern ranges. During the site assessments, Parks Victoria staff and Aboriginal community members located a large number of unrecorded sites in the burnt-out landscapes. The greater visibility and access to previously unassessed rock outcrops, also occasioned a small number of other unrecorded sites to be reported by bushwalkers, rock climbers and Parks Victoria staff involved in other activities.

The initial peak period of recording activity in the 1960s derived from the work of the local Field Naturalist Clubs from 1956 to 1973. Some of these sites were found during field trips exploring the 'natural' world of the park, but other rock art sites were identified during dedicated trips searching for rock art as new areas of the then Grampians State Forest were made more accessible with the construction of new logging tracks (Ian McCann and Eric Barber, local long-time residents, pers. comm. 1981). Following the findings of these keen amateurs, the National Museum of Victoria was contacted and Massola then recorded and published the sites.

What we have learned

The geographical pattern of site locations throughout Greater Gariwerd was essentially set by the work of the Field Naturalist members in the 1960s (Figure 7.8). This pattern was expanded during the 1980s–1990s, and then again in the most recent concerted efforts. With each pulse of activity, new areas have been surveyed and previous areas consolidated with additional surveys. From personal observation and from reviewing of aerial photographs, however, several large areas of the National Park and surrounding ranges still remain to be systematically surveyed. From the amount of exposed rock outcrops in these unexplored areas, we anticipate that the density of sites away from the Victoria Range will likely increase with further surveys.

Our knowledge of the art has also continually expanded over time. In the 1950s, with 10 known sites, the art was seen to consist of red paintings and hand stencils, and a single site containing white painting. Today, with 155 known sites, we have a repertoire comprised of paintings, drawings, stencil and prints in red; paintings and drawings in white; paintings in yellow and drawings in black as well as a small number of scratchings, poundings and abradings (Gunn and Goodes 2018; Gunn et al. 2019). In contrast, the range of motifs has changed little from the earliest recordings, confirming that there is a standard repertoire of rock art types throughout Greater Gariwerd over time, with only minor local variations. The red paintings are dominated by elongated, static or standardised anthropomorphic stick figures, rows of short bars, long lines, ovals and bird tracks; red drawings are dominated by animated anthropomorphic stick figures and bar rows; black drawings are dominated by animated stick figures, emu-like birds and bar rows; and white paintings by bird tracks, bar clusters and animated stick figures. Petroglyphs (scratched, abraded and pounded) have been reported from only two sites to date (Gunn 1981, 1987d; and pers. observations).

Red is the most frequent and widespread colour. Some motif types occur in relatively high numbers at one particular site while occurring only in small numbers elsewhere: hand stencils at Manya in the Victoria Range; hand prints at Gulgurn Manya at the northern tip of Gariwerd; red bars at Billimina; red elongated anthropomorphic stick figures at Gunangidura in the centre of the Victoria Range; white anthropomorphic stick figures at Ngamadjidj in northern Gariwerd, while drawings in red or black are widespread throughout.

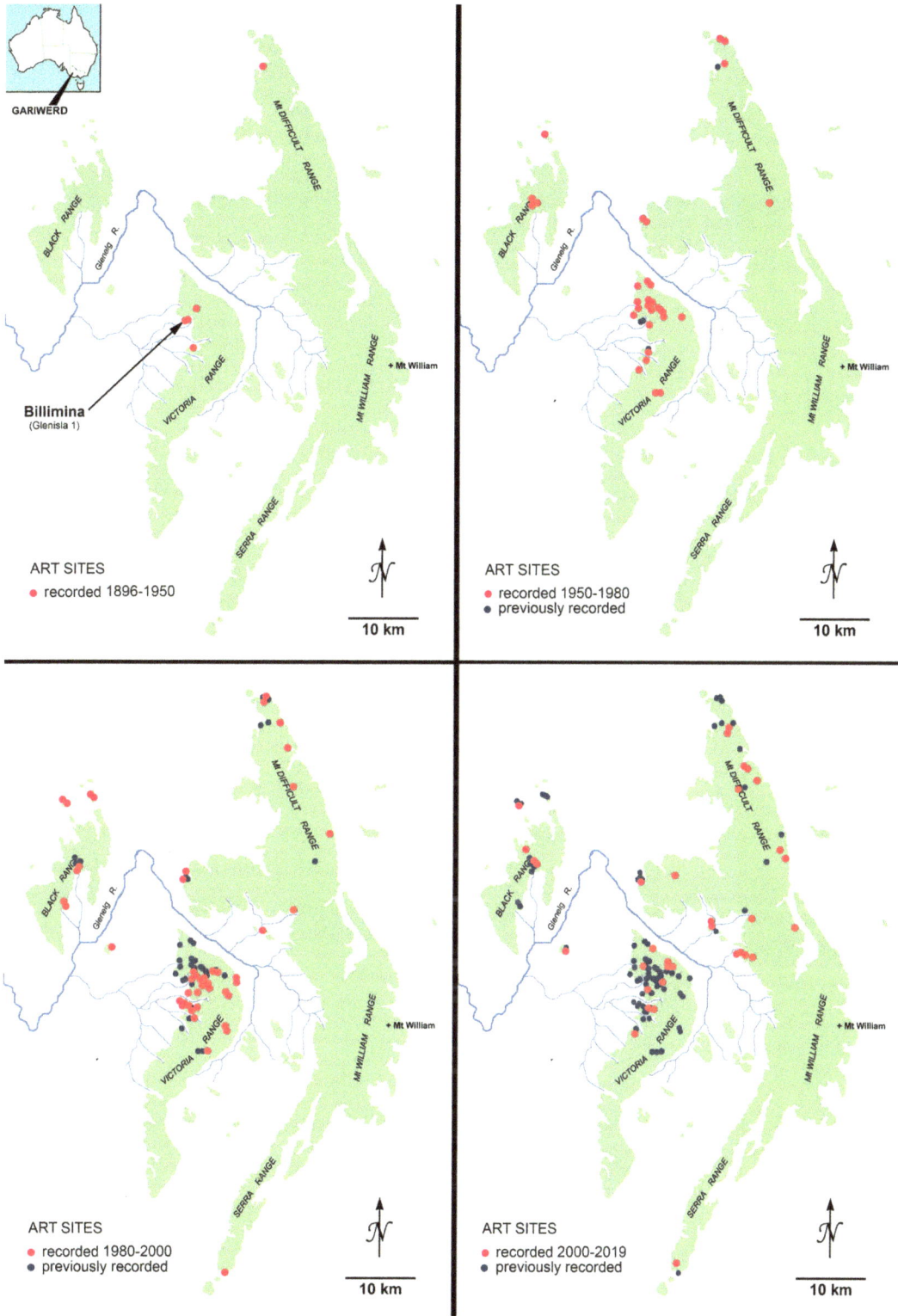

Figure 7.8: Patterns of site recording 1896–2019.

Source: Photograph by Robert G. Gunn.

One of the most recent findings was not made in the field but in the studies of Ian Clark from Federation University, Ballarat. Following his lifelong interest in the region, he came across an early record of a cosmogonic story that connects Gariwerd to Bunjil's shelter in the granite rocks of the Black Range (Clark 2017). This story describes the descent of Bunjil and his family (including his mother-in-law) down the eastern cliffs of Gariwerd, Bunjil's fight with the Bunyip at Mokepilly waterhole, midway between Gariwerd and the Black Range, where Bunjil's shelter is located, and the subsequent painting of the event in Bunjil's shelter (see also Howitt 1904). The representation of Bunjil in the Black Range, in a very different style to other rock art images known from Gariwerd, along with its linking originary story, now requires that the Greater Gariwerd rock art region be expanded from the sandstone ranges to include this exceptionally important but otherwise isolated art site (Figure 7.1).

Conclusion

The story of Gariwerd and its rock art has a long history, but it also has a living presence and encouraging future. This paper has only considered the rock art and what we have learned about it. It highlights the lack of Aboriginal involvement prior to the 1990s, but also looks forward to a period of greater participation and leadership in documenting and assessing the irreplaceable realities of the rock art of Greater Gariwerd. There is much more to be done and so the story must continue.

Acknowledgements

We thank the three Traditional Owner groups (Barengi Gadjin Land Council Aboriginal Corporation, Eastern Maar Aboriginal Corporation and Gunditj Mirring Traditional Owners Aboriginal Corporation) who have supported this and other rock art projects within Greater Gariwerd. The work has also been assisted by Parks Victoria, Halls Gap. We are grateful to Leigh Douglas and two anonymous referees who made helpful suggestions with content and grammar.

References

Adam, L. 1952. The rock paintings near Glen Isla, Victoria Range, Victoria. *Mankind* 4:343–344. doi. org/10.1111/j.1835-9310.1952.tb00260.x.

Agar, J.M. 1966. A new painted rock shelter in the Victoria Range. *Victorian Naturalist* 83:199–201.

Ah Kit, J. 1995. Aboriginal rock art imagery and ownership of 'research'. In G.K. Ward and L.A. Ward (eds), *Management of rock imagery*, pp. 36–38. Occasional AURA Publication No 9. Australian Rock Art Research Association, Melbourne.

AUSLIG 1990. Terrestrial photography, Aboriginal rock art, the Grampians, Victoria. Unpublished report of the Australian Surveying and Land Information Group, Department of Administrative Services, Canberra.

Barrett, C. 1929a. Cave hunting and what we found. *Australian Museum Magazine* 3(12):414–419.

Barrett, C. 1929b. Mysterious cave in the Grampians. *Herald,* 2 March 1929:1.

Barrett, C. 1943. New primitive art gallery. *Wildlife* 5:124–126.

Bird, C.F.M. 1986. Excavations at Mount Talbot 1 (VAS 7323/75). Unpublished report to the Victoria Archaeological Survey, Melbourne.

Bird, C.F.M. 1989. Archaeological field survey in the Grampians National Park, 1988. Unpublished report. Department of Archaeology, La Trobe University, Bundoora.

Bird, C.F.M. 1995. Mount Talbot 1: A rock-shelter in the southern Wimmera, Victoria. *The Artefact* 18:12–21.

Bird, C.F.M. and D. Frankel 2005. *An archaeology of Gariwerd: From Pleistocene to Holocene in Western Victoria.* Tempus 8. University of Queensland, St Lucia.

BOM (Bureau of Meteorology) 2019. *Climate statistics for Australian locations.* Available at: www.bom. gov.au/climate/data/index.shtml (accessed 23 April 2019).

Calder, J. 1987. *The Grampians: A noble range.* Victorian National Parks Association, Melbourne.

Cayley, R.A. and D.H. Taylor 1997. *Grampians special map area geological report.* Geological Survey Report 107. Natural Resources and Environment, Melbourne.

Cekalovic, H. 2000. Archaeological surveys of Boroka and Balconies/Reed Visitor nodes, Grampians. Unpublished report of Biosis Research to Parks Victoria.

Clark, I.D. 1990a. *Aboriginal languages and clans: An historical atlas of Western and Central Victoria 1800–1900.* Monash Publications in Geography Number 37. Monash University, Clayton.

Clark, I.D. 1990b. The difficulty of determining pre-contact Aboriginal spatial organisation: Case studies from south western Victoria. *Melbourne History Journal* 20:66–85.

Clark, I.D. 1991a. Billimina Shelter ('Glenisla Shelter') VAS Site 7323/1: A history of management and intervention. Unpublished report to the Victoria Archaeological Survey, Melbourne.

Clark, I.D. 1991b. Manya Shelter ('Cave of Hands') VAS Site 7323/4: A history of management and intervention. Unpublished report to the Victoria Archaeological Survey, Melbourne.

Clark, I. 1995. *Scars in the landscape.* Australian Institute of Aboriginal and Torres Strait Islander Studies, Canberra.

Clark, I.D. 2002. Rock art sites in Victoria, Australia: A management history framework. *Tourism Management* 23:455–464. doi.org/10.1016/s0261-5177(02)00011-0.

Clark, I.D. 2017. Bunyip, Bunjil and mother-in-law avoidance: New insights into the interpretation of Bunjils shelter, Victoria, Australia. *Rock Art Research* 34(2):189–192.

Clark, I.D. and L.L. Harradine 1990. *The restoration of Jardwajali and Djab wurrong names for rock art sites and landscape features in and around the Grampians National Park.* Submission to the Victorian Place Names Committee by the Koorie Tourism Unit of the Victorian Tourism Commission, Melbourne.

Clark, I., A. Long and R.G. Gunn 1999. History of scientific research and documentation. In A. Long (ed.), Billimina shelter (AAV 7323-1) management plan, pp. 21–36. Unpublished report to the South West Rock Art Committee.

Clarkson, C., Z. Jacobs, B. Marwick, R. Fullagar, L. Wallis, M. Smith, R.G. Roberts, E. Hayes, K. Lowe, X. Carah, S.A. Florin, J. McNeil, D. Cox, L.J. Arnold, Q. Hua, J. Huntley, H.E.A. Brand, T. Manne, A. Fairbairn, J. Shulmeister, L. Lyle, M. Salinas, M. Page, K. Connell, G. Park, K. Norman, T. Murphy and C. Pardoe 2017. Human occupation of northern Australia by 65,000 years ago. *Nature* 547:306–310. doi.org/10.1038/nature22968.

Coutts, P.J.F. 1981. *Readings in Victorian prehistory,* Vol. 2. Ministry for Conservation, Melbourne.

Coutts, P.J.F. 1982a. Victoria Archaeological Survey activities report 1979–80. *Records of the Victoria Archaeological Survey* 13:1–28.

Coutts, P.J.F. 1982b. Management of Aboriginal cultural heritage in Victoria. *Records of the Victoria Archaeological Survey* 13:85–114.

Coutts, P.J.F. and M. Lorblanchet 1982. *Aborigines and rock art in the Grampians.* Records of the Victoria Archaeological Survey No 12. Ministry for Conservation, Melbourne.

Coutts, P.J.F., R.K. Frank and P. Hughes 1978. *Aboriginal engineers of the Western District, Victoria.* Records of the Victorian Archaeological Survey 7. Ministry for Conservation, Melbourne.

Coutts, P.J.F., D. Witter, M. McIlwraith and R. Frank 1976. *The mound people of Western Victoria.* Records of the Victoria Archaeological Survey No 1. Ministry for Conservation, Melbourne.

Curr, E.M. 1886. *The Australian race: Its origins, languages, customs, places of landing in Australia, and the routes by which it spread itself over that continent.* Volume 1. Victorian Government Printer, Melbourne.

Davidson, D.S. 1936. *Aboriginal Australian and Tasmanian rock carvings and paintings.* Memoirs of the American Philosophical Society No 5. American Philosophical Society, Philadelphia.

Day, J.C., G.A. McGregor and P.D. Johnstone 1984. *Grampians National Park: Inventory of resources and uses.* National Parks Service, Melbourne.

Edmonds, V. 1992. Mt Arapiles – Tooen State Park archaeological survey. Unpublished report to the Goolum-Goolum Aboriginal Cooperative, Horsham.

Gale, F. and J.M. Jacobs 1987. *Tourism and the national estate.* Australian Government Publishing Service, Canberra.

Gunn, R.G. 1981. *The prehistoric rock art sites of Victoria: A catalogue.* Occasional Report Series No 5. Victoria Archaeological Survey, Melbourne.

Gunn, R.G. 1983a. *Aboriginal rock art in the Grampians.* Records of the Victorian Archaeological Survey No 16. Ministry for Conservation, Melbourne.

Gunn, R.G. 1983b. *The Cave of Ghosts Aboriginal rock art site.* Occasional Report Series No 12. Victorian Archaeological Survey, Melbourne.

Gunn, R.G. 1984. Fire and the preservation of rock art: Assessment of the effects of a fuel reduction burn on archaeological sites in the Victoria Range, Grampians. Unpublished report to the Victoria Archaeological Survey, Melbourne.

Gunn, R.G. 1987a. Aboriginal rock art in Victoria. Unpublished report to the Victoria Archaeological Survey, Melbourne.

Gunn, R.G. 1987b. Flat Rock 1 Aboriginal rock art site. Unpublished report to the Victoria Archaeological Survey, Melbourne.

Gunn, R.G. 1987c. BR2 and the art of the Black Range, Western Grampians. Unpublished report to the Victoria Archaeological Survey, Melbourne.

Gunn, R.G. 1987d. Second catalogue of Victorian rock art sites. Unpublished report to the Victoria Archaeological Survey, Melbourne.

Gunn, R.G. 1989. Alternative names for rock art sites and natural features in the Grampians National Park. Unpublished report to Victorian Tourist Commission, Melbourne.

Gunn, R.G. 1999. Grampians National Park development sites: Archaeological survey. Unpublished report to Parks Victoria, Halls Gap.

Gunn, R.G. and J. Goodes 2018. Wartook Lookout 1 (WO-1) and the Gariwerd rock art sequence, Victoria. In C. Spry, E. Foley, D. Frankel, S. Lawrence, I. Berelov and S. Canning (eds), *Excavations, surveys and heritage management in Victoria* 7, pp. 7–11. La Trobe University, Melbourne.

Gunn, R.G. and J. Goodes 2020. Grampians National Park SPAs: Aboriginal rock art site impact assessments. Unpublished report to Parks Victoria, Melbourne.

Gunn, R.G. and S. Lowish 2017. The Morellian method and its potential in rock art research. *Rock Art Research* 34(2):193–205.

Gunn, R.G., C.L. Ogleby, D. Lee and R.L. Whear 2010. A method to visually rationalise superimposed pigment motifs. *Rock Art Research* 27(2):131–136.

Gunn, R.G. J. Goodes and L.C. Douglas 2019. Gariwerd petroglyphs and their situation within the Gariwerd rock art sequence. *The Artefact* 42:17–27.

Harman, J. 2008. Using decorrelation stretch to enhance rock art images. *DStretch.* Available at: www. dstretch.com/AlgorithmDescription.html (accessed 12 April 2009). Paper originally presented at American Rock Art Research Association Annual Meeting, 2005.

Harman, J. 2015. Using DStretch for rock art recording. *INORA* 72:24–30.

Harris, E.C. and R.G. Gunn 2018. The use of Harris Matrices in rock art research. In B. David and I. McNiven (eds), *The Oxford handbook of the archaeology and anthropology of rock art*, pp. 911–926. Oxford University Press, Oxford. doi.org/10.1093/oxfordhb/9780190607357.013.18.

Howitt, A.W. 1904. *The native tribes of South Eastern Australia*. MacMillan, London.

Kenyon, A.S. 1912. Camping places of the Aborigines of south-east Australia. *Victorian Historical Magazine* 2:97–110.

Kenyon, A.S. 1929a. *Australian Aboriginal art*. National Museum of Victoria, Melbourne.

Kenyon, A.S. 1929b. Correspondence. *Ararat Advertiser,* 11 April 1929:1.

Kosinova Thorn 1988. Bunjils Cave: A report on the removal of recent overpaint. Unpublished report to the Victoria Archaeological Survey, Melbourne.

Langford, R. 1983. Our heritage – your playground. *Australian Archaeology* 16:1–6. doi.org/10.1080/03 122417.1983.12092875.

Lorblanchet, M. 1975. Erosion in the Grampians Mountains. Unpublished report to the Australian Institute of Aboriginal Studies, Canberra.

Massola, A. 1956a. Aboriginal paintings at the Flat Rock shelter. *Victorian Naturalist* 73:21–23.

Massola, A. 1956b. More paintings at Flat Rock. *Victorian Naturalist* 73:65–67.

Massola, A. 1957. Bunjil's cave found. *Victorian Naturalist* 74:19–22.

Massola, A. 1958. New Aboriginal rock paintings in the Victoria Range. *Victorian Naturalist* 75:73–78.

Massola, A. 1960a. Two new painted shelters at Glenisla. *Victorian Naturalist* 76:234–235.

Massola, A. 1960b. The shelter at the Camp of the Emu's Foot. *Victorian Naturalist* 77:188–191.

Massola, A. 1962. The Cave of Ghosts. *Victorian Naturalist* 78:335–337.

Massola, A. 1963. Black Range shelters. *Victorian Naturalist* 79:169–176.

Massola, A. 1964a. Records of new shelters in the Black Range. *Victorian Naturalist* 81:15–17.

Massola, A. 1964b. Victoria Range shelters. *Victorian Naturalist* 81:169–176.

Massola, A. 1967. Honeysuckle Creek rock shelters. *Victorian Naturalist* 84:264–266.

Massola, A. 1968. *Bunjil's cave: Myth, legends and superstitions of the Aborigines of south-eastern Australia.* Lansdowne Press, Melbourne.

Massola, A. 1970. *Aboriginal mission stations in Victoria.* Hawthorn Press, Melbourne.

Massola, A. 1971a. Boggy Creek painted shelter: A new locality recorded. *Victorian Naturalist* 88:152–154.

Massola, A. 1971b. Aboriginal paintings at Muline Creek. *Victorian Naturalist* 89:139–141.

Massola, A. 1972. Honeysuckle Creek No. 4 Aboriginal shelter. *Victorian Naturalist* 89:196–197.

Massola, A. 1973a. Report on new discoveries and notes on an older Aboriginal painted shelter in the Victoria Range, Grampians. *Victorian Naturalist* 90:280–285.

Massola, A. 1973b. The 'Matterhorn' Aboriginal shelter and its possible mythological significance. *Victorian Naturalist* 90(11):326–327.

Massola, A. 1973c. An Avoca River–-Wirrengren Plain Aboriginal track route. *Victorian Naturalist* 90:126–131.

Mathew, J. 1896. Notes on an Aboriginal rock painting in the Victoria Range, County of Dundas. *Proceedings of the Royal Society of Victoria* 9:29–33.

McConnell, A. 1981. Preliminary report: Grampian's art conservation project 1977–1981. Unpublished report of the Victoria Archaeological Survey, Melbourne.

Mitchell, T.L. 1839. *Three expeditions into the interior of eastern Australia.* Boone, London.

Parks Victoria 2020. *Greater Gariwerd landscape draft management plan.* Parks Victoria, Melbourne.

Pearson, C. (ed.) 1978. *Conservation of rock art.* ICCM, Sydney.

Presland, G. (ed.) 1978. *Journals of George Augustus Robinson: March–May 1847.* Records of the Victorian Archaeological Survey No 5. Ministry for Conservation, Melbourne.

Richards, T., C. Pavlides, K. Walshe, H. Webber and R. Johnston 2007. Box Gully: New evidence for Aboriginal occupation of Australia south of the Murray prior to the Last Glacial Maximum. *Archaeology in Oceania* 42:1–11. doi.org/10.1002/j.1834-4453.2007.tb00001.x.

Rosenfeld, A. 1988. *Rock art conservation in Australia.* Australian Government Publishing Service, Canberra.

Stockdale, J. (ed.) 1789. *The voyage of Governor Phillip to Botany Bay.* John Stockdale, London.

Tugby, D.J. and E. Tugby 1980. The Reverend John Mathew and painted rock: Perception and cognition in the recording and reproduction of an Aboriginal rock painting in the Grampians, Victoria. *The Artefact* 5:123–143.

Wallace, P. and N. Wallace 1977. *Killing me softly: The destruction of a heritage.* Nelson, Melbourne.

Wettenhall, G. 1999. *The people of Gariwerd: The Grampians' Aboriginal heritage.* Aboriginal Affairs Victoria, Melbourne.

Wilkie, B. 2020. *Gariwerd: An environmental history of the Grampians.* CSIRO Publishing, Melbourne. doi.org/10.1071/9781486307692.

8

'Like broad arrows': A history of encounters with Central Australian rock art

June Ross and Mike A. Smith

Dedication

To those Aboriginal people in Central Australia who have, over 40 years, shared our interests in the lives of the 'old people' and to the Traditional Owners who generously granted permission to us to undertake research at rock art sites.

Introduction

Research on rock art in Central Australia[1] has moved from a basic record of its presence (1870–1890), where it was mostly approached as an ethnographic curiosity, to more nuanced understandings of the sociocultural contexts underpinning production of rock art that emerged from anthropological research between 1890 and 1940. It was not until 1965, with pioneering research by Bob Edwards, that rock art moved to centre stage of archaeological studies and became the focus of dedicated research. Specialised rock art research in Central Australia involving rock paintings, engravings and post-European contact graphics increased after 1990 with a range of studies that approached rock art as a historical record of cultural geography, looking at changing style, structure and composition of the art and its likely age. Despite this proliferation of studies, detailed regional surveys of rock art in Central Australia did not begin until 1988.

Early accounts

Before 1950, observers of rock art were mostly interested in Central Australia as part of an emerging picture of the ethnography of the region. Most accounts provided only a basic description of the art itself. Sometimes, these included speculation about its meaning, or the techniques used in producing the paintings and engravings. Sometimes just a record of its presence was documented. Early accounts rarely provided detailed descriptions of individual panels or of their composition, the superimposition of motifs, or any evidence for the likely age of art panels.

---

1   In this chapter, Central Australia encompasses a topographically varied area of the arid zone centred round Alice Springs. It includes the central ranges, sand ridge deserts, expansive sand plains and riverine corridors. The area is bounded in the north at latitude 22°S – thus it includes the southern reaches of Walpiri country. It extends south to latitude 27°S and incorporates Anangu-Pitjantjatjara-Yankuntjatjara Lands. It extends east as far as longitude 138°E and to the west to longitude 129°E.

Explorers: 1860–1891

The first British exploration parties to enter Central Australia (Giles 1889; Gosse 1973; Stuart 1865; Sturt 1865; Tietkens 1891; Warburton 1981) either saw no rock art or did not comment on it. John McDougall Stuart, however, did notice inscribed trees at several locations (Hardman 1865:250, 258), perhaps because, as a surveyor, he was predisposed to notice blazed trees. For instance, at Marchant Springs on the Finke River (22 February 1861), Stuart noted a tree marked with a barred-circle, and bird tracks, which he described using a surveyor's lexicon as 'like "broad arrows"' (Hardman 1865:250). This was, he said, 'the first attempt at representation by the natives of Australia which I had ever seen' (Hardman 1865:250). Later, on the Hugh River (15 March 1861), he noted another tree inscribed with 'broad arrows and a wavy line' (Hardman 1865:250).

Explorers did not always notice rock art near the wells and waterholes they depended on. For instance, Stuart did not comment on a large vertical panel of pecked cupules at Annas Reservoir, which he visited and named in April 1860. Nor does he appear to have seen engravings at a waterhole on the Hugh River that he visited on 15 March 1861. Here he noted another inscribed tree, but not the small panel of old rock engravings, a circle enclosing a pair of macropod tracks above the waterhole (this site was relocated in 2007 during archaeological surveys (Ross and Smith 2007)). Nevertheless, Stuart's account of marked trees provides the first glimpse of the distinctive graphic systems used in Central Australia.

The construction of the Overland Telegraph Line from 1871 to 1872 brought more activity to Central Australia. Ernest Giles used the telegraph line as a springboard for exploring country to its west. Giles was taken with the 'romance of exploration' and, not surprisingly, often commented on the rock art he saw. His journals provide the first accounts of rock paintings in Central Australia. He vividly describes paintings at Tarn of Auber (Tjungkupu), but apparently did not notice the rock engravings on surrounding rock pavements. Giles was an unusually reflective observer who commented on the likely techniques used to apply the paintings and the way natural features of the rock were incorporated into the rock art. His journal entry on 5 October 1872 notes that:

> One device represents a snake going into a hole; the body of the reptile is curled round and round the hole, though its breadth is out of proportion to its length, being seven or eight inches thick, and only two to three feet long. It is painted with charcoal ashes which had been mixed up with some animal's or reptile's fat. (Giles 1889:78–79)

South-west of the Tarn of Auber, at a campsite that Giles called Glen Thirsty (Yatajirra) (see Smith and Ross 2008a), he subsequently described rock art in several rock-shelters, which he dubbed the 'Aboriginal National Gallery of painting and hieroglyphics', writing that:

> We … found a Troglodytes' cave ornamented with the choicest specimens of aboriginal art. The rude figures of snakes were the principal objects, but hands, and other devices for shields were also conspicuous. One hieroglyphic was most striking; it consisted of two Roman numerals – a V and an I, placed together and representing the figure VI; they were both daubed over with spots, and were painted with red ochre. (Giles 1889:101) (Figure 8.1)

Figure 8.1: Explorer Ernest Giles's 'Aboriginal National Gallery', Glen Thirsty.
Source: Photograph by June Ross.

Work parties for the Overland Telegraph Line also occasionally observed rock art. Ooraminna Rockhole, just south of Alice Springs had become an important waypoint for these parties moving through the region. By 1873, the vivid paintings above the rock hole, mostly emu tracks and 'shield' motifs, had attracted comment (Overlander 1891). Another party under Arthur J. Giles, thought to have been a worker on the telegraph line, observed a large panel of rock engravings near the Finke River in 1873 (Worsnop 1897:45), which he described as consisting of pecked dots, track lines, arcs and lines. This is the earliest account of rock engravings in Central Australia and is also noteworthy because A.J. Giles was the first to seek information from Aboriginal people to interpret rock art. He was unsuccessful in this respect and in lieu of a better explanation decided that the engravings might represent some sort of lunar calendar made by the lost Leichhardt expedition of 1848 (Worsnop 1897:45–46).

Anthropologists and ethnographers: 1891–1942

Ernest Giles's remarks remained the only detailed observations of rock art in Central Australia until anthropological research commenced two decades later. However, for anthropologists and missionaries of the region, rock art was only an incidental interest. For a number of different reasons, they were mostly interested in the ethnography of Aboriginal societies and their traditions. Notwithstanding this, they had the advantage that they could usually communicate with local people, either in broken English or rudimentary Arrernte, though at first only mission-raised T.G.H. Strehlow was fluent in a local language.

Elder Expedition

The Elder Expedition of 1891–1892 was one of the most elaborate scientific exploration expeditions of its time (Lindsay 1893). Although it subsequently fell apart, it entered the Everard Ranges in 1891 where the naturalist, Richard Helms, made detailed notes on Aboriginal culture, including local rock paintings (Helms 1896). He left a remarkable account of the local rock art he recorded, illustrating each major panel of rock paintings (Figure 8.2). He commented, that 'they were not executed simply for idle sport becomes more evident the longer one looks at them. They probably possess a symbolic meaning, which I confess myself unable to elucidate' (Helms 1896:265). In his discussion of individual panels of paintings, Helms took pains to note any evidence of age or superimposition. In one case, he noted that 'the designs are undoubtedly of different age, and in many instances, particularly on the roof, which is nearly black, are obliterated by smoke' (1896:262). At another site, he observes that: 'It is a very old painting and was much obliterated, and … is painted over with bustard-tracks' (1896:262, Plate IX). Helms also commented on the incorporation of natural features into the rock art, observing at one site that 'the readiness with which the blacks adapt already existing outlines to their intended designs is here particularly well exemplified. A natural depression in the rock resembling the shape of an eye is utilised to represent that organ' (1896:262). Helms saw rock engravings ('broad arrows') but did not give them the attention that he devoted to the paintings (1896:265).

Figure 8.2: Rock paintings recorded by Richard Helms in the Everard Ranges in 1891.
Source: Helms 1896: Plate IX.

Horn Expedition and Baldwin Spencer

The Horn Expedition of 1894 was the first scientific expedition to enter the Alice Springs district (Spencer 1896). Its primary aim was to investigate the natural history of the centre of the continent, but its investigations initiated some of the most influential anthropological studies of the nineteenth century (Mulvaney and Calaby 1985). The research of Spencer and Gillen (1899, 1927) represents a quantum leap from earlier works, in that while not focused on rock art, it explored in some detail the cultural context in which Central Australian rock art was produced.

An initial report of the area's anthropology by E.C. Stirling, director of the South Australian Museum, illustrated representative motifs from several rock painting sites in the George Gill Range, at the Tarn of Auber and at Ayers Rock (Uluru), with unsupported interpretations of what they were thought to represent (Stirling 1896). Baldwin Spencer and Frank Gillen's later work across the region (1899, 1927) was fundamental in providing deeper insights into Aboriginal social systems, totemic beliefs and their elaborate cosmologies, which centred on the travels of Ancestral Beings over the landscape in the Altyerre, a creation-time that Spencer dubbed the 'Dreamtime' (see Mulvaney and Calaby 1985; Mulvaney et al. 1997). Spencer's partnership with F.J. Gillen, local postmaster and protector of Aborigines in Alice Springs, gave this research a deeper reach into Aboriginal cosmologies than any previously, as well as an ability to interact with local people.

Spencer and Gillen's research led them to the view that much of the art, including rock art, body decorations and designs on *tjurrunga* (sacred boards or plaques) were grounded in the religious beliefs of the 'Dreamtime', mostly as visual evidence signifying the presence of Ancestral Beings and their creative actions. As part of their attempts to understand such cosmologies, Spencer and Gillen published descriptions of the rock art motifs at three sites: Emily Gap (Anthwerrke), Quiurnpa (Kweyunpe) and Watarrka (1927:Plates II, III, IV).

Their most detailed account was of the large, striped totemic designs painted in red and white pigments in a gorge at Emily Gap (Spencer and Gillen 1899:171, Figure 132). This painting site, they reported, was associated with Utnerrengatye caterpillar ancestors, and the apparent 'eyes' represent caterpillar eggs. At these three sites, we can see that Spencer and Gillen had begun to understand that much of the art is linked with the totemic belief system, although neither yet fully appreciated the degree to which this system codified links between people and place. These art sites also gave them a glimpse of the way in which local interpretations of the rock art was contingent on place and context, with a labile rather than fixed iconography. They also began to see that motifs in the rock art were linked to designs used in ceremonial body decoration.

Their research also led them to appreciate the direct role that some rock art played in Arrernte ceremonial activity (Spencer and Gillen 1899:193–201). For instance, at Undiarra (Indiarra), they learned that, as part of ceremonies, the prominent red and white stripes would be repainted and blood from men's arms allowed to flow over the painting while other men sang the songs associated with the activities of kangaroo ancestors. Although Spencer and Gillen (1899:1927) interpreted this as an 'increase' ceremony, what they had described was more likely to have been concerned with maintenance of species and ritual stewardship of the land. As part of this research, Spencer and Gillen began to make a conceptual distinction between sacred art and ordinary or secular art.

North-West Prospecting Expedition

Herbert Basedow, prospector on the South Australian Government North-West Prospecting Expedition into the Mann and Musgrave Ranges in 1903, made extensive notes on local ethnography explicitly to allow comparison with the records of the Elder Expedition, the Horn Expedition and the works of Spencer and Gillen (Basedow 1904). His report included basic descriptions of panels of rock paintings (1904:41–46) as well as descriptions of bruised or pounded rock engravings that he referred to as 'primitive rock scratchings' (1904:38). In particular, Basedow noted the extent to which many rock paintings had been over-painted or repainted (1904:41). He also apparently saw track-line motifs in the rock art and thought that they represented 'route maps' (1904:42). On the 1903 expedition, Basedow was only 22 years old and commencing his career as a self-taught anthropologist. Although his notes on the ethnography of the regions the expedition traversed were detailed, it is perhaps not surprising that there is little in his account of the rock art beyond a basic record.

T.G.H. Strehlow

T.G.H. Strehlow did more than any other scholar to deepen understanding of the cultural history of Central Australia. With an academic interest in literature and a fluency in Arrernte that came from a childhood on Hermannsburg Mission, he was able to show the poetry and detail in the elaborate song cycles of the region. He was also able to demonstrate that in the elaborate totemic geography of Central Australia, each Dreaming story was fundamentally linked to a particular place (Strehlow 1947, 1971). He provided the first formal description of the graphic systems used in Central Australian art (1964) and its landesque nature, noting that:

- Each totemic centre was associated with sacred patterns that were 'believed to have been provided by the local supernatural beings' (1964:50). These patterns were 'rigidly formalised' and adhered to, although changes could be made to designs in the secular domain.

- Each sacred pattern was tied to a 'specific location' rather than to the associated 'mythology'.

Strehlow, however, gave little attention to rock art, largely dismissing it from consideration:

> The rock paintings and rock carvings of inland Australia may be mentioned only in passing … none of the works at these inland sites can compare with the rock paintings and carvings found in certain other parts of the continent, especially in northern and north-western Australia. (Strehlow 1964:55)

C.P. Mountford

Charles Mountford led ethnographic expeditions into Central Australia in 1938–1942. Travelling from Ernabella to Ayers Rock and into the Warburton, Mann and Musgrave Ranges, he mostly worked in what are now the Anangu-Pitjantjatjara-Yankuntjatjara Lands (APY Lands) (Mountford 1948, 1955, 1960, 1965, 1968, 1976). He gave much more attention to Aboriginal rock art and graphic systems than other anthropologists had, disseminating his work in a slew of publications over the next three decades. In some cases, he was able to directly observe people painting designs, or ritual interactions with existing paintings. For instance, at the Ngama site, near Yuendumu, which he visited in 1951 with an expedition initiated by the Board for Anthropological Research in Adelaide, he observed a senior man take the hand of a male initiate and guide it to key designs (1968:69–70).

Mountford's work is notable as he was the first researcher to attempt to follow an entire Dreaming track on the ground, which he described in a book-length study of the Dreaming track of the mulga snake (Jarapiri) (Mountford 1968). He also produced ethnographic studies of rock paintings at Ayers Rock (1965) and made a detailed record of the painted assemblage at Cave Hill (Walinynga) (1976:65–72, Plate 15, Figure 8). His book, *Ayers Rock, its people, their beliefs and their art* (1965) was based on his Master of Arts (MA) thesis at the University of Adelaide in 1964. His magnum opus, *Nomads of the Australian desert* (1976), is a remarkable catalogue of the Dreaming tracks and the associated actions of the Ancestral Beings throughout the Mann–Musgrave Ranges. Even today, this remains the most detailed and systematic account of the tapestry of cosmologies in any region, except possibly those given in Land Claim books in the 1980s. Mountford also recorded panels of rock engravings at Ewaninga, near Alice Springs in 1959 (Mountford 1960), which he regarded as an archaic art form with similarities to the engravings in north-eastern South Australia with which he was familiar. Like other recorders of rock art in this region, he found that his Aboriginal informants invariably attributed the origin of the art to the Dreaming, stating that it was not made by men but by a 'mythical hero during the creation period' (Mountford 1960:145).

Figure 8.3: Post-contact drawn horse and rider, Watarrka National Park.

Source: Photograph by June Ross.

Mountford's work marked a watershed for rock art research in Central Australia, because he showed that the art remained a 'living art' among the Aboriginal people in this region, noting:

- Some sites had acquired new paintings between 1930 and 1940, as testified by a comparison of photographs.

- Some sites included post-European contact motifs such as horses and camel trains (Figure 8.3).

- He observed an Aboriginal man painting a motif at Ayres Rock by applying red ochre and pipeclay with a finger and outlining the motif with a brush made from bark (Mountford 1948:87–88).

- He observed men 'bruising' motifs by pounding rock surfaces (Mountford 1955).

Mountford's work also extended our understanding of the sociocultural dimensions of this 'living art', showing that:

- Traditional interpretations of rock art were often contingent on social and territorial context, and the right to produce paintings was entangled with primary rights in a site.

- The production of rock art was a continual process, as evident in the repainting or over-painting of motifs, and additions to pre-existing painted friezes.

- There were a range of ways people interacted with rock paintings.

Mountford had also begun to appreciate that rock art was often as much about performance and practice as display. At the Ngama painting site in 1951, he saw:

> An old Aboriginal, taking the right hand of each initiate in turn, rubbed it on the rock from the tail to the head of the snake painting, then, retracing his steps, placed the hand of the initiate on each individual design, at the same time explaining its mythical significance. (Mountford 1968:69–70)

Rock art researchers

From 1890 to 1960, work on rock art in Central Australia moved from interest in its place in the ethnography of the region to a much more nuanced understanding of the sociocultural aspects of the function and production of rock art. Charles Mountford was a highly influential figure in this shift. Until the 1960s, however, he was the only researcher working specifically on rock art in Central Australia, although Richard Gould had also observed men making rock paintings in the late 1960s (Gould 1968). Much of Mountford's primary fieldwork in the region was carried out before 1942 and published later (1955–1965) in a series of books and articles on the rock art. It was not until 1965 that the archaeology of rock art became the primary concern of research projects, and that the art itself became the core focus of research.

Bob Edwards: 1965–1970

The key figure in the shift to a more archaeological approach to the study of rock art in Central Australia (and especially rock engravings) was Robert Edwards (Smith et al. 2020). In a break with earlier work, the rationale for Edwards's approach (see below) was that the rock engravings might be 'of great antiquity' and derive from a period predating the ethnography (although he did not flag a specific time period).

Edwards's research in Central Australia (undertaken between 1965 and 1968) occurred during a decade when archaeological research in Australia was rapidly expanding and he was undoubtedly influenced by this milieu (Mulvaney 1969; Griffiths 2018). His work essentially marks the beginning of systematic archaeological exploration of Central Australia. For instance, Richard Gould did not begin his pioneering excavations at Puntutjarpa until 1967 (Gould 1968) and at James Range East (Intirtekwerle) until 1974 (Gould 1978). Eugene Stockton undertook the first archaeological excavation in the Alice Springs region, digging at Kerringke rockhole in 1969 (Stockton 1971). Apart from Edwards work, broad-ranging archaeological reconnaissance of Central Australia only began with surveys in 1973 by L.K. Napton and A. Albee (1973) and by Mike Smith from 1980 to 1988 (Smith 1988).

Edwards was curator of anthropology at the South Australian Museum (1965–1973) where, under the mentorship of Mountford, he had developed his interests in engravings as relics of an ancient Australia. Edwards's program of work on rock engraving sites began in the Flinders Ranges some time prior to 1962, and subsequently developed into a major survey of engraving sites in the Olary region of South Australia, centred on Panaramitee Station. By 1965, Edwards had extended his work into Central Australia, comparing the frequency of different motifs at six localities in north-east South Australia (Florinna, Panaramitee, Pitcairn, Tiverton, Nackara and Winnininnie) with several localities in Central Australia (Tukulnga, Keringke and at Roma and N'Dhala gorges). Between 1962 and 1971, he published nine research papers on rock engravings (Edwards 1964, 1965a, 1965b, 1966, 1968b, 1971; Mountford and Edwards 1962, 1963, 1964).

Edwards's involvement with Central Australia was funded by a grant from the then Australian Institute of Aboriginal Studies (AIAS) in 1965 to photograph and record rock art sites across the Northern Territory. In this, he had the support of the existing principal of AIAS, Fred McCarthy, who had strong interests in rock art. In 1967 he was also commissioned by the institute to visit Thomas Reservoir (Alalya) in the Cleland Hills, west of Alice Springs, to record the first of a series of engravings of faces (Edwards 1968a, 1968b), a type of motif now widely known from the interior (Brady and Carson 2012; McDonald 2005; Ross and Smith 2009) (Figures 8.4 and 8.5). To allow his research to develop into a more systematic survey of rock art sites in

Central Australia, Edwards convinced a newly established newspaper, *The Australian* (first published in July 1964), to fund an expedition across the Centre in return for a six-part serialised account of his fieldwork (1970). As a result, he was able to embark on an extensive 10-week journey through Central Australia in 1969. During this, he travelled north into the Tanami, into the area west of Alice Springs (including a second trip to the Cleland Hills, this time guided by Kukatja-Luritja man Timmy Tjukadai) and into the APY Lands across to the Blackstone Range. On his second visit to the Cleland Hills, he also made a series of latex casts of the distinctive 'face' designs. He was also the first person to suggest a site museum of desert rock art at the prominent rock painting site at Cave Hill (Walinynga) in the APY Lands (Edwards 1975).

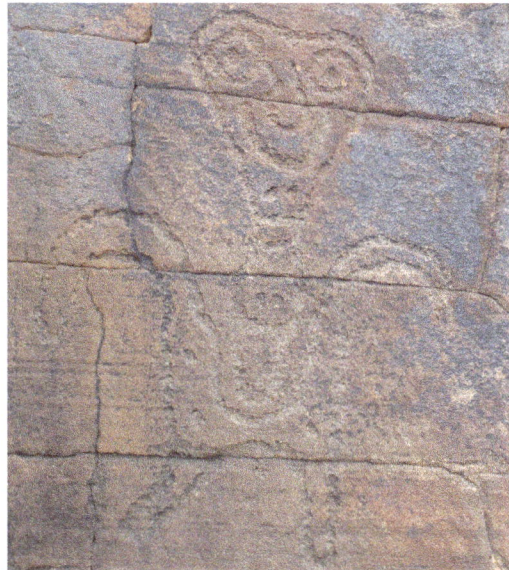

Figure 8.4: One of 17 engraved archaic faces at Alalya, Cleland Hills.
Source: Photograph by June Ross.

Figure 8.5: Engraved archaic face with body, Alalya, Cleland Hills.
Source: Photograph by June Ross.

Edwards's approach to recording and analysing engraving sites was a break with previous work in Central Australia. He approached this as a systematic, quantitative and comparative survey of rock engravings in north-eastern South Australia and Central Australia. Sometime before 1965, Edwards had begun to collect a range of quantitative data, mostly on motif frequencies within sites. To gain a first-order overview of the structure of the art, he grouped his motif counts into broad motif classes, concatenating data on the dimensions of motifs, styles and compositions into

10 motif types. At this scale, his results showed an overall similarity in the engraved art at sites across southern and Central Australia, suggesting to Edwards that the engravings represented an ancient pan-continental art style (1966a).

In another break with previous work, Edwards was also concerned with the location and condition of the engraving sites. In 1971, he summarised his views on the antiquity of the engravings (1971), noting:

- the high degree of weathering, patination and break-up of engraved pavements
- their proximity to scatters of large stone artefacts that he presumed were archaic types
- the location of engraving sites near water, which he implied was different to the distribution of recent art sites.

To Edwards, both the archaic stone tools and evidence of an arid landscape suggested an early Holocene antiquity for the engravings, though later scholars have sometimes assumed a Late Pleistocene age for Panaramitee-style rock engravings (but see Rosenfeld 1991; Smith et al. 2020).

Although the idea of Panaramitee as an ancient pan-continental phenomenon is a legacy of Edwards's rock art research that frames much rock art research in Central Australia (e.g. Clair Smith 1992; Forbes 1982; Franklin 2004; Maynard 1979; Rosenfeld and Mumford 1996), the basis for this proposition has been questioned by later researchers (see Rosenfeld 1991; Smith et al. 2020).

The proliferation of rock art research: 1988–2000

Bob Edwards put rock art research in Central Australia firmly on an archaeological footing. A significant return to ethnographic research on the structure of the graphic system was the seminal 1973 publication by Nancy Munn (*Walbiri iconography*), who analysed the production of sand drawings in a social anthropological study of Warlpiri graphic conventions. A concern with both the archaeology and social anthropology was characteristic of rock art research as it proliferated after 1988. From this time, rock art research across Central Australia routinely approached paintings and engravings as records of social geography, variously looking at social boundaries, and relationships of the art to place, land tenure and cosmology. The social and ontological contexts of art production, and subsequent ritual interactions with rock art surfaces, were also given more attention. The focus of research mostly moved back to rock paintings, looking in detail at individual site complexes, with a consideration of style, structure, colour and composition.

Academic research

Working on a finer scale than Edwards, Sarah Forbes (1982) undertook a formal analysis of engravings at a large site complex at N'Dhala Gorge, east of Alice Springs, to investigate the degree of internal uniformity of the assemblage. The notion of a single ancient period of rock engravings became more problematic as Forbes (1982), and later Franklin (1991), Rosenfeld and Mumford (1996) and Ross (2003) showed that there was significant spatial and temporal patterning within individual rock complexes of rock engravings, despite overall use of a common core vocabulary.

The social context of rock art production was emphasised in several studies. Ursula Frederick (1999) related patterning in rock art production in the George Gill Range (Watarrka) to changes in Aboriginal society during the European contact period, showing that, despite the ongoing use of a core graphic vocabulary consisting of circles, arcs and tracks, there had been changes in the site locations, motif types and techniques used during this period. Other researchers also gave specific attention to changes in rock art (paintings, stencils, prints, drawings and engravings) across Central Australia in the colonial period (Ross 2018). Galt-Smith (1997) found that assemblages of rock paintings within the region were most diverse at sites otherwise identified as important totemic sites. Rosenfeld (Rosenfeld and Mumford 1996; Rosenfeld and Smith 2002) explored social contexts of rock art production in an overview of research data from several rock art complexes, Watarrka, Wallace Rock Hole (Thuiparta) and Puritjarra, suggesting that two broad categories of paintings were present:

- **Secular art**, consisting of track alignments and hand stencils or prints. This type of rock art is widespread and commonly found in association with evidence of everyday occupation.
- **Sacred art**, consisting of elaborate formal or heraldic motifs associated with Dreaming stories.

Rosenfeld proposed that the secular art articulated daily economic and social geographies of groups associated with their foraging ranges, while sacred art was anchored in totemic geography (see also Gunn 1997c).

In a formal analysis of rock paintings, engravings, stencils and drawings investigating the repetition of motifs across space and through time, Ross and Davidson (2006) argued that ritual practices, both sacred and secular, were responsible for the production of much of Central Australia's rock art.

Impact of government agencies

By far the majority of rock art recording in Central Australia, undertaken between 1990 and 2015, has been commissioned by government agencies such as the Aboriginal Areas Protection Authority (formerly the Sacred Sites Authority), the Central Land Council (CLC) and the Conservation Commission of the Northern Territory (CCNT), latterly renamed the Parks and Wildlife Commission/Service of the Northern Territory (PWCNT) and now the Department of Environment, Parks and Water Security. These agencies found that they needed to improve site documentation to protect and manage cultural sites on lands for which they were responsible. The trigger for this proliferation of rock art recording programs seems to have been, in the case of the CLC, a shift from a core business concerned with land rights and land ownership in the 1970s and 1980s (land claims under the *Aboriginal Land Rights (Northern Territory) Act 1976* had a statutory 'sunset' clause), to a greater focus on the management of Aboriginal lands and Land Trusts in the 1990s. The requirement for parks and reserves administered by PWCNT to be jointly managed by Aboriginal Traditional Owner groups was initiated with passage of the *Territory Heritage Conservation Act 1991* (NT) and became widespread with the passing of the *Parks and Reserves (Framework for the Future) Act 2003* (NT).

Collectively, these studies created detailed coverage of the corpus of rock art in Central Australia, mostly in the MacDonnell, James and George Gill ranges, along the Finke, Hugh, Todd and Palmer rivers, and on the margins of the Simpson Desert, with some rock art complexes recorded multiple times by different researchers. Kimber (1991), Gunn (1995b) and Ross (2003) undertook comprehensive surveys of sites in Rainbow Valley (Urre) south of Alice Springs. Taçon (1994), Worrall (1994) and Ross (2003) documented assemblages of engravings at or in the vicinity of Roma Gorge in the West MacDonnell Ranges. Rosenfeld undertook rock art surveys, in addition to her academic research in Watarrka National Park (Rosenfeld 1990, 1993, Smith and Rosenfeld 1992; see also Ross 2003, 2009). Brown (1993, 1994) and Gunn (1989a, 1999b) completed site recording and condition assessments at the Ewaninga engraving site and at Kyunba just outside Alice Springs.

The most extensive body of recording has been by the indefatigable R.G. 'ben' Gunn who, over a decade of work from 1988, made detailed records of nearly two dozen rock art complexes at Illararri (Gunn 1988), Ewaninga (Gunn 1989a), several sites in the Dulcie Range (Gunn 1989b, 1992, 1993a, 1997b), Ooraminna (Gunn 1991a), Erota and Inangne (Gunn 1991b), Therreyererte (Gunn 1993b), Kwerlpe (Gunn 1994a), Kulpi Mara (Gunn 1995a), Rainbow Valley (Gunn 1995b), Keringke (Gunn 1995c), Inteyerre (Gunn 1997a), Intirtekwerle (Gunn 1998), Emily, Jessie and Heavitree gaps (Gunn 1999a), Kuyunba (Gunn 1999b), Akewlpe (Gunn 2001), Alyemperrke (Gunn 2002b), Irtikiri (Gunn and Thorn 1997a), Kulpitjata (Gunn and Thorn 1997b), and Yamaparnta (Gunn 1994b), one of the few sites recorded in Warlpiri Country during this phase of work.

Although many rock art studies from this phase of work involve detailed recording of individual rock art complexes, they are almost all unpublished in-house reports without peer review. With the exception of R.G. Gunn, who used a quantitative methodology (motif counts), these reports provide little scope for formal analysis of the art. The need to work closely with traditional custodians to document contemporary Aboriginal significance of each site complex has allowed some researchers, particularly Gunn, to record details of the sacred geography, Dreaming stories and totemic affiliations of many rock art sites. Gunn observed that, for Aboriginal people, rock art is only one of a number of elements that structure the totemic significance of a locality, and that the totemic geography is largely vested in natural features (Gunn 1995a:125, 1997c). In a comparison with the totemic geography outlined by Spencer and Gillen a century earlier, Gunn (2000) also found that large, bichrome, geometric motifs were distinctive at each site where they occurred – indeed, distinctly different in design from those at other sites.

This impressive phase of rock art recording produced a large and exceptionally detailed body of data on rock art assemblages across Central Australia. This primary literature is essentially a grey literature, mostly inaccessible to scholars, although there has sometimes been a sharing of reports among individual rock art researchers, and Gunn (2004) has published an outline of his accumulated rock art data.

Survey and synthesis

We could expect that a period that saw the rapid accumulation of new data would be followed by a period of synthesis. In Central Australia, despite an avalanche of rock art research after 1991, the fragmentation of studies undertaken for different purposes made broad-scale synthesis difficult, although two overall syntheses have emerged from programs of research by R.G. Gunn and June Ross.

Gunn provided an overview of Central Australian rock art (2004) and a series of studies exploring regional and spatial patterns in the rock art (Gunn 1995d, 2002a, 2011). He also revisited ideas about its articulation with land tenure and Dreamings (Gunn 1997c, 2011). Gunn used changes in motif frequencies in rock paintings to compare and contrast rock art in the central ranges (including the MacDonnell, James, Waterhouse, Harts, Deep Well and Rodinga ranges) with that recorded at complexes to the south-west of Central Australia (including the George Gill Range; Gunn 1995d, 2002a, 2011). Quantitative analysis of frequencies of motif type, technique, size and colour allowed Gunn to test ideas about the relative richness and diversity of rock art in these two regions, finding greater use of complex geometric designs in the central ranges where Strehlow contended there had been greater social complexity resulting from more favourable environments (Gunn 2002a).

Figure 8.6: Painted pole designs at Back Canyon, Watarrka National Park.

Source: Photograph by June Ross.

June Ross, working across a wide arc of Central Australia (1999–2003) in collaboration with PWCNT, was also able to take a regional approach based on her research at 51 site complexes (Ross 2003, 2005). The majority of these rock art sites were in the central ranges (see above), the George Gill Range, or in the riverine corridors of the Finke River and its tributaries. These data allowed a fine-grained characterisation of the structure and composition of rock art in Central Australia, building on the approach taken by Rosenfeld a decade earlier. Analysing the spatial distribution of rock art assemblages at a range of scales, Ross (2003) found that variability across the region was subtle and articulated in a core graphic vocabulary that had been employed at regional scale, within site complexes, within sites and over single panels irrespective of technique (engraving, painting, stencilling, printing or drawing) (Ross 2002). Specifically, she found that individual site complexes feature specific dominant motifs that, while they may not have been predominant quantitatively, had been produced in a manner that creates a visual dominance either by placement, size, colour or repetition (Ross and Davidson 2006) (Figure 8.6). She related the creation of these motifs to the totemic geography documented in ethnographic accounts. In order to understand the spatial placement of rock art in the central ranges, Ross and Abbott compared the significance of the Dreamings recorded at sites and the associated art with the distribution of reliable water sources, the geological rock type, the associated archaeological material, and the medium or size of the rock art assemblage at site complexes. They concluded that no one element could be flagged as the defining feature for the selection of locations for the production of rock art (Ross and Abbott 2004), and many of the most significant Dreaming sites today contained no rock art at all.

The issue of chronology

The chronological dimensions of Central Australian rock art have received less attention than its anthropological aspects or its sociocultural contexts. Unlike in northern Australia, rock art researchers in Central Australia have not generally recognised a clear dichotomy in rock paintings between early and late rock art styles (comparable to the distinction between Gwion and Wanjina art in the Kimberley, or between Dynamic Figure and x-ray art in western Arnhem Land). The closest analogue to this is where some researchers have assumed that the engraved art of Central Australia uniformly represents an archaic body of art substantially older than other pigment art in Central Australia (contra Maynard 1979), a notion that has unfortunately persisted among some researchers since the 1960s, despite identified similarities in the structure and composition of the younger engraved and painted assemblages (Ross 2002). Ross's study supported Rosenfeld's contention that some engravings were produced into the recent past in a gestural manner and style similar to recent pigment motifs indicating that the two assemblages were contemporaneous (see also Frederick 1997).

Absolute dating

Central Australian rock art research has not seen major investments in direct dating of rock art, unlike projects undertaken in the Western Desert and northern, Australia where direct dating of rock paintings has emerged as an important line of rock art research (e.g. David et al. 2013; Finch et al. 2020; McDonald et al. 2014; McDonald and Veth 2012; Ross et al. 2016). This may be, in part, due to the failure of earlier attempts at dating engravings in the Olary region using cation-ratio techniques (Dorn et al. 1988).

Field evidence from several Central Australian studies has also shown that engravings were produced over an extended period of time and into the late Holocene. A fragment of an engraving was recovered from excavations at Keringke, where its position in a late Holocene deposit provides only a *terminus ante quem* for engravings (Stockton 1971:57). More secure evidence that rock engravings were produced during the last few millennia was provided by a large slab with engraved bird tracks found buried within late Holocene deposits at Intirtekwerle (James Range East) (Gould 1978:120, 122; Smith 1986). Smith et al. (2009) dated the formation of calcium oxalate crusts on rock slabs and boulders containing engravings at two sites, Wanga East in the George Gill Range and Puritjarra, and established that oxalate had begun forming in the early Holocene (NZA27388, 7970-8161BP), extending over the engravings in the mid-Holocene (from NZA27393 4840-4965BP). The age estimates for formation of the oxalate crusts were cross-checked against radiocarbon ages for sediments excavated from beneath the fallen rock slabs and boulders, providing a maximum age for the engravings (Figure 8.7). Noting widespread evidence for pulses in the production of engravings, Smith (2013) used a state-and-transition model to suggest that any major challenge to land tenure or territory posed by rapid changes in population or environment would see accelerated production of rock art, followed by a period when existing rock art was curated, remarked or refreshed once the social geography had once again stabilised.

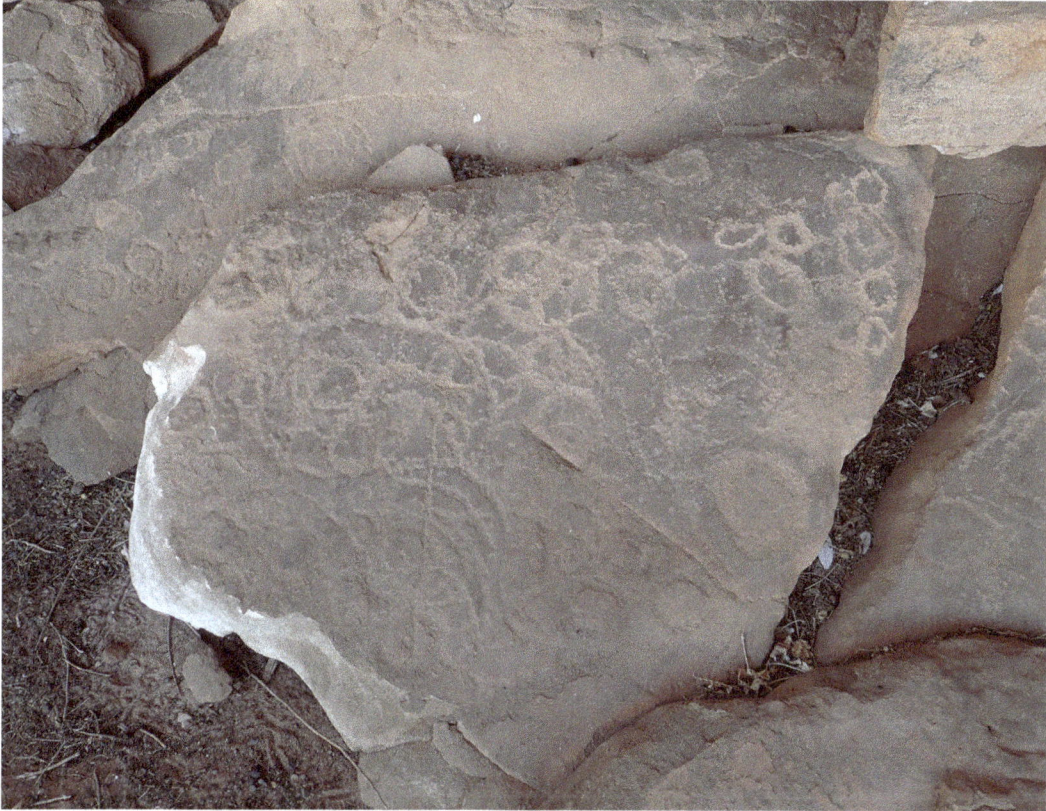

Figure 8.7: Engraved circles covered in calcium oxalate crust sampled for dating, Wanga East, Watarrka National Park.

Source: Photograph by June Ross.

Relative sequences

A number of researchers have identified relative sequences in panels of paintings or engravings at individual art site complexes, primarily using superimposition of motifs and degrees of patination (Rosenfeld and Mumford 1993; Rosenfeld and Smith 2002; Ross 2003). A handful of studies have attempted to integrate changes in rock art assemblages into programs of excavation at archaeological sites (Rosenfeld and Smith 2002; Smith et al. 1998; Smith and Ross 2008a; Thorley and Gunn 1996).

At a regional scale, Gunn (2002a) proposed a five-phase rock art sequence based on technique, suggesting that the range of techniques used to produce rock art have broadened over time. A detailed study of relative chronology at both the regional level and within individual site complexes was carried out by Ross (2003) in a fine-grained analysis of superimposition, weathering and relative patination of motifs at rock art sites across Central Australia. Although this was not a straightforward task, given that a core graphic vocabulary was used throughout the period of rock art production, and the composition of earlier and later art varied from complex to complex, her work showed that there was a substantial increase in production of rock art during the last millennium (see Ross 2005; Smith and Ross 2008b). Using site data from Ross (2003), Smith (2013) used a similarity matrix to show greater differentiation in motif types, techniques and frequency between sites. Based on these results, he proposed that rock art produced within the last millennium had responded to the emergence of distinctive clan territories that underpinned ethnographic land tenure with its focus on site-specific proprietorial knowledge.

Proposing a detailed relative sequence of rock art for Central Australia, Ross (2003, 2005) argued that the earliest surviving rock art consisted of small deeply pecked circles, or circles and pits, concentric circles, and individual or paired intaglio bird or macropod tracks. These motifs continued to be produced over time but were supplemented by a range of new motifs. Initially, these additions included figurative and outline designs (bird, macropod and lizard motifs), with additions in more recent art including meandering or straight track lines, spoked wheels, fans, ferns, complex poles, sinuous lines and anthropomorphic figures with headdresses and/or carrying boomerangs or spears (Figure 8.8). The early pigment assemblage includes a similar range of motifs with the addition of hand stencils. Stencils, including stencilled objects, continued to be produced into the recent past, although printed or drawn hands became more common forms of hand representation. A proliferation of charcoal and ochre drawings, both European contact subjects and roughly rendered traditional motifs, mark the last phase of rock art production.

Figure 8.8: Pounded figurative motifs among the most recent art at Rainbow Valley.
Source: Photograph June Ross.

Conclusion

The history of rock art research in Central Australia over the past century shows an evolution from documented encounters with the graphic systems showing they were poorly understood, to a more nuanced appreciation of the social and ideological system in which the rock art is embedded. The work of Charles Mountford is especially important in this regard, as he combined interests in the ethnography and anthropology of the region with a strong focus on rock art. The work of Robert Edwards in the 1960s was seminal in putting rock art research in this region on an explicit archaeological footing, and also because he introduced a quantitative perspective with his methodology of using motif counts as a central element of his analysis. Research by scholars after 1990 involved studies of the social and geographical context of rock art production, its structure and its social geography. The plethora of studies documenting individual rock art complexes commissioned by government agencies between 1990 and 2015 created a large, unpublished literature on rock art across Central Australia. This saw subsequent analyses of regional patterns in the rock art of the region as well as the first attempts to systematically extract relative and absolute chronological details for this geographically expansive corpus of art. The intensification and expansion of data on the rock art of this region after 1960, documenting both its cultural and chronological dimensions, places future rock art research in a strong strategic position to contribute more comprehensively to understandings of the archaeology of this region.

References

Basedow, H. 1904. Anthropological notes made on the South Australian Government North–West Prospecting Expedition, 1903. *Transactions of the Royal Society of South Australia* 28:12–51.

Brady, L.M. and A. Carson 2012. An archaic face from the Woodstock Abydos Protected Reserve, north-western Western Australia. *Australian Archaeology* 74:98–102. doi.org/10.1080/03122417.2012.116 81938.

Brown, R. 1993. Ewaninga rock carvings conservation reserve: Site recording and condition assessment. Conservation Commission Northern Territory, Alice Springs.

Brown, R. 1994. Kuyunba conservation reserve: Site recording and condition assessment. Conservation Commission Northern Territory, Alice Springs.

David, B., B. Barker, F. Petchey, J.J. Delannoy, J.M. Geneste, C. Rowe, M. Eccleston, L. Lamb and R. Whear 2013. A 28,000 year old excavated painted rock from Nawarla Gabarnmang, northern Australia. *Journal of Archaeological Science* 40:2493–2501. doi.org/10.1016/j.jas.2012.08.015.

Dorn, R.J., M. Nobbs and T.A. Cahill 1988. Cation-ratio dating of rock-engravings from the Olary Province of arid South Australia. *Antiquity* 62:681–689. doi.org/10.1017/S0003598X00075074.

Edwards, R. 1964. Rock engravings and stone implements of Pitcairn station, north-eastern South Australia. *Records of the South Australian Museum* 14:643–662.

Edwards, R. 1965a. Rock engravings and incised stones: Tiverton Station, northeast South Australia. *Mankind* 6:223–231. doi.org/10.1111/j.1835-9310.1965.tb00352.x.

Edwards, R. 1965b. Rock engravings and Aboriginal occupation at Nackara Springs in the north-east of South Australia. *Records of the South Australian Museum* 15:9–29.

Edwards, R. 1966. Comparative study of rock engravings in south and central Australia. *Transactions of the Royal Society of South Australia* 90:33–8.

Edwards, R. 1968a. Unique rock art in Central Australia. *Hemisphere* May 1968:2–7.

Edwards, R. 1968b. Prehistoric rock engravings at Thomas Reservoir, Cleland Hills, western Central Australia. *Records of the South Australian Museum* 15:647–670.

Edwards, R. 1970. The rock engravers. Parts 1–6. *The Australian* (Sydney), 14–19 April 1970.

Edwards, R. 1971. Art and Aboriginal prehistory. In D.J. Mulvaney and J. Golson (eds), *Aboriginal man and environment in Australia*, pp. 356–367. The Australian National University, Canberra.

Edwards, R. (ed.) 1975. *Proposal to establish a site museum of desert culture at Cave Hill, South Australia.* National Seminar on Aboriginal Antiquities in Australia – the preservation of Australia's Aboriginal heritage, May 1972. pp. 141–146. Prehistory and Material Culture Series 11. Australian Institute of Aboriginal Studies, Canberra.

Finch, D., A. Gleadow, J. Hergt, V. Levchenko, P. Heaney, P. Veth, S. Harper, S. Ouzman, C. Myers and H. Green 2020. 12,000-Year-old Aboriginal rock art from the Kimberley region, Western Australia. *Science Advances* 6(6):eaay3922. doi.org/10.1126/sciadv.aay3922.

Forbes, S. 1982. Aboriginal rock engravings at N'Dhala Gorge: An analysis of a Central Australian 'Panaramitee Style' rock art site. Unpublished B Litt thesis, The Australian National University, Canberra.

Franklin, N.R. 1991. Explorations of the Panaramitee style. In P. Bahn and A. Rosenfeld (eds), *Rock art and prehistory: Papers presented to Symposium G of the AURA Congress, Darwin 1988,* pp. 120–135. Oxbow Monograph 10, Oxbow Books, Oxford.

Franklin, N.R. 2004. *Explorations of variability in Australian prehistoric rock engravings.* British Archaeological Reports, International Series 1318. British Archaeological Reports, Oxford. doi.org/10.30861/9781841713878.

Frederick, U.K. 1997. Drawing in differences: Changing social contexts of rock art production in Watarrka (Kings Canyon) National Park, Central Australia. Unpublished MA thesis, The Australian National University, Canberra.

Frederick, U.K. 1999. At the centre of it all: Constructing contact through the rock art of Watarrka National Park, central Australia, *Archaeology in Oceania* 34:132–144. doi.org/10.1002/j.1834-4453.1999.tb00443.x.

Galt-Smith, B. 1997. Motives for motifs: Identifying aggregation and dispersion settlement patterns in the rock art assemblages of central Australia. Unpublished BA (Hons) thesis, University of New England, Armidale.

Giles, E. 1889. *Australia twice traversed: The romance of exploration, being a narrative compiled from the journals of five exploring expeditions into and through Central South Australia, and Western Australia, from 1872 to 1876* [Facsimile edition 1964]. Libraries Board of South Australia, Adelaide.

Gosse, W.C. 1973. *Report and diary of Mr. W. C. Gosse's Central and Western Exploring Expedition, 1973.* Government Printer, Adelaide. Reprinted 1973 as Australian Facsimile Editions.

Gould, R.A. 1968. Preliminary report on excavations at Puntutjarpa rockshelter near the Warburton Ranges, Western Australia. *Archaeology and Physical Anthropology in Oceania* 3:161–85.

Gould, R.A. 1978. James Range East rock Shelter, Northern Territory, Australia: A summary of the 1973 and 1974 investigations. *Asian Perspectives* 21:85–126.

Griffiths, B. 2018. *Deep time Dreaming: Uncovering ancient Australia.* Black Inc, Melbourne.

Gunn, R.G. 1988. Recording and assessment of rock art sites at Illararri, Tempe Downs Station, N.T. Unpublished report to the Central Land Council, Alice Springs, and the Australian Heritage Commission, Canberra.

Gunn, R.G. 1989a. Comments on the management of Ewaninga Reserve. Unsolicited report to Conservation Commission of the Northern Territory and Aboriginal Areas Protection Authority, Alice Springs.

Gunn, R.G. 1989b. Dulcie Range rock art survey. Unpublished report to Aboriginal Areas Protection Authority, Alice Springs.

Gunn, R.G. 1991a. Urrememe (Oorammina) rock art survey. Unpublished report to Aboriginal Areas Protection Authority, Alice Springs, and the Australian Heritage Commission, Canberra.

Gunn, R.G. 1991b. The rock art of Erota and Inangne, Central Australia. Unpublished report to Aboriginal Areas Protection Authority, Alice Springs and the Australian Heritage Commission, Canberra.

Gunn, R.G. 1992. Dulcie Range rock art survey II. Unpublished report to Aboriginal Areas Protection Authority, Alice Springs, and the Australian Heritage Commission, Canberra.

Gunn, R.G. 1993a. Dulcie Range rock art survey III. Report to the Aboriginal Areas Protection Authority, Alice Springs, and Australian Institute of Aboriginal and Torres Strait Islander Studies, Canberra.

Gunn, R.G. 1993b. The rock art of Therirrerte (Rodinga Range), Central Australia. Unpublished report to Aboriginal Areas Protection Authority, Alice Springs, and the AHC, Canberra.

Gunn, R.G. 1994a. The rock art of Kwerlpe (James Range), Central Australia. Unpublished report to Aboriginal Areas Protection Authority, Alice Springs, and the Australian Heritage Commission, Canberra.

Gunn, R.G. 1994b. Yamapamta: A Warlpiri occupation, ritual and rock art site. Unpublished report to Aboriginal Areas Protection Authority, Alice Springs.

Gunn, R.G. 1995a. Kulbi Maru and the rock art of the KM Site Complex, Central Australia. Unpublished report to Aboriginal Areas Protection Authority, Alice Springs.

Gunn, R.G. 1995b. Rainbow Valley rock art recording. Unpublished report to Aboriginal Areas Protection Authority and Conservation Commission of the Northern Territory, Alice Springs.

Gunn, R.G. 1995c. Keringke: An Eastern Arrernte ritual and rock art site. Unpublished report to Aboriginal Areas Protection Authority, Alice Springs, and the Australian Heritage Commission, Canberra.

Gunn, R.G. 1995d. Regional patterning in the Aboriginal rock-art of Central Australia: A preliminary report. *Rock Art Research* 12:117–128.

Gunn, R.G. 1997a. Inteyerre: A southern Arrernte rock art and ritual site complex, Central Australia. Unpublished report to Aboriginal Areas Protection Authority, Alice Springs, and Australian Heritage Commission, Canberra.

Gunn, R.G. 1997b. Taperraperre: An Akarre Arrernte rock art and mythological site, Dulcie Ranges, Central Australia. Unpublished report to the Traditional Owners for the Aboriginal Areas Protection Authority, Alice Springs, and Australian Heritage Commission, Canberra.

Gunn, R.G. 1997c. Rock-art, occupation and myth: The correspondence of symbolic and archaeological sites within the Arrernte rock-art complexes of Central Australia. *Rock Art Research* 14:12–36.

Gunn, R.G. 1998. Intertekwerle: An Arrernte rock art and Dreaming site, Central Australia. Unpublished report to Aboriginal Areas Protection Authority, Alice Springs, and Australian Heritage Commission, Canberra.

Gunn, R.G. 1999a. The rock art of Nthwerrke, Atherrke & Intriyapa (Emily Gap, Jessie Gap & Heavitree Gap): Near Alice Springs, Central Australia. Unpublished report to the Aboriginal Areas Protection Authority, Alice Springs, and Australian Heritage Commission, Canberra.

Gunn, R.G. 1999b. Kweyernpe: An Arrernte rock art and Dreaming site in Central Australia. Unpublished report for the Traditional Custodians to the Aboriginal Areas Protection Authority, Alice Springs, and Australian Heritage Commission, Canberra.

Gunn, R.G. 2000. Spencer and Gillen's contribution to Australian rock-art studies. *Rock Art Research* 17:56–64.

Gunn, R.G. 2001. Akewelpe: An Arrernte rock-art and Dreaming site in Central Australia. Unpublished report to Traditional Custodians to the Aboriginal Areas Protection Authority, Alice Springs, and Australian Heritage Commission, Canberra.

Gunn, R.G. 2002a. 'Our country, their country': Preliminary comparisons of the rock-art across the Western Desert/Arrernte borderlands. *Tempus* 7:109–119.

Gunn, R.G. 2002b. Alyemperrke: An Eastern Arrernte rock-art and Dreaming site. Unpublished report to Traditional Custodians to the Aboriginal Areas Protection Authority, Alice Springs, and Australian Heritage Commission, Canberra.

Gunn, R.G. 2004. The rock-art of Central Australia: An overview. *Australian Aboriginal Studies* 2004(1):54–68.

Gunn, R.G. 2011. Eastern Arrernte rock art and land tenure. *Rock Art Research* 28:225–239.

Gunn, R.G. and A. Thorn 1997a. The rock art of lrtikiri: A recording and conservation assessment. Unpublished report to the Aboriginal Areas Protection Authority, Alice Springs, and Australian Heritage Commission, Canberra.

Gunn, R.G. and A. Thorn 1997b. Kulpitjata: A Yankunytjatjara rock art complex in Central Australia. Unpublished report to the Site Custodians for Anungu tours, Yulara, and the Australian Institute of Aboriginal and Torres Strait Islander Studies, Canberra.

Hardman, W. 1865. *Explorations in Australia: The journals of John McDouall Stuart during the years 1858, 1859, 1860, 1861, & 1862* [Facsimile edition 1984]. Hesperian Press, Carlisle.

Helms, R. 1896. Anthropology. *Transactions of the Royal Society of South Australia* 16(3):238–386.

Kimber, R.G. 1991. Aboriginal rock art survey: Rainbow Valley. Unpublished report for CCNT, Alice Springs.

Lindsay, D. 1893. Journal of the Elder Scientific Exploring Expedition, 1891-2. C.E. Bristow, Government Printer, Adelaide.

Maynard, L. 1979. The archaeology of Australian Aboriginal art. In S.M. Mead (ed.), *Exploring the visual art of Oceania*, pp. 83–110. University of Hawai'i Press, Honolulu.

McDonald, J. 2005. Archaic faces to headdresses: The changing role of rock art across the arid zone. In P.M. Veth, M. Smith and P. Hiscock (eds), *Desert peoples: Archaeological perspectives,* pp. 116–141. Blackwell, Oxford. doi.org/10.1002/9780470774632.ch7.

McDonald, J. and P. Veth 2012. Western Desert iconography: Rock art mythological narratives and graphic vocabularies. *Diogenes* 58:7–21. doi.org/10.1177/0392192112452078.

McDonald, J., K.L. Steelman, P. Veth, J. Mackey, J. Loewen, C.R. Thurber and T.P. Guilderson 2014. Results from the first intensive dating program for pigment art in the Australian arid zone: Insights into recent social complexity. *Journal of Archaeological Science* 46:195–204. doi.org/10.1016/j.jas.2014.03.012.

Mountford, C.P. 1948. *Brown men and red sand: Journeyings in wild Australia*. Robertson and Mullens, Melbourne.

Mountford, C.P. 1955. An unrecorded method of Aboriginal rock marking. *Records of the South Australian Museum* 11:345–352.

Mountford, C.P. 1960. Simple rock engravings in Central Australia. *Man* 60:145–147. doi.org/10.2307/2797057.

Mountford, C.P. 1965. *Ayers Rock, its people, their beliefs and their art*. East-West Center Press, Honolulu.

Mountford, C.P. 1968. *Winbaraku and the myth of Jarapiri*. Rigby, Adelaide.

Mountford, C.P. 1976. *Nomads of the Australian desert*. Rigby, Adelaide.

Mountford, C.P. and R. Edwards 1962. Aboriginal rock engravings of extinct creatures in South Australia. *Man* 62:97–99. doi.org/10.2307/2796665.

Mountford, C.P. and R. Edwards 1963. Rock engravings of Panaramitee Station, north-eastern South Australia. *Transactions of the Royal Society of South Australia* 86:131–146.

Mountford, C.P. and R. Edwards 1964. Rock engravings in the Red Gorge, Deception Creek, northern South Australia. *Anthropos* 59:849–859.

Mulvaney, D.J. 1969. *The prehistory of Australia*. Penguin Books, London.

Mulvaney, D.J. and J.H. Calaby 1985. *'So much that is new': Baldwin Spencer (1860–1929)*. Melbourne University Press, Parkville.

Mulvaney, D.J., H. Morphy and A. Petch (eds) 1997. *'My dear Spencer': The letters of F.J. Gillen to Baldwin Spencer*. Hyland House, Melbourne.

Munn, N.D. 1973. *Walbiri iconography: Graphic representation and cultural symbolism in a Central Australian society*. Cornell University Press. Ithaca, New York.

Napton, L.K. and A. Albee 1973. Field notes. Unpublished manuscript. Museums and Art Galleries of the Northern Territory, Darwin.

Overlander 1891. Across the continent–No. 11, The MacDonnell Ranges. *Advertiser*, 20 May 1891:6.

Rosenfeld, A. 1990. Rock art in Watarrka National Park. Unpublished report for the Conservation Commission of the Northern Territory, Alice Springs.

Rosenfeld, A. 1991. Panaramitee: Dead or Alive? In P. Bahn and A. Rosenfeld (eds), *Rock art and prehistory: Papers presented to Symposium G of the AURA Congress, Darwin 1988*, pp. 136–144. Oxford University Press, Oxford.

Rosenfeld, A. 1993. The emergence of rock art in Australia. In M.A. Smith, M. Spriggs and B. Fankhhauser (eds), *Sahul in review: Pleistocene archaeology in Australia, New Guinea and Island Melanesia*, pp. 71–80. Occasional Papers in Prehistory 24. Department of Prehistory, Research School of Pacific Studies, The Australian National University, Canberra.

Rosenfeld, A. and W. Mumford 1993. The rock engravings at Thuiparta, Wallace Rockhole, near Alice Springs, Northern Territory. Unpublished report for the Wallace Rockhole community.

Rosenfeld, A. and W. Mumford 1996. The Thuiparta rock engravings at Erowalle, Wallace Rock Hole, James Range, Northern Territory. In S. Ulm, I. Lilley and A. Ross (eds), *Australian archaeology: Proceedings of the 1995 Australian Archaeological Association Annual Conference, Tempus 6*, pp. 247–255. University of Queensland, Brisbane.

Rosenfeld, A. and M.A. Smith 2002. Rock-art and the history of Puritjarra Rock Shelter, Cleland Hills, Central Australia. *Proceedings of the Prehistoric Society* 68:103–124. doi.org/10.1017/S0079497X00001468.

Ross, J. 2002. Rocking the boundaries, scratching the surface: An analysis of the relationship between paintings and engravings in the central Australian arid zone. In S. Ulm, C. Westcott, J. Reid, A. Ross, I. Lilley, J. Prangnell and L. Kirkwood (eds), *Barriers, borders, boundaries: Proceedings of the 2001 Australian Archaeological Association Annual Conference, Tempus 7*, pp. 83–91. University of Queensland, Brisbane.

Ross, J. 2003. Rock art, ritual and relationships: An archaeological analysis of rock art from the central Australian arid zone. Unpublished PhD thesis, School of Human and Environmental Studies, University of New England, Armidale.

Ross, J. 2005. Rock art of the Red Centre. In M.A. Smith and P. Hesse (eds), *23ºS: Archaeology and environmental history of the Southern Deserts*, pp. 217–230. National Museum of Australia Press, Canberra.

Ross, J. 2009. The prehistory of Watarrka National Park. Unpublished report prepared for Northern Territory Parks & Wildlife Service, Alice Springs.

Ross, J. 2018. Shifting worlds: Post-contact rock art in Central Australia. *Australian Archaeology* 84:219–231. doi.org/10.1080/03122417.2018.1547949.

Ross, J. and L. Abbott 2004. 'These things take time': Central Australian rock art in context. *Australian Aboriginal Studies* 1:69–78. Australian Institute of Aboriginal and Torres Strait Islander Studies, Canberra.

Ross, J. and I. Davidson 2006. Rock art and ritual: An archaeological analysis of rock art in arid Central Australia. *Journal of Archaeological Method and Theory* 13:304–340. doi.org/10.1007/s10816-006-9021-1.

Ross, J. and M.A. Smith 2007. An archaeological appraisal of Owen Springs Reserve, Central Australia. Unpublished report to the Northern Territory Parks & Wildlife Service, Alice Springs.

Ross, J. and M.A. Smith 2009. An engraved 'Archaic Face' in the north-eastern Simpson Desert. *Australian Archaeology* 69:68–70. doi.org/10.1080/03122417.2009.11681902.

Ross, J., K. Westaway, M. Travers, M. Morwood and J. Hayward 2016. Into the past: A step towards a robust Kimberley rock art chronology. *PLOS ONE* 11:e0161726. doi.org/10.1371/journal.pone.0161726.

Smith, C. 1992. Colonising with style: Reviewing the nexus between rock art, territoriality and the colonisation and occupation of Sahul. *Australian Archaeology* 34:34–42. doi.org/10.1080/03122417.1992.11681450.

Smith, M.A. 1986. A revised chronology for Intirtekwerle (James Range East) Rockshelter, Central Australia. *The Beagle: Occasional Papers of the Northern Territory Museum of Arts and Sciences* 3(1):123–130. doi.org/10.5962/p.260878.

Smith, M.A. 1988. The pattern and timing of prehistoric settlement in Central Australia. Unpublished PhD Thesis, Department of Archaeology and Palaeoanthropology, University of New England, Armidale.

Smith, M.A. 2013. *The archaeology of Australia's deserts*. Cambridge University Press, New York.

Smith, M.A. and A. Rosenfeld 1992. Archaeological sites in Watarrka National Park: The northern sector plateau. Report to Conservation Commission of the Northern Territory, Alice Springs.

Smith, M.A. and J. Ross 2008a. Glen Thirsty: The history and archaeology of a desert well. *Australian Archaeology* 66:45–59. doi.org/10.1080/03122417.2008.11681867.

Smith, M.A. and J. Ross 2008b. What happened at 1500–1000 BP in Central Australia? Timing, impact and archaeological signatures. *The Holocene* 18(3):379–388. doi.org/10.1177/0959683607087928.

Smith, M.A., B. Fankhauser and M. Jercher 1998. The changing provenance of red ochre at Puritjarra rock shelter, central Australia: Late Pleistocene to present. *Proceedings of the Prehistoric Society* 64:275–292. doi.org/10.1017/S0079497X00002243.

Smith, M.A., A. Watchman and J. Ross 2009. Direct dating indicates a mid-Holocene age for archaic desert rock engravings in arid Central Australia. *Geoarchaeology* 24:191–203. doi.org/10.1002/gea.20262.

Smith, M.A., J. Ross and R.G. Kimber 2020. Robert Edwards and the history of Australian rock art research. *Historical Records of Australian Science* 32(1):41–51. doi.org/10.1071/HR20011.

Spencer, W.B. (ed.) 1896. *Report on the work of the Horn Scientific Expedition to Central Australia*. 4 volumes [Facsimile edition, Corkwood Press 1994, Melbourne]. Melville, Mullen and Slade.

Spencer, W.B. and F.J. Gillen 1899. *The Native Tribes of Central Australia* [Facsimile edition, Anthropological Publications 1969, Melbourne]. Macmillan, London.

Spencer, W.B. and F.J. Gillen 1927. *The Arunta: A study of a stone age people.* Macmillan, London.

Stirling, E.C. 1896. *Report on the work of the Horn Scientific Expedition to Central Australia*. Part IV [Facsimile edition, Corkwood Press 1994, Melbourne]. Melville, Mullen and Slade.

Stockton, E.D. 1971. Investigations at Santa Teresa, Central Australia. *Archaeology and Physical Anthropology in Oceania* 6:44–61.

Strehlow, T.G.H. 1947. *Aranda traditions.* Melbourne University Press, Melbourne.

Strehlow, T.G.H. 1964. The art of circle, line and square. In R.M. Berndt (ed.), *Australian Aboriginal art*, pp. 44–59. Ure Smith, Sydney.

Strehlow, T.G.H. 1971. *Songs of Central Australia.* Angus and Robertson, Sydney.

Stuart, J.M. 1865. *Explorations in Australia: The journals of John McDouall Stuart.* W. Hardman (ed.). Saunders Otley and Co, London.

Sturt, C. 1865. *Journal of the Central Australian expedition 1844–45.* J. Waterhouse (ed.). Caliban, London.

Taçon, P.S.C. 1994. Socialising landscapes: The long-term implications of signs, symbols and marks on the land. *Archaeology in Oceania* 29:117–129. doi.org/10.1002/arco.1994.29.3.117.

Thorley, P. and R.G. Gunn 1996. Archaeological research from the eastern borderlands of the Western Desert. Paper prepared for the Western Desert Origins workshop, Australian Linguistic Institute, Canberra.

Tietkens, W.H. 1891. *Journal of the Central Australian Exploring Expedition, 1889, under command of W.H. Tietkens.* C.E. Bristow, Government Printer, Adelaide.

Warburton, P.E. 1981. *Journey across the Western interior of Australia.* Sampson, Lowe, Marston, Low and Steale, London. Facsimile reprinted in 1981 by Hesperian Press, Western Australia.

Worrall, R.H. 1994. Rock art survey, Roma Gorge: Western MacDonnell National Park, Central Australia. Unpublished MA thesis, Department of Archaeology and Palaeoanthropology, University of New England.

Worsnop, T. 1897. *The prehistoric arts, manufactures, works, weapons, etc., of the aborigines of Australia.* C.E. Bristow, Government Printer, Adelaide.

9

Without them – what then? People, petroglyphs and Murujuga

Ken Mulvaney

Introduction

From the late 1960s, apart from the Traditional Owners, it has been 'foreigners' that have made known the stories of Murujuga (Dampier Archipelago including Burrup Peninsula) in northern Western Australia. Early work carried out by Italian Dampier Salt Company Projects Manager Enso Virili and French archaeologist Michel Lorblanchet involved detailed archaeological investigations and engagements with local Aboriginal groups. Weaving through these early investigations was Austrian Robert Bednarik, photographing the petroglyphs and then later generating political and public focus on the conflicting issues of commercial development. Local West Australians started recording the archaeology of the place prior to industrial construction, mainly by the Western Australian Museum Department of Aboriginal Sites (DAS) staff, such as Peter Randolph, Vera Novak and John Clarke, based in Perth 1500 km to the south. Bruce Wright, as the DAS registrar, fetched yet others into engagement with Murujuga, initially documenting sites prior to construction of a petrochemical processing facility. One of these, South African-born Pat Vinnicombe, brought with her a wealth of experience and a particular way of investigating rock art. Her influence guided future work and engagement with Traditional Owners. All these 'foreigners' have contributed to understanding the globally significant petroglyphs of Murujuga. These people have endeavoured to ensure that a few decades of industrial utilisation did not wipe out tens of thousands of years of priceless cultural productivity.

Murujuga, the Aboriginal name for what modern Australia calls Burrup Peninsula and the Dampier Archipelago, is a spectacular group of 42 islands, islets and rock exposures projecting into the Indian Ocean on Australia's north-west coast (Figure 9.1). This land has belonged to the Aboriginal people of north-west Australia for at least 50,000 years, when evidence suggests they first came into this part of the continent (Veth et al. 2017). It has only been since the mid-seventeenth century that others ventured to these shores, and it is merely since 1863 that foreigners came to settle the land. Then, 100 years later, industrial developments generated archaeological interests in Murujuga. Industry brought the first of those to study the cultural heritage of this place. A trait of those who came is their dedication to making others aware of the immense cultural heritage values present at Murujuga and in engaging with the Aboriginal custodians.

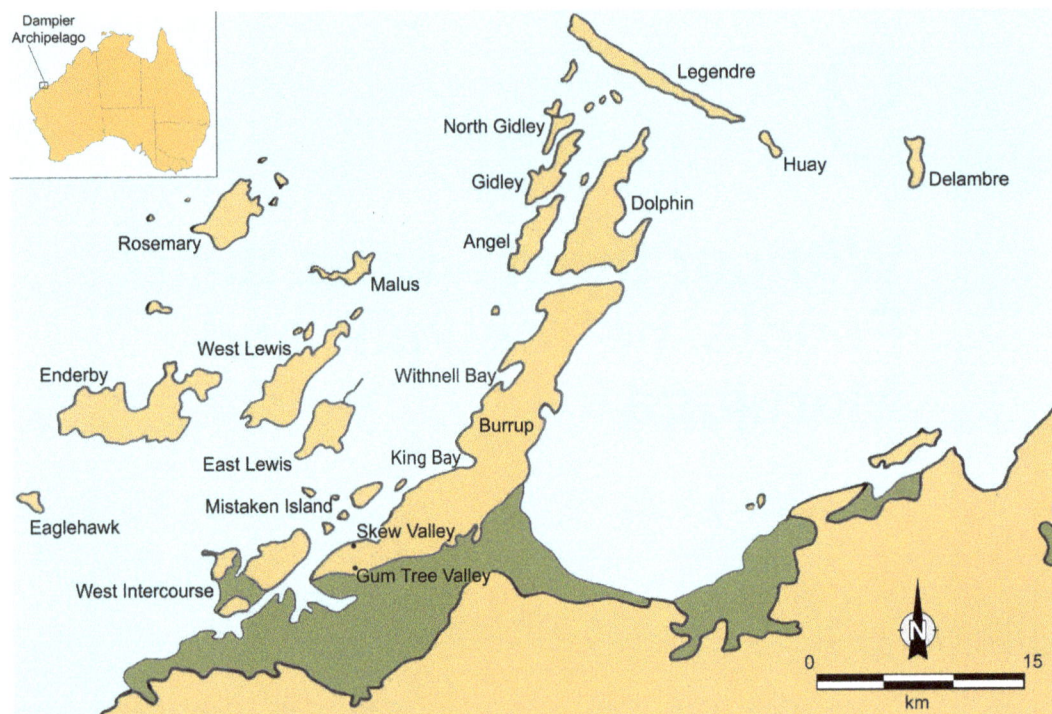

Figure 9.1: Map showing the Dampier Archipelago with the location of places mentioned in the text.

Source: Map by Ken Mulvaney.

Murujuga is in the traditional lands of the Yaburara, a people decimated in 1868 during the events known as the Flying Foam Massacre (Sholl 1868; see Gara 1983). Due to the spiritual significance of Murujuga and with few Yaburara remaining, today there are five language groups, including Yaburara, who look after this Country, represented by the Murujuga Aboriginal Corporation (MAC). It is these adjacent Aboriginal groups that hold the role of custodians of the land and lore.

In July 2007, the Dampier Archipelago including Burrup Peninsula was placed on Australia's National Heritage List, in recognition of its spectacular rock art (petroglyphs) and exceptional stone arrangements (McDonald and Veth 2009). Then, in January 2013, the long-awaited declaration of Murujuga National Park occurred (with a signed agreement for this in 2003). The Aboriginal people through MAC own and co-manage this conservation estate with the Western Australian Department of Biodiversity, Conservation and Attractions. The National Park covers 5134 ha of this land, with non-industrial gazetted lands representing 43 per cent of the Burrup Peninsula. Early in 2020, Murujuga was placed on the UNESCO World Heritage Tentative List, the culmination of efforts for such recognition having begun 40 years earlier.

Josephine Flood makes the observation that Australian rock art research is:

> a saga full of personal feuds, bitter rivalries and competition for 'territory' … added to this is the explosive mix in the rock art world of so-called 'professionals' and 'amateurs', all with chips on both shoulders. (Flood 1997:xi)

Happily, with one possible exception (see Bednarik 2006, 2016), this situation does not seem to have marred Murujuga research. Possibly tempered by political expediency around dealing with impacts of industrial developments, amateurs and professionals alike, often working with the Traditional Owners and in collaboration with others, have progressed our understanding of and promoted protection for the unique cultural landscape that is Murujuga.

Murujuga

Many of the islands of Murujuga comprise distinctive steep basaltic rocky slopes and rock piles interspersed with spinifex scrubland and white gum-lined valley slopes and creek channels (Figure 9.2). Other islands are low-lying limestone and consolidated beach-rock platforms. All feature mangroves, shallow embayments and sandy beaches, habitats for a myriad of plant and animal species. The islands and surrounding waters are a haven for wildlife and marine biodiversity, with migratory birds using the resources to feed and rest after flying in from the northern hemisphere. Dugong, dolphins, whales, turtles, rays and hundreds of fish species inhabit the waters. Their images along with terrestrial fauna can be found in Murujuga's rock art.

The archipelago formed c. 7000 years ago when rising sea levels flooded what were once coastal plains. This changed the ecological nature of the area – a feature that is recorded in the petroglyphs (McDonald 2015; Mulvaney 2015a; Ward et al. 2013). Prior to this, the ancient rugged rocky landscape, interspersed with sheltered freshwater rock pools and creeks, presented as a series of short, low ranges rising some 100 metres above a vast coastal plain, that at times extended out some 100 to 160 kilometres to the continental shelf. It is the abundance of environmental resources that provided for the residential population over some 50,000 years (see Veth et al. 2017), and it is the profusion of the rock art that has brought scholars to Murujuga over the past 50 years.

It is not just the natural and Aboriginal cultural landscape of Murujuga that is impressive. The extensive industrial estate that rises incongruously about the rugged slopes also has an impact on visitors. The leases that Hamersley Iron and Dampier Salt hold predate the implementation of the *Aboriginal Heritage Act 1972* (WA). Yet despite protection and awareness of this culturally rich place, Murujuga is now home to Australia's largest oil and gas operations. Marketed by the state government as the Burrup Strategic Industrial Area, companies seem unconcerned by the priceless Aboriginal cultural heritage situated on the same area of land. The Burrup Strategic Industrial Area is a concept conceived decades ago by people far removed from Murujuga and ignorant of the remarkable cultural heritage they condemned to destruction.

Figure 9.2: Landscape of Murujuga, a 50,000-year-old cultural wonderland that is often mistaken for a mining-created landscape of mullock heaps.

Source: Photograph by Ken Mulvaney.

Historical shift

One of the first to document the archaeology of the Dampier Archipelago and notify relevant statutory authorities of its importance was Enso Virili, employed at Dampier Salt from 1970 to 1974. Virili had arrived from Italy to take up the role of a civil engineer with Comalco, the company engaged in construction of the solar salt ponds. Just as with many others that have come to this remote part of north-west Australia, Virili became enchanted by the petroglyphs. One of the features of Virili's work is that he engaged with the local Aboriginal people, bringing knowledgeable persons out to sites, not only to discuss the rock art but also to consult on industrial development impacts (Figure 9.3). He successfully negotiated through the Traditional Owners the accompaniment of a turtle-engraved rock with the first shipment of salt to Japan in 1973, gifted by the Western Australian Museum to Tokyo National Museum (*Hamersley News* 1973:1).

A collaborative engagement established early between Virili and staff of the Western Australian Museum DAS was led by Warwick Dix, then registrar of Aboriginal sites. This association resulted in a number of publications and attendance at the formative Canberra rock art conference held in 1974 by the Australian Institute of Aboriginal Studies (AIAS) and elsewhere (Dix 1977; Dix and Virili 1977; Virili 1977). This meeting in Canberra was very much a gathering of academic members of AIAS, as well as national and international invitees. That Virili attended may relate to the fact that Dix had taken up a position as deputy principal at AIAS. Nevertheless, this collaboration and attendance as an amateur demonstrates the regard held of Virili's work within the Dampier Archipelago. Virili not only brought this cultural landscape to the attention of archaeologists and professional institutions, he also contributed to the safeguarding of sites, even before there existed heritage protection legislation (*Hamersley News* 1970:2; *Aluminium* 1972:1–7).

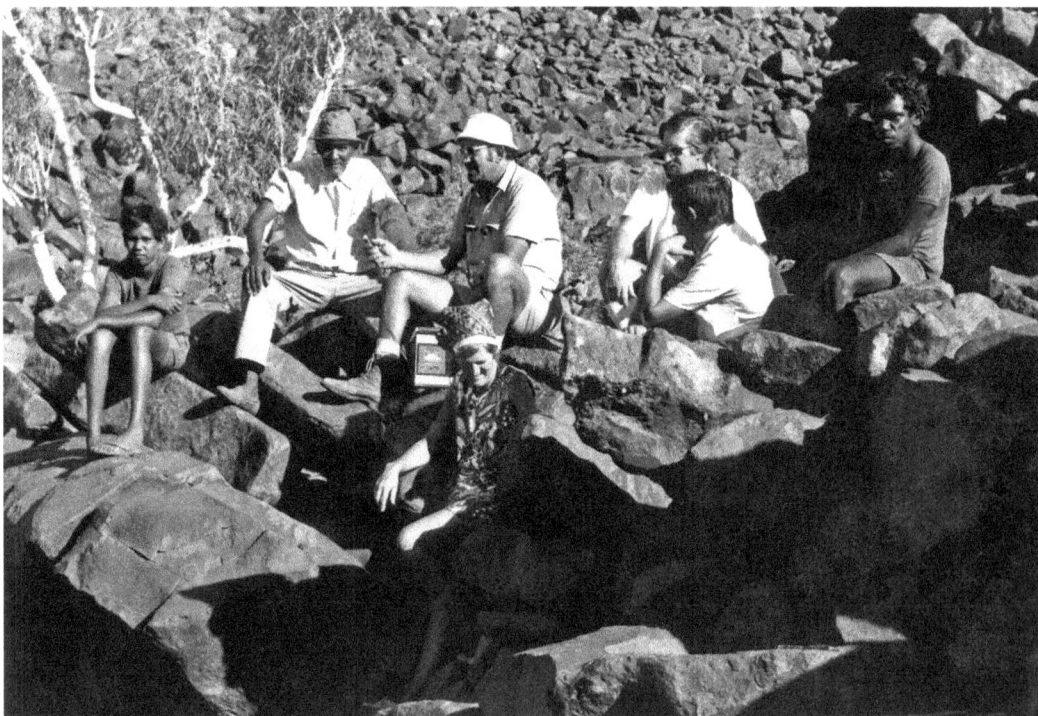

Figure 9.3: Enso Virili (in hat) with Traditional Custodian Coppen Dale and others at Gum Tree Valley.
Source: From *Aluminium* 7, December 1972:3.

Figure 9.4: Herbert Parker and Algie Paterson, senior Pilbara lawmen and active in the National Aboriginal Conference, with whom Lorblanchet consulted.

Source: Photograph by Ken Mulvaney, taken at Red Hill Station 1984.

Virili's efforts to protect rather than destroy sites is a theme running through all those that have engaged with the Murujuga cultural landscape. A figure that has loomed large in this respect is Austrian Robert Bednarik, who established the Australian Rock Art Research Association (AURA) in 1984 and who has published widely on the need to protect Murujuga's rock art (e.g. Bednarik 2006 and references therein). Although Bednarik arrived in the Pilbara in the late 1960s and states he witnessed destroyed rock art near King Bay (Bednarik 1977:51), it was not until early in the twenty-first century that he began a campaign of public awareness and the associated push against industrial development on Murujuga (see below).

One outcome of the 1974 Canberra conference was that the French rock art expert Michel Lorblanchet, newly appointed as an AIAS researcher, among other duties, was directed to carry out work within Murujuga. He focused activities at two locations identified by Virili as of particular cultural richness: Skew Valley and Gum Tree Valley (see Figure 9.1 and 9.2). These places are near the southern end of what is Dampier Island, the northern half now named Burrup Peninsula. Lorblanchet conducted two major field seasons, in 1975–1976 and again in 1983– 1984 (Lorblanchet 1983, 1992). In addition to bringing several Indigenous staff from AIAS, Lorblanchet contacted the local Aboriginal community for their advice and involvement; two of these men were Herbert Parker and Algie Paterson (Figure 9.4). The experience enhanced his own understanding of rock art production, which he brought to bear to his interpretations of European Upper Palaeolithic cave art when he returned to France (Lorblanchet 2018).

In their activities within Murujuga, Virili and Lorblanchet brought many professionally employed archaeologists to the area, as well as engaging with local residents. This included not just the white community but also Indigenous peoples. This improved understanding of the rock art and meant that more people became aware of the adverse impacts that industry was imposing on this cultural landscape. Of the heritage professionals brought in, most were state employees of DAS. Peter Randolph, a graduate of the University of Western Australia, arguably has had the longest association with Murujuga, other than local Aboriginal people. Although, like many others, he did not have formal training in rock art research, Randolph had an enthusiasm typical of those who have recorded cultural heritage places within the archipelago.

The second rock art specialist to come to Murujuga was South African–born Patricia (Pat) Vinnicombe, arriving in Western Australia in 1979 after a stint in New South Wales (Figure 9.5). Recognised for her groundbreaking work in the Drakensberg, KwaZulu-Natal (Vinnicombe 1976), Vinnicombe brought a particular energy to rock art recording with a combination of scientific rigour and cross-cultural insight. Her ability to learn about how to understand the rock art from local Aboriginal peoples, as she had done among the Drakensberg San, stood her well for research in Australia. Vinnicombe's theoretical approach to the rock art was that it did not just represent simple pictures, or an inventory of daily encounters, but rather reflected the beliefs and cosmological perspectives of that culture. Without diminishing the important recording work of her predecessors including Lorblanchet, Vinnicombe's entry into Western Australia transformed the documentation of Murujuga from inventory into engaged rock art research.

It was Bruce Wright, as registrar of Aboriginal sites, that instigated the rescue archaeology work linked to the construction of a petrochemical plant within Murujuga, known as the Dampier Archaeological Project (DAS 1979, 1980). While working for the state education department, Wright (1965, 1968) researched and published on Pilbara rock art, and through numerous but limited surveys conducted by DAS staff, understood 'that the Dampier Archipelago is a rich archaeological resource which has the potential to yield substantial scientific insights' (DAS 1980:1). During work in the Pilbara, Wright had established strong connections within the Pilbara Aboriginal community. Discussions were held with Traditional Owners in relation to the Dampier Archaeological Project. However, as a consequence of Noonkanbah, where Kimberley Aboriginals were demonstrating against desecration of their sacred sites (see Hawke and Gallagher 1989), the state government would not consent to direct Aboriginal involvement, fearing community opposition to Murujuga's petrochemical plant construction.

Figure 9.5: Pat Vinnicombe, flies and all, taking photograph of petroglyph during the 1980 Dampier Archaeological Project, Burrup Peninsula.

Source: Photograph by Ken Mulvaney.

Figure 9.6: Ken Mulvaney, Bill Arthur and Peter Veth having a morning cuppa while sheltering from the cold wind and noise of machinery, Withnell Bay 1981.

Source: Photograph by Peter Ridgway.

Instead of carrying out research with the traditional artists of the Kimberley region, as she had wanted, Vinnicombe was coopted by Wright into the Murujuga work. Her influence was directed to the bevy of newly qualified and employed DAS staff, Peter Veth and myself among them (Figure 9.6), to record cultural features and archaeological sites prior to their destruction to make way for a massive petrochemical (liquified natural gas, LNG) plant and allied services (Vinnicombe 1987). Initially Jim Rhoads, an American archaeologist who had carried out his doctoral research in New Guinea through The Australian National University in Canberra, was employed to manage a group of three other staff as the LNG project team. However, once they had started, it became clear that the density and complexity of the archaeological sites and artefacts meant that additional people were required to keep ahead of construction activities. At one stage, in late 1980, 17 people worked on documenting Murujuga's archaeology in the area between King Bay and Withnell Bay (see Figure 8.1). In total the Dampier Archaeological Project covered some 13.4 km², recording 720 archaeological sites including documentation of 9744 petroglyph panels (DAS 1984:12). A lasting impression gained by all concerned was that of the needless annihilation of cultural heritage and landscapes taking place.

Given that the gas deposits were offshore, over a hundred kilometres away, and the fact that there existed plenty of less culturally and environmentally significant land elsewhere along the coast that could have better accommodated industrial construction, such disregard for Australia's cultural heritage was soul-destroying for the archaeologists and Traditional Owners. All of the heritage professionals came away with a sense that there must be better options and that the protection of Murujuga's cultural heritage should be paramount. By the early 1980s, with legislation now in place to manage Aboriginal heritage, coupled with the greater awareness of just how significant the place was, it was felt by some that Murujuga was now recognised as a unique and significant cultural landscape unsuited to further industrial development. Alas, government and industry did not budge from their perspective that the legislation was there to facilitate development, not to protect heritage. Risks to the cultural heritage of Murujuga continue today with proposals for the establishment of various petrochemical and fertiliser companies, requiring extra effort from heritage professionals to dissuade such outcomes.

Vinnicombe returned to Murujuga on a number of occasions, carrying out surveys of land allocated for industrial development (Vinnicombe 1997a, 1997b, 2002). Fortunately, unlike with the earlier LNG project, work with the Traditional Owners was by then a legal requirement. Vinnicombe formed strong relationships with Elders like David Daniel and his wife Tootsie. In fact, throughout the 1990s there was increased engagement with Aboriginal people out on surveys and in consultation over projects (e.g. National Estates Programme survey: Veth et al. 1993). Tragically, when Vinnicombe died in March 2003, she was in the middle of yet another round of meetings, attempting to shift government and industry attitude. Respected by all, Vinnicombe's measured words and tactful approach had done much in protecting Murujuga over the intervening 20+ years since she first engaged with Murujuga.

Since Vinnicombe's death, industrial development has come back to Burrup Peninsula and now there are plans underway for expansion of existing petrochemical facilities, with the addition of a urea production plant (*Pilbara News* 2018:14), all this impacting the cultural heritage (see Bednarik 2002; Black et al. 2017a; Mulvaney 2011, 2015b). Others have taken up the baton of Vinnicombe's legacy and continue to shame industry and government, not least of all American Tom Perrigo (National Trust of Australia (WA) (NTWA)) and Englishman the Hon. Robin Chapple (Greens MLC).

Concern over additional destruction of petroglyphs in 2004 prompted the NTWA to take action to request National Heritage listing (Haynes and Waldmann 2004) – one of three applications to the federal government, another by Bednarik (AURA) and a third on behalf of Traditional Owners. This endeavour was the culmination of increased efforts by people to change the way commercial interests regarded Murujuga, that it is not simply just industrial real estate. Selected areas at both ends of Burrup Peninsula and the site known as Climbing Men were protected until a change in legislation, under the then Federal Register of National Estate.

Such was the concern of land clearance and damage through corrosive emissions that the World Monument Fund (WMF) added Murujuga to their global list of the 100 most-threatened sites. It was the first Australian site to go on the list, prompting a visit by the WMF president, Bonnie Burnham, in early 2004. Burnham flew into Karratha on her way home to the United States, having just come from a trip to Antarctica. Aboriginal Elders, Greens MLC Robin Chapple, Robert Bednarik and myself escorted Burnham around Murujuga. Bednarik and Burnham subsequently met with state ministers and other government officials. The upshot was an investment of funds managed by the NTWA, part of which went into the production of a much-needed, widely available publication on Murujuga cultural heritage by two English-born academics with longstanding connections to Murujuga and Australian archaeology (Bird and Hallam 2006).

As a consequence of Bednarik's actions in raising public awareness of the industrial emissions threat to Murujuga petroglyphs, COBRA (Champions of Burrup Rock Art), a locally based advocacy group, was formed. This local association later expanded into a national organisation, Friends of Australian Rock Art (FARA). It was the efforts of FARA and NTWA, not those of the Bednarik associations (e.g. AURA and the International Federation of Rock Art Organisations (IFRAO)), that the federal minister acknowledged when Murujuga was included on the National Heritage List (Media statement 3 July 2007: Hon. Malcom Turnbull MP).

However, Bednarik was in the fray, holding meetings, writing letters and engaging in a media campaign. As the then president of AURA, I was also part of this campaign, writing letters to state and federal ministers urging effective protection of Murujuga's cultural heritage. Importantly, statements by Bednarik (2002) that industrial emissions were destroying the rock art pressured the state government to establish the Burrup Rock Art Monitoring Management Committee (BRAMMC). This committee was tasked with overseeing the implementation of a program of 'scientific' studies that ran in 2004–2005 and 2007–2008 (CSIRO 2009; SKM 2009). They included the monitoring of air quality, microbiological analyses, mineral spectrometry, dust deposition, accelerated weathering experiments, surface-colour readings and air dispersion modelling. Belgium-born English rock art specialist (teacher of many students and researcher of both Australian and international rock art) Professor Andrée Rosenfeld was an initial member of this committee. Rosenfeld died in 2008 and no suitably qualified rock art expert replaced her on the committee. Her absence may explain the BRAMMC final report's conclusion, that 'there is no scientific evidence to indicate measurable impact of emissions on the rate of deterioration of the Aboriginal rock art in the Burrup' (BRAMMC 2009). The colour monitoring at seven selected sites has continued annually, with the addition of three locations linked to the Yara Technical Ammonia Nitrate Plant environmental approval conditions (e.g. Markley et al. 2015).

FARA has been very active as lobbyists and facilitators, helping in June 2013 with taking two Murujuga custodians Tim Douglas and Wilfred Hicks to Canberra to petition then Environment Minister Tony Burke (Figures 9.7 and 9.8). These men, in addition to presenting Burke with a letter signed by other custodians, explained the sacred nature of the place and requested Murujuga be progressed to World Heritage recognition. Sadly, shifting politics overshadowed this appeal and Murujuga had to wait another seven years for movement on this (Media statement 28 January 2020: Hon. Stephen Dawson MLC).

Figure 9.7: Traditional Owner Wilfred Hicks addressing visitors on the FARA tour of 2015.
Source: Photograph by Ken Mulvaney.

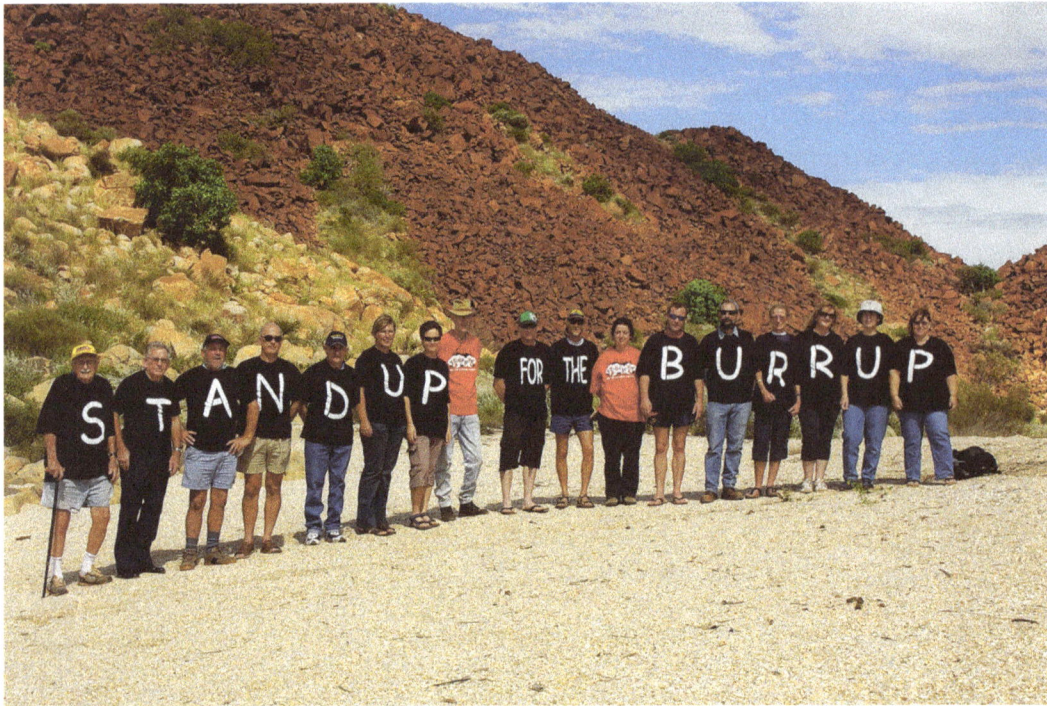

Figure 9.8: Part of the FARA 'Stand Up for the Burrup' action, Hearson Cove 2007, a campaign that has gone international.

Source: Photograph by Robbin Chapple.

As part of increasing public awareness of Murujuga, FARA facilitated an annual tour with a focus on visiting rock art sites. On one of these expeditions was retired CSIRO animal scientist John Black and his wife Claire. Their brief visit resulted in Black devoting enormous time and money to bringing an accurate scientific understanding of industrial emissions and effects on rock art. One of the first things Black did was to reanalyse the BRAMMC raw data, not publicly available and derived from the state government but paid for by industry. On reviewing the raw data, Black concluded that the published reports were flawed in terms of scientific methods, analyses and inferences, a view accepted by the Senate Environment and Communications Reference Committee (ECRC 2018). The conclusion drawn in these original reports and publicised by BRAMMC and the state was that industrial emissions would not have impacted the rock art, a finding that government used to justify further industrial development and to not impose emissions control measures.

Black is not the first to have applied a scientific methodology to understanding the geochemistry of Murujuga's rock art. Ian MacLeod, another English expatriate, based at the Museum of Western Australia, has been interested in the surface pH and microbiology on Murujuga's rocks. As with Black, there was concern that the rock varnish or patina, an iron and manganese-rich accretion, will dissolve under high acidic conditions, exposing the underlying, weathered, altered clay-rich layer, resulting in removal of the petroglyphs (Black et al. 2017a, 2017b; MacLeod 2005). At issue is that the pH readings taken on rock surfaces of Murujuga have gone from near-neutral (7) to between 4.2 and 3.6, representing a ten-thousandfold increase in acid conditions, seen as a consequence of industrial airborne emissions (Ian MacLeod pers. comm. 2017). Although recently it has been suggested that ammonia emissions, sea-spray and periodic rainfall events decrease the acidity (MacLeod and Fish 2021; see Smith et al. 2022 for contra view).

Figure 9.9: University students under the tutelage of Ben Gunn recording rock art at a site within the Hamersley Iron lease, Burrup Peninsula, during the 2010 field school.
Source: Photograph by Ken Mulvaney.

Once a member of the CSIRO team tasked by the state's BRAMMC with conducting the scientific studies into emissions and rock art, Eric Ramanaidou has continued his research involvement into Murujuga's petroglyphs. Following on from my own research into understanding the rock art sequence (Mulvaney 2015a), Ramanaidou attempted to provide age approximations for the petroglyphs using a field portable reflectance spectrometer, giving numerical values to the colour-contrast between the engraved surface and the adjacent rock surface (Ramanaidou and Fonteneau 2019). This research is admirable, but as with the original CSIRO studies, would have benefited from the inclusion of rock art experts' advice in the application of the investigation, thus resulting in more accurate and applicable data.

The Centre for Rock Art Research and Management (CRAR+M) at the University of Western Australia was established in 2010 with funding assistance from Rio Tinto. CRAR+M's director, Jo McDonald, who came on board in 2012, developed a research institution attracting numerous other rock art scholars, most from overseas including Liam Brady (Canada by way of Monash University), Jamie Hampson (UK), Sven Ouzman (South Africa) and Leslie Zubieta (Mexico). Another of these, Englishman Ben Smith, arrived from South Africa in 2013, and is currently involved along with Black and geochemist Ron Watkins in a FARA-sponsored study. The focus is on Murujuga rock samples to develop methods for determining the impacts of emissions on the chemistry and morphology of the rock patina. In addition, the program aims to develop ways of determining the microbes present on the rocks and the impacts of pollutants on microbial types and numbers. It is these microbes that develop the accretion that slow down the rate of erosion of the rock surface.

Research into the petroglyphs and other aspects of Murujuga archaeology continues today through CRAR+M, much of this by way of an Australian Research Council Linkage Project: Murujuga Dynamics of the Dreaming (LP140100393) and through an annually run field school jointly managed with Rio Tinto (Figure 9.9). Increases in research have provided the opportunity for Traditional Owners to re-engage with Murujuga outside the usual industrial development remit. Engagements with heritage professionals have enabled MAC staff to gain specialist experience and for Elders to pass on site-restricted knowledge to the next generation. The benefit to understanding the National Heritage Place is that there is a much more accurate and digitised record of the character of the heritage values across the islands. With nearly 32,000 petroglyphs, over 1000 grinding patches, and 680 stone features documented, archaeological excavation occurring at 15 locations and 117 new radiocarbon dates, the efforts of CRAR+M and Rio Tinto have greatly increased our understanding of the archaeology of Murujuga.

Discussion

Many Australians generally have been and continue to be slow to recognise and appreciate the cultural heritage values of this continent, preferring to conjure historical realities from a Eurocentric perspective. This was so clearly exemplified by Australian Prime Minister Scott Morrison's mistaken notion of a Cook 'circumnavigation' re-enactment as the way to celebrate the 250th anniversary of Cook's entry into Botany Bay, NSW. Bednarik (2006:Figure 135 caption) made the observation and asked:

> Western Australia is one million square miles of mostly unoccupied land. It has one of the world's lowest densities of population. Why does one of the world's greatest cultural assets and most sacred places have to share its location with the continent's largest industrial estate?

This is an issue raised by many since the 1970s, with the most active voices being those from people not born in Australia. Is it that individuals from other countries, holding a deep interest and awareness of their own nations' cultural past, show a keener interest than the home-grown white population in what they find when in Australia?

Understandably, people in the resource sector are eager for commercial ventures, such as Woodside CEO Peter Coleman who wants his 'Burrup Hub' realised, a concept of Murujuga housing the largest gas and oil-processing operations in the world. His vision is driving state government thinking about Murujuga, exposing the problematic notion that industry and cultural heritage can 'coexist'. Physically this cannot be the case, for putting industry anywhere on Murujuga results in the devastation of cultural heritage. This belief of coexistence is in fact a collision over heritage and commerce, driven by people with the desire to continue industrial expansion across Murujuga regardless of the impact to environment and heritage. As many concerned individuals and conservation groups have said, there is plenty of suitable land for industry elsewhere, especially when considering the distances required in moving the product.

Mexican researcher José Antonio González Zarandona has written extensively on the clash of perspectives, where Murujuga's contested space of iron ore, petroleum and fertiliser product has pushed aside an ancient, inscribed landscape (e.g. Zarandona 2011). Appalled by what he saw, Zarandona (2020) equates what is happening with Murujuga as to that of the 2001 Taliban militias' destruction of the Bamiyan Buddha statues in Afghanistan.

When the Australian Heritage Council included Murujuga on the National Heritage List, they described the place as 'a masterpiece of human creative genius', reiterating this opinion a number of years later (AHC 2012:2). For many, it is intolerable that such a culturally rich place should be at risk by industry, as well as associated footprint impacts, population pressures and chemical emissions. Over the decades, there have been many people, of sundry nationalities, devoting time and effort into raising public awareness of the cultural significance of Murujuga. Why, then, is it that individuals in particular positions within industry and government employ, can have so much influence? What system of society negates those voices calling for reason and protection?

This does not need to be the case. It is not simply a matter of conservation versus industry, for since 2003 the iron ore company transporting products out through Murujuga ports has employed a heritage professional to advise the company on matters pertinent to Murujuga to ensure the company maintains Virili's legacy of site protection and management. Company values were never diminished by such actions, and shareholders did not lose out. Instead, a social licence to operate and 'green' credibility were gained.

The federal government website on National Heritage Places states that '[a] balance between heritage management and economic prosperity is being achieved' (Australian Government Department of Agriculture, Water and the Environment n.d.a). But how can this be so, given the rapacious mining interests coupled with inept government ministers and public servants that has seen the progressive degradation of the cultural landscape? Even when there is legislation intended to manage and protect, there is often reticence to enforce. The Federal Department of Environment and Energy's own findings show that 20 per cent of projects were in breach of their approval conditions. However, a departmental spokesperson stated that no company was prosecuted, instead the department 'relied on administrative measures such as variations to conditions of approval, revisions to management plans, conservation agreements and warnings' (Australian Government Department of Environment and Energy 2016). Despite the potential of harm to National Heritage Values through breaches of operational conditions, the department has not changed its way of operating, as evidenced during the Senate enquiry a couple of years later (ECRC 2018).

Concerns over the impacts of industrial emissions, as mentioned above, were raised 20 years ago, particularly by Bednarik (2002), that eventually resulted in the establishment of the state-sponsored formation in 2003 of BRAMMC. As these findings are now discredited, additional studies are necessary to understand the potential of the rock art to survive airborne industrial emissions (Black et al. 2017a; ECRC 2018). This new program of investigation is part of the state government's Murujuga Rock Art Strategy of 2017. Although new scientific studies are yet to be implemented, further industrial expansion is approved by the state government.

The Burrup Rock Art Strategy, now rebranded as the Murujuga Rock Art Strategy, has replaced the BRAMMC, with the intention to be a monitoring, analysis and decision-making framework to protect Aboriginal rock art located on Murujuga (DWER 2019). As part of the strategy, Murujuga Rock Art Stakeholder Reference Group exists to provide advice to the state department and minister; to consult, inform and educate other stakeholders, and inform others on state government matters relating to Murujuga rock art (DWER 2019:53). The Reference Group comprises 16 members: a MAC representative and an independent chair; one local, seven state and one federal representative; three representatives from industry; a CRAR+M representative, and Dr John Black as the only named individual member. Only the CRAR+M representative among these 16 members has any specialist expertise in rock art, and few have a primary interest in the protection of Murujuga petroglyphs.

Science does show that the pH levels on the rocks have become more acidic over time, and that the iron and magnesium compounds are mobilising, breaking down the protective skin that has formed on the rock surfaces and protected the images for many tens of millennia (Black et al. 2017b; Pillans et al. 2008; Pillans and Fifield 2013). The only conceivable source for this is the airborne industrial emissions, but no qualitative or quantitative data exists on anthropogenic emissions and impact on Murujuga rock art. Given that the damaging effects of acid rain and altered pH levels is well known globally, it would be prudent under the precautionary principle that zero emissions is the only acceptable level. The National Pollutant Inventory managed by the Department of Environment and Water for the year 2018–2019 recorded that over 58,000 tonnes of emissions were released from Burrup industry (Australian Government Department of

Agriculture, Water and the Environment n.d.b). Currently, Woodside Petroleum has applied to expand their operations to allow development of their Scarborough and Browse gas resources through Woodside's proposed Burrup Hub. Such expansion would see a total carbon footprint of around 6 billion tonnes over its 50-year life, with combined annual emissions of 139 million tonnes (Robin Chapple pers. comm. 2020).

In recent years, the parliamentary effort of Hon. Robin Chapple (MLC) to hold the government to account over commercial decisions that are counter to the protection of Murujuga's rock art has been relentless. His numerous Legislative Council 'Questions Without Notice' reveal the bias of the answering ministers, the ineptitude of their advisers and obfuscation by departmental staff. In consort with FARA and John Black, Chapple continues to defend the unique, ancient and irreplaceable petroglyphs of Murujuga through regulatory processes. Without their efforts, few in Western Australia would be aware of, or object to, the continued destruction wrought by industry on Murujuga.

'Cultural landscapes' and 'intangible heritage', concepts that have been understood for decades, are becoming more widely utilised in heritage management institutions. Traditional Owners have rights to access ancestral places and responsibilities in protection of their cultural heritage. There is also the principle of intergenerational equity that should ensure this matchless heritage is there for the benefit of all generations to come. This is a concept that neither the State Environment Protection Authority nor the Department of Agriculture, Water and Environment (formally Department of Environment and Energy) seem to understand when making deliberations on commercial development applications or when investigating regulatory breaches. Industry is an anathema to this cultural landscape. Many countries around the world would not knowingly put industry in a place of such cultural importance.

Conclusion

There is no doubt that the petroglyphs of Murujuga are a masterpiece of human creativity; it is also evident that right from the early days of rock art research, practitioners engaged with the Aboriginal custodians of the place. Imbued with singular personalities, international backgrounds and commercial and political influences, the last 50 years has seen a shift from site documentation and attribute analysis to one of attempting to place the rock art into its wider sociocultural context. Engaging the Traditional Custodians not just as knowledge holders but as the rightful owners of this world-significant cultural heritage has been instrumental in the progress to better recognition and management.

The documentation of the Murujuga petroglyphs transcends the shift in rock art research from the notion of images as simple narratives of everyday encounters, what people saw and hunted, to understanding that they reflect Dreaming beings, have spiritual essence and are integral to the belief systems of the Aboriginal people. Much of this conceptual shift was aided by the influence of Pat Vinnicombe. In her tranquil and professional way, Vinnicombe influenced government decision-making, brought rock art into professional archaeology and assisted meaningful Aboriginal engagement. Her premature death in 2003 certainly put back the progress to international recognition and held back formation of adequate protection and management of Murujuga's petroglyphs.

World Heritage nomination processes have commenced after some 40 years. I know of no other place that demonstrates 50,000 years of human ingenuity marked by so many petroglyphs. Yet for many Australians, Murujuga, like most of the Pilbara, is seen as a place of mineral wealth, and the petroglyph-adorned rock slopes as the mullock heaps of mining operations (see Figure 9.2).

Essentially, it has been the efforts of foreign individuals that have endeavoured to get Murujuga into the national consciousness, working for Aboriginal cultural heritage to be valued and for appreciation of its cultural significance. It cannot be clearer: for the Murujuga petroglyphs to survive, industrial emissions must be eliminated, or reduced to as near zero as technology allows, and any future industrial development has to be placed away from the Dampier Archipelago. Industrial representatives and those in government continue with the mantra of coexistence, but what has occurred in the last 50 years proves that 50,000 years of culture heritage can be unhesitatingly erased from existence.

References

AHC (Australian Heritage Council) 2012. *The potential outstanding universal value of the Dampier Archipelago site and threats to that site.* Australian Heritage Council, Canberra.

Aluminium 1972. Rock art of the Dampier archipelago. Number 7(December):1–7.

Australian Government Department of Agriculture, Water and the Environment n.d.a. *National Heritage Places – Dampier Archipelago (including Burrup Peninsula).* Report. Available at: www.environment. gov.au/heritage/places/national/dampier-archipelago (accessed 1 April 2020).

Australian Government Department of Agriculture, Water and the Environment n.d.b. *National Pollutant Inventory.* Available at: www.npi.gov.au/npidata (accessed 14 April 2020).

Australian Government Department of Environment and Energy 2016. Compliance monitoring program 2016–2017. Department of Environment and Energy, Canberra.

Bednarik, R.G. 1977. A survey of prehistoric sites in the Tom Price region, north Western Australia. *Archaeology and Physical Anthropology in Oceania* 12(1):51–76.

Bednarik, R.G. 2002. The survival of the Murujuga (Burrup) petroglyphs. *Rock Art Research* 19(1):29–40.

Bednarik, R.G. 2006. *Australian apocalypse: The story of Australia's greatest cultural monuments.* Occasional AURA Publication No. 14. Australian Rock Art Research Association, Melbourne.

Bednarik, R.G. 2016. *Myths about rock art.* Archaeopress Publishing Ltd, Oxford. doi.org/10.2307/j.ctvx rq1jr.

Bird, C. and S.J. Hallam 2006. *A review of archaeology and rock art in the Dampier Archipelago.* National Trust of Australia (WA), Perth.

Black, J., I Box and S. Diffey 2017a. Inadequacies of research used to monitor change to rock art and regulate industry on Murujuga ('Burrup Peninsula'), Australia. *Rock Art Research* 34(2):130–148.

Black, J.L., I. MacLeod and B.W. Smith 2017b. Theoretical effects of industrial emissions on colour change at rock art sites on Burrup Peninsula, Western Australia. *Journal of Archaeological Science: Reports* 12(2017):457–462. doi.org/10.1016/j.jasrep.2017.02.026.

BRAMMC (Burrup Rock Art Monitoring Management Committee) 2009. *Report and recommendations to the Minister for State Development.* Report. Available at: www.dsd.wa.gov.au/burruprockart (accessed 1 March 2009).

CSIRO (Commonwealth Scientific and Industrial Research Organisation) 2009. *Burrup Peninsula Aboriginal petroglyphs 2004-8: Colour change and spectral mineralogy.* CSIRO Publishing, Clayton.

DAS (Department of Aboriginal Sites, Western Australian Museum) 1979. Dampier Archipelago liquefied natural gas project: A survey for Aboriginal sites. Unpublished. Aboriginal Sites Department, Western Australian Museum, Perth.

DAS 1980. A proposal for the archaeological investigation of and preservation of Aboriginal sites in Dampier Archipelago. Unpublished. Aboriginal Sites Department, Western Australian Museum, Perth.

DAS 1984. Dampier Archaeological Project: Survey and salvage of Aboriginal sites on portion of the Burrup Peninsula for Woodside Offshore Petroleum Pty Ltd. Catchment areas, geomorphic zones and tabulations. Department of Aboriginal Sites, Western Australian Museum, Perth.

Dix, W.C. 1977. Facial representations in Pilbara rock engravings. In P.J. Ucko (ed.), *Form in Indigenous art: Schematisation in the art of Aboriginal Australia and prehistoric Europe,* pp. 277–285. Australian Institute of Aboriginal Studies, Canberra.

Dix, W.C. and F.L. Virili 1977. Prehistoric petroglyphs of the Dampier Archipelago, north western Australia. *Bollettino del Centro Camuno di Studi Preistorici* 16:87–110.

DWER (Department of Water and Environmental Regulation, Western Australia) 2019. *Murujuga rock art strategy.* Department of Water and Environmental Regulation, Perth.

ECRC (Senate Environment and Communications Committee) 2018. *Protection of Aboriginal rock art of the Burrup Peninsula.* The Senate Printing Unit, Parliament House, Canberra.

Flood, J. 1997. *Rock art of the Dreamtime: Images of ancient Australia.* Angus & Robertson, Hong Kong.

Gara, T.J. 1983. The Flying Foam massacre: An incident on the north-west frontier, Western Australia. In M. Smith (ed.), *Archaeology at ANZAAS 1983,* pp. 86–94. Western Australian Museum, Perth.

Hamersley News 1970. Rock engravings 1 May 1970:2.

Hamersley News 1973. First carving to Japan. 25 January 1973:1.

Hawke, S. and M. Gallagher 1989. *Noonkanbah: Whose land, whose law.* Fremantle Arts Centre Press, Fremantle.

Haynes, K.C. and H. Waldmann 2004. Dampier rock art precinct. *Trust News* 220:4–9.

Lorblanchet, M. 1983. Chronology of the rock engravings of Gum Tree Valley and Skew Valley near Dampier, WA. In M. Smith (ed.), *Archaeology at ANZAAS 1983,* pp. 189–184. Western Australian Museum, Perth.

Lorblanchet, M. 1992. The rock engraving of Gum Tree Valley and Skew Valley, Dampier, Western Australia: Chronology and functions of the sites. In J. McDonald and I.P. Haskovec (eds), *State of the art: Regional rock art studies in Australia and Melanesia,* pp. 39–59. AURA Publications, Melbourne.

Lorblanchet, M. 2018. *Archaeology and petroglyphs of Dampier (Western Australia): An archaeological investigation of Skew Valley and Gum Tree Valley.* Technical Reports of the Australian Museum, Online, Number 27. doi.org/10.3853/j.1835-4211.27.2018.

MacLeod, I.D. 2005. Effects of moisture, micronutrient supplies and microbiological activity on the surface pH of rocks in the Burrup Peninsula. In I. Verger (ed.), *14th triennial meeting, The Hague, 12–16 September 2005: Preprints (ICOM Committee for Conservation),* pp. 386–393. Earthscan Ltd, Den Haag.

MacLeod, I. and W. Fish 2021. Determining decay mechanisms on engraved rock art sites using pH, chloride ion and redox measurements with an assessment of the impact of cyclones, sea salt and nitrate ions on acidity. Paper presented to the ICOM-CC 19th Triennial Conference Preprints, Beijing, 17–21 May 2021.

Markley, T., M. Wells, E. Ramanaidou, D. Lau and D. Alexander 2015. *Burrup Peninsula Aboriginal Petroglyphs: Colour change & spectral mineralogy 2004–2014.* Confidential Report t # EP1410003. CSIRO, Australia.

McDonald, J. 2015. I must go down to the seas again: Or, what happens when the sea comes to you? Murujuga rock art as an environmental indicator for Australia's north-west. *Quaternary International* 385:124–135. doi.org/10.1016/j.quaint.2014.10.056.

McDonald, J. and P. Veth 2009. Dampier Archipelago petroglyphs: Archaeology, scientific values and national heritage listing. *Archaeology in Oceania* 44:49–69. doi.org/10.1002/j.1834-4453.2009. tb00068.x.

Mulvaney, K.J. 2011. Dampier Archipelago: Decades of development and destruction. *Rock Art Research* 28(1):17–25.

Mulvaney, K.J. 2015a. *Murujuga Marni – Rock art of the macropod hunters and the mollusc harvesters.* UWA Press, Perth.

Mulvaney, K.J. 2015b. Burrup Peninsula: Cultural landscape and industrial hub, a 21st century conundrum. *Landscape Research* 20(6):759–772. doi.org/10.1080/01426397.2015.1057804.

Pilbara News 2018. Urea factory a step closer. 2 May 2018:14.

Pillans, B. and L.K. Fifield 2013. Erosion rates and weathering history of rock surfaces associated with Aboriginal rock art engravings (petroglyphs) on Burrup Peninsula, Western Australia, from cosmogenic nuclide measurements. *Quaternary Science Reviews* 69(2013):98–106. doi.org/10.1016/j.quascirev.2013. 03.001.

Pillans, B., R.A. Eggelton, S.M. Eggins, L.K. Fifield and R.G. Roberts 2008. The nature, age and weathering history of rock surfaces associated with petroglyphs at Burrup Peninsula, Western Australia. Unpublished. The Australian National University, Canberra.

Ramanaidou, E.R. and L.C. Fonteneau 2019. Rocky relationships: The petroglyphs of the Murujuga (Burrup Peninsula and Dampier Archipelago) in Western Australia. *Australian Journal of Earth Sciences* 66(5):671–698. doi.org/10.1080/08120099.2019.1577299.

Sholl, R.J. 1868. Murder of policeman Griffis and three others by the natives. *Perth Gazette & W.A. Times.* 3 April:3.

SKM (Sinclair Knight Merz) 2009. *Burrup Rock Art Monitoring Program – Summary of study reports.* Sinclair Knight Merz, Perth.

Smith, B.W., J.L. Black, S. Hœrlé, M.A. Ferland, S.M. Diffey, J.T. Neumann and T. Geisler 2022. The impact of industrial pollution on the rock art of Murujuga, Western Australia. *Rock Art Research* 39(1):3–14.

Veth, P., E. Bradshaw, T. Gara, N. Hall, P. Haydock and P. Kendrick 1993. Burrup Peninsula Aboriginal Heritage Project. Unpublished. Department of Conservation and Land Management, Perth.

Veth, P., I. Ward, T. Manne, S. Ulm, K. Ditchfield, J. Dortch, F. Hook, F. Petchey, A. Hogg, D. Questiaux, M. Demuro, L. Arnold, N. Spooner, V. Levchenko, J. Skippington, C. Byrne, M. Basgall, D. Zeanah, D. Belton, P. Helmholz, S. Bajkan, R. Bailey, C. Placzek and P. Kendrick 2017. Early human occupation of a maritime desert, Barrow Island, north-west Australia. *Quaternary Science Reviews* 168:19–29. doi.org/10.1016/j.quascirev.2017.05.002.

Vinnicombe, P. 1976. *People of the eland: Rock paintings of the Drakensberg Bushman as a reflection of their life and thought.* University of Natal Press, Pietermaritzburg.

Vinnicombe, P. 1987. *Dampier Archaeological Project: Resource document, survey and salvage of Aboriginal sites, Burrup Peninsula, Western Australia.* Western Australian Museum, Perth.

Vinnicombe, P. 1997a. King Bay – Hearson Cove Aboriginal heritage survey. Unpublished. West Pilbara Land Council, Department of Resources Development, Perth.

Vinnicombe, P. 1997b. Maitland Heavy Industry Estate: Aboriginal heritage survey. Unpublished. West Pilbara Land Council, Department of Resources Development, Perth.

Vinnicombe, P. 2002. Petroglyphs of the Dampier Archipelago: Background to development and descriptive analysis. *Rock Art Research* 19(1):3–27.

Virili, F.L. 1977. Aboriginal sites and rock art of the Dampier Archipelago. In P.J. Ucko (ed.), *Form in Indigenous art: Schematisation in the art of Aboriginal Australia and prehistoric Europe*, pp. 439–451. Australian Institute of Aboriginal Studies, Canberra.

Ward, I., P. Larcombe, K. Mulvaney and C. Fandry 2013. The potential for the discovery of new submerged archaeological sites near Dampier Archipelago, Western Australia. *Quaternary International* 308–309(2013):216–229. doi.org/10.1016/j.quaint.2013.03.032.

Wright, B.J. 1965. Some Aboriginal rock engravings in the Roebourne-Hamersley Range area. *The Western Australian Naturalist* 9(5):97–118.

Wright, B.J. 1968. *Rock art of the Pilbara region, North-West Australia*. Occasional Papers in Aboriginal Studies 11. Australian Institute of Aboriginal Studies, Canberra.

Zarandona, J.A.G. 2011. The destruction of heritage: Rock art in the Burrup Peninsula. *The International Journal of the Humanities* 9(1):325–342. doi.org/10.18848/1447-9508/cgp/v09i01/43116.

Zarandona, J.A.G. 2020. *Murujuga: Rock art, heritage and landscape iconoclasm*. Penn Press, Pennsylvania. doi.org/10.9783/9780812296983.

10

Histories of rock art research in Western Australia's Kimberley, 1838–2000

Joakim Goldhahn, Sam Harper, Peter Veth and Sven Ouzman

Introduction

This article frames the history of rock art research in the Kimberley in north-western Australia through four tropes of colonialism. We distinguish three phases of research, starting with 'Explorers and colonisers' from 1838 to the early 1900s, followed by the move 'Towards an Indigenous understanding of Australian rock art' that derived from early missionary and ethnographic studies conducted during the first half of the twentieth century up to 1960, before developing into 'Diverging fields of rock art research' from the 1960s. We conclude our discussion around the year 2000 but refer to current research topics and discourses when apposite.

The Kimberley

Australia's Kimberley is acknowledged globally for the quantity and diversity of its rock art (Bindon 1997; Clottes 2002; David and McNiven 2018; McDonald and Veth 2012), some of which are still being produced and curated. Senior Traditional Owner Yornadaiyn Woolagoodja (2020:170) of the Woddordda Clan explains:

> There were special people who did that job to repaint the Wandjina. The people who belong to the area are supposed to go and paint the Wandjina to make them fresh. They knew what time to do it. It was not like a job, they just knew when to go. They would paint over and over the images so that the Wandjina knows the people are looking after him. They have been doing this since the Wandjina put themselves in Country.

Situated in north-west Australia, the Kimberley is a geographically and culturally distinct region that covers approximately 423,000 km² (Figure 10.1). Archaeological evidence shows the area was settled by people more than 50,000 years ago (Veth et al. 2019), though we acknowledge Aboriginal ontologies that recognise Aboriginal people have always been there. During the Last Glacial Maximum, some 26,500 to 19,000 years ago, the land area of the Kimberley would have been at least double its current size and constituted part of the now-submerged Sahul Shelf. Current sea levels stabilised approximately 7,000 to 6,000 years ago with a subtropical climate (Wood et al. 2016). The landscape is varied but dominated by Devonian sandstone formations crisscrossed by large river systems that transport annual monsoonal rains to the sea.

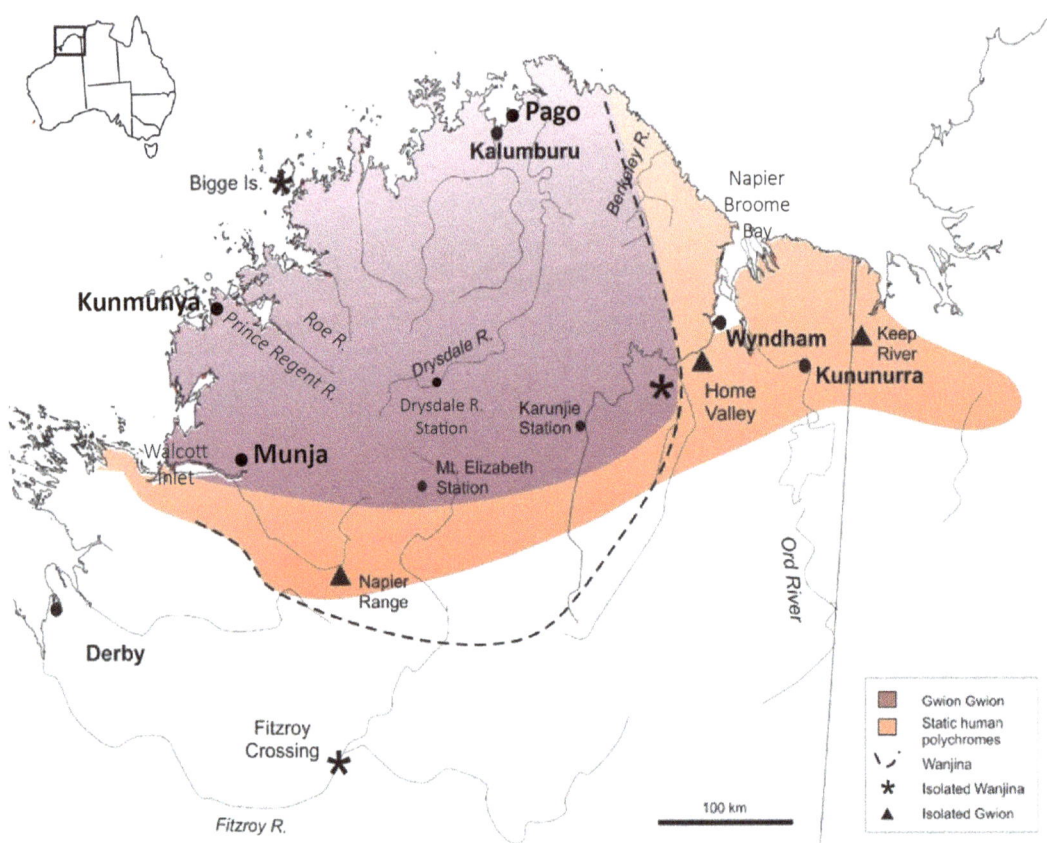

Figure 10.1: Australia's Kimberley, showing places mentioned.

Source: Map developed by Harper from Akerman 2016 and Walsh 2000.

When first encountered by outsiders, there were at least 50 Aboriginal languages spoken in the Kimberley. Today four major languages are practised, Bunaban, Jarragan, Nyul Nyulan and Worrorran, each with up to nine distinguishable dialects. These are part of the non-Pama-Nyungan language bloc stretching across the northern coast of Australia eastward to Cape York (McConvell 1996). Since 1992, Native Title determinations have resulted in c. 84 per cent of the Kimberley now being managed through Indigenous Protected Areas and Aboriginal Corporations, with 13 ranger groups who 'Care for Country'. There are also non-Aboriginal pastoral, industrial and tourism leases that, together with Commonwealth and National Park lands, both hinder and promote Aboriginal access to traditional lands and cultural sites. Programs and projects aiming to reconnect people to Country are ongoing, and rock art plays an increasingly important role as a heritage and health asset, as reflected in various Healthy Country Plans (e.g. Balanggarra/KLC 2011).

Both genetic research (Malaspinas et al. 2016; Nagle et al. 2017) and archaeological reconstructions (Veth et al. 2019, 2021; Wood et al. 2016) confirm what Kimberley Aboriginal people have stated as their primary origin narrative: that they have always been on Country. More broadly, archaeological analyses that focus on symbolic behaviours increasingly indicate that the creation of art was part of peoples' cultural repertoire from the time they first settled Australia (Aubert et al. 2017; Clarkson et al. 2017; Veth et al. 2019). To date, the oldest directly dated rock art of *in situ* naturalistic depictions of Irregular Animal Infill and Gwion Gwion imagery is determined at c. 17,000 BP and 12,000 BP, respectively (Finch et al. 2020; Finch et al. 2021), although the dating of the art has only just begun and further results may reveal a broader range of dates. There is also a 28,000 BP charcoal marked plaque from Arnhem Land (David et al. 2013). However, if one broadens our definition of 'rock art', this date can be pushed back to at least 42,700 BP to account for the pigment sprayed on a rock slab from Carpenters Gap in the southern Kimberley (O'Connor and Fankhauser 2001).

All Kimberley rock art was created by Aboriginal people, although again we acknowledge Aboriginal belief systems that what we call 'rock art' are often entities in their own right, created independently of human agency. Some rock art is still made and maintained. For example, Wandjina (also 'Wanjina') are repainted/refreshed according to cultural protocols (Blundell and Woolagoodja 2005; Woolagoodja 2020). Aboriginal people enrich our Western understanding in sharing knowledge that some Wandjina 'put themselves' or their 'shadows' in the landscape during the time of creation, known to them as *lalai* or *larlan* (e.g. Blundell and Woolagoodja 2005; Chalarimeri 2001; Mangolamara et al. 2018; Mowaljarlai and Malnic 1993; Ngarjno et al. 2000). Other rock art traditions such as Gwion Gwion (formerly 'Bradshaw') are said to be created by Kujon, the sandstone shrike thrush (*Colluricincla woodwardi*), an ancestral being who taught people how to dance and conduct ceremonies, and who also created rock art (Ngarjno et al. 2000:120; Schulz 1956:47; cf. Rainsbury 2009:60). Many other rock art 'styles', 'traditions' and place markings exist in the Kimberley, not all of which have been documented or described in academic contexts.

Picturing Kimberley rock art research

Histories of archaeology in general, and the history of Kimberley rock art research in particular, are often pictured through a modernistic world view outlining defining moments in time: watersheds that delineate a 'before and after'. The first dating of an Aboriginal occupation site in Australia to the Pleistocene (Mulvaney 1964) or Maria Sanz de Sautuola's discovery of the bison in Altamira cave in Spain (Madariga de la Campa 2001), are classic examples used to generate synchronic picture histories of archaeology. Stories about how outsiders first 'discovered' and made known Kimberley rock art are no exception (see Akerman 2016; Crawford 1968; Rainsbury 2009; Walsh 2000). Such stories are often redeployed as a tactic to centre and legitimise archaeological practice, including rock art research. These accounts also naturalise otherwise politicised knowledge projects by presenting a history of archaeology as a natural and noble part of outsiders' research quest to learn more about the past. Seldom are these events discussed from an Indigenous perspective (but see Mangolamara et al. 2018; O'Connor et al. 2008; Woolagoodja 2020), and how Aboriginal people had agency and participated in such 'discoveries'. Pioneering examples of the latter include Olsen and Russell's (2019) chronicling of how Aboriginal people, with their profound knowledge of Country, constitute an essential part of outsiders' mapping of the flora and fauna in Australia. The same is true for Kimberley rock art research (e.g. Blundell and Woolagoodja 2005; Crawford 2001; Redmond 2017), but many of these stories still wait to be written.

Some reasons for such 'dissociative' history writing are explored by McNiven and Russell (2005) in their unpacking of how Australian archaeology was forged through a double manoeuvre that removed Aboriginal people from their past while archaeology appropriated it (i.e. Trigger 1984). This imperial and colonial history unfolded as distinct tropes, primarily:

- *Progressivism* viewed European history as exceptional and progressive, which left Indigenous cultures and other nations as 'living fossils' of earlier stages of human evolution.
- *Migrationism* suggested that First Australians were not the 'original inhabitants' but had replaced an earlier 'race' often described as 'alien' and/or 'mystic' with a 'higher degree of culture'.
- *Diffusionism,* often focused on why some cultural traits among First Australians were 'advanced' by invoking contact with outsiders holding advanced aesthetic practices.

- *Subjectation* casts First Australians as objects for specific scientific and academic endeavours using an alienating esoteric language and academic jargon that 'diminishes the level to which laypeople can interact with the discipline' (McNiven and Russell 2005:7–9; e.g. Lubbock 1870; Nilsson 1868).

We touch on some of these entangled tropes but also reveal more progressive processes that have empowered Aboriginal people to achieve increased control over their cultural heritage and engage in a relational 'two-way of learning' with academics (e.g. Porr and Bell 2012). Because colonial tropes have a penchant to re-emerge, especially during periods of conservatism, we structure our history of research along a familiar linear timeline. We start with 'Explorers and colonisers' from 1838, pass through 'Towards an Indigenous understanding of Australian rock art', which explores early missionaries and ethnographic studies during the first half of the twentieth century, before concluding with 'Diverging fields of rock art research' that occurred from the 1960s onwards. We conclude our discussion around 2000 albeit with reference to current research topics and discourses (e.g. Akerman 2015a, 2016; David et al. 2019; Finch et al. 2020; Gunn et al. 2019; Harper et al. 2020; O'Connor et al. 2013; Ross and Travers 2013; Travers and Ross 2016; Veth et al. 2018, 2019).

Explorers and colonisers (1838–1920)

Despite centuries of sporadic visits of Dutch, French and English explorers, and visits by Macassan trepangers that predate European incursions (Crawford 2001; Mulvaney 1989), the earliest known documentation of Kimberley rock art was made by Lieutenant George Grey in 1838. Grey, who later occupied influential positions such as governor of South Australia, governor of the Cape of Good Hope and governor and premier of New Zealand, led an expedition to map the north-western corner of Australia in an attempt to expand economic opportunities for the emerging Swan River Colony centred in Fremantle.

Grey and his party's relationships with Aboriginal people were characterised by mistrust and fear. During his journey, local Wororran (Worrorran) people were observed through smoke on the horizon from fires, and more directly through encounters with habitation sites, fireplaces, scattered objects, 'a very neat Native oven', with Grey frequently spotting 'rude drawings scratched upon the tree' (Grey 1841:176, 113). Their first physical encounter was disastrous. On 22 December 1837 Grey's party was 'attacked' (Grey 1841:105–106), probably because they did not follow established cultural protocols on how to enter and travel through other people's Country (Blundell et al. 2018). There was another attack in February, when Grey was struck by several spears and one Aboriginal man was killed (McGlashan 2012:64). Grey would later enact the *Aboriginal Witnesses Act 1844*, which excluded Aboriginal witnesses in genocide/mass murder trials.

Rock art was first spotted on 11 March 1838 during the exploration of what Grey named the Glenelg River (Grey 1841:175). After this first 'discovery', Grey's party became more observant and started to look for art sites more enthusiastically. The most 'remarkable paintings' were 'discovered' on 26 March, at a site known today as Gonjorong's Cave (Blundell et al. 2018). When entering the gallery, Grey (1841:201) looked up to discover 'a most extraordinary large figure peering down upon' him (Figure 10.2), which he goes on to describe thus:

> It would be impossible to convey in words an adequate idea of this uncouth and savage figure … Its head was encircled by bright red rays, something like the rays which one sees proceeding from the sun when depicted on the sign-board of a public house; inside of this came a broad stripe of very brilliant red, which was coped by lines of white, but both inside and outside of this red space were narrow stripes of a still deeper red, intended probably to mark its boundaries; the face was painted vividly white, and the eyes black, being however surrounded by red and yellow lines; the body, hands, and arms were outlined in red, the body being curiously painted with red stripes and bars. (Grey 1841:202)

Figure 10.2: Grey's documentations of rock art during his 1838 trip to west Kimberley.
Source: Grey 1841.

This is the first known recording of Kimberley rock art. Grey noticed about 50–60 paintings in this cave. In another part of this site complex – today known as Dondandjik – he spotted four 'vividly coloured' heads of Wandjina, which Sam Woolagoodjah later identified as Mulu Mulu, a malevolent form of Wandjina (Crawford 1968:65; cf. Schulz 1956:16–17). He also saw an 'ellipse being of a bright yellow dotted over with red lines and spots', and a 'rather humorous sketch (Number 4) which represented a native in the act of carrying a kangaroo'. He also noticed 'the stamp of a hand and arm' (Grey 1841:202–204). Leaving the shelter, Grey encountered an 'intaglio' of a human head 'cut in a rock' (Grey 1841:205–206), which has subsequently been re-located and is a natural rock feature (Figure 10.2; see Crawford 1968:65, Figures 47–48; McGlashan 2012:66). He 'sketched' these images and published them in his ensuing travelogue (Figure 10.2).

Three days later the party encountered another shelter with paintings. In a secluded area, Grey found a slab that 'formed a natural seat' and on the ceiling above he spotted an alluring Wandjina, described as:

> a man, ten feet six inches in length, clothed from the chin downwards in a red garment which reached to the wrists and ankles; beyond this red dress the feet and hands protruded and were badly executed. The face and head of the figure were enveloped in a succession of circular bandages or rollers, or what appeared to be painted to represent such. These were coloured red, yellow, and white; and the eyes were the only features represented on the face.

> Upon the highest bandage or roller a series of lines were painted in red, but, although so regularly done as to indicate that they have some meaning, it was impossible to tell whether they were intended to depict written characters or some ornament for the head. (Grey 1841:214)

Grey published his travelogue in 1841. His sketches sparked great scholarly interest, not least since Grey depicted the anthropomorphic beings wearing clothes (Figure 10.2) while noting that the Aboriginal people he encountered 'were in a perfect state of nature' (Crawford 1968:66). Grey's coloured illustration included red finger strokes in the headdress of the Wandjina (Figure 10.2), which subsequent scholars misunderstood as letters and which led to speculation including their representing a writing system that 'proved' non-Aboriginal authorship of this rock art (Crawford 1968:67; McCarthy 1958:56–57). Grey (1841:263) was not convinced Aboriginal people made this art and left their authorship open to conjecture:

> With regard to the age of these paintings we had no clue whatever to guide us. It is certain that they may have been very ancient … but, whatever may have been the age of these paintings, it is scarcely probable that they could have been executed by a self-taught savage. Their origin therefore I think must still be open to conjecture.

The site was re-located in 1947 by Howard Coate, who painted his name and date there. It was revisited in 1948 by Elkin (1948) when it became clear that Grey's documentation was very much a product of its time – careful but incorrect in many details (Donaldson 2013:254–259; Rainsbury 2009:17). This colonial migrationist idea disassociates the rock art from Aboriginal authorship – a legacy that still reverberates today (e.g. Weiler and Weiler 2017).

Just over half a century later, Gwion Gwion (formerly 'Bradshaw') rock art was described and documented by pastoralist Joseph Bradshaw who had taken up a lease of a million acres that he called Marigui, situated in the area now covered by Drysdale River Station. After reaching what he erroneously thought to be the Prince Regent River (actually, the Roe River), Bradshaw stated in his diary of 16 April 1891 that he encountered: 'Aboriginal paintings which appeared to be of great antiquity, and I do not attribute them to the present representations of the Black race' (quoted in Walsh 2000:9). The day after he made 'some sketches of the native drawings' – four to be precise (Rainsbury 2013). He announced the 'discoveries' in a lecture given at the Royal Geographic Society of Australia in Melbourne in September 1891. In the ensuing account of the journey, Bradshaw stated that he encountered 'numerous caves and recesses in the rocks, the walls of which were adorned with native paintings, coloured in red, black, brown, yellow white and pale blue' (Figure 10.3), and he described how:

> Some of the human figures were life-size, the bodies and limbs very attenuated, and represented as having numerous tassel-shaped adornments appended to the hair, neck, waist, arms, and legs; but the most remarkable fact in connection with these drawings is that wherever a profile face is shown the features are of a most pronounced aquiline type, quite different from those of any natives we encountered. Indeed, looking at some of the groups, one might almost think himself viewing the painted walls of an Egyptian temple. These sketches seemed to be of great age, but over the surface of some of them were drawn in fresher colors smaller and more recent scenes, and rude forms of animals, such as the kangaroo, wallaby, porcupine, crocodile, &c. (Bradshaw 1892:100)

Bradshaw was entranced with the aesthetic quality of the Gwion Gwion figures, which clashed with his (mis)perception of Aboriginal people. He was aware of Grey's travelogue, as he observed 'in one or two places … alphabetical characters somewhat similar to those seen by Sir George Grey' (Bradshaw 1892:100). Revealingly, none of these rock paintings were sketched. The 'Bradshaw' type site remained 'lost' for over a century – primarily because Bradshaw's geography was confused – he was on the Roe River rather than the Prince Regent. The site was finally re-located in 1997 (Parker et al. 2007) and published by Walsh three years later (2000:8–12, Plates 19, 21–25).

Figure 10.3: Examples of Bradshaw's documentation of Gwion Gwion rock art from his visit to Kimberley in 1891.

Source: The original drawings are in the Berndt Museum of Anthropology at the University of Western Australia, published with their kind permission.

During the 1800s and early 1900s, the Kimberley became a moving colonial frontier, sparked by short-lived gold rushes, and crisscrossed by non-Indigenous explorers. Many outsiders could not avoid noticing and occasionally documenting rock art (e.g. Basedow 1925; Basset-Smith 1894; Conigrave 1938; Easton 1922; Explorer 1896; Forrest 1880; Mjöberg 1915, 2012; see Akerman 2016; Rainsbury 2016). Besides Grey and Bradshaw, Brockman's 1901 expedition was the next-most significant, as it systematically used photography to document much of the rock art encountered (Brockman 1902:Figures 4–6, 10, 12–13, 15–20, 23–26). For example, rare instances of portable stone slabs with Wandjina were recorded (Brockman 1902:Figures 20, 25). Brockman (1902:12) found the rock art intriguing but made only short notes about this 'remarkable custom'. He states that 'over the area in which these paintings occur, I frequently found the pigments used at the native camps' (Brockman 1902:12), which explicitly links the rock art with local Aboriginal people. In Appendix C to the report, F.M. House, the project photographer, like Grey, found that the depicted anthropomorphic beings wore 'clothes', which for him indicated that the artworks must 'date back before the advent of the first known white men' visited the Kimberley (Brockman 1902:18).

Grey's travelogue served to spark interest in Kimberley rock art. Bradshaw's 1891 lecture revitalised this interest. While only one of his four rock art sketches was published in 1892, some of the others were published two years later by Reverend J. Mathew (1894). Mathew opened his article with a blunt statement that said more about his world view than the artwork he tried to comprehend: 'The art of painting, has been so little practised by the aborigines [sic] of Australia, that to say they were ignorant of it altogether would not be far from the truth' (Mathew 1894:42). Grey's depiction of Wandjina was described as 'nearly in the military attitude of "Attention"'. Mathew (1894:44) thought the markings in the 'head-dress' resembled 'plain Roman letters'. His contemporaries suggested Morian or Japanese letters (Crawford 1968:67). Mathew proposed that the rock art was made by 'sacred men' from Sumatra (Mathew 1894:51). Turning to the artworks documented by Bradshaw, Mathew offered many suggestions for the foreign origin of the artists, including 'Phoenicians, Spaniards, Portuguese, and Hindus' (Mathew 1894:45), and even argued that they were depictions of Hindu gods (Mathew 1894:50).

Reverend Mathew is but one out of many nineteenth-century dilettantes who tried to make sense of the rock art documented and published by Grey and Bradshaw. Few if any unequivocally suggested Aboriginal authorship, in keeping with the nineteenth and early twentieth-century colonial milieu that held that 'certain elements of Australian Aboriginal culture are defined as advanced and therefore anomalous and exotic in origin' (McNiven and Russell 2005:8). This idea can be followed throughout twentieth-century rock art research (e.g. Walsh 1994, 1997a, 1997b, 2000), and it still finds new advocates in popular culture (e.g. Parker et al. 2007; Wilson 2006; Weiler and Weiler 2017; cf. Gray 2018; McNiven 2011; Porr 2017; Redmond 2002).

Towards an Indigenous understanding of Australian rock art (1900–1960)

Replacing such fact-absent colonial notions with substantive narratives describing the rock art and acknowledging Aboriginal authorship and custodianship was work undertaken by a diverse collection of individuals who took an active interest in Aboriginal culture and spent the time to learn about their customs and world views firsthand (Gray 2007). Spencer and Gillen's 1899 study *The native tribes of Central Australia* had a lasting impact on rock art research in Australia (e.g. Brady et al. 2018; Gunn 2000), and elsewhere (Bahn 1998; Goldhahn 2013; Layton 1992; Lewis-Williams 2002), and it is often celebrated as a decisive turning point. An often unsung hero in this context was R.H. Mathews (1893, 1896, 1898, N.B. unrelated to the Reverend Mathew), who published a series of dedicated studies on Aboriginal rock paintings and engravings in the 1890s and the early twentieth century (see Elkin 1949; McDonald 2008). Through his profession as a surveyor, Mathews came to know many Aboriginal people and started to conduct anthropological work with them (Elkin 1975). His studies about Aboriginal culture, objects, artworks, social structure, language and 'mythology' helped shape Australian anthropology and rock art research (Thomas 2007).

Missionaries and rock art

Pioneering studies of rock art using informed methodologies started in the Kimberley in the early 1900s through some of the earliest Christian missions (Blundell and Woolagoodja 2005). A pivotal example of this was Father Nicholas d'Emo who worked at the Cistercian Drysdale River mission at Pago, established in 1908 (Perez 1977). The missionaries were given a harsh welcome by the Wunambal. Inspired by Grey's travelogue, and after a more friendly relationship had been established, d'Emo started to document nearby rock art sites, and some of these recordings were published anonymously (Walsh 2000:12). By 1909, the mission had moved to the King Edward River and today's Kalumburu community. In 1910, d'Emo was visited by the naturalist Hill, who documented rock art at Napier Broome Bay and Parry Harbour, which included some Gwion Gwion figures that Mountford published in 1937. d'Emo continued to document rock art at more than 90 sites until 1913, with hundreds of figures, but most of these would remain unknown to rock art scholars until the end of the century (Rainsbury 2017). Copies of his documentation are kept in the Western Australian Museum, while Hill's are kept in the South Australian Museum.

Missions like Kalumburu and Kunmunya, as well as some 'refuge' homesteads (cf. Paterson and Wilson 2009), grew into safe havens where Aboriginal people from different clans and language groups in the west Kimberley could avoid the worst of the colonial excess (e.g. Elder 2003; Owen 2016). Such communities became nodes where people could gather, exchange experiences, and transfer cultural knowledge and protocols to coming generations (Blundell and Woolagoodja 2005; Crawford 2001; see also May et al. 2020 for a comparable situation in Arnhem Land). These enclaves enabled the noteworthy work of Reverend Love (1917) among the Worora.

Arriving in 1914 to work at the Presbyterian mission at Walcott Inlet, Love conducted research about the Worora, including the meaning and significance of their rock art. Love witnessed new paintings being made (Love 1917:35–36). He was one of the first outsiders to explore cosmologies connected to Wandjina and established their relationship to rain and maintenance ceremonies (Love 1917:37). Love left Kunmunya in 1915 but returned in 1927 when he took over as the leader of the mission.

Through close dialogue with the local Worora, Love recorded that every Wandjina has a proper name that relates to an ancestral being of a specific patrilineal clan. He recorded that rock art was crucial for some maintenance rituals, stating: 'they are to ensure the food supply of the present generation' (Love 1930:3–4). In early 1929, Love (1930:7) documented how Kánaway, an Adbalandi man of Malandum clan, described as a 'doctor' and *Ináiiri* by Love, went out on Country to 'take care of it'. A week later Love (1930:7) found 'three new paintings of a kunjáwarinya (freshwater tortoise), a bulgúja (dugong), and a liver of a stingray "ubúnu"'. Aboriginal people at the mission confirmed that these paintings were created by Kánaway. Around this time Love witnessed two senior men, named Indamoi and Wallamurra, repaint the Namarali Wandjina at Karndirrim, which would later appear through Yornadaiyn Woolagoodja's agency at the opening of the Sydney Olympic Games in 2000 (Blundell and Woolagoodja 2005:85–89; Woolagoodja 2020). He also made important observations about painting techniques and other cultural practices and beliefs concerning rock art (Love 1930).

In the end, Love (1930:7) found himself 'pleased to have established the fact that the rock paintings … are mainly subject to renewal, or fresh execution, periodically, by Worora men now living'. His popular book that describes his experience of living with *Stone Age Bushmen of today* (republished with the primary title *Kimberley people* by Welch in 2009) made a lasting impact in Australia and overseas and sparked a new interest in Aboriginal culture.

Early ethnographic research

The era between the Great War and World War II marks the beginning of a mostly positive change in attitudes towards Aboriginal people in Australia. This movement grew stronger when anthropological studies started to uncover some of the more obvious shortcomings of colonial social science (see Gray 2007). Spencer and Gillen's landmark study in 1899 was followed by new studies of Aboriginal people and their lifeworlds (e.g. Spencer 1914; see Elkin 1934) that led to a growing interest in Aboriginal culture. The first exhibition on *Australian Aboriginal art* was held in Melbourne in 1929 (Barrett and Kenyon 1929). It included bark paintings as well as photographs and documentations of rock art (e.g. Morphy 1998; Petersen et al. 2008). Several new scholars, such as F.D. McCarthy and C.P. Mountford, dedicated their careers to exploring Aboriginal artworks (see Clarke et al. Chapter 2, this volume). The first synthesis on 'Aboriginal Australian and Tasmanian rock carvings and paintings' was published by Davidson in 1936, in which he argued for an Aboriginal authorship of rock art in Australia (Davidson 1936:121–134).

This renewed interest in Aboriginal culture fostered ethnographic studies, with A.P. Elkin being the earliest scholar to conduct extensive fieldwork in the Kimberley (Wise 1985). Assisted by the now-reviled A.O. Neville, the 'Chief Protector of Aborigines' in Western Australia (Gray 1997) – and still known as 'Neville the Devil' among Kimberley people – Elkin dedicated 11 weeks between 1927 and 1928 to study rock art, mainly 'in the country of the Ungarinyin' (Elkin 1930a:257).

After visiting three rock art sites around Walcott Inlet close to Munja Station together with Traditional Owners, and sharing some of their cultural knowledge, Elkin found no reason to doubt the authorship of Wandjina: 'There do not seem to be any features of the wondjina and associated paintings that might be supposed foreign to the ideas and practices of the natives' (Elkin 1930a:274). In Beleguldo Cave, he obtained detailed information about the meaning of certain paintings and their significance, such as some head-ornaments of the figures, which had counterparts in ceremonial practices of his informants (Figure 10.4). On the puzzling question of why certain 'wondjina' were not depicted with a mouth, he got a frank answer: 'It cannot be done'. Through Elkin's dialogue with senior men, he could start to correct many earlier misinterpretations about Wandjina (Elkin 1930a:260–262, 274). For instance, from the state of the art, Elkin could see that they were repainted regularly, and some were even repainted during his visit:

> This operation should only be done at the beginning of the wet season, for the retouching causes rain to fall. As a matter of fact, a blackfellow who was with me retouched the eyes of the large wondjina with some charcoal while I was visiting the pictures, and, strangely enough, some light showers fell a few days later in the midst of the dry season. This did much to strengthen the aborigines' faith, and they did not fail to draw my attention to the cause of this unprecedented rain. (Elkin 1930a:261)

Contemporary understandings among Kimberley Aboriginal people suggests that Wandjina are kept 'fresh' so that their powers are regained and retained. This should be done regularly, or when they start to lose their lustre. Scientific analyses conducted by Morwood et al. (2010:5–6) revealed 38 layers of paint on a 'Wandjina-style snake depiction', spanning a c. 375-year period, suggesting repainting (on average) at least once a decade.

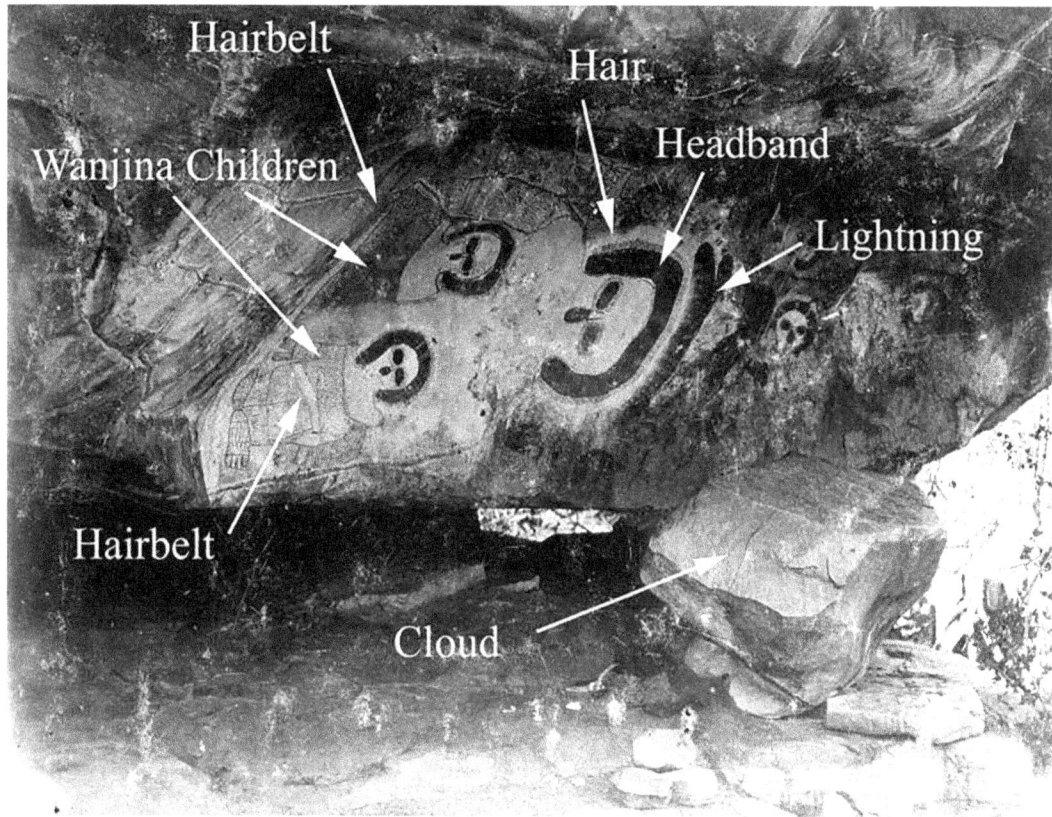

Figure 10.4: Photograph from Elkin's fieldwork in the late 1950s.
Source: Akerman 2016.

Elkin's enquiries into the meaning of Wandjina showed that many were linked to 'increase rituals' – that is, maintenance rituals. Certain Wandjina in the cave of Wiri Modangeri, on the Charnley River, were said to depict female Spirit Figures, and by repainting these 'women will have babies' (Elkin 1930a:262). Other images at the same site were said to help certain animals and bush food to procreate (Elkin 1930a:263). The third cave Elkin described was Bindjibi and it provided more of a challenge for him. The rock art gave plenty of evidence for repainting and contemporary use, but the 'somewhat faded red ochre' Gwion Gwion figures made Elkin (1930a:266) wonder about their authorship: 'It must, however, be admitted that the realistic and life-like representation is certainly superior to that which is usually seen in native galleries' (Elkin 1930a:265). Later in the same article, he concluded that 'The shape of heads, head-dress and body-forms suggests an origin and workmanship other than native' (Elkin 1930a:275), demonstrating the persistent colonial trope of migrationism (see also Capell 1939; Lommel 1966; Mountford 1937).

That said, Elkin did consult with Traditional Owners and recounted many significant cultural practices and objects in the caves and shelters, as well as in their surroundings, such as some stone arrangements that were described as manifestations of *Ungud* (Elkin 1930b), often referred to as the Rainbow Serpent by outsiders. Elkin's (1930a:272) statement that 'It is, however, hazardous to propose meanings without the assistance of the men … to which the gallery belongs', still holds.

Love and Elkin's studies included an active dialogue with Aboriginal people to learn from their cultural knowledge about Kimberley rock art. It opened up new understandings and made it clear that a more holistic approach was needed to understand Aboriginal lifeworlds. Elkin's novel study of rock art was soon followed by analyses of other aspects of Aboriginal culture, including Aboriginal stone arrangements (Love 1929), 'mythology' (Capell 1939; Elkin 1930b;

Love 1935), social organisation (Elkin 1932), totemism (Elkin 1933), and more (Elkin 1945). Some of this work was groundbreaking. For example, Phyllis Kaberry (1935, 1936, 1939), a student of Elkin's, spent three years in the East Kimberley, pioneering anthropological work with Aboriginal women exploring different aspects of their sacred lifeways (Williams 1988), including their agency with rock art production and ochreous applications. Kaberry (1939:206) was told how an old woman 'touched up the painting of the rainbow serpent in her country so that the spirit-children might increase' (see also Kaberry 1936:398). She documented how a women took a stone, painted an image and 'covered it with feathers' whereafter she 'sung it' as part of a sorcery ritual (Kaberry 1939:250). Women also created images on their bodies and on material culture in 'love magic corroborees' (Kaberry 1939:254–268). Kaberry's focus on the lifeworlds of women was groundbreaking, both as a result of her access as a female anthropologist in a male-dominated field, and in the material she chose to document.

The 22nd Frobenius Expedition

Analyses of Aboriginal lifeworlds where rock art could be understood as an integrated part of culture practices led to the most ambitious Kimberley rock art project up until that time. This was the Frobenius 'Institut für Kulturmorphologie' Expedition of 1938 (Beinssen-Hesse 1991; Porr and Doohan 2017). The expedition consisted of two ethnographers, A. Lommel and H. Petri, and two female artists, G. Kleist and A. Schulz. Since Love (1936) had already presented an account on Worora, Petri (1954) decided to concentrate his fieldwork among Ngarinyin people at the Munja government station (Figure 10.5), while Lommel (1952) focused on Wunambal (Unambal) in the Wurewurí area.

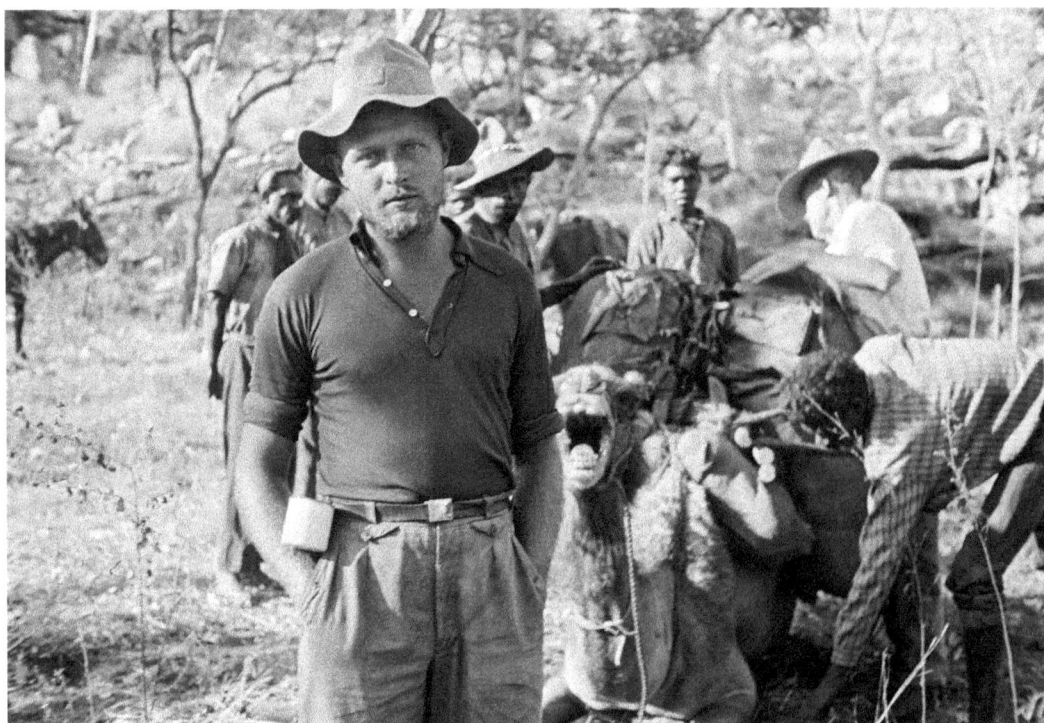

Figure 10.5: Helmut Petri during fieldwork at the Munja Government Station in 1938.
Source: Frobenius Institute in Frankfurt am Main, Germany, published with their kind permission.

Frobenius's interest in rock art was grounded in a Hegelian world view. He understood languages and artworks as an essential aspect of the *Geist* of a people's mentality and culture (Kuper 1988). 'Myths' and legends decoded information that could reveal hidden aspects of human cultural history (Porr and Doohan 2017). This idea of progressivism considered Aboriginal people as 'frozen fossils' of previous evolutionary stages that European nations had surpassed through the Neolithic revolution (e.g. Childe 1925). Frobenius and his co-workers were convinced that Aboriginal people of Australia were a 'dying race' (Petri 1954), soon to be replaced by the 'higher civilization' that was brought to Australia by its colonisers. Following this stance, the Frobenius Expedition aimed to save traces of the vanishing original Aboriginal culture before it became 'extinct'. This meant that their ethnographic work had a pronounced focus on Aboriginal cosmologies and the role of ritual specialists (Lommel 1952; Petri 1952a, 1953, see also Coate 1966; Elkin 1945; Lommel and Mowaljarlai 1994).

World War II and postwar conditions delayed publications from the Frobenius Expedition. Some of Petri's (1954:97) fieldnotes on 'mythology' were lost when his office storage was bombed (Schulz 1956:45). Also, most of its proceedings were published in German in the 1950s (Lommel 1949, 1950, 1952; Petri 1950, 1952a, 1952b, 1953, 1954), leading to this work having a relatively low profile in Australia (cf. Peterson and Kenny 2017). One exception is Schulz's well-cited article on rock art from 1956, which was published in English (cf. Schulz 1971). Schulz (1956:8) underlined the necessity of including the 'mythology' connected with rock art to understand its meaning:

> In primeval times, the Wond-inas, conceived as mythic beings and totemic heroes, wandered on the earth. They made the landscape in its present form … On the completion of their earthly activities the Wond-inas went partly down into the earth, partly up to heaven. On earth the spot is mostly indicated by some never-drying waterhole where Wond-ina survives, generally in the shape of the rainbow serpent Ungud. From him comes the rain on which the preservation and renewal of all life depend. In these Ungud places the aborigines find the spirit children, mythic impersonations of the all-essential substance, man's vital power but for which no children are born.

Schulz (1956:15–16) named some of her informants in her article and their close affiliation to specific Wandjina images through the patrilineal kinship system and she retold Dreaming stories connected to some artworks. Where possible, she used Aboriginal names of the specific Wandjina and offered a summary of the necessity to refresh these figures, or as one of her anonymous informants formulated it, 'to make 'm pretty fellows' (Schulz 1956:57): 'The portrait is regarded as a living thing and is treated as such. When the shadow on the rock wall fades away, the Wond-ina being vanishes, and thus end rain and fertility' (Schulz 1956:9). Moreover, Schulz (1956:32) made novel use of older photographic documentation, such as that of A.E. House taken during Brockman's 1901 study, to reveal the repainting of images and, sometimes, the addition of new imagery in the shelters that she studied.

Schulz's article demonstrated a growing interest in the relationship between Wandjina and Gwion Gwion rock art, an inquiry that would become central in the following decades. She underlined the stylistic differences and also the cosmological explanations embedded in these artworks (Schulz 1956:48). She bluntly declared: 'There is no room for [Gwion Gwion] in present-day aboriginal culture'. However, in the following sentence she cited her informants who interpreted them as '*D'imi*, bush spirits' (Schulz 1956:12, 44). Her Ungarinyin guide had the following information to add:

> Pointing east he said: That way are many more rocks high up the hills like Malan, with similar paintings. The black-fellows have nothing to do with them. Long ago Kujon a black bird, painted on the rocks. He struck his bill against the stones so that it bled, and with the blood he painted. He painted no animals, only human-shaped figures which probably represent spirits. It is long since he did so. (Schulz 1956:47)

As Porr and Doohan (2017) have argued, there is an ambivalence in Schulz's reading of Gwion Gwion. On one hand, she wrote that 'these paintings present the same difficulties as most of the rock paintings which have come down to us from by-gone peoples about which we know little or nothing' (Schulz 1956:44) and even defined them as 'peculiar and un-Australian paintings' (Schulz 1956:12). On the other hand, she defined Gwion Gwion as an older style whose similarities over large geographical distances in the Kimberley indicated that a 'culture once extended over the area between the picture places known to us and that further evidence of it may be found' (Schulz 1956:48). She rejected external and exotic explanations of Gwion Gwion (Schulz 1956:47). Similar thoughts were expressed by Lommel (1958a), but his description of the transition from Gwion Gwion to Wandjina rock art defined this shift in colonial terms as a 'Degeneration und Verprimitivierung des eleganten und bewegten Bradshawstiles zu plumpen und skurrilen' (Lommel 1958b:33): in short, as a degeneration of the elegant and dynamic Bradshaw style into clumsy and bizarre imageries.

The missionary Worms (1955) expressed a similar view when he described Gwion Gwion as 'prehistoric rock miniatures'. Worms (1955:547, 555) argued that the Kwini Elders he worked with did not show the 'slightest interest in them' and that 'the present natives are of the opinion that another people' had created these artworks. The state of preservation of these 'masterpieces' led him to suggest that these artworks were prehistoric and created by a now-extinct 'pygmoid race' (Worms 1955:555, 558, 561, 563–566).

It has been claimed that the disputed nomenclature of 'Bradshaw Figures' was coined by Schulz (1956:45–48), but it had already been used by Elkin (1948:15). However, as Kwini Senior Traditional Owner Ambrose Chalarimeri (2001:72, 72–78) has argued: 'Aboriginal painting shouldn't have white man name'. Recently, the core studies from the Frobenius Expedition have been translated into English (Akerman 2015b; Lommel 2007; Petri 2011, 2014), making these studies more accessible. They have, however, also attracted criticism for being published while not meeting today's best standard practice of consulting the descendent Aboriginal groups beforehand (Porr and Doohan 2017).

This period of research, searching for an ethnographic understanding of Aboriginal rock art, established the conditions of possibility for the divergent research paths that were to follow from the 1960s.

Diverging fields of rock art research (1960–2000)

In his first overview of *Australian Aboriginal rock art*, F.D. McCarthy (1958:53) declared that no other rock art area in Australia 'has caused so much interest nor produced a larger body of literature' than the Kimberley (also McCarthy 1967:57). However, 36 years later when Morwood and Smith (1994) presented an overview of Australian rock art research between 1974 and 1994, the study of Kimberley rock art seemed to have played a more modest role. From the 1960s onwards, other rock art regions dominated the research scene (see Morwood and Smith 1994:31–38), and the established research traditions of the Kimberley changed in four main ways.

First, few if any missionaries continued to write about rock art. Secondly, with archaeology having established itself as an academic discipline in Australia, rock art developed – after some hesitation (i.e. Mulvaney 1969:174) – as one of its major research areas (Griffith 2018). Crawford's classic 1968 study *The art of the Wandjina*, and his subsequent research (Crawford 1972, 1973, 1977, 1997, 2001, 2007), is an early example of this trend.

Thirdly, from the 1970s, we can witness an increased interest in Kimberley rock art from avocational researchers, such as bushwalkers, tour operators, station owners, doctors and other devotees (see Donaldson 2012a, 2012b, 2013; Donaldson and Kennealley 2007; Kennealley et al. 1997; Stubbs 1974). New organisations such as the Australian Rock Art Research Association (1983–present), The Kimberley Society (1992–2019), and The Kimberley Foundation, Australia (1993–2020, renamed Rock Art Australia), helped channel this interest by providing funding, logistical support and a community of practitioners. The main aims of these avocational researchers were to find 'new' sites (Schmiechen 1993, 1995) and use superimposition sequences to analyse the distribution of specific rock art styles in time and space (e.g. Walsh 1994, 2000; Walsh and Morwood 1999; Welch 1990, 1993c, 1995, 1996b). Increasingly, archaeologists developed partnerships with these avocationalists, applying new scientific methods to date and contextualising rock art styles and their modes of production (e.g. Morwood et al. 1994; Morwood and Walsh 1993; Roberts et al. 1997; Watchman 1997; Watchman et al. 1997). This development produced mixed results, with some very reputable work alongside uninformed speculation based on arguably colonial ideas.

The fourth change was the empowerment of Aboriginal people to express their knowledge through their own ontological frameworks about Kimberley rock art and associated heritage. This process gained momentum after the 1967 referendum that granted Aboriginal people civil rights, followed by the demand for repatriation of Aboriginal land, human remains and significant material culture. As a part of these processes, which still pertain, Aboriginal people started to express concerns about Indigenous intellectual property rights (see Frederick and O'Connor 2009, and Gray 2018, for two relevant case studies). This impetus was augmented with calls for land rights and Native Title in the 1980s and the 1990s, resulting in a growing number of research articles and books with Aboriginal authorship (Mowaljarlai 1992; Mowaljarlai and Malnic 1993; Mowaljarlai and Peck 1987; Mowaljarlai et al. 1988; Utemorrah and Vinnicombe 1992). A way to visualise these trends is to graph authorship of articles on Kimberley rock art (Figure 10.6).

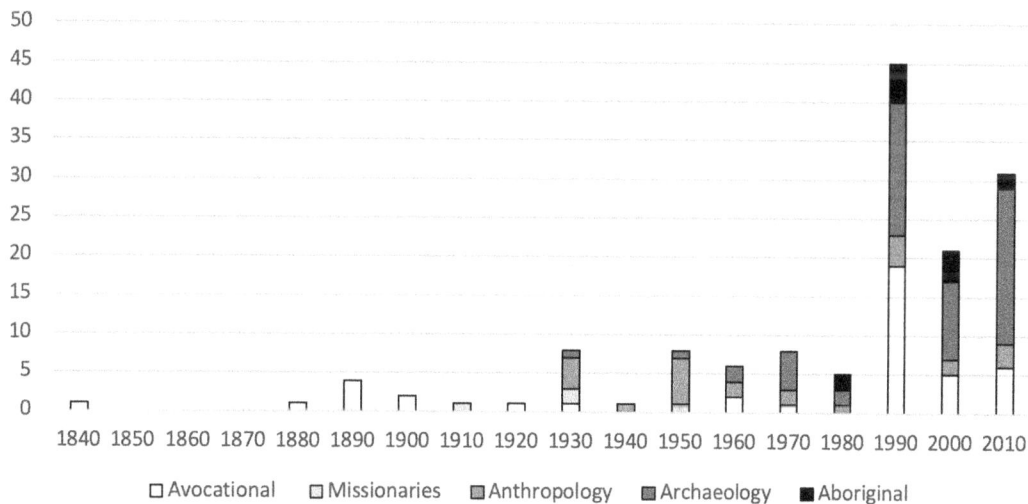

Figure 10.6: Kimberley rock art publications 1841–2020 according to authorship.

(i) Avocational researchers, (ii) missionaries, (iii) anthropologists, (iv) archaeologists and (v) Aboriginal authors. Co-authored publication has been assembled according to the specific author, which means that there are more authors than publications in this graph.

Source: Authors' summary.

All these changes led to new relationships and dialogues concerning Kimberley rock art. Sometimes, this led to tensions and oppositional positions regarding access to sites, how to understand and interpret different rock art assemblages, and who could use and speak for rock art. We here highlight some of these discourses and clashes.

Anthropology versus archaeology

The enduring presence of anthropologists in the Kimberley from the late 1920s saw a new generation in the 1970s who were eager to refigure their discipline towards more contemporary social perspectives and issues (Morphy 2007). Many of these academics were dedicated to standing up against social injustices, engaging in Aboriginal land rights, and working towards closing the economic and social gap between Aboriginal and non-Aboriginal Australians. In some instances, this has led to decades-long partnerships between Aboriginal groups and specific anthropologists. Researchers such as Blundell (1974; Blundell and Woolagoodja 2005; Blundell et al. 2018) and Akerman (2016; Ryan and Akerman 1993) have dedicated decades of fieldwork in the Kimberley and explored contemporary Aboriginal understandings of rock art (see also Crawford 2001; Layton 1992; Redmond 2002, 2017).

Archaeology, by contrast, tends to explore human histories from a diachronic perspective. For Kimberley rock art, Schulz's (1956) article marks a growing awareness of the temporality of different rock art styles. She focused on iconography, spatial distributions and differences in the preservation of Wandjina and Gwion Gwion rock art, suggesting that the latter must be much older. At the time, Australia was thought to have been inhabited for a relatively short period, usually measured in a few thousand years. The significant deep-time history of Aboriginal people in Australia started to unfold with the increased application and development of radiocarbon dating in the 1960s (Mulvaney 1964). Radiometric dating of Aboriginal sites advanced knowledge of first human colonisation from a few thousand years ago (Mulvaney 1969), to about 20,000 years (cf. Mulvaney 1975), to, now, at least 50,000 years for the Kimberley (Veth et al. 2019).

When locating rock art in a Western chronological framework, current analyses indicate that some East Kimberley Irregular Infill Animal period art is around 17,300 years old (Finch et al. 2021), with some Gwion Gwion figures created c. 12,000 BP, and others possibly up to 18,000 BP (Finch et al. 2020; cf. Lewis 1997; Roberts et al. 1997). Unquestionably, some surviving rock art imagery and styles are older yet (Finch et al. 2020; Finch et al. 2021; Veth et al. 2018). The current earliest age for a disputed Wandjina-style figure is 5100 ± 240 BP (Ross et al. 2016:19). Whether a Wandjina or not, it is part of a noticeable 'explosion' of different, visually vivid rock arts created during the late Holocene. Interestingly, this is close to the time when current ocean levels stabilised, suggesting a possible recursive relationship between environmental changes and the multiplicity of recent Kimberley rock art traditions or 'styles'. It may also be taphonomic in that more recent art and its diversity is better represented in galleries, overall. Importantly, the Wandjina tradition is still practised, with art produced or renewed today, and Aboriginal people thus find more recent dates more valent on account of their linkage to known histories and people (Ouzman 2021, for instance; see also Blundell and Woolagoodja 2005; Blundell et al. 2018; Chalarimeri 2001; Crawford 2001; Mangolamara et al. 2018; Mowaljarlai and Malnic 1993; Ngarjno et al. 2000; Woolagoodja 2007, 2020) – an important contradistinction with archaeology, where 'oldest' dates are typically prized.

Archaeologists' growing awareness of some rock art traditions' deep-time origins resulted in a difference in analytical approaches to Australian rock art, described by Taçon and Chippindale (1998) as 'Informed' and 'Formal' methodologies. The former explores rock art through an anthropological and contemporary perspective, mainly focusing on the significances of Wandjina-style rock art (e.g. Arndt 1964; Blundell 1974, 1982; Capell 1972; Crawford 1968; Playford 1960, 1997, 2007) and how these and other ancestral imageries inspire contemporary artists in the Kimberley (e.g. Ryan and Akerman 1993; Woolagoodja 2007, 2020). Archaeologists applying formal methodologies focused on revealing the sequence and age of rock art traditions, and how these changed – that is, the art is seen from a long-term diachronic perspective, often in relation to environmental change. This research trajectory was particularly pronounced between 1960 and 2000, with these varied research interests subsequently beginning to merge. It should be noted, though, that an increasing number of archaeologists used the dual lens of anthropology well before 2000 (e.g. Mowaljarlai and Vinnicombe 1995; Mowaljarlai et al. 1988; Utemorrah and Vinnicombe 1992; Vinnicombe 1992, 1997).

Rock art chronologies

Based on states of preservation, it had become evident that some rock art is of considerable antiquity while other forms and styles are more recent. Despite being just two of many rock art styles and expressions, Gwion Gwion and Wandjina have received the most attention (e.g. Crawford 1968). This is especially true for research before 2000, which left the broader Kimberley rock art repertoire unexplored (cf. Gunn et al. 2019 for new 'styles'). By suggesting a transformation of earlier styles to later ones, Crawford (1977) became one of the first scholars to advocate for continuity between Gwion Gwion and Wandjina rock art styles. However, it was not until the early 1990s that Walsh (1994) and Welch (1993a) presented more developed rock art chronologies using formal analyses, particular readings of superimposition and interpretations of specific styles' preservation.

Welch (1993a) classified and sequenced rock art by technique (such as cupules, engravings and paintings). Then he analysed iconographic details, such as anthropomorphic body position (i.e. bent knee or straight parts) and attributes (e.g. tassels, material culture). However, he did not apply consistent variables between the six 'periods' he distinguished: Archaic, Tasselled, Bent Knee, Straight Parts, Wandjina, Contact (Figure 10.7). Walsh (1994) identified similar broad categories and formed similar relative chronological conclusions, but his chronology included three 'Epochs', each subdivided into two parts:

- *Archaic Epoch*, subdivided into 'Pecked Cupule' and 'Irregular Infill Animal period'
- *Erudite*, subdivided into 'Bradshaw' and 'Clothes Peg'
- *Aborigine*, which he subdivided into 'Clawed Hand' and 'Wanjina'.

An important difference between their chronologies is that Welch (1993a, 1993b, 1996a, 1997, 2007) argued for a clear Aboriginal authorship throughout his 'periods', whereas Walsh (1994) revitalised the colonial trope of migrationism and argued for discontinuities between his 'epochs' (McNiven and Russell 1997). The implied non-Aboriginal authorship of his two earliest 'epochs' were argued to match some recorded site abandonments recorded archaeologically (cf. O'Connor et al. 1999). Significantly, archaeological work has now demonstrated a clear continuity of Aboriginal people in the Kimberley from the time this region was settled to the present era (e.g. Malaspinas et al. 2016; Nagle et al. 2017; Travers and Ross 2016; Veth et al. 2019; Veth et al. 2021). Intellectually, much of Walsh's theoretical framework has been superseded, retaining traction is some pseudoarchaeologial circles, while his detailed multi-decadal recordings giving rise to the superimposition sequence remains largely intact.

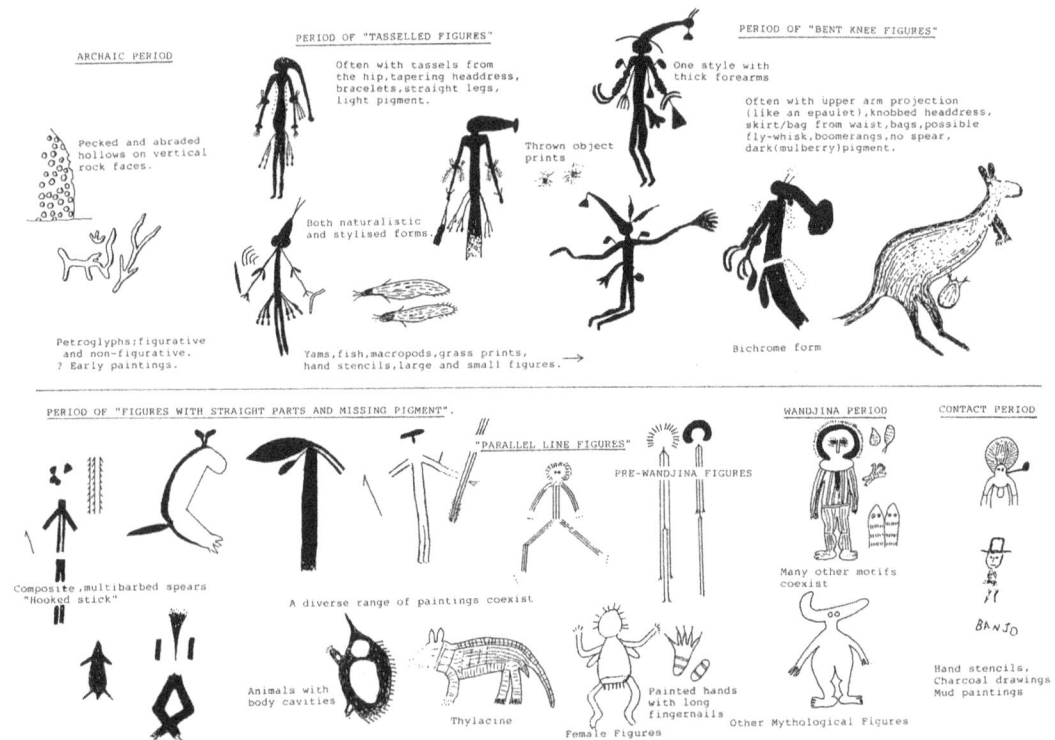

Figure 10.7: A 1993 version of Welch's rock art chronology for the Kimberley.

Source: Welch 1993a:1, Figure 1, published with kind permission by Welch (cf. Welch 2016).

Another way to establish Kimberley rock art's age has been to apply indirect or direct dating methods. The former has been done by OSL (optically stimulated luminescence) analyses of mud wasp nests lying under or over the art, thus giving maximum or minimum ages for the art (Roberts et al. 1997), or AMS (accelerator mass spectrometry) radiocarbon-dating mineral crusts that grow under or over paintings (Walsh 2000:41). The direct radiocarbon dating of charcoal or beeswax art has also been undertaken (e.g. Watchman et al. 1997; Walsh 2000; see also Harper et al. 2020; Morwood et al. 2010). When first applied in the Kimberley, many of these methods were in their infancy, and results were not always reliable (Aubert 2012). Today, more advanced methods are available, such as the AMS dating of differentiated organics in the mud wasp nest stubs above and below the art (Finch et al. 2019; Finch et al. 2020; Finch et al. 2021), geomorphological dating (David et al. 2019), uranium-thorium dating of mineral crusts (Green et al. 2021a; Green et al. 2021b) and geomicrobiology (Hoy 2020). Both Irregular Infill Animal Paintings and Gwion Gwion rock art now have secure dates, at least for the east Kimberley.

Conservation versus repainting

The growing insight about some rock art's great antiquity saw a mounting awareness about its preservation. Debate began around how this cultural heritage could be 'saved' so that coming generations could enjoy it (Crawford 1968:137–139). Since the 1970s, this led to different national organisations launching rock art conservation and restoration programs (Edwards 1974; Lambert 1989; Pearson and Swartz 1991; Rosenfeld 1985; Ward and Sullivan 1989; see also Callaghan 2007; MacLeod et al. 1997). Trials were carried out in the Kimberley to learn more about the properties and durability of various pigments that were used in creating the rock art (Clarke 1977; Clarke and North 1976), a research field that has recently rapidly advanced (cf. Chalmin and Huntley 2018; Ford et al. 1994; Huntley et al. 2014; Lenehan et al. 2017; Popelka-Filcoff and Zipkin 2021; Roberts et al. 2015; Ward et al. 2001).

Fading rock art was not news to Aboriginal people, but their responses differed to those of many non-Aboriginal people. In the Kimberley, a long tradition of repainting Wandjina according to cultural protocols kept images fresh (Blundell and Woolagoodja 2005). In the 1980s, several senior Elders felt a need for the next generation to 'step up'. In an act of resilience and cultural pride, several senior Elders argued for continuing the tradition of repainting Wandjina. David Banggal Mowaljarlai (1928–1997), a senior Ngarinyin man who had a long history of working as an informant for outsiders (see Love 1936; Coate 1966; Crawford 1968; Lommel and Mowaljarlai 1994), became a leading spokesman for this movement. A government-sponsored project was launched in 1986 (Mowaljarlai and Peck 1987), which created a heated debate about who should have authority about management of Aboriginal cultural heritage and traditions (cf. Bowdler 1988; Clarke and Randolph 1992; Mowaljarlai 1992; Mowaljarlai et al. 1988; Vinnicombe 1992; Walsh 1992, 2000).

The Australian Archaeological Association took a stand in favour of Aboriginal people's rights to continue their cultural practices and traditions. Others voiced conflicting arguments, especially when it came to 'older' artworks such as Gwion Gwion and the application of non-traditional pigments (Ward 1992). Walsh (1992, 1994, 2000) was a vigorous opponent of such practices. He considered older artworks disassociated from contemporary Aboriginal people and argued that they had a transcending and global significance. He noted these paintings had sometimes been described by Traditional Owners as 'rubbish paintings'. In doing so, Walsh relied heavily on earlier researchers' evaluations, such as Schulz (1956:30), Worms (1955:547, 555) and Crawford (1968:86), rather than contemporary Aboriginal understandings of their own cultural expressions (i.e. Mowaljarlai and Malnic 1993). To support his viewpoint, Walsh quoted senior Aboriginal people who did not identify with or share information about these particular paintings (Walsh 2000:429, 444–446).

An interesting aspect of this debate was that all outsiders, from Love to Walsh, considered at face value the information that Aboriginal people had shared with them. They never considered the possibility that some restricted cultural information could have been filtered or withheld from them (see Brady et al. 2020 for a theoretical discussion). They also did not consider that different clans and persons could have varied or contextual understandings of these artworks. Some clarity is provided by recourse to emic taxonomy (Brady et al. 2020). Redmond (2002:58), for example, observed that in the Kimberley, 'rubbish' is often used in Aboriginal English to mean 'someone who is very old and maybe no longer active'. It can also mean 'not dangerous, friendly' and/ or 'someone who is too young and inexperienced for an important political role'. According to Redmond, in Ngarinyin relations to Gwion Gwion, the notion of 'rubbish' may refer to:

> the total visual and cosmological Gestalt that has made *Wanjina* a 'well-known bloke' and *Gwion,* a more background one; forever present but not interacted with in the same way as the *Wanjina*. While the focus of living connection may have shifted long ago to the *Wanjina,* the *Gwion* form an essential part of a living sense of identity for many contemporary Ngarinyin and related groups in much the same way that the early paintings are overlaid by but seldom entirely obscured by, the Wanjina. (Redmond 2002:58)

Clearly there can be more to a word than is first understood; as is well known, words cannot just be naively translated, but need to be understood in relation to their specific ontological contexts. This and other related debates are far from settled, though older interpretations of Kimberley rock art that voice colonial ideas seem to reappear in a range of social and cultural contexts through time. A constructive outcome of such colonial discourses is that it has made academics more cognisant (Crawford 2001; Gray 2018; McNiven and Russell 2005; McNiven 2011; Porr 2017), and Aboriginal people more determined to express their own opinions about the meaning of their ancestors' artworks, including their right to define and control their cultural heritage

(Blundell and Woolagoodja 2005; Blundell et al. 2018; Chalarimeri 2001; Mangolamara et al. 2018; Mowaljarlai and Malnic 1993; Ngarjno et al. 2000; Woolagoodja 2007, 2020; see also Somerville 1997).

Conclusion

Kimberley rock art research at the close of the twentieth century can be seen as diverse and diverging, with embedded and persistent colonial tropes. However, the last two decades are witness to new cross-cultural collaborations with a common interest in rock art, with a gradual but active progression towards a relational dialogue and a 'two-way of learning' (Porr and Doohan 2017). This is not to say that the history of Kimberley rock art research can be ignored, nor that different methodologies and interpretations built upon colonial ideas have been erased. The development of contextualised research, both with Kimberley people and within broader archaeological and environmental datasets, allows for continued improvements in deepening different understandings of the Kimberley's rich rock art repertoire. Today, Kimberley rock art acts as an intergenerational medium for the transmission of cultural knowledge among Aboriginal people, and these powerful images are also used to educate non-Aboriginal people about their rich history and culture, about what 'always was, always will be'.[1]

References

Akerman, K. 2015a. A review of the Indigenous watercraft of the Kimberley region, Western Australia. *The Great Circle* 37(1):82–111.

Akerman, K. (ed.) 2015b. *Cologne to the Kimberley: Studies of Aboriginal life in Northwest Australia by five German scholars in the first half of the 20th Century.* Hesperian Press, Carlisle.

Akerman, K. 2016. *Wanjina: Notes on some iconic Ancestral Beings of the northern Kimberley.* Hesperian Press, Carlisle.

Arndt, W. 1964. The Australian evolution of the Wandjinas from rain clouds. *Oceania* 34(3):161–169. doi.org/10.1002/j.1834-4461.1964.tb00259.x.

Aubert, M. 2012. A review of rock art dating in the Kimberley, Western Australia. *Journal of Archaeological Science* 39(3):573–577. doi.org/10.1016/j.jas.2011.11.009.

Aubert, M., A. Brumm and P.S.C. Taçon 2017. The timing and nature of human colonization of Southeast Asia in the Late Pleistocene: A rock art perspective. *Current Anthropology* 58(17):553–566. doi.org/10.1086/694414.

Bahn, P.G. 1998. *The Cambridge illustrated history of prehistoric art.* Cambridge University Press, Cambridge.

Balanggarra Aboriginal Corporation/KLC (Kimberley Land Council) 2011. *Balanggarra Healthy Country plan.* Balanggarra Aboriginal Corporation/Kimberley Land Council, Wyndham/Broome.

Barrett, C.L. and A.S. Kenyon 1929. *Australian Aboriginal art.* National Museum of Victoria, Melbourne.

Basedow, H. 1925. *The Australian Aboriginal.* F.W. Preece and Sons, Adelaide.

Basset-Smith, P.W. 1894. The Aborigines of north-west Australia. *Journal of the Royal Anthropological Institute* 23:324–231. doi.org/10.2307/2842084.

---

1   See: australian.museum/learn/first-nations/always-will-be-aboriginal-land, accessed 21 February 2022.

Beinssen-Hesse, S. 1991. The study of Australian Aboriginal culture by German anthropologists of the Frobenius Institute. In D. Walker and J. Tampke (eds), *From Berlin to the Burdekin: The German contribution to the development of Australian science, exploration and the arts*, pp. 135–152. New South Wales University Press, Kensington.

Bindon, P. 1997. Kimberley aboriginal art in the Australian and world context. In K.F. Kenneally, M.R. Lewis, M. Donaldson and C. Clement (eds), *Aboriginal rock art of the Kimberley*, pp. 9–12. Occasional Paper 1. Kimberley Society, Perth.

Blundell, V. 1974. The Wandjina cave paintings of northwest Australia. *Arctic Anthropology* 11:213–223.

Blundell, V. 1982. Symbolic systems and cultural continuity in Northwest Australia: A consideration of Aboriginal cave art. *Culture* 2(1):3–20.

Blundell, V. and D. Woolagoodja 2005. *Keeping the Wanjinas fresh*. Fremantle Press, Fremantle.

Blundell, V., D. Woolagoodja, J. Oobagooma and L. Umbagai 2018. Visiting Gonjorong's Cave. In B. David and I.J. McNiven (eds), *The Oxford handbook of the archaeology and anthropology of rock art*, pp. 1181–1104. Oxford University Press, Oxford. doi.org/10.1093/oxfordhb/9780190607357.013.16.

Bowdler, S. 1988. Repainting Australian rock art. *Antiquity* 62 (236):517–523. doi.org/10.1017/S0003598X00074639.

Bradshaw, J. 1892. Notes on a recent trip to Prince Regent's River. *Royal Geographical Society of Australia (Victorian Branch) Transactions* 9(2):90–103.

Brady, L.M., R.G. Gunn, C. Smith and B. David 2018. Rock art and ethnography in Australia. In B. David and I.J. McNiven (eds), *The Oxford handbook of the archaeology and anthropology of rock art*, pp. 545–564. Oxford University Press, Oxford. doi.org/10.1093/oxfordhb/9780190607357.013.55.

Brady, L., S.K. May, J. Goldhahn, P.S.C. Taçon and P. LamiLami 2020. What painting? Encountering and interpreting the archaeological record in western Arnhem Land. *Archaeology in Oceania* 55:106–117. doi.org/10.1002/arco.5208.

Brockman, F.S. 1902. *Report on exploration of north-west Kimberley, 1901. Report to Minister for lands, Western Australia*. WM Alfred Watson, Government Printer, Perth.

Callaghan, D. 2007. Natural deterioration of rock art. In M.J. Donaldson and K.F. Kenneally (eds), *Rock art of the Kimberley*, pp. 111–126. Kimberley Society, Perth.

Capell, A. 1939. Mythology in northern Kimberley, north-west Australia. *Oceania* 9(4):382–404. doi.org/10.1002/j.1834-4461.1939.tb00246.x.

Capell, A. 1972. *Cave painting myths: Northern Kimberley*. Oceania Publications 18. University of Sydney, Sydney.

Chalarimeri, A.M. 2001. *The man form the Sunrise side*. Magabala Books, Broome.

Chalmin, E. and J. Huntley 2018. Characterizing rock art pigments. In B. David and I.J. McNiven (eds), *The Oxford handbook of the archaeology and anthropology of rock art*, pp. 885–909. Oxford University Press, Oxford. doi.org/10.1093/oxfordhb/9780190607357.013.48.

Childe, V.G. 1925. *The dawn of European civilization*. Kegan Paul, Trench, Trubner & Co, London.

Clarke, I. and P. Randolph 1992. Repainting of Kimberley Wandjina rock art sites. In G.K. Ward (ed.), *Retouch: Maintenance and conservation of Aboriginal rock imagery*, pp. 17–22. Occasional AURA Publication 5. Australian Rock Art Research Association, Melbourne.

Clarke, J. 1977. Deterioration analysis of rock art sites. In C. Pearson (ed.), *Conservation of rock art: Proceedings of the international workshop on the conservation of rock art,* pp. 54–63. Institute for the Conservation of Cultural Materials, Perth.

Clarke, J. and N. North 1976. Two Aboriginal rock art pigments from Western Australia: Their properties, use, and durability. *Studies in Conservation* 21(3):134–142. doi.org/10.1179/sic.1976.023.

Clarkson, C., Z. Jacobs, B. Marwick, R. Fullagar, L. Wallis, M. Smith, R.G. Roberts, E. Hayes, K. Lowe, X. Carah, S.A. Florin, J. McNeil, D. Cox, L.J. Arnold, Q. Hua, J. Huntley, H.E.A. Brand, T. Manne, A. Fairbairn, J. Shulmeister, L. Lyle, M. Salinas, M. Page, K. Connell, G. Park, K. Norman, T. Murphy and C. Pardoe 2017. Human occupation of northern Australia by 65,000 years ago. *Nature* 547:306–310. doi.org/10.1038/nature22968.

Clottes, J. 2002. *World rock art.* The Getty Conservation Institute, Los Angeles.

Coate, H.H.J. 1966. The Rai and the third eye: North-west Australian beliefs. *Oceania* 37(2):93–123. doi.org/10.1002/j.1834-4461.1966.tb01790.x.

Conigrave, C.P. 1938. *Walk-about.* Dent, London.

Crawford, I.M. 1968. *The art of the Wandjina.* Oxford University Press, Melbourne.

Crawford, I.M. 1972. Function and change in Aboriginal rock art, Western Australia. *World Archaeology* 3(3):301–312. doi.org/10.1080/00438243.1972.9979512.

Crawford, I.M. 1973. Wandjina paintings. In R.M. Berndt and E.S. Philiphs (eds), *The Australian Aboriginal heritage: An introduction,* pp. 108–117. Ure Smith, Sydney.

Crawford, I.M. 1977. The relationship of Bradshaw and Wandjina art in North-West Kimberley. In P. Ucko (ed.), *Form in Indigenous art: Schematisation in the art of Aboriginal Australia and prehistoric Europe,* pp. 357–369. Australian Institute of Aboriginal Studies, Canberra.

Crawford, I.M. 1997. Wandjina: A western perspective. In K.F. Kenneally, M.R. Lewis, M. Donaldson and C. Clement (eds), *Aboriginal rock art of the Kimberley,* pp. 47–52. Occasional Paper 1. Kimberley Society, Perth.

Crawford, I.M. 2001. *We won the victory: Aborigines and outsiders on the north-west coast of the Kimberley.* Fremantle Arts Centre Press, Fremantle.

Crawford, I.M. 2007. Reminiscences of 1960s field work for *The art of Wandjina.* In M.J. Donaldson and K.F. Kenneally (eds), *Rock art of the Kimberley,* pp. 101–110. Kimberley Society, Perth.

David, B. and I.J. McNiven (eds) 2018. *The Oxford handbook of the archaeology and anthropology of rock art.* Oxford University Press, Oxford. doi.org/10.1093/oxfordhb/9780190607357.001.0001.

David, B., B. Barker, F. Petchey, J.-J. Delannoy, J.-M. Geneste, C. Rowe, M. Eccleston, L. Lamb and R. Whear 2013. A 28,000 year old excavated painted rock from Nawarla Gabarnmang, northern Australia. *Journal of Archaeological Science* 40:2493–2501. doi.org/10.1016/j.jas.2012.08.015.

David, B., J.-J. Delannoy, F. Petchey, R. Gunn, J. Huntley, P. Veth, K. Genuite, R.J. Skelly, J. Mialanes, S. Harper, S. Ouzman, Balanggarra Aboriginal Corporation, P. Heaney and V. Wong 2019. Dating painting events through by-products of ochre processing: Borologa 1 Rockshelter, Kimberley, Australia. *Australian Archaeology* 85(1):57–94. doi.org/10.1080/03122417.2019.1603263.

Davidson, S.D. 1936. *Aboriginal Australian and Tasmanian rock carvings and paintings.* Memoirs of the American Philosophical Society, Philadelphia.

Donaldson, M.J. 2012a. *Kimberley rock art: Mitchell Plateau area.* Wildrocks Publications, Mount Lawley.

Donaldson, M.J. 2012b. *Kimberley rock art: North Kimberley.* Wildrocks Publications, Mount Lawley.

Donaldson, M.J. 2013. *Kimberley rock art: Rivers and ranges*. Wildrocks Publications, Mount Lawley.

Donaldson, M.J. and K.F. Kenneally (eds) 2007. *Rock art of the Kimberley*. Kimberley Society, Perth.

Easton, W.R. 1922. *Report on the north Kimberley district of Western Australia, Kimberley Expedition 1921*. Western Australian Government Printer, Perth.

Edwards, R. (ed.) 1974. *Aboriginal rock paintings considerations for their future*. The Australian Museum, Sydney.

Elder, B. 2003. *Blood on the wattle: Massacres and maltreatment of Aboriginal Australians since 1788*. New Holland Publishers, Chatswood.

Elkin, A.P. 1930a. Rock-paintings of north-west Australia. *Oceania* l(3):257–279. doi.org/10.1002/j.1834-4461.1930.tb01649.x.

Elkin, A.P. 1930b. The Rainbow Serpent myth in North-West Australia. *Oceania* 1(3):349–352. doi.org/10.1002/j.1834-4461.1930.tb01655.x.

Elkin, A.P. 1932. Social organization in the Kimberley Division, North-Western Australia. *Oceania* 2(3):296–333. doi.org/10.1002/j.1834-4461.1932.tb00031.x.

Elkin, A.P. 1933. Totemism in North-Western Australia: (The Kimberley Division). *Oceania* 3(3):257–296. doi.org/10.1002/j.1834-4461.1933.tb01679.x.

Elkin, A.P. 1934. Anthropology and the future of the Australian Aborigines. *Oceania* 5(1):1–18. doi.org/10.1002/j.1834-4461.1934.tb00128.x.

Elkin, A.P. 1945. *Aboriginal men of high degree: Initiation and sorcery in the world's oldest tradition*. Australasian Publishing, Sydney.

Elkin, A.P. 1948. Grey's northern Kimberley cave-paintings re-found. *Oceania* 19(1):1–15. doi.org/10.1002/j.1834-4461.1948.tb00492.x.

Elkin, A.P. 1949. The origin and interpretation of petroglyphs in South-East Australia. *Oceania* 20(2):119–157. doi.org/10.1002/j.1834-4461.1949.tb00522.x.

Elkin, A.P. 1975. R.H. Mathews: His contribution to Aboriginal studies. *Oceania* 46(2):126–152. doi.org/10.1002/j.1834-4461.1975.tb01901.x.

Explorer [Aeneas Gunn] 1896. Natives and native carvings in north Australia. *The Leader* June 27:6–7.

Finch, D., A. Gleadow, J. Hergt, V.A. Levchenko and D. Fink 2019. New developments in the radiocarbon dating of mud wasp nests. *Quaternary Geochronolgy* 51:140–154. doi.org/10.1016/j.quageo.2019.02.007.

Finch, D., A. Gleadow, J. Hergt, V.A. Levchenko, P. Heaney, P. Veth, S. Harper, S. Ouzman, C. Myers and H. Green 2020. 12,000-Year-old Aboriginal rock art from the Kimberley region, Western Australia. *Science Advanced* 6(6):eaay3922. doi.org/10.1126/sciadv.aay3922.

Finch, D., A. Gleadow, J. Hergt, P. Heaney, H. Green, C. Myers, P. Veth, S. Harper, S. Ouzman and V.A. Levchenko 2021. Ages for Australia's oldest rock paintings. *Nature Human Behaviour* 5(2021):310–318. doi.org/10.1038/s41562-020-01041-0.

Ford, B., I. MacLeod and P. Haydock 1994. Rock art pigments from the Kimberley region of Western Australia: Identification of the minerals and conservation mechanisms. *Studies in Conservation* 39:57–69. doi.org/10.1179/sic.1994.39.1.57.

Forrest, A. 1880. *North-west exploration: Journal of expedition from DeGrey to Port Darwin*. Parliamentary Paper 3. Government Printer, Perth.

Frederick, U. and S. O'Connor 2009. Wandjina, graffiti and heritage: The power and politics of enduring imagery. *Humanities Research* 15(2):153–183. doi.org/10.22459/HR.XV.02.2009.10.

Goldhahn, J. 2013. *Bredarör på Kivik – en arkeologisk odyssé*. Kalmar Studies in Archaeology IX, Kalmar.

Gray, G. 1997. 'Mr Neville did all in [His] power to assist me': A.P. Elkin, A.O. Neville and anthropological research in northwest Western Australia, 1927–1928. *Oceania* 68(1): 27–46. doi.org/10.1002/j.1834-4461.1997.tb02640.x.

Gray, G. 2007. *A cautious silence: The politics of Australian anthropology*. Australian Studies Press, Canberra.

Gray, S. 2018. Cultural and intellectual property rights in rock art: A case study of Australian Indigenous art. In B. David and I.J. McNiven (eds), *The Oxford handbook of the archaeology and anthropology of rock art*, pp. 971–992. Oxford University Press, Oxford. doi.org/10.1093/oxfordhb/9780190607357.013.56.

Green, H., A. Gleadow, D. Finch, C. Myers and J. McGovern 2021a. Micro-stromatolitic laminations and the origins of engraved, oxalate-rich accretions from Australian rock art shelters. *Geoarchaeology* 36(6):964–977. doi.org/10.1002/gea.21882.

Green, H., A. Gleadow, V.A. Levchenko, D. Finch, C. Myers, J. McGovern, P. Heaney and R. Pickering 2021b. Dating correlated microlayers in oxalate accretions from rock art shelters: New archives of paleoenvironments and human activity. *Science Advances* 7(33). doi.org/10.1126/sciadv.abf3632.

Grey, G. 1841. *Journals of two expeditions of discovery in north-west and Western Australia during the years 1837, 38 and 39*. T&W Boone, London.

Griffith, B. 2018. *Deep time Dreaming: Uncovering ancient Australia*. Black Inc., Carlton.

Gunn, R.G. 2000. Spencer and Gillen's contribution to Australian rock art studies. *Rock Art Research* 17(1):56–64.

Gunn, R., B. David, L. Douglas, J.-J. Delannoy, S. Harper, P. Heaney, S. Ouzman and P. Veth 2019. Kimberley Stout Figures: A new rock art style for Kimberley rock art, north-western Australia. *Australian Archaeology* 82(2):151–169. doi.org/10.1080/03122417.2019.1681129.

Harper, S., P. Veth and S. Ouzman 2020. Kimberley rock art. In C. Smith (ed.), *Encyclopedia of global archaeology*. Springer, New York. doi.org/10.1007/978-3-319-51726-1_3449-1.

Hoy, J. 2020. The origins and Paleoclimate potential of oxalate glazes of the Kimberley region, Western Australia. Unpublished MSc thesis, University of Melbourne, Melbourne.

Huntley, J., H. Brand, M. Aubert and M.J. Morwood 2014. The first Australian synchrotron powder diffraction analysis of pigment from a Wanjina motif in the Kimberley, Western Australia. *Australian Archaeology* 78:33–38. doi.org/10.1080/03122417.2014.11681996.

Kaberry, P.M. 1935. The Forrest River and Lyne River tribes of North-West Australia. *Oceania* 5(4):408–436. doi.org/10.1002/j.1834-4461.1935.tb00163.x.

Kaberry, P.M. 1936. Spirit-children and spirit-centres of the North Kimberley Division, West Australia. *Oceania* 6(4):392–400. doi.org/10.1002/j.1834-4461.1936.tb00202.x.

Kaberry, P.M. 1939. *Aboriginal women, sacred and profane*. George Routledge and Sons Ltd, London.

Kenneally, K.F., M.R. Lewis, M. Donaldson and C. Clement (eds) 1997. *Aboriginal rock art of the Kimberley*. Occasional Paper 1. Kimberley Society, Perth.

Kuper, A. 1988. *The invention of primitive society: Transformations of an illusion*. Routledge, London.

Lambert, D. 1989. *Conserving Australian rock art: A manual for site managers.* Aboriginal Studies Press, Canberra.

Layton, R. 1992. *Australian rock art: A new synthesis.* Cambridge University Press, Cambridge.

Lenehan C.E., S.S. Tobe, R.J. Smith and R. Popelka-Filcoff 2017. Microbial composition analyses by 16S rRNA sequencing: A proof of concept approach to provenance determination of archaeological ochre. *PLoS ONE* 12(10):e0185252. doi.org/10.1371/journal.pone.0185252.

Lewis, D. 1997. Bradshaws: The view from Arnhem Land. *Australian Archaeology* 44(1):1–16. doi.org/10.1080/03122417.1997.11681585.

Lewis-Williams, J.D. 2002. *A cosmos in stone: Interpreting religion and society through rock art.* AltaMira Press, Walnut Creek.

Lommel, A. 1949. Notes on sexual behaviour and initiation, Wunambal Tribe, North-Western Australia. *Oceania* 20(2):158–164. doi.org/10.1002/j.1834-4461.1949.tb00523.x.

Lommel, A. 1950. Modern culture influences on the Aborigines. *Oceania* 21(1):14–24. doi.org/10.1002/j.1834-4461.1950.tb00170.x.

Lommel, A. 1952. *Die Unambal: Ein Stamm in Nordwest-Australien.* Monographien zur Völkerkunde herausgegeben vom Hamburgischen Museum für Völkerkunde 11, Hamburg.

Lommel, A. 1958a. Australische Felsbilder und ihre ausseraustralischen Parallelen. *Baessler-Archiv, Neue Folge* V:267–283.

Lommel, A. 1958b. Fünf neue Felsbildstellen in Nordwest-Australien. *Zeitschrift für Ethnologie* 83(1):1–33.

Lommel, A. 1966. *Prehistoric and primitive man.* Prentice Hall, London.

Lommel, A. 2007. *The Unambal.* Takarakka Nowan Kas Publications, Carnarvon Gorge.

Lommel, A. and D. Mowaljarlai 1994. Shamanism in northwest Australia. *Oceania* 64(4):277–287. doi.org/10.1002/j.1834-4461.1994.tb02472.x.

Love, J.R.B. 1917. Notes on the Wororra tribe of North-Western Australia. *Royal Society of South Australia Transactions* 41:20–38.

Love, J.R.B. 1929. Illustrations of stone monuments of the Worora. *Records of the South Australian Museum* 6(2):137–142.

Love, J.R.B. 1930. Rock paintings of the Worora and their mythological interpretation. *Journal of the Royal Society of Western Australia* 16:1–24.

Love, J.R.B. 1935. Mythology, totemism and religion of the Worora Tribe of North-West Australia. *Australian and New Zealand Association for the Advancement of Science, Report* 22:222–231.

Love, J.R.B. 1936. *Stone-Age Bushman of to-day: Life and adventure among a tribe of savages in North-Western Australia.* Blackie & Son Limited, London and Glasgow.

Lubbock, J. 1870. *The origin of civilisation and the primitive condition of man: Mental and social condition of savages.* Longman, London.

MacLeod, I., P. Haydock and B. Ford 1997. Conservation management of the west Kimberley rock art: Micro-climate studies and decay mechanisms. In K.F. Kenneally, M.R. Lewis, M. Donaldson and C. Clement (eds), *Aboriginal rock art of the Kimberley,* pp. 65–70. Occasional Paper 1. Kimberley Society, Perth.

Madariga de la Campa, B. 2001. *Sanz de Sautuola and the discovery of the caves of Altamira.* Fundación Marcelino Botín, Santander.

Malaspinas, A.S., M.C. Westaway, C. Muller, V.C. Sousa, O. Lao, I. Alves, A. Bergström, G. Athanasiadis, J.Y. Cheng, J.E. Crawford, T.H. Heupink, E. MacHoldt, S. Peischl, S. Rasmussen, S. Schiffels, S. Subramanian, J.L. Wright, A. Albrechtsen, C. Barbieri, I. Dupanloup, A. Eriksson, A. Margaryan, I. Moltke, I. Pugach, T.S. Korneliussen, I.P. Levkivskyi, J.V. Moreno-Mayar, S. Ni, F. Racimo, M. Sikora, Y. Xue, F.A. Aghakhanian, N. Brucato, S. Brunak, P.F. Campos, W. Clark, S. Ellingvåg, G. Fourmile, P. Gerbault, D. Injie, G. Koki, M. Leavesley, B. Logan, A. Lynch, E.A. Matisoo-Smith, P.J. McAllister, A.J. Mentzer, M. Metspalu, A.B. Migliano, L. Murgha, M.E. Phipps, W. Pomat, D. Reynolds, F.X. Ricaut, P. Siba, M.G. Thomas, T. Wales, C.M.R. Wall, S.J. Oppenheimer, C. Tyler-Smith, R. Durbin, J. Dortch, A. Manica, M.H. Schierup, R.A. Foley, M.M. Lahr, C. Bowern, J.D. Wall, T. Mailund, M. Stoneking, R. Nielsen, M.S. Sandhu, L. Excoffier, D.M. Lambert and E. Willerslev 2016. A genomic history of Aboriginal Australia. *Nature* 538:207–214. doi.org/10.1038/nature18299.

Mangolamara, S., L. Karadada, J. Oobagooma, D. Woolagoodja and J. Karadada 2018. *Nyara pari kala niragu (Gaambera), gadawara ngyaran-gada (Wunambal), inganinja gubadjoongana (Woddordda): We are coming to see you*. Edited by K. Doohan. Dambimangari Aboriginal Corporation and Wunambal Gaambera Aboriginal Corporation, Derby.

Mathew, J. 1894. The cave paintings of Australia: Their authorship and significance. *The Journal of the Anthropological Institute of Great Britain and Ireland* 23:42–52. doi.org/10.2307/2842314.

Mathews, R.H. 1893. Rock paintings of the Aborigines in caves on Bulgar Creek, near Singleton. *Journal of the Royal Society of NSW* 27:353–358.

Mathews, R.H. 1896. The rock paintings and carvings of the Australian Aborigines. *Journal of the Anthropological Institute of Great Britain and Ireland* 25:145–163. doi.org/10.2307/2842395.

Mathews, R.H. 1898. The rock paintings and carvings of the Australian Aborigines (Part II). *Journal of the Anthropological Institute* 27:532–541. doi.org/10.2307/2842773.

May, S.K., L. Rademaker, D. Nadjamerrek and J. Narndal Gumurdul 2020. *The Bible in Buffalo Country: Oenpelli mission 1925–1931*. Aboriginal History Monographs. ANU Press, Canberra. doi.org/10.22459/BBC.2020.

McCarthy, F.D. 1958. *Australian rock art*. Australian Museum, Sydney.

McCarthy, F.D. 1967. *Australian rock art*. 3rd ed. Australian Museum, Sydney.

McConvell, P. 1996. Backtracking to Babel: The chronology of Pama-Nyungan expansion in Australia. *Archaeology in Oceania* 31(3):125–144. doi.org/10.1002/j.1834-4453.1996.tb00356.x.

McDonald, J. 2008. *Dreamtime superhighway: Sydney basin rock art and Prehistoric information exchange*. ANU E Press, Canberra. doi.org/10.22459/DS.08.2008.

McDonald, J. and P. Veth (eds) 2012. *A companion to rock art*. Wiley-Blackwell, Chichester. doi.org/10.1002/9781118253892.

McGlashan, H. 2012. George Grey's expeditions 1837–1838: First European penetration of the Kimberley interior. In C. Clement, J. Gresham and H. McGlashan (eds), *Kimberley history: People exploration and development*, pp. 61–69. The Kimberley Society, Perth.

McNiven, I.J. 2011. The Bradshaw debate: Lessons learned from critiquing colonialist interpretations of Gwion Gwion rock paintings of the Kimberley, Western Australia. *Australian Archaeology* 72:35–44. doi.org/10.1080/03122417.2011.11690529.

McNiven, I.J. and L. Russell 1997. 'Strange paintings' and 'mystery races': Kimberley rock art, diffusionism and colonialist constructions of Australia's Aboriginal past. *Antiquity* 71(274):801–809. doi.org/10.1017/S0003598X00085744.

McNiven, I.J. and L. Russell 2005. *Appropriated pasts: Indigenous people and the colonial culture of archaeology.* AltaMira Press, Walnut Creek.

Mjöberg, E. 1915. *Bland vilda djur och folk i Australien.* Bonnier, Stockholm.

Mjöberg, E. 2012. *Among wild animals and people in Australia.* Hesperian Press, Carlisle.

Morphy, H. 1998. *Aboriginal art.* Phaidon Press, London.

Morphy, H. 2007. *Becoming art: Exploring cross-cultural categories.* Berg, New York.

Morwood, M.J. and C.E. Smith 1994. Rock art research in Australia 1974–94. *Australian Archaeology* 39:19–38. doi.org/10.1080/03122417.1994.11681525.

Morwood, M.J. and G.L. Walsh 1993. A mark in time. *Australian Natural History* 24:40–45.

Morwood, M.J., G.L. Walsh and A. Watchman 1994. The dating potential of rock art in the Kimberley, N.W. Australia. *Rock Art Research* 11(2):79–87.

Morwood, M.J., G.L. Walsh and A.L. Watchman 2010. AMS radiocarbon ages for beeswax and charcoal pigments in north Kimberley rock art. *Rock Art Research* 27(1):3–8.

Mountford, C.P. 1937. Examples of Aboriginal art from Napier Broome Bay and Parry Harbour, North-Western Australia. *Royal Society of South Australia, Transactions* 61:30–40.

Mowaljarlai, D. 1992. Ngarinyin perspective of repainting: Mowaljarlai's statement. In G.K. Ward (ed.), *Retouch: Maintenance and conservation of Aboriginal rock imagery,* pp. 8–9. Occasional AURA Publication 5. Australian Rock Art Research Association, Melbourne.

Mowaljarlai, D. and J. Malnic 1993. *Yorro Yorro: Everything standing up alive.* Magabala Books, Broome.

Mowaljarlai, D. and C. Peck 1987. Ngarinyin cultural continuity: A project to teach the young people the culture including the re-painting of Wandjina rock art sites. *Australian Aboriginal Studies* 7:71–78. search.informit.org/doi/10.3316/informit.189872533135934.

Mowaljarlai, D. and P. Vinnicombe 1995. Perspectives of the origin of rock images in the Western Kimberley. In G. Wards and L.A. Wards, (eds), *Management of rock imagery,* pp. 42–52. Occasional AURA Publication 9. Australian Rock Art Association, Melbourne.

Mowaljarlai, D., P. Vinnicombe, G.K. Ward and C. Chippindale 1988. Repainting images on rock in Australia and the maintenance of Aboriginal culture. *Antiquity* 62(237):690–696. doi.org/10.1017/S0003598X00075086.

Mulvaney, J.D. 1964. The Pleistocene colonization of Australia. *Antiquity* 38(152):263–267. doi.org/10.1017/S0003598X00031161.

Mulvaney, J.D. 1969. *The prehistory of Australia.* Thames and Hudson, London.

Mulvaney, J.D. 1975. *The prehistory of Australia.* Revised ed. Penguin Books, Ringwood.

Mulvaney, J.D. 1989. *Encounters in place: Outsiders and Aboriginal Australians, 1606–1985.* University of Queensland Press, St. Lucia.

Nagle, N., K.N. Ballantyne, M. van Oven, C. Tyler-Smith, Y. Xue, S. Wilcox, L. Wilcox, R. Turkalov, R.A.H. van Oorschot, S. van Holst Pellekaan, T.G. Schurr, P. McAllister, L. Williams, M. Kayser, R.J. Mitchell and The Genographic Consortium 2017. Mitochondrial DNA diversity of present-day Aboriginal Australians and implications for human evolution in Oceania. *Journal of Human Genetics* 62:343–353. doi.org/10.1038/jhg.2016.147.

Ngarjno, Unugudman, Banggal and Nyawarra 2000. *Gwion Gwion: Secret and sacred pathways of the Ngarinyin, Aboriginal people of Australia.* Edited by J. Doring. Könemann, Köln.

Nilsson, S. [1838–1843] 1868. *The primitive inhabitants of Scandinavia. An essay on comparative ethnography, and a contribution to the history of mankind.* 3rd ed. Longmans, Green, and Co, London.

O'Connor, S. and B.L. Fankhauser 2001. Art at 40,000BP? One step closer: An ochre covered rock from Carpenter's Gap Shelter 1, Kimberley Region, Western Australia. In A. Anderson, I. Lilley and S. O'Connor (eds), *Histories of old ages: Essays in honour of Rhys Jones*, pp. 287–300. Pandanus Books, Canberra.

O'Connor, S., A. Barham and D. Woolagoodja 2008. Painting and repainting in the Kimberley. *Australian Aboriginal studies* 2008(1): 22–38.

O'Connor, S., P. Veth and A. Barham 1999. Cultural versus natural explanations for lacunae in Aboriginal occupation deposits in northern Australia. *Quaternary International* 59(1):61–70. doi.org/10.1016/S1040-6182(98)00072-X.

O'Connor, S., J. Balme, J. Fyfe and J. Oscar 2013. Marking resistance? Change and continuity in the recent rock art of the southern Kimberley, Australia. *Antiquity* 87(336):539–554. doi.org/10.1017/S0003598X00049115.

Olsen, O. and L. Russel 2019. *Australia's first naturalists. Indigenous people's contribution to early zoology.* National Library of Australia, Canberra.

Ouzman, S. 2021. Archaeologies of Austral: Australian identities from the Pleistocene to the Anthropocene. *Journal of Australian Studies* 45(2):152–164. doi.org/10.1080/14443058.2021.1910857.

Owen, C. 2016. *Every mother's son is guilty: Policing the Kimberley frontier of Western Australia 1882–1905.* University of Western Australia, UWA Publishing, Perth.

Parker, A., J. Bradshaw and C. Done 2007. *A Kimberley adventure: Rediscovering the Bradshaw Figures.* Gecko Books, Marleston.

Paterson, A. and A. Wilson 2009. Indigenous perceptions of contact at Inthanoona, Northwest Western Australia. *Oceania* 44:99–111. doi.org/10.1002/j.1834-4453.2009.tb00071.x.

Pearson, C. and B. Swartz (eds) 1991. *Rock art and posterity: Conserving, managing and recording rock art.* Occasional AURA Publication 4. Australian Rock Art Research Association, Melbourne.

Perez, E. 1977. *Kalumburu: The Benedictine Mission and the Aborigines 1908–1975.* Kalumburu Benedictine Mission, Kalumburu.

Peterson, N. and A. Kenny (eds) 2017. *German ethnography in Australia.* ANU E Press, Canberra. doi.org/10.22459/GEA.09.2017.

Peterson, N., L. Allen and L. Hamby (eds) 2008. *The makers and making of Indigenous Australian museum collections.* Melbourne University Press, Melbourne.

Petri, H. 1950. Das Weltende im Glauben Australischer Eingeborener. *Paideuma* 4:349–362.

Petri, H. 1952a. Der australische Medizinmann. *Annali Lateranensi* 16:159–317.

Petri, H. 1952b. Rituelle Vermehrungs-Handlungen in Den Kimberleys (Nordwest Australia). *Paideuma* 5(4):189–200.

Petri, H. 1953. Der australische Medizinmann. *Annali Lateranensi* 17:157–225.

Petri, H. 1954. *Sterbende Welt in Nordwest-Australien.* Kulturgeschichtliche Forschungen 5. A. Limbach, Braunschweig.

Petri, H. 2011. *Dying world in northwest Australia.* Hesperian Press, Carlisle.

Petri, H. 2014. *The Australian medicine man.* Hesperian Press, Carlisle.

Playford, P.E. 1960. Aboriginal rock paintings of the west Kimberley region, Western Australia. *Journal of Royal Society of Western Australia* 43:111–122.

Playford, P.E. 1997. Rock art of the western Kimberley. In K.F. Kenneally, M.R. Lewis, M. Donaldson and C. Clement (eds), *Aboriginal rock art of the Kimberley*, pp. 19–24. Occasional Paper 1. Kimberley Society, Perth.

Playford, P.E. 2007. Aboriginal rock art in the limestone ranges of the west Kimberley. In M.J. Donaldson and K.F. Kenneally (eds), *Rock art of the Kimberley*, pp. 126–152. Kimberley Society, Perth.

Popelka-Filcoff, R.S. and A.M. Zipkin 2021. The archaeometry of ochre *sensu lato*: A review. *Journal of Archaeological Science* 137(2022). doi.org/10.1016/j.jas.2021.105530.

Porr, M. 2017. Myths that refuse to die. Kimberley rock art and the interpretation of Australian Indigenous heritage. Available at: www.decolonisinghumanorigins.com/2017/01/myths-that-refuse-to-die.html (accessed 6 June 2020).

Porr, M. and H.R. Bell 2012. 'Rock-art', 'animism' and two-way thinking: Towards a complementary epistemology in the understanding of material culture and 'rock-art' of hunting and gathering people. *Journal of Archaeological Method and Theory* 19(1):161–205. doi.org/10.1007/s10816-011-9105-4.

Porr, M. and K. Doohan 2017. From pessimism to collaboration: The impact of the German Frobenius-Expedition (1938–1939) on the perception of Kimberley art and rock art. *Journal of Pacific Archaeology* 8(1):88–99. pacificarchaeology.org/index.php/journal/article/view/216.

Rainsbury, M.P. 2009. *River and coast: Regionality in north Kimberley rock art.* Unpublished PhD thesis, Department of Archaeology, Durham University, Durham. Available at: core.ac.uk/works/3255931 (accessed 20 June 2020).

Rainsbury, M.P. 2013. Mr Bradshaw's drawings: Reassessing Joseph Bradshaw's sketches. *Rock Art Research* 30(2):248–253.

Rainsbury, M.P. 2016. Forgotten images: Charles Price Conigrave and the Kimberley Exploring Expedition of 1911. *Rock Art Research* 33(1):99–102.

Rainsbury, M.P. 2017. Rock art water colours: The Kimberley paintings of Hill and d'Emo. *Rock Art Research* 34(2):211–214.

Redmond, A. 2002. 'Alien abductions', Kimberley Aboriginal rock-paintings, and the speculation about human origins: On some investments in cultural tourism in the northern Kimberley. *Australian Aboriginal Studies* 2:54–64. search.informit.org/doi/10.3316/informit.595248307027622.

Redmond, A. 2017. Tracks and shadows: Some social effects of the 1938 Frobenius Expedition to the north-west Kimberley. In N. Peterson and A. Kenny (eds), *German ethnography in Australia*, pp. 413–434. ANU E Press, Canberra. doi.org/10.22459/GEA.09.2017.16.

Roberts, A., I. Campbell, A. Pring, G. Bell, A. Watchman, R. Popelka-Filcoff, C. Lenehan, C. Gibson and N. Franklin 2015. A multidisciplinary investigation of a rock coating at Ngaut Ngaut (Devon Downs), South Australia. *Australian Archaeology* 80(1):32–39. doi.org/10.1080/03122417.2015.11682042.

Roberts, R., G. Walsh, A. Murray, J. Olley, R. Jones, M.J. Morwood, C. Tuniz, E. Lawson, M. Macphail, D. Bowdery and I. Naumann 1997. Luminescence dating of rock art and past environments using mud-wasp nests in northern Australia. *Nature* 387(6634):696–699. doi.org/10.1038/42690.

Rosenfeld, A. 1985. *Rock art conservation in Australia*. Special Australian Heritage Publication 2. Australian Government Publishing Service, Canberra.

Ross, J. and M. Travers 2013. 'Ancient mariners' in northwest Kimberley rock art: An analysis of watercraft and crew depictions. *The Great Circle* 35(2):55–82.

Ross, J., K. Westaway, M. Travers, M.J. Morwood and J. Hayward 2016. Into the past: A step towards a robust Kimberley rock art chronology. *PLoS One* 11(8):e0161726. doi.org/10.1371/journal.pone. 0161726.

Ryan, J. and K. Akerman 1993. *Images of power: Aboriginal art of the Kimberley.* National Gallery of Victoria, Melbourne.

Schmiechen, J. 1993. *Shadows in stone: A report on Aboriginal rock art survey expeditions 1988 and 1991. Drysdale River National Park, Kimberley, Western Australia.* AIATSIS, Canberra.

Schmiechen, J. 1995. Drysdale River National Park, Western Australia: Aboriginal Cultural Heritage, management problems and potential. In G.K. Ward and L.A. Ward (eds), *Management of rock art imagery*, pp. 71–81. Occasional AURA Publication 9. Australian Rock Art Association, Melbourne.

Schulz, A. 1956. North–west Australian rock paintings. *Memoirs of Museum Victoria* 20:7–57. doi.org/ 10.24199/j.mmv.1956.20.01.

Schulz, A. 1971. *Felsbilder in Nord-Australien.* Steiner, Wiesbaden.

Somerville, C. 1997. Cultural importance of rock art to today's Aboriginal people. In K.F. Kenneally, M.R. Lewis, M. Donaldson and C. Clement (eds), *Aboriginal rock art of the Kimberley*, pp. 5–8. Occasional Paper 1. Kimberley Society, Perth.

Spencer, B. 1914. *Native tribes of the Northern Territory of Australia.* Macmillan, London.

Spencer, B., and F.J. Gillen 1899. *The native tribes of Central Australia.* MacMillan & Co, London.

Stubbs, D. 1974. *Prehistoric art of Australia.* The Macmillan Company of Australia Pty Ltd, Sydney.

Taçon, P.S.C. and C. Chippindale 1998. An archaeology of rock art through informed and formal methods. In C. Chippindale and P.S.C. Taçon (eds), *The archaeology of rock art*, pp. 1–10. Cambridge University Press, Cambridge.

Thomas, M. (ed.) 2007. *Culture in translation: The anthropological legacy of R.H. Mathews.* ANU E Press, Canberra. doi.org/10.22459/CT.09.2007.

Travers, M. and J. Ross 2016. Continuity and change in the anthropomorphic figures of Australia's northwest Kimberley. *Australian Archaeology* 82(2):148–167. doi.org/10.1080/03122417.2016.1210 757.

Trigger, B.G. 1984. Alternative archaeologies: Nationalist, colonialist, imperialist. *Man* 19(3):355–370. doi.org/10.2307/2802176.

Utemorrah, D. and P. Vinnicombe 1992. Northwestern Kimberley belief systems. In M.J. Morwood and D.R. Hobbs (eds), *Rock art and ethnography*, pp. 25–26. Occasional AURA Publication 5. Australian Rock Art Research Association, Melbourne.

Veth, P., C. Myers, P. Heaney and S. Ouzman 2018. Plants before farming: The deep history of plant-use and representation in the rock art of Australia's Kimberley region. *Quaternary International* 489:26–45. doi.org/10.1016/j.quaint.2016.08.036.

Veth, P., K. Ditchfield, M. Bateman, S. Ouzman, M. Benoit, A.P. Motta, D. Lewis, S. Harper and Balanggarra Aboriginal Corporation 2019. Minjiwarra: Archaeological evidence of human occupation of Australia's northern Kimberley by 50,000 BP. *Australian Archaeology* 85(2):115–125. doi.org/10.1080/03122417.2019.1650479.

Veth, P., S. Harper and K. Ditchfield 2021. The case for continuity in the Kimberley occupation and rock art. In A. McGrath and L. Russell (eds), *Routledge companion to Indigenous global history*, pp. 195–220. Routledge, New York.

Vinnicombe, P. 1992. Kimberley ideology and the maintenance of sites. In G.K. Ward (ed.), *Retouch: Maintenance and conservation of rock art imagery*, pp. 10–11. Occasional AURA Publication 5. Australian Rock Art Research Association, Melbourne.

Vinnicombe, P. 1997. Aspects of the value system associated with Wandjina art. In K.F. Kenneally, M.R. Lewis, M. Donaldson and C. Clement (eds), *Aboriginal rock art of the Kimberley*, pp. 13–18. Occasional Paper 1. Kimberley Society, Perth.

Walsh, G.L. 1992. Rock art retouch: Can a claim of Aboriginal descent establish curation rights over humanity's cultural heritage? In M.J. Morwood and D.R. Hobbs (eds), *Rock art and ethnography*, pp. 46–59. Occasional AURA Publication 5. Australian Rock Art Association, Melbourne.

Walsh, G.L. 1994. *Bradshaws: Ancient rock paintings of north-west Australia*. Carouge-Bradshaw Foundation, Geneva.

Walsh, G.L. 1997a. Ancient rock art of the Kimberley. In K.F. Kenneally, M.R. Lewis, M. Donaldson and C. Clement (eds), *Aboriginal rock art of the Kimberley*, pp. 25–38. Occasional Paper 1. Kimberley Society, Perth.

Walsh, G.L. 1997b. Wandjinas and recent rock art of the Kimberley. In K.F. Kenneally, M.R. Lewis, M. Donaldson and C. Clement (eds), *Aboriginal rock art of the Kimberley*, pp. 53–64. Occasional Paper 1. Kimberley Society, Perth.

Walsh, G.L. 2000. *Bradshaw art of the Kimberley*. Takarakka Nowan Kas Publications, Toowong.

Walsh, G.L. and M.J. Morwood 1999. Spear and spearthrower evolution in the Kimberley region, NW Australia: Evidence from rock art. *Archaeology in Oceania* 34(2):45–58. doi.org/10.1002/j.1834-4453.1999.tb00428.x.

Ward, G.K. (ed.) 1992. *Retouch: Maintenance and conservation of rock art imagery*. Occasional AURA Publication 5. Australian Rock Art Research Association, Melbourne.

Ward, G.K. and S. Sullivan 1989. The Australian Institute of Aboriginal Studies rock art protection program. *Rock Art Research* 6:54–62.

Ward, I., A. Watchman, N. Cole and M.J. Morwood 2001. Identification of minerals in pigments from Aboriginal art in the Laura and Kimberley Regions, Australia. *Rock Art Research* 18(1):15–23.

Watchman, A.L. 1997. Dating the Kimberley rock paintings. In K.F. Kenneally, M.R. Lewis, M. Donaldson and C. Clement (eds), *Aboriginal rock art of the Kimberley*, pp. 39–46. Occasional Paper 1. Kimberley Society, Perth.

Watchman, A.L., G.L. Walsh, M.J. Morwood and C. Tuniz 1997. AMS radiocarbon age estimates for early rock paintings in the Kimberley, NW Australia: Preliminary results. *Rock Art Research* 14:18–25.

Weiler, A. and R. Weiler 2017. *Australia's forgotten rock paintings*. Hanse-Wisenschaftskolleg, Oldenburg.

Welch, D.M. 1990. The bichrome art period in the Kimberley, Australia. *Rock Art Research* 7(2):110–124.

Welch, D.M. 1993a. Stylistic change in the Kimberley rock art, Australia. In M. Lorblanchet and P.G. Bahn (eds), *Rock art studies: The post-stylistic era or where do we go from here?* pp. 99–113. Oxbow Books, Oxford.

Welch, D.M. 1993b. The early rock art of the Kimberley, Australia: Developing a chronology. In J. Steinbring, A. Watchman, P. Faulstich and P.S.C. Taçon (eds), *Time and space: Dating and spatial considerations in tock art research*, pp. 13–21. Occasional AURA Publication 8. Australian Rock Art Research Association, Melbourne.

Welch, D.M. 1993c. Early 'naturalistic' human figures in the Kimberley, Australia. *Rock Art Research* 10(1):24–37.

Welch, D.M. 1995. Beeswax rock art in the Kimberley, Western Australia. *Rock Art Research* 12(1):23–28.

Welch, D.M. 1996a. Material culture in Kimberley rock art, Australia. *Rock Art Research* 13(2):104–123.

Welch, D.M. 1996b. Simple figures in Kimberley rock art, Western Australia. *The Artefact* 19:73–89.

Welch, D.M. 1997. Fight or dance? Ceremony and the spear thrower in Northern Australian rockart. *Rock Art Research* 14(2):88–112.

Welch, D.M. 2007. Bradshaw art of the Kimberley. In M.J. Donaldson and K.F. Kenneally (eds), *Rock art of the Kimberley*, pp. 81–100. Kimberley Society, Perth.

Welch, D.M. 2016. *From Bradshaw to Wandjina: Aboriginal paintings of the Kimberley Region, Western Australia*. Australian Aboriginal Culture Series 12, Coolalinga.

Williams, N.M. 1988. 'She was the first one:' Phyllis Kaberry in the east Kimberley: *Aboriginal History* 12(1/2):84–102. doi.org/10.22459/AH.12.2011.07.

Wilson, I. 2006. *Lost world of the Kimberley: Extraordinary glimpses of Australia's Ice Age ancestors*. Alan and Unwin, Crows Nest.

Wise, T. 1985. *The self-made anthropologist: The life of A.P. Elkin*. Allen & Unwin, Sydney.

Wood, R., Z. Jacobs, D. Vannieuwenhuyse, J. Balme, S. O'Connor and R. Whitau 2016. Towards an accurate and precise chronology for the colonization of Australia: The example of Riwi, Kimberley, Western Australia. *PloS ONE* 2016. doi.org/10.1371/journal.pone.0160123.

Woolagoodja, D. 2007. Rock art as inspiration for contemporary Aboriginal painting. In M.J. Donaldson and K.F. Kenneally (eds), *Rock art of the Kimberley*, pp. 25–38. Kimberley Society, Perth.

Woolagoodja, Y. 2020. *Yornadaiyn Woolagoodja*. Magabala Books, Broome.

Worms, E.A. 1955. Contemporary and prehistoric rock paintings in central and northern Kimberley. *Anthropos* 50(4/6):546–566.

Part C: North, north-east and beyond

11

The history of Arnhem Land rock art research: A multicultural, multilingual and multidisciplinary pursuit

Paul S.C. Taçon

Introduction

Arnhem Land rock art, including that of Kakadu National Park, has been known to the outside world since the early 1800s but it was not until the 1940s that it became a subject of serious investigation (e.g. see McCarthy 1955, 1960; Rose 1942). Eight key research themes developed over time with different approaches, questions and subjects of concern. These themes, from an initial one of discovery and reporting to the most recent employing digital technology, structure this paper. However, the focus is on the multicultural investigation of Arnhem Land rock art and the ways in which this has shaped the history and course of research, including the testing and adoption of many pioneering approaches to rock art recording, interpretation, dating, conservation, management and tourism. Over 100 non-Indigenous individuals from 12 countries have contributed to our understanding of Arnhem Land rock art, with Australians, Brits, Czechs and Canadians, in particular, advancing knowledge. But there has always equally been a strong interest from Aboriginal Australians in better understanding, promoting and protecting their rock art heritage with over 100 key individuals from across Arnhem Land and beyond actively participating in Arnhem Land research. Consequently, Indigenous and non-Indigenous research perspectives have been intertwined for over 70 years, resulting in a deservedly rich and enriched rock art research history.

The history of Australian rock art research has been outlined in various forums, with Layton (1992) providing detail for different periods of time scattered across a number of book chapters and Taçon (2001) undertaking a focused review. Aspects of the history of Arnhem Land rock art research can be found in the background chapters of various PhD theses, such as Gunn (2016), Hayward (2016), Johnston (2018), Jones (2017), Marshall (2020), Taçon (1989) and Wesley (2014), including discussion of the varying styles and stylistic chronologies that have been proposed (e.g. Brandl 1973; Chaloupka 1993; Chippindale and Taçon 1998; David et al. 2013; Jones et al. 2016; Lewis 1988; Taçon and Brockwell 1995; Taçon and Chippindale 2008; various papers in David, Taçon, Geneste et al. 2017). The chronology continues to be refined (e.g. Jones et al. 2020; May, Taylor et al. 2020; Taçon et al. 2020). Marshall's (2020) PhD thesis is particularly important for the rock art conservation history of Arnhem Land (see also Haritos's 2006 Honours thesis on rock art management). Recently, a comprehensive Arnhem

Land rock art research history was also published (David, Taçon, Gunn et al. 2017). All of these studies essentially take a timeline approach, focusing on what was achieved over time. However, in this paper the rise of rock art research themes over time is explored to highlight the strong collaborations and friendships that were formed between Indigenous and non-Indigenous researchers, as well as to show that this led to pioneering developments that not only advanced Arnhem Land and Australian rock art research but also benefited the study of rock art worldwide.

Over 20,000 rock art sites have been reported and/or recorded in varying ways across Arnhem Land since the early 1800s. Each year hundreds of previously undocumented sites are located by various teams. The region is especially famous for its painted and stencilled rock art imagery, sometimes in huge rock-shelter complexes in many overlapping styles (e.g. for Djulirri see May et al. 2010; Taçon, Langley et al. 2010; Taçon, May et al. 2010; for Mt. Gilruth see Chaloupka 1993; Haskovec 1992; and for Nawarla Gabarnmang see David et al. 2011; David, Taçon, Geneste et al. 2017; David et al. 2013; Gunn et al. 2012), as well as what is reputed to be Australia's oldest dated archaeological site with rock art, Madjedbebe (see Clarkson et al. 2017).

Summaries of the western Arnhem Land rock art can be found in May et al. (2015) and May and Taçon (2014), while detailed accounts are in Brandl (1973), Chaloupka (1993), Lewis (1988) and Taçon (1989). It is beyond the scope of this paper to list the entire literature on Arnhem Land rock art, let alone describe it, but comprehensive databases of Australian rock art publications can be found in Australian Heritage Commission (1990) and Marymor (2018, 2019). Instead, the focus is on the people who undertook the research, the earliest discoveries and reports on rock art and the development of rock art tourism.

Arnhem Land researchers

An early attempt to list which non-Indigenous researchers worked in Kakadu National Park can be found in May et al. (2015) but until now there has not been a comprehensive list of the key players in greater Arnhem Land rock art research. In the short lists or research summaries that do exist, Aboriginal individuals who participated are rarely named. In the two tables below the names, countries of origin, specialties and periods when they were most active are listed for non-Indigenous and Indigenous people, as well as Indigenous–non-Indigenous collaborations.

Non-Indigenous people who contributed to Arnhem Land rock art research are listed in Table 11.1. In summary, 78 Australians (55 male and 23 female) and 29 individuals from 11 other countries (21 male and eight female) were identified, for a total of 107 non-Indigenous individuals. In terms of people from outside Australia contributing to knowledge about the rock art of Arnhem Land, most were from the United Kingdom (eight), then Canada (five) and Czechoslovakia (now Czech Republic) (five). George Chaloupka, originally from Czechoslovakia, and Paul Taçon, originally from Canada, were most active, 44 years (1967–2011) and 40 years (1981–ongoing), respectively. There were also a lot of students and volunteers working with a range of people from the 1980s to the present who are not listed in the table. Paddy Cahill has not been included as, although he investigated some rock-shelters with art, possibly as early as the 1880s and certainly since 1909 (see below), he did not publish descriptions of what he saw unlike others who 'discovered' sites in the 1800s and early 1900s. However, he did direct various people to sites who then published accounts.

Table 11.1: Non-Aboriginal people in Arnhem Land rock art research.

Name	Country	Primary approaches	Period most active
W. Arndt	Australia	Recording, analysis & ethnography	1960s
Charles Barrett	Australia	Recording, Wessel Islands	1939
Herbert Basedow	Australia	Recording	1900s–1920s
Annie Clarke	Australia	Survey, recording & analysis	1995–1996, 2018–present
John Clarke	Australia	Pigment analysis & conservation	1986–1989
Peter Cooke	Australia	Survey, recording, ethnography & management	2007–present
David Cooper	Australia	Ethnography & management	Late 1980s – early 1990s
Phil Crews	Australia	Parks Australia survey, recording & management	1990s
Isabelle Dangas	Australia	Conservation	1989
Charles Dashwood	Australia	Reporting discovery	1895
Bruno David	Australia	Survey, recording, analysis	2009–present
Graham Davidson	Australia	Recording	1976
Max Davidson	Australia	Tourism	1986–2017
Janet Davill	Australia	Survey & recording	2008–present
Phil Davill	Australia	Survey & recording	2008–present
Leigh Douglas	Australia	Survey & recording	2008–2012
Alfred J. Dyer	Australia	Reporting discovery & some ethnography	Late 1920s & early 1930s
Robert Edwards	Australia	Recording & analysis	1964–mid-1970s
A.P. Elkin	Australia	Recording & ethnography	1949–1952
Ursula K. Frederick	Australia	Survey, recording & analysis	1995–1996, 2018–present
Fay Gale	Australia	Tourism & management	1982–1983
Murray Garde	Australia	Survey, recording, analysis & ethnography	1990s–present
Dan Gillespie	Australia	Conservation & management	1980s
Pina Giuliani	Australia	Survey, recording, archiving	1980s–2015
Robert (ben) Gunn	Australia	Survey, recording, ethnography, management, analysis & digital applications	1987–present
Nicholas Hall	Australia	Recording, analysis & conservation	2006–2018
Judith Hammond	Australia	Master of Arts thesis	2016
Helen Haritos	Australia	Management	2005–2006
Fred Hunter	Australia	Reporting discovery	1960s
Jillian Huntley	Australia	Pigment analysis	2018–present
Phil Hughes	Australia	Conservation	1980s
Gary Jackson	Australia	Recording & ethnography	Early 1990s – present
Daniel James	Australia	Survey, recording & analysis	2009–2016
Iain Johnston	Australia	Survey, recording & analysis	2012–present
Tristen Jones	Australia	Survey, recording, analysis & dating	2008–present
Bill Harney	Australia	Reporting	1957
John Hayward	Australia	Survey, recording & analysis	2012–present
Dave Lambert	Australia	Conservation	1997–1999
Darrel Lewis	Australia	Survey, recording & analysis	1970s & 1980s
Dave Lindner	Australia	Management	2008
N.W.G. Macintosh	Australia	Recording	1949–1977

Name	Country	Primary approaches	Period most active
Fred McCarthy	Australia	Survey & recording	1940s–1950s
Jo McDonald	Australia	Survey & recording	1986
Fiona McKeague	Australia	Survey & recording, rock art tourism research	2008–present
Kim McKenzie	Australia	Film	1982, 2002–2013
Dehne McLaughlin	Australia	Survey & recording	Late 1970s – early 1980s
Melissa Marshall	Australia	Survey, recording, analysis & conservation	1990s–present
Elsie Masson	Australia	Reporting discovery	1913
Sally K. May	Australia	Survey, recording, analysis, digital applications & ethnography	1998–present
Emily Miller	Australia	Survey, recording & analysis	2016–present
Charles Mountford	Australia	Survey & recording	1948, 1949
Neil North	Australia	Pigment analysis	1986–1988
Gabrielle O'Loughlin	Australia	Parks Australia survey, recording, management	2000s–present
Adrian Parker	Australia	Recording & analysis	Early 2000s
Alistair Paterson	Australia	Recording & analysis	2008
Axel Poignant	Australia	Reporting discovery & ethnography	1953
Andy Ralph	Australia	Tourism	1990s–2015
Marie Reay	Australia	Recording	1960s
Leo J. Rivett	Australia	Photogrammetry	1984
David Andrew Roberts	Australia	Recording & analysis	Early 2000s
Colin Simpson	Australia	Reporting	1948
Claire Smith	Australia	Recording, analysis & ethnography	1990s–present
W. Baldwin Spencer	Australia	Reporting discovery	1912
Allan Stewart	Australia	Tourism	1960s
Hilary Sullivan	Australia	Parks Australia survey, recording, tourism, conservation & management	1980s & 1990s
Andrew Thorn	Australia	Conservation	1992–1993
Norman Tindale	Australia	Recording	1920s
David Turner	Australia	Recording	1969
Georgia Vallance	Australia	Survey, recording & management	2010–present
Mark Viney	Australia	Survey & recording	1978
Carl Warburton	Australia	Reporting	1919
Alan Watchman	Australia	Dating, conservation	1980s
Ray Whear	Australia	Survey & recording	1990s–present
David Welch	Australia	Survey & recording	1980s–present
Daryl Wesley	Australia	Survey, recording & analysis	1990s–present
Trent Wilkinson	Australia	Management	2008–present
Meredith Wilson	Australia	Survey, recording & analysis	1996
Duncan Wright	Australia	Survey, recording & analysis	2012–2018
Megan Berry	Canada	Master of Liberal Arts thesis	2011
Liam Brady	Canada	Survey, recording, analysis & ethnography	2016–present
Laura Jacobs	Canada	Pigment analysis	2018
Erle Nelson	Canada	Dating	1990s

Name	Country	Primary approaches	Period most active
Paul S.C. Taçon	Canada	Survey, recording, analysis, dating, ethnography, conservation, digital applications	1981–present
Eric Brandl	Czechoslovakia	Survey, recording, analysis, ethnography	1960s & 1970s
George Chaloupka	Czechoslovakia	Survey, recording, analysis, dating, ethnography	1967–2011
Ivan Haskovec	Czechoslovakia	Parks Australia survey, recording, analysis, tourism, conservation & management	1980s & 1990s
Jan Jelinek	Czechoslovakia	Survey, recording & analysis	1969–1973
Stanislav Novotny	Czechoslovakia	Survey, recording & analysis	1969
Jean-Jacques Delannoy	France	Recording, analysis & digital applications	2009–present
Jean-Michel Geneste	France	Recording & analysis	2009–present
Sabine Hoeng	Germany	Curation of Chaloupka collection at MAGNT & survey	2009–2017
Ludwig Leichhardt	Germany	Reporting discovery	1846
Agnes Schultz	Germany	Recording	1954–1955
Harry Allen	New Zealand	Survey & recording	1970s
Knut Dahl	Norway	Reporting discovery	1894
Andrea Jalandoni	Philippines	Photogrammetry, 3D, digital applications	2016–present
Ines Domingo Sanz	Spain	Survey, recording, analysis, digital applications	2008–present
Joakim Goldhahn	Sweden	Survey, recording & analysis	2013–present
Christopher Chippindale	United Kingdom	Survey, recording, analysis & dating	1990–2010
Matthew Flinders	United Kingdom	Reporting discovery	1803
John Lewis	United Kingdom	Reporting discovery	1874
Judy Opitz	United Kingdom	Tourism study	2001–2008
Frederick Rose	United Kingdom	Recording	1938–1939, 1941
Harry Stockdale	United Kingdom	Reporting discovery	1891
William Westall	United Kingdom	Painting	1803
Peter Worsley	United Kingdom	Recording	1953
Peggy Grove	USA	Recording & analysis	Late 1990s
Grand total = 107			

Note: MAGNT = Museum and Art Gallery of the Northern Territory.
Source: Author's summary.

As can be seen in Table 11.2, 99 Indigenous individuals (78 male and 21 female), one family (Yantarrnga), a ranger group (Njanjma), an Aboriginal Association (Jawoyn Association Aboriginal Corporation), an art centre (Injalak Arts) and a land management rock art group (Warddeken) could be named with information about who they collaborated with and when. Chaloupka (1993:249) listed another five individuals and two families but without any information and many more have participated in group activities, such as Kakadu National Park research and management programs, the activities of the Warddeken Land Management rock art group, Injalak Arts artist engagements with rock art and the Jawoyn Association's Jawoyn Rock Art and Heritage Project. Additionally, hundreds of local Aboriginal community members, such as local Aboriginal school groups, Elders, rangers and sometimes recently deceased site managers or owners (in the local Aboriginal sense) participated in some projects but were not named in publications because of a combination of factors including appropriate local protocols. They come from right across Arnhem Land and other parts of the Territory's 'Top End'. Moreover, three Aboriginal individuals from New South Wales undertook research and co-authored or significantly contributed to publications (Wayne Brennan, Sue McPherson and Toni Wickey). Local Indigenous woman and Parks Australia employee Mary Blyth was more active than anyone, working with rock art over a period of 31 years, from 1984 to 2014. She knew and interacted with all of the major non-Aboriginal players who worked on Kakadu National Park rock art since the park's declaration on 5 April 1979.

Table 11.2: Aboriginal people in Arnhem Land rock art research.

Name	Language & Country	Primarily with	Period
Jimmy (Fabian) Ah Toy	Kundjeyhmi, Djuwarr (Deaf Adder Gorge)	I. Haskovec, H. Sullivan & P. Taçon	1985–1986
Mick Alderson	Mayali, Jim Jim Creek	G. Chaloupka, E. Nelson, C. Chippindale & P. Taçon	1980s & 1990s
Larry Atkinson	Jawoyn	R. Gunn, R. Whear, L. Douglas	2008–2012
Thomas Balmana	Kunwinjku	G. Chaloupka	1970s
Peter Balmanidbal	Kundjeyhmi, Mirarr country	G. Chaloupka	1960s and 1970s
Balumba (Old Sam)	Anindilyakwa, Wuramara local group, Bikerton Island	D. Turner	1969
Sandy Barraway	Jawoyn, Southern Kakadu Stage 3	P. Taçon, R. Gunn	1980s & 1990s
Big Bill Birriyabirriya	Kuninjku, Lower Liverpool River	M. Garde & P. Taçon	2003–2004
Mary Blyth	Iwaidja, Murganella	Parks Australia	1984–2014
Peter Bolgay	Jawoyn	R. Gunn	2000s–2010s
Queenie Brennan	Dalabon	I. Haskovec & H. Sullivan	1985
Wayne Brennan	Gamilaraay, Gamilaraay country (NSW)	P. Taçon & S. May	2008–present
Nipper Brown	Jawoyn, Southern Kakadu Stage 3	R. Gunn, P. Taçon	1980s
Jacky Bunkarniyal	Dangbon/Rembarrnga/Kune, Cadell River	E. Brandl, S. Novotny	1970s
David Canari (Nadulwinj)	Kundjeyhmi, Djuwarr (Deaf Adder Gorge)	P. Taçon, C. Chippindale	1980s & 1990s
Victor Cooper	Minitja, north Kakadu	Parks Australia, S. May, own tourism business	1993–present
Djimongurr (Old Nym)	Kundjeyhmi, Warddjak clan country	A. Stewart	1963–1965
Hector Djorlom	Mawng, Born country	G. Chaloupka	1960s & 1970s
Ivan Milliken Donborr	Burarra, East of Maningrida	M. Garde, P. Taçon	1993 & 1994
Sarah Flora	Jawoyn	R. Gunn	2010s
Frank Ganangu	Kunwinjku	G. Chaloupka	1970s
Toby Gangale	Kundjeyhmi, Mirarr country	P. Taçon	1970s & 1980s
Douglas Hunter (Namara Bunja)	Kundjeyhmi, Bolmo Dedjrungi country, upper East Alligator River	S. May, P. Taçon, J. Goldhahn, I. Johnston, J. Hayward	2012–2014
Jenny Hunter (Ngaljalkarrdi)	Kundjeyhmi, Bolmo Dedjrungi country, upper East Alligator River	Parks Australia, S. May, tourism business	1990s–present
Injalak Arts artists	Kunwinjku and various other	Themselves, S. May, P. Taçon and others	1980s–present
Peter Jatbula	Jawoyn, Greater Katherine Gorge & southern Kakadu Stage 3	G. Chaloupka, R. Gunn, P. Taçon, C. Chippindale	1980s & 1990s

Name	Language & Country	Primarily with	Period
Jawoyn Association Aboriginal Corporation's Jawoyn Rock Art and Heritage Project (lots of individuals)	Jawoyn	R. Gunn, R. Whear, L. Douglas	2005–2012
Kanaula (also Kanowla)	Oenpelli	A.J. Dyer, C. Mountford	1930s, 1940s
Nipper Kapirigi	Kundjeyhmi, Djuwarr (Deaf Adder Gorge)	G. Chaloupka, P. Taçon	1970s–1987
Margaret Katherine	Jawoyn, Birndalak area of the upper Mann River	B. David, R: Gunn, J. Geneste, J. Delannoy, D. James	2000s–2018
Mick Kubarkku	Kuninjku, Lower Mann River	M. Garde, P. Taçon	1990s
Kumbiala	Anindilyakwa, Groote Eylandt	F. McCarthy	1948
Lamderod (Lamjorrotj)	Jawoyn	A.P. Elkin, N.W.G. Macintosh	Early 1950s
Lazarus Lamilami	Mawng, Namunidjbuk	A. Poignant, G. Chaloupka	Late 1920s, 1952, 1970s
Leonard Lamilami	Mawng, Namunidjbuk	P. Taçon, S. May, D. Wesley	2000s–present
Lloyd Lamilami	Mawng, Namunidjbuk	P. Taçon	2018
Patrick Lamilami	Mawng, Namunidjbuk	P. Taçon, S. May, D. Wesley	2000s–present
Ronald Lamilami	Mawng, Namunidjbuk	P. Taçon, S. May, D. Wesley, G. Chaloupka	2000s–present
Jeffrey Lee	Kundjeyhmi, Nourlangie/ Burrungkuy (Djok country)	Parks Australia, G. O'Loughlin, S. May, P. Taçon, J. Goldhahn	1990s–present
Robert Lee	Jawoyn	R. Gunn, P. Taçon	Late 1980s – early 1990s
McGuiness McGee	Kundjeyhmi	P. Taçon	1981 & 1985
Peter McLevitt (Anamak)	Kundjeyhmi, Deaf Adder Gorge	P. Taçon, C. Chippindale	1995
Sue McPherson	Wirradjuri, Wagga Wagga, NSW but mother from Arnhem Land	P. Taçon	1991
Peter Manabaru	Jawoyn	C. Smith, G. Jackson	1992
Wally Mandarrg	Dangbon/Rembarrnga/Kune, Cadell River	E. Brandl, G. Chaloupka	1970s
Kenneth Mangiru	Kunwinjku, Tin Camp Creek	T. Wilkinson, P. Taçon, E. Nelson, S. May	1990s–present
Moses Mangiru	Kunwinjku, Tin Camp Creek	P. Taçon, E. Nelson, C. Chippindale	1990s
Josie Maralngurra	Kundjeyhmi, Warddjak clan country	S. May. J. Goldhahn, P. Taçon	2018–2019
Yvonne Margarula	Kundjeyhmi, Mirarr	S. May	1990s–present
John Mawurndjul	Kuninjku, Lower Mann River	M. Garde, P. Taçon	1993 & 1994
Jimmy Midjaw Midjawu	Kunwinjku, Minjalang, Croker Island	G. Chaloupka	1970s, early 1980s
Kadeem May	Larrakia, Darwin	Parks Australia, G. O'Loughlin, S. May, P. Taçon, M. Marshall, J. Huntley, L. Jacobs	2015–present
Colin Moore	Mayali	P. Taçon, C. Chippindale	1992–1995
Charlie Mungulda	Amurdak, Awunbarna	M. Davidson, S. Hoeng, P. Taçon, A. Parker, D. Roberts, G. Chaloupka, S. May	1990s–present

Name	Language & Country	Primarily with	Period
Mandy (Marrgam) Muir	Mayali, Jim Jim Creek	S. Sullivan, I. Haskovec, own tourism business	Late 1980s – early 1990s, 2015–present
Dick Nadjalorro	Kuninjku, Lower Mann River	M. Garde, P. Taçon	1993–1994
Natasha (Mungumurru) Nadji	Gagudju, Bunidj country	P. Taçon, N. Hall, tourism business	2013–present
Lofty Bardayal Nadjmerrek	Kundedjnjenghmi, Upper Mann and Liverpool rivers	G. Chaloupka, P. Cooke, M. Garde, R. Gunn, P. Taçon	1990s–2009
Djawida Nadjongorle	Kunwinjku, Kudjekbinj & Djalbangurr areas	G. Chaloupka	1980s
Fred Nagawali	Kunwinjku, Rol clan	I. Dargas, I. Haskovec, H. Sullivan	1980s
Najombolmi	Kundjeyhmi, Deaf Adder Gorge	A. Stewart	1963–1965
Frank Nalowerd	Kunwinjku, greater Nabarlek area	G. Chaloupka	1970s
Paddy Compass Namadbara	Iwaidja, Croker Island	G. Chaloupka	Late 1960s & early 1970s
Namuluda	Amurdak & Iwaidja Awunbarna	A. Poignant	1920s & 1950s
Jacky Namandali	Kundedjnjenghmi/Kundjeyhmi	I. Haskovec, H. Sullivan	1980s
Namandkragg (Butcher Knight)	Mayali, Jim Jim Creek	G. Chaloupka, P. Taçon	1980s
Elijah Namarabundja	Kundjeyhmi	G. Chaloupka	1970s
Paul Namarinjmak	Kuninjku, Lower Mann River	M. Garde, P. Taçon	1993 & 1994
Kalarriya (Jimmy) Namarnyilk	Kundedjnjenghmi, Upper Cadell River	M. Garde, P. Cooke, S. May, P. Taçon	1990s–2012
George Namingum	Kundjeyhmi, Deaf Adder Gorge	G. Chaloupka, P. Taçon	1970s & 1980s
Don Namundja	Kunwinjku, Mankorlod	P. Taçon, E. Nelson, D. Wesley	1992 & 2000s
Wilfred Nawirridj	Kunwinjku, Mirarr	S. May, P. Taçon	1990s–2013
Alfred Nayinggul	Kunwinjku/Urningangk, Manilakarr country	T. Jones, T. Wilkinson, N. Hall, M. Marshall, S. May, D. Wesley	2000s–present
Anita Nayinggul	Kunwinjku/Urningangk, Manilakarr country	T. Jones	2013–2017
Connie Nayinggul	Kunwinjku/Urningangk, Manilakarr country	T. Jones, T. Wilkinson, N. Hall, S. May, M. Marshall, D. Wesley	2000s–present
Jacob Nayinggul	Kunwinjku/Urningangk, Manilakarr country	G. Chaloupka, P. Taçon, S. May, D. Wright, D. Wesley, T. Jones	Late 1970s–2012
Katie Nayinggul	Kunwinjku/Urningangk, Manilakarr country	T. Jones	2013–2017
Manbiyarra (Grant) Nayinggul	Kunwinjku/Urningangk, Manilakarr country	T. Jones, T. Wilkinson, N. Hall, D. Wesley	2000s–present
Samuel Nayinggul	Kunwinjku/Urningangk, Manilakarr country	T. Jones	2013–2017
Big Bill Neidjie	Gagudju, Bunidj country	G. Chaloupka, P. Taçon, D. Gillespie	1980s–2002
Bobby Barrdjaray Nganjmira	Kunwinjku, Malworn (residence)	G. Chaloupka, P. Taçon	1980s–1992
Thompson (Thommo) Nganjmira	Kunwinjku, Gunbalanya	Injalak Arts, tourism	1990s–present
Ken Ngindjalakku	Kuninjku, Lower Mann River	M. Garde, P. Taçon	1993 & 1994
Dick Nguleingulei Murrumurru	Dangbon & Kunwinjku, Liverpool River	G. Chaloupka	1980s

Name	Language & Country	Primarily with	Period
Njanjma Rangers not listed individually	Mostly Kunwinku	T. Jones, N. Hall, D. Wesley, T. Wilkinson	2015–present
Catherine Ralph (Gundjulk)	Kundjeyhmi	Parks Australia, Warddeken Land Management rock art group, Jenny Hunter	2018–present
Sybil Ranch	Jawoyn	R. Gunn	2010s
Norman Ross (Namandjalawokwok)	Kundjeyhmi, Warddjak country	P. Taçon	1985–1986
Peter Rotumah	Amurdak, Awunbarna	A. Parker, D. Roberts	Early 2000s
Peter Sullivan	Mayali/Jawoyn, upper East Alligator River, upper Katherine River (Wunkomku clan)	Parks Australia, P. Taçon, C. Chippindale	1985–1992
Ben Tyler	Mayali	Parks Australia, S. May, P. Taçon	2012–2014
Warddeken Land Management rock art group (many individuals)	Bininj Kunwok, Warddeken Indigenous Protected Area	P. Cooke, G. Vallance, M. Garde, K. McKenzie	2007–present
Jenny Wellings	Mayali	Parks Australia, S. May	2017–present
Toni Wickey	Wiradjuri Wiradjuri country (NSW)	P. Taçon, M. Garde, E. Nelson	1994
Wilirra	Kunwinjku	Mountford, G. Chaloupka	1948, 1970s
Julie Williams	Jawoyn	R. Gunn	2010s
Lilly Willika	Jawoyn	C. Smith, G. Jackson	Early 1990s
George, Winungoyd (Winungoid)	Mawng, Namunidjbuk	A. Poignant, G. Chaloupka	1952, 1970s
Phyllis Wiynjorroc	Jawoyn	C. Smith, G. Jackson, R. Gunn	1990s
Galijawa Wuramarba	Anindilyakwa, Bikerton Island	D. Turner	1969
Yantarrnga family	Anindilyakwa, Yantarrnga (Central Hill) to cast, Groote Eylandt	A. Clarke, U. Frederick	1995 & 1996
Dolly Yarnmalu	Gagudju, Bunidj country	G. Chaloupka, P. Taçon	Late 1970s – mid-1980s
Kennedy Yiddunu	Kuninjku, Lower Mann River	M. Garde, P. Taçon, E. Nelson	1994
Thompson Yulidjirri	Kunwinjku	P. Taçon, S. May	1990s
Total = 104+			
Kalinowa	No info	G. Chaloupka (see 1993:249)	No info
Kulanjinga	No info	G. Chaloupka (see 1993:249)	No info
Madjandi	No info	G. Chaloupka (see 1993:249)	No info
Namilg	No info	G. Chaloupka (see 1993:249)	No info
Yorawadj	No info	G. Chaloupka (see 1993:249)	No info
Marlangura family	No info	G. Chaloupka (see 1993:249)	No info
Wagbara family	No info	G. Chaloupka (see 1993:249)	No info
Grand total = 114 +			

Source: Author's summary.

Arnhem Land rock art research and management phases, 1803 to the present

After tens of thousands of years of Aboriginal occupation of Arnhem Land's rock-shelters, as well as rock art production, curation, inspiration, contemplation and renewal, outsiders began to take an interest. This began in 1803 with an initial phase of non-Indigenous encounter with rock art, followed by focused research. Seven main research themes that developed over time can be identified. However, they are not so much discrete time periods but instead signal changes in the topics of rock art research of interest, with each new theme continuing aspects of previous ones but with added elements, concerns and orientations:

- *Theme 1: Initial non-Aboriginal discovery and brief reporting, early 1800s to 1950s*
- *Theme 2: Survey, recording and archaeological approaches, 1940s onward*
- *Theme 3: Tourism, since the 1950s*
- *Theme 4: Chronological frameworks, 1950s to present*
- *Theme 5: Ethnography of rock art, primarily 1960s to present*
- *Theme 6: Conservation and management, 1980s to present*
- *Theme 7: Scientific dating, 1980s to present*
- *Theme 8: Digital recording, laser scanning, 2008 to present*

In what follows, the focus is on the history of the first three themes. Although not formally identified as such, Themes 4–8 have been extensively discussed by others (see Introduction above and Discussion below).

Theme 1: Initial non-Aboriginal discovery and brief reporting, early 1800s to 1950s

Matthew Flinders (1814:188–189) was the first to report on Arnhem Land rock art, finding rock art on Chasm Island on Wednesday 12 January 1803:

> In the steep sides of the chasms were deep holes or caverns, undermining the cliffs; upon the walls of which I found rude drawings, made with charcoal and something like red paint upon the white ground of the rock. These drawings represented porpoises, turtle, kangaroos, and a human hand; and Mr. Westall, who went afterwards to see them, found the representation of a kangaroo, with a file of thirty-two persons following after it.

Artist William Westall, who accompanied Flinders on his voyage, made watercolour reproductions of some of the imagery (see Clarke and Frederick 2008:156; Findley 1998:39; Flinders 1814:189).

Ludwig Leichhardt (1846:3) was the first to remark on the rock art and other art forms of the deep interior of Arnhem Land, specifically some from the Alligator Rivers region after observing it in December 1845:

> We saw the foot of an emu cut very carefully and accurately into the bark of a tree, and other fanciful forms which we could not understand: A turtle was depicted very accurately on a rock with red ochre, and a fish in caves, in which the natives were accustomed to paint themselves for corroberies. It is extremely interesting to compare these efforts of the Australian natives with those of more advanced nations, and we are involuntarily induced to suppose meanings which we know as belonging to the latter. These imitations of the human body were, however, too near and too easy, and could be as well the produce of play and accident as conventional design.

Thus, since 1846, theories of 'art for art's sake' and 'art and ritual' were being explored to explain the meaning of the art and from the outset there was a warning of not reading one's own cultural experience into Aboriginal rock art.

John Lewis (1922:132) encountered rock art east of the East Alligator River in what is probably the Mount Borradaile area while searching for missing explorers Pemain and Borradaile in 1874:

> Near to the Head of the Alligator were numbers of old castle-like rocks, some with native paintings on them, and many parcels and packets of bones we found in the melaleuca bark; also stones wrapped in some sort of tartan cloth and blue serge. Where these came from I could not find out.

In 1891, explorer Harry Stockdale reported the discovery of 40 'caves' with paintings in the Alligator Rivers region over the course of about 100 miles. The sites were located during an overland journey to Port Essington (see Stockdale 1891). Some of Stockdale's descriptions were published by Worsnop (1895, 1897):

> These drawings and hieroglyphs are very remarkable indeed, being made in some cases on the roof and in others on the sides of caves. They consist of animals, birds, reptiles, men, women, canoes with men in them, &c., and a great many of the drawings of the men exhibit all the features of the face, several being (apparently) Europeans …

> There were quite 200 different drawings, though sometimes one cave would have seen quite seven or eight different representations more or less mixed together. (Worsnop 1897:38; see also Stockdale 1891 and Edwards 1979:38–39)

In 1894, Charles Dashwood visited the Alligator Rivers region and described rock art near where the McKinley Expedition camped for three weeks on the western side of the East Alligator River in 1866:

> Under an immense slab of sandstone, which was resting on other slabs, affording good shelter for man and beast, an aboriginal gallery of pictures was seen – alligators, kangaroo, fish, wallabies, birds, and human figures were drawn with coloured chalks. (Dashwood 1895:8)

The rock art Dashwood saw may be the main gallery of what is now known as the Ubirr complex. To the south, at a locality called 'Three Pools', is a shelter with paintings of men on horseback, considered to be a depiction of McKinley and part of his group (Chaloupka 1979).

Also, in 1894, Knut Dahl made note of rock art near the Katherine River:

> One day when approaching the storekeeper's place I came across some large rocks in the forest. On the face of these rocks I found a good many ochre drawings executed by the natives. There were clumsy drawings of men and kangaroos, the usual stencilled pictures of hands, etc. I found, also, however, some contour drawings of fishes very well done, so well, indeed, that I could easily recognise the common squirting fish (*Toxotes jaculator*), which was very often captured by the blacks. Perhaps the reason for the faithfulness of these drawings was that the fish's outline had been traced on the rock. (Dahl 1926:251)

Paddy Cahill may have been the first non-Aboriginal person to see the rock art near his settlement of Oenpelli, from his arrival in the early 1900s (Mulvaney 2004:3–4) onward, and may have investigated some sites on seasonal visits to the Alligator Rivers region since the 1880s (Edwards 1979:38). He showed Baldwin Spencer many Aboriginal bark paintings and took him to rock-shelters with art near Oenpelli when Spencer (1914, 1928) visited him in 1912:

> Up on the hill sides, among the rocks, wherever there is an overhanging shelter where the native can screen himself from the sun and rain, these drawings are certain to be found in the country of the Kakadu.

The colours used are red, white, black and yellow. They represent the animals with which the natives come in contact, and also their ideas in regard to the nature of certain mythical and mischievous spirits. So far as the animals are concerned, it is interesting to notice that the drawings are always more or less anatomical, that is, they represent not only the external form, but, to a certain extent, the internal structure. The backbone is almost always represented, as are the heart and main features of the alimentary canal. (Spencer 1914:432–433)

Spencer (1914:439), clearly impressed with what he saw, stated 'the bark and rock drawings of Kakadu, Gembio, and Umoriu tribes represent, I think, the highest artistic level amongst Australian aboriginals with the possible exception of the Melville and Bathurst Islanders'. Thus, comparisons with the art of other peoples also began early.

It is not known exactly which rock art sites Spencer was taken to. Elsie Masson, one of the first women to travel to remote areas outside Darwin and to visit Oenpelli (Lydon 2018), arrived in 1913. She was the first to publish a photograph of the main gallery of Injalak Hill, in 1915, taken by Dr Mervyn Holmes (Masson 1915:opposite page 108). Both visited Oenpelli in 1913 (see Cahill's letter to Spencer, dated 9 October 2013 in Mulvaney 2004:85). She also described the discovery of another site while travelling from the East Alligator River to Oenpelli on foot:

> We climbed up a cleft between two rocks through a tangle of creeper, crawled on our hands and knees up a dark tunnel, with little bats softly hitting our faces, and emerged on a sunny platform, surrounded by great rocks and smelling sweetly of spinifex. The underside of one of these was covered with crude images in red, yellow, and white clay. It seemed a native picture gallery we had discovered. For the most part the paintings seemed to be of birds and fishes, but here and there was an unmistakable alligator or a human form; and scattered amongst them all was an imprint of a human hand. We longed for someone learned in black lore to tell us if the paintings were old, or lately made. The place, so silent, remote, and smelling sweetly, gave the impression that it had been a sacred spot for long ages, and that not one man but the artists of many generations had come there alone to spend sunny hours, lying on their backs below the rock and daubing it with their coloured clays. (Masson 1915:107–108)

Masson remarked that the location of the rock art she discovered had a sense of spirituality about it and that she was very interested in the age of the rock art. A few years later buffalo shooter Carl Warburton (1934:92) reported entering a 'cave' and finding rock art near Cannon Hill (now in Kakadu National Park) in 1919:

> In the flickering light of the torch our eyes suddenly alighted upon a group of aboriginal paintings along one side. They held us in amazement. Exceptionally lifelike reproductions of kangaroos, turtles, crocodiles, emus, nude lubras with well developed breasts, and hands, had been painted with red, yellow and white ochre. We tested the paint but it gave no sign of smearing.
>
> There were also drawings and carvings. I had no idea that aboriginal art could reach such a high level.

The earliest recorded statement about the significance of some Arnhem Land rock art by an Aboriginal person was made by Namuluda (Figure 11.1) in the late 1920s as told by Lazarus Lamilami who was with him at the time. They travelled from Goulburn Island to Oenpelli to the south of the Wellington Range with four other men (Lamilami 1974:121). On the return trip they camped 'at the top of Angarlban Creek, where there are many caves' (1974:124) and saw some rock paintings including some high up on rock-shelter walls:

> I hadn't seen paintings like that before and I wondered how they could be so high up. Then Namuluda told us, 'these paintings are done by *mimi*. *Mimi* can make these at the top of the caves to come down very close to paint. Then when they are finished they say some magic words or blow some wind and the paintings go up to the normal place. That's how it's done'. These *mimi* are good spirits that our people told us about. Still we wondered if it was true or not. (Lamilami 1974:124–125)

Figure 11.1: Namuluda, Goulburn Island in 1925.

Source: Photograph by Herbert Read in Paul S.C. Taçon collection.

Later, in 1952, Namuluda, Lazarus Lamilami and George Winungoyd visited a site with photographer Axel Poignant and Namuluda pointed out a painting made by his cousin (Poignant 1995:4).

Also, in the late 1920s/early 1930s, a man named Kanowla related the following to missionary Alfred J. Dyer who established the Oenpelli Mission in 1925:

> If a native misses a fish with his spear he later returns to the cave and draws in careful detail the lines in the x-ray drawing of the fish as a warning that he had better aim straighter next time, or ask the spirit to help him, by biting harder the kidney fat bag. (Dyer 1934:36ii)

Dyer was the first to use the term 'x-ray' in relation to Arnhem Land rock art (Taçon 1989:30) and also remarked on an 'x-ray woman; drawn with all the internal organs' he saw in a shelter near Oenpelli (Dyer 1934:36ii). He first saw rock art at 'Oenpelli Hill' (Injalak) in 1915 and 'took a sketch of a debbil debbil drawing and knelt in prayer' (Dyer 1962:9).

Tindale (1925–26:117–119) briefly mentioned some of the rock art of Groote Eylandt in his treatise on the Aboriginal people of Groote. He also published on some of the rock art of Oenpelli (Tindale 1928), briefly describing some paintings and hand stencils in three rock-shelters in 1928. Two photographs of paintings of fish were included. From these we know he was at the main gallery of Injalak Hill and others nearby. He made note of depictions of the internal anatomy of painted creatures. Also in 1928, Herbert Basedow recorded rock art with Donald MacKay near the Liverpool River (Basedow 1928a, 1928b; Garde and Kohen-Raimondo 2004; MacKay 1929). Basedow (1928b:9) was particularly impressed with the quality of the rock paintings, stating 'The drawings in the Liverpool River district are particularly good and displayed no mean degree of artistic taste and talent'.

He also published a photograph of one of the galleries showing numerous paintings with the caption 'A native art gallery, Liverpool River.

Among the designs are a crocodile, fish, and a human figure'. Garde and Kohen-Raimondo (2004) found his photographs important for comparison with recent photographs, as new paintings made after Basedow and MacKay's visit could be seen. These showed that traditional designs and subject matter continued to be made after contact with outsiders in recent centuries. Basedow (1928b:9) stated that:

> The local tribes are very proud of their works of art, and never missed a chance of conducting our party to any of their art galleries which happened to be located in the districts we traversed. Our interest in and admiration of the work were greatly appreciated.

In early 1939, Rev. Theodor Webb found a number of rock-shelters with burials and rock paintings in the Wessel Islands of north-east Arnhem Land. Later, in 1939, Charles Barrett visited the sites with Webb and made a photographic record. Some of these were later published, including what he interpreted as rock paintings of the crew of a Japanese lugger (Barrett 1943:opp. 72). In one cave were paintings of two large serpents 'with the head surrounded by a rainbow; one snake having a forked tail: the missionary's guide, a Wessel Islander, declared that this was a water-snake which lived in a nearby lagoon' (Barrett 1943:70).

Bill Harney was an acting patrol officer and protector of 'Aborigines' for the Northern Territory Government from 1940 to 1947. He also was an adviser for the 1948 American–Australian Scientific Expedition to Arnhem Land. During this period, he visited many rock art sites, some of which he described in detail (Harney 1957:115–118). In his 1957 book opposite page 17, there is a photograph of him with four adult Aboriginal males and an Aboriginal boy sitting in front of the main gallery of Ubirr, discovered during the expedition and now one of Kakadu National Park's main rock art areas for tourists to visit (opened in 1979; see Commonwealth of Australia 1999:133).

Theme 2: Survey, recording and archaeological approaches, 1940s to present

Following on from Tindale (1925–26), Rose (1942) was one of the first to describe some Groote Eylandt rock paintings in an extensive publication. However, methodical detailed recording began with Frederick McCarthy and Charles Mountford in 1948 as part of the aforementioned American–Australian Scientific Expedition to Arnhem Land (see May 2009 and Thomas and Neale 2011). As David, Taçon, Gunn et al. (2017:2) note, this 'expedition to Arnhem Land put the art and archaeology of the region on the world map'. McCarthy and Mountford made extensive records of the Injalak Hill and other Oenpelli paintings, as well as elsewhere in Arnhem Land (see Mountford 1956). On Groote and Chasm Islands 'McCarthy recorded some 2400 rock art motifs at three key complexes: Chasm Island, Angoroko and Junduruna' (Clarke and Frederick 2011:135; and see McCarthy 1955, 1960). Clarke and Frederick (2011:135–136) contend:

> This body of work still constitutes the most detailed recording of Groote Eylandt rock art published to date. The rock art recordings enabled McCarthy to provide descriptions of the motifs and to propose a schema of stylistic changes in the art over time. His application of a systematic field methodology to record the art and his subsequent interpretations mark a definitive period in the development of rock art research in Australia.

This important movement in Arnhem Land rock art recording is explored in Chapter 2 of this volume. Not much rock art–related activity took place in the 1950s or most of the 1960s other than some analysis by Arndt (1962a, 1962b, 1966). Things picked up in 1969 and the 1970s with the work of Brandl, Chaloupka, Jelinek and the 1969 Czech Expedition to Arnhem Land. Afterwards, 'the recording and analysis of rock art flourished through the 1980s to the present' (David, Taçon, Gunn et al. 2017:3).

Theme 3: Tourism, since the 1950s

It can be argued that Arnhem Land rock art tourism began with Paddy Cahill in the early 1900s at Oenpelli, with visitors sometimes taken to Injalak and nearby galleries. 'It was the show place for visitors' (Dyer 1962:95). Besides some of those mentioned above (such as Masson and Holmes in 1913), there were other visitors who photographed rock paintings but did not publish them. For instance, in a 1922 photo album now in the possession of the Northern Territory Library, Roy Maxwell Edwards, then 16, included two such photographs taken during a visit to Paddy Cahill's station that year (Figure 11.2). Rev. Dyer was taken to the Injalak galleries when he first visited Paddy Cahill in 1915, and later he took mission visitors to Injalak (Dyer 1962:95). However, official rock art tours in greater Arnhem Land began in the 1950s, after tourist pressure increased from the mid-1940s, as Ronald and Catherine Berndt (1970:203) have documented:

> Renewed interest in Aboriginal culture from a research and recording point of view coincides with increased government and commercial enthusiasm for its tourist potential. Mission stations throughout Arnhem Land have been under pressure since the middle 1940s to admit tourists, but now it is stronger and on a much bigger scale. So many unheralded visitors without official permits to enter have been crossing into the reserve by the dry-season road that Oenpelli mission has agreed to regularize the situation by sponsoring guided tours of local cave paintings.

Figure 11.2: One of the earliest 'tourist' photos of Arnhem Land rock art, 1922, Oenpelli area.

Source: Photograph by Roy Maxwell, reproduced here with permission of Northern Territory Library (PH0274-0069).

The rock art of Oenpelli was brought to the attention of international tourists in a profound way with the 1954 UNESCO publication of *Australia: Aboriginal paintings – Arnhem Land* by The New York Graphic Society, as part of the UNESCO World Art Series. This oversize book is beautifully illustrated. After an introduction by Herbert Read and an essay by Charles Mountford that includes a large black-and-white photograph of Aboriginal men in front of the main gallery of Ubirr, there are 15 colour plates of rock art photographed at Ubirr and Injalak (Oenpelli) galleries and a further 17 colour plates of bark paintings. The photograph on page 10 has some of the same Aboriginal people, including the boy, that are with Bill Harney in the photograph he published in 1957 mentioned above, although they are naked in this one and have cloth around their waists in Harney's photo. The photographs were taken in an Australian Government–sponsored expedition in October–November 1949, by W. Brindle (UNESCO 1954:16).

Allan Stewart and Fred Hunter are thought to have been the first to bring tourists to Anbangbang Gallery, Nourlangie in the 1960s, in what is now Kakadu National Park. This included a visit by David Attenborough for the TV series *Quest under Capricorn* in 1963 (Attenborough 1963; Stewart 1969a:53).

Later that year, Hunter noted the existence of what later came to be called 'Dynamic Figures' (one of the styles referred to as 'Mimi' paintings elsewhere) higher up Nourlangie rock (Stewart 1969a:54). In March 1969, Allan Stewart advocated not only the promotion of Arnhem Land rock art but also its protection, as well as predicting many more galleries would be found, in a full-page article in *The Northern Territory News*:

> As the encroaching roads snake into remote Arnhem Land from the west, and south-west, to gouge out the mineral wealth of the Territory, 'the world's richest mine', more and more galleries of paintings will be found – galleries that should be respected and protected from the hoodlum elements, who desecrate, evidence of which I have seen left by ill-disciplined and undiscerning visitors to the area.

> Rich in animal life, anthropological antiquities, and scenic beauty, we are lucky to have such an area to preserve for Australian and overseas visitors to see – which I predict will rival Yellowstone and Kruger one day.

> It is time that the Australian Tourist Commission and our own Territory Tourist Board in their promotion, realised what an asset, provided rigid control is enforced – that this area can be to the Territory and Australia. (Stewart 1969b:8)

Stewart worked closely with rock painters Nayombolmi and Djimongurr, also known as Old Nym (May et al. 2019; Stewart 1969a; see also Figure 11.3). Rock art tourism has grown ever since, especially after Kakadu National Park was established in 1979. In that year the Nourlangie and Ubirr galleries were officially opened to the public for general visitation, both non-escorted and escorted by rangers or tour operators (Commonwealth of Australia 1999:133). Nourlangie's Anbangbang Main Gallery, for instance, receives tens of thousands of visitors each year (May et al. 2019:1), and Nourlangie and Ubirr continue to be the most visited rock art complexes in western Arnhem Land. Galleries in Nitmiluk, at the southern end of Arnhem Land, have also become popular with tourists.

Figure 11.3: Allan Stewart with Djimongurr (Old Nym) and 'Roy' at Nanguluwurr, Kakadu National Park, 1959.

Source: Photograph by Ern McQuillian 1959.

Nanguluwurr (Hayward et al. 2021; Jelinek 1977) also opened for general visitation in 1979, while those undertaking bushwalks encounter a wide range of sites not advertised. Some sites in the Hawk Dreaming area north of Ubirr were also available for tourist visitation for about 10 years until 2018. Across the East Alligator River, Injalak Hill sites remain very popular, and various tourism businesses also take people to some of the Red Lily area sites on the way. Since the late 1990s, rock art sites of the Mount Borradaile area have also become very popular, with this area accessible for paid tours between April and October each year.

Discussion and conclusions

Interest and research on Arnhem Land rock art by non-Aboriginal people has a lengthy history spanning well over 200 years, but with most studies and reporting undertaken during the past century. A consistent theme that runs through the early discoveries is how impressive and stunning the rock art was for those encountering it.

During much of the past 70 years, Arnhem Land rock art research has been a highly collaborative venture between local Aboriginal people associated with the rock art and a wide range of non-Aboriginal people from across Australia and a dozen other countries. Over 200 people have contributed to Arnhem Land rock art research in significant ways, more than half being Aboriginal Australians. Between a quarter and a third of non-Aboriginal people who contributed to the reporting and study of Arnhem Land rock art are female, whether from Australia or overseas, and about a fifth of Aboriginal participants are female. Thus, Arnhem Land rock art research has long been a multicultural, multilingual and multidisciplinary pursuit with a wide range of individuals with different forms of knowledge, experience, status as Traditional Owners (e.g. site owners, site managers) and expertise.

Besides those individuals listed in Tables 11.1 and 11.2, many other people have contributed to our understanding of Arnhem Land rock art in very significant ways. For example, Luke Taylor's analysis of related bark paintings detailed in numerous publications (e.g. 2016 and see references therein) has added significant insights into recent rock art, especially x-ray paintings. Numerous journalists have promoted the rock art of Arnhem Land, beginning with author Colin Simpson when he was with the ABC and attached to the 1948 National Geographic expedition to Arnhem Land. This experience led to an exploration of Aboriginal anthropology and rock art features in his first book, *Adam in ochre: Inside Aboriginal Australia* (Simpson 1951; see especially pages 17–26 and photo opposite page 66). Injalak Arts in Gunbalanya has long promoted western Arnhem Land rock art to the broader public, and for many years has run tours of the Injalak rock art galleries with local Aboriginal community members as guides. In the 1980s and 1990s, the then Australian Institute of Aboriginal Studies (now Australian Institute of Aboriginal and Torres Strait Islander Studies) (Canberra), the Aboriginal Areas Protection Authority (Darwin) and the Northern Land Council (Darwin) were major sponsors of Arnhem Land rock art research. Filmmakers, such as Kim McKenzie, also promoted Arnhem Land rock art, as did museum curators responsible for displays in the Australian Museum (Sydney) and the Museum and Art Gallery of the Northern Territory (Darwin).

The major turning point in the study of the rock art of Arnhem Land was the American–Australian Scientific Expedition to Arnhem Land in 1948. With the work of McCarthy (1960) and Mountford (1956), and promotion of the rock art by Harney (1957), Simpson (1951) and UNESCO (1954), word rapidly spread across the world about the importance and impressiveness of Arnhem Land's rock art. All of this helped heighten international interest, leading to the Czech Expedition to Arnhem Land in 1969 and rock art research by Brandl (e.g. 1968, 1973, 1980; working with Traditional Owners Wally Mandarrg and Jacky Bunkarniyal), Jelinek (1976, 1977, 1978a, 1978b, 1989), Novotny (1975) and others. This set the stage for Chaloupka's

(Figure 11.4) passionate pursuit of Arnhem Land rock art and his extensive research with Aboriginal collaborators, especially Nipper Kapirigi (Figure 11.5) and George Namingum.

George Chaloupka first encountered western Arnhem Land rock art in 1958:

> when, in the heartland of the region's rock art at the East Alligator River, I entered a rock shelter whose wall and ceiling were ablaze with multicoloured layers of painted images. Some were identifiable as representing the natural species that inhabited the riverine environment, others were of human figures and some, as I was to learn later, were beings from the Dreaming. In the stillness of the day I stood spellbound by their magic, captivated by their unique form and the brilliance of their execution. (Chaloupka 1993:8)

After visiting many sites in the 1960s and early 1970s, Chaloupka joined the Museum and Art Gallery of the Northern Territory in 1973 to pursue the study of rock art full-time, with a particular focus on western Arnhem Land. Chaloupka (e.g. 1984, 1993) was the first to move beyond the simple Mimi–x-ray dichotomy of Arnhem Land rock art chronology that began with Mountford (1956) and was later subdivided and expanded by Brandl (1973). In this sense, Chaloupka's research can be considered the second major step forward in the study of Kakadu–Arnhem Land rock art, although Lewis (1988) provided an alternative perspective and many others have elaborated chronologies since (Theme 4). Chaloupka worked most closely with brothers Nipper Kapirigi and George Namingum. They were his closest friends and mentors (Chaloupka 1993:249), but he also worked with over 30 other Traditional Owners from across the breadth of western Arnhem Land (see Chaloupka 1993:249 and Table 2), as he was very interested in the ethnography of rock art (Theme 5; see also Turner 1973 for Bickerton Island and Groote Eylandt in eastern Arnhem Land).

Figure 11.4: George Chaloupka in the field in 1988.

Source: Photograph by Paul S.C. Taçon.

Figure 11.5: Nipper Kapirigi and David Canari at Yuwenjgayay, Kakadu National Park in 1986.
Source: Photograph by Paul S.C. Taçon.

Figure 11.6: Sally K. May (far left) with Josie Maralngurra (fourth from the left) and PhD candidate Emily Miller (far right) and others at Nanguluwur, Kakadu in 2019.

Source: Photograph by Paul S.C. Taçon.

Since 1981, this author has worked with over 40 Traditional Owners for collaborative rock art research, while other researchers have also worked closely with dozens of Aboriginal colleagues over several decades. The friendships and collaborations, all of them formed with Traditional Owners, have contributed most of what can be considered the ethnography of Arnhem Land rock art, and these collaborations continue today throughout broader Arnhem Land (Brady et al. 2020; and see Figure 11.6).

Taçon's collaborative research with Traditional Owners, which began with PhD research in 1985–1989 (Taçon 1989), expanded to joint research in the 1990s with Christopher Chippindale (e.g. Chippindale and Taçon 1993, 1998; Taçon and Chippindale 1994; Taçon et al. 2004; Figure 11.7) and has continued since with numerous people of varied disciplinary backgrounds, especially Murray Garde, Sally K. May, Erle Nelson and Daryl Wesley, leading to numerous publications and new methods (e.g. the first use of Harris Matrices for rock art anywhere – Chippindale and Taçon 1993). Chaloupka published his landmark book *Journey in time* in 1993 and undertook much fieldwork. The 1990s also saw some pioneering rock art dating by Erle Nelson with Chaloupka, Chippindale and Taçon (Theme 7, e.g. see Nelson 2000; Nelson et al. 1995; Taçon et al. 2004), built on earlier experimental work by Alan Watchman (e.g. 1987). This combined research and the resulting publications can be considered the third major step forward in terms of advancing knowledge about Arnhem Land rock art. Robert (ben) Gunn also contributed to this third advancement with much field research and many reports and publications since the late 1980s (e.g. Gunn 1992; Gunn et al. 2012; and see extensive list in Gunn 2016).

Figure 11.7: From left to right, Christopher Chippindale, Sue McPherson, Paul S.C. Taçon and Peter Sullivan recording rock paintings at the key sequence site of Kungurrul in Kakadu National Park, 1991 (see Chippindale and Taçon 1993).

Source: Photograph by Paul S.C. Taçon.

In recent years, PhD students Géraldine Castets (2016), Samuel Dix (2021), Robert Gunn (2016), John Hayward (2016), Iain Johnston (2018), Tristan Jones (2017; and Jones et al. 2016 for recent dating), Melissa Marshall (2020) and Daryl Wesley (2014) have continued to make advancements. Melissa Marshall (2020 and various reports and papers listed therein; Marshall and Taçon 2014), in particular, has contributed much to Arnhem Land rock art conservation and management (Theme 6), something begun with the establishment of Kakadu National Park in 1979 (Gillespie 1983). Géraldine Castets's (2016) PhD thesis, in French, has not yet been published in English, but includes very detailed analysis of the chemistry of excavated pigments from Nawarla Gabarnmang (Jawoyn Country, central Arnhem Land Plateau), and how these relate to on-rock paintings. Two Masters theses have also resulted from data analysis (Berry 2011; Hammond 2016; see also Hammond 2019).

A fourth major advancement is now occurring with the rise of the digital era (Theme 8), with digital applications for survey and recording (e.g. iPad and android-based recording systems, photogrammetry, 3D laser scanning, drones and so forth), as well as interpretation (DStretch, pXRF, etc.) and conservation/management (employing all of the above as well as multifunctional digital data management systems) (see Jalandoni et al. 2018; Jalandoni and May 2020 and May, Huntley et al. 2020 for examples). Even machine learning is being developed to identify features suitable for distinguishing styles of rock art (Kowlessar et al. 2021).

A very important aspect of Arnhem Land rock art research over the past 200 years is the active participation and, at times, direction by Aboriginal Traditional Owners, Custodians and other community members. Well over 100 Aboriginal individuals and several organisations were identified as having worked closely with at least 107 non-Aboriginal researchers. These are the major players in the history of Arnhem Land rock art research, although, undoubtedly, others who have not yet been named played various roles. It is worth mentioning in this regard that on at least a number of publications, recently deceased Elders and younger Traditional Owners were mentioned without being named, following appropriate local Aboriginal protocols.

But despite the vast amount of research on the rock art of the Arnhem Land region by over 200 people, of varied backgrounds, and over half of whom are Aboriginal, hundreds of previously recorded rock art sites are found each year and there is much more survey, recording, dating, interpretation and conservation research to be done. Indeed, it will be interesting to see what is achieved over the next 70, 100 or 200 years, the state of the rock art and the new methods and technologies employed. The study of greater Arnhem Land's rock art is a continuing story full of adventure, discovery, friendship and the generous sharing of Aboriginal imagery and knowledge with the global community.

References

Arndt, W. 1962a. The Nargorkun-Narlinji cult. *Oceania* 32(4):298–320. doi.org/10.1002/j.1834-4461.1962.tb01784.x.

Arndt, W. 1962b. The interpretation of Delamere lightning paintings and rock engravings. *Oceania* 32(3):163–177. doi.org/10.1002/j.1834-4461.1962.tb01759.x.

Arndt, W. 1966. Seventy year old records and new information on the Nargorkun-Narlinji cult. *Oceania* 36(3):231–239. doi.org/10.1002/j.1834-4461.1966.tb00288.x.

Attenborough, D. 1963. *Quest under Capricorn*. Lutterworth Press, London.

Australian Heritage Commission 1990. *Australia's rock art*. Australian Heritage Commission Bibliography Series. Australian Government Publishing Service, Canberra.

Barrett, C. 1943. Art in Arnhem Land. In C. Barrett and R.H. Croll (eds), *Art of the Australian Aboriginal*, pp. 67–75. The Bread and Cheese Club, Melbourne.

Basedow, H. 1928a. Diary of the Mackay exploring expedition in Arnhem Land. Mitchell Library: ML MSS 161 Item 5 and CY Reel 892, frames 78–161. Sydney.

Basedow, H. 1928b. Through unknown Arnhem Land – work of the Mackay exploring expedition: Art and customs of the native tribes. An account of the Mackay exploring expedition, *The Brisbane Courier*, 5 September:9.

Berndt, R.M. and C.H. Berndt 1970. *Man, land & myth in north Australia*. The Gunwinggu people. Ure Smith, Sydney.

Berry, M. 2011. Dissecting yams: 'Yam' Figures in the rock art of Kakadu. Unpublished Master of Liberal Arts thesis, The Australian National University, Canberra.

Brady, L., S.K. May, J. Goldhahn, P.S.C. Taçon and P. Lamilami 2020. What painting? Encountering and interpreting the archaeological record in western Arnhem Land, northern Australia. *Archaeology in Oceania* 55(2):106–117. doi.org/10.1002/arco.5208.

Brandl, E.J. 1968. Aboriginal rock designs in beeswax and description of cave painting sites in Western Arnhem Land. *Archaeology and Physical Anthropology in Oceania* 3(1):19–29.

Brandl, E.J. 1973. *Australian Aboriginal paintings in western and central Arnhem Land, temporal sequences and elements of style in Cadell River and Deaf Adder Creek art*. Australian Institute of Aboriginal Studies, Canberra.

Brandl, E.J. 1980. Some notes on faunal identification and Arnhem Land rock paintings. *Australian Institute of Aboriginal Studies Newsletter,* New Series No. 14:6–13.

Castets, G. 2016. Apports de l'analyse des matières colorantes et colorées dans l'étude intégrée d'un site orné: Application au site de Nawarla Gabarnmang (Terre d'Arnhem, Territoire du Nord – Australie). Unpublished PhD thesis, Université Grenoble Alpes, Grenoble.

Chaloupka, G. 1979. Pack bells on the rock face: Aboriginal paintings of European contact in north-western Arnhem Land. *Aboriginal History* 3(2):92–95.

Chaloupka, G. 1984. *From Palaeoart to casual paintings.* Monograph Series 1. Northern Territory Museum of Arts and Sciences, Darwin.

Chaloupka. G. 1993. *Journey in time: The world's longest continuing art tradition: The 50.000-year story of the Australian Aboriginal rock art of Arnhem Land.* Reed, Chatswood.

Chippindale, C. and P.S.C. Taçon 1993. Two old painted panels from Kakadu: Variation and sequence in Arnhem Land rock art. In J. Steinbring, A. Watchman, P. Faulstich and P.S.C. Taçon (eds), *Time and space: Dating and spatial considerations in rock art research*, pp. 32–56. Occasional AURA Publication No. 8. Archaeological Publications, Melbourne.

Chippindale, C. and P.S.C. Taçon 1998. The many ways of dating Arnhem Land rock-art, north Australia. In C. Chippindale and P.S.C. Taçon (eds), *The archaeology of rock-art*, pp. 90–111. Cambridge University Press, Cambridge.

Clarke, A. and U. Frederick 2008. The mark of marvelous ideas: Groote Eylandt rock art and the performance of cross-cultural relations. In P. Veth, P. Sutton and M. Neale (eds), *Strangers on the shore. Early coastal contacts in Australia*, pp. 148–164. National Museum of Australia, Canberra.

Clarke, A. and U. Frederick 2011. Making a sea change: Rock art, archaeology and the enduring legacy of Frederick McCarthy's research on Groote Eylandt. In M. Thomas and M. Neale (eds), *Exploring the legacy of the 1948 Arnhem Land expedition*, pp. 135–155. ANU Press, Canberra. doi.org/10.22459/ELALE.06.2011.07.

Clarkson, C., Z. Jacobs, B. Marwick, R. Fullagar, L. Wallis, M. Smith, R.G. Roberts, E. Hayes, K. Lowe, X. Carah, S.A. Florin, J. McNeil, D. Cox, L.J. Arnold, Q. Hua, J. Huntley, H.E.A. Brand, T. Manne, A. Fairbairn, J. Shulmeister, L. Lyle, M. Salinas, M. Page, K. Connell, G. Park, K. Norman, T. Murphy and C. Pardoe 2017. Human occupation of northern Australia by 65,000 years ago. *Nature* 547:306–310. doi.org/10.1038/nature22968.

Commonwealth of Australia 1999. *Australia's Kakadu: Protecting world heritage.* Environment Australia, Canberra.

Dahl, K. 1926. *In savage Australia. An account of a hunting and collecting expedition to Arnhem Land and Dampier Land.* Phillip Allan and Co., London.

Dashwood, C.J. 1895. The government resident's trip to the Alligator Rivers. In C.J. Dashwood (ed.), The government resident's report on the Northern Territory for the year 1894. *South Australia Parliamentary Papers* 2(24):8.

David, B., J.-M. Geneste, R. Whear, J.-J. Delannoy, M. Katherine, R.G. Gunn, C. Clarkson, H. Plisson, P. Lee, F. Petchey, C. Rowe, B. Barker, L. Lamb, W. Miller, S. Hoerle, D. James, E. Boche, K. Aplin, I. McNiven, T. Richards, A. Fairburn and J. Matthews 2011. Nawarla Gabarnmang, a 45,180+/-910 cal BP site in Jawoyn country, southwest Arnhem Land plateau. *Australian Archaeology* 73:73–77. doi.org/10.1080/03122417.2011.11961928.

David, B., B. Barker, F. Petchey, J.-J. Delannoy, J.-M. Geneste, C. Rowe, M. Eccleston, L. Lamb and R. Whear 2013. A 28,000 year old excavated painted rock from Nawarla Gabarnmang, northern Australia. *Journal of Archaeological Science* 40:2493–2501. doi.org/10.1016/j.jas.2012.08.015.

David, B., P.S.C. Taçon, J.-M. Geneste and J.-J. Delannoy (eds) 2017. *The archaeology of rock art in western Arnhem Land*. Terra Australis 47. ANU Press, Canberra. doi.org/10.22459/TA47.11.2017.

David, B., P.S.C. Taçon, R. Gunn, J.-J. Delannoy and J.-M. Geneste 2017. The archaeology of western Arnhem Land's rock art. In B. David, P.S.C. Taçon, J.-M. Geneste and J.-J. Delannoy (eds), *The archaeology of rock art in western Arnhem Land*, pp. 1–17. Terra Australis 47. ANU Press, Canberra. doi.org/10.22459/TA47.11.2017.01.

Dix, S. 2021. Understanding contact, hybridity, conservatism, and innovation in archaeological superimposition of rock art. Djulirri, Arnhem Land, Northern Territory, Australia. Unpublished PhD thesis, Griffith University, Gold Coast.

Dyer, A.J. 1934. The story of A.J. Dyer: Experiences in Arnhem Land 1915 to 1934. Typescript manuscript lodged at the Australian Institute of Aboriginal and Torres Strait Islander Studies, Canberra.

Dyer, A.J. 1962. Typescript manuscript 18 NTRS 693/P1. Northern Territory Archive Service, Darwin.

Edwards, R. 1979. *Australian Aboriginal art: The art of the Alligator Rivers region, Northern Territory*. Australian Institute of Aboriginal Studies, Canberra.

Findlay, E. 1998. *Arcadian quest: William Westall's Australian sketches*. National Library of Australia, Canberra.

Flinders, M. 1814. *A voyage to Terra Australis*, Volume 2. G & W Nicol, London.

Garde, M. and A. Kohen-Raimondo 2004. Putting Herbert Basedow back in focus: The 1928 expedition to Arnhem Land. *Australian Aboriginal Studies* 2004(1):26–36.

Gillespie, D. (ed.) 1983. *The rock art sites of Kakadu National Park – Some preliminary research findings for their conservation and management*. Australian National Parks and Wildlife Service and Commonwealth of Australia, Canberra.

Gunn, R.G. 1992. Bulajang – A reappraisal of the archaeology of an Aboriginal cult. In J. MacDonald and I.P. Haskovec (eds), *State of the art*, pp. 174–194. Occasional AURA Publication No. 6. Australian Rock Art Research Association, Melbourne.

Gunn, R.G. 2016. Art of the ancestors: Spatial and temporal patterning in the rock art of Nawarla Gabarnmang, a major Jawoyn cultural site on the Arnhem Land plateau. Unpublished PhD thesis, Monash University, Melbourne.

Gunn, R.G., R.L. Whear and L.C. Douglas 2012. Dating the present at Nawarla Gabarnmang: Time and function in the art of a major Jawoyn rock art and occupation site in western Arnhem Land. *Australian Archaeology* 75:55–65. doi.org/10.1080/03122417.2012.11681950.

Hammond, J.W. 2016. Yam culture in Arnhem Land: An analysis of cultural life related to Dioscorea yams from the 'Yam Figure' rock paintings to the present day. Unpublished Master of Arts thesis, University of New England, Armidale.

Hammond, J.W. 2019. The spatial distribution of unique motifs featuring *Dioscorea bulbifera*, the round yam, in western Arnhem Land rock art. *Australian Archaeology* 85(2):215–219. doi.org/10.1080/031 22417.2019.1686237.

Haritos, H. 2006. Does management matter? A case study of two rock art sites Balauru and Djuwarr 1 in the Deaf Adder sites complex. Unpublished BA Honours thesis, Charles Darwin University, Darwin.

Harney, W.E. 1957. *Life among the Aborigines*. Robert Hale Ltd., London.

Haskovec, I.P. 1992. Mt Gilruth revisited. *Archaeology in Oceania* 27(2):61–74. doi.org/10.1002/j.1834-4453.1992.tb00285.x.

Hayward, J. A. 2016. Reading the signs: Depictions of people and things in the rock art of Mirarr Country, Northern Territory, Australia. Unpublished PhD thesis, The Australian National University, Canberra.

Hayward, J., S.K. May, J. Goldhahn, A. Jalandoni and P.S.C. Taçon 2021. A spatial analysis of motif clusters at Nanguluwurr rock art site, Kakadu National Park, N.T. Australia. *Journal of Field Archaeology* 46(6):414–428. doi.org/10.1080/00934690.2021.1926698.

Jalandoni, A. and S.K. May 2020. How 3D models (photogrammetry) of rock art can improve recording veracity: A case study from Kakadu National Park, Australia. *Australian Archaeology* 86(2):137–146. doi.org/10.1080/03122417.2020.1769005.

Jalandoni, A., I. Domingo Sanz and P.S.C. Taçon 2018. Testing the value of low-cost Structure-from-Motion (SfM) photogrammetry for metric and visual analysis of rock art. *Journal of Archaeological Science: Reports* 17:605–616. doi.org/10.1016/j.jasrep.2017.12.020.

Jelinek, J. 1976. The social meaning of north Australian rock paintings. *Anthropologie* 14:83–87.

Jelinek, J. 1977. Nangalore: A gallery of rock paintings in Western Arnhem Land. *Anthropologie* 15:3-26.

Jelinek, J. 1978a. Mimi or the archaic art of Arnhem Land. *Archaeology and Physical Anthropology in Oceania* 13:229–233.

Jelinek, J. 1978b. Obiri – A rock art gallery in Arnhem Land. *Anthropologie* 16:35–65.

Jelinek, J. 1989. *The great art of the early Australians: The study of the evolution and role of rock art in the society of Australian hunters and gatherers*. Moravian Museum-Anthropos Institute, Brno.

Johnston, I. 2018. The Dynamic Figure art of Jabiluka: A study of ritual in early Australian rock art. Unpublished PhD thesis, The Australian National University, Canberra.

Jones, T. 2017. Disentangling the styles, sequences and antiquity of the early rock art of western Arnhem Land. Unpublished PhD thesis, The Australian National University, Canberra.

Jones, T., V.A. Levchenko, P.L. King, U. Troitzsch, D. Wesley, A. Williams and A. Nayingull 2016. Radiocarbon age constraints for a Pleistocene–Holocene transition rockart style: The Northern Running Figures of the East Alligator River region, western Arnhem Land, Australia. *Journal of Archaeological Science: Reports* 11:80–89. doi.org/10.1016/j.jasrep.2016.11.016.

Jones, T., D. Wesley, S.K. May, I.G. Johnston, C. McFadden and P.S.C. Taçon 2020. Rethinking the age and unity of large naturalistic animal forms in early western Arnhem Land rock art, Australia. *Australian Archaeology* 86(3):238–252. doi.org/10.1080/03122417.2020.1826080.

Kowlessar, J., J. Keal, D. Wesley, I. Moffat, D. Lawrence, A. Weson, A. Nayinggul and Mimal Land Management Aboriginal Corporation 2021. Reconstructing rock art chronology with transfer learning: A case study from Arnhem Land, Australia. *Australian Archaeology* 87(2):115–126. doi.org/10.1080/03122417.2021.1895481.

Lamilami, I. 1974. *Lamilami speaks*. Ure Smith, Sydney.

Layton, R. 1992. *Australian rock art: A new synthesis*. Cambridge University Press, Cambridge.

Leichhardt, L. 1846. Dr Leichardt's lectures (Lecture II). Delivered at School of Arts, on Tuesday, August 25. *The Sydney Morning Herald*, Thursday 27 August 1846.

Lewis, D. 1988. *The rock paintings of Arnhem Land, Australia: social, ecological and material culture change in the post-glacial period*. British Archaeological Reports, International Series 415. British Archaeological Reports, Oxford.

Lewis, J. 1922. *Fought and won*. W.K. Thomas and Co., Adelaide.

Lydon, J. 2018. Hidden women of history: Elsie Masson, photographer, writer, intrepid traveller. *The Conversation*, 31 December 2018.

McCarthy, F.D. 1955. Notes on the cave paintings of Groote and Chasm Islands in the Gulf of Carpentaria. *Mankind* 5(2):69–75. doi.org/10.1111/j.1835-9310.1955.tb01422.x.

McCarthy, F. D. 1960. The cave paintings of Groote Eylandt and Chasm Island. In C.P. Mountford (ed.), *Records of the American–Australian Scientific Expedition to Arnhem Land. Volume 2: Anthropology and nutrition*, pp. 297–414. Melbourne University Press, Carlton.

Mackay, D. 1929. An expedition in Arnhem Land. *Geographical Journal* 74:568–71. doi.org/10.2307/1785164.

Marshall. M. 2020. Rock art conservation and management: 21st Century perspectives from northern Australia. Unpublished PhD thesis, The Australian National University, Canberra.

Marshall, M. and P.S.C. Taçon 2014. Past and present, traditional and scientific: The conservation and management of rock art sites in Australia. In T. Darvill and A.P.B. Fernandes (eds), *Open-air rock art conservation and management: State of the art and future perspectives*, pp. 214–228. Routledge, London.

Marymor, L. 2018. Australian rock art bibliography extracted from the rock art studies bibliographic database for the years 1841 to 2018 – Part 1. *Rock Art Research* 35(2):188–248.

Marymor, L. 2019. Australian rock art bibliography extracted from the rock art studies bibliographic database for the years 1841 to 2018 – Part 2. *Rock Art Research* 36(1):49–93.

Masson, E.R. 1915. *An untamed territory: The Northern Territory of Australia*. MacMillan, London.

May, S.K. 2009. *Collecting cultures: Myth, politics, and collaboration in the 1948 Arnhem Land Expedition*. AltaMira Press, Lanham.

May, S.K. and P.S.C. Taçon 2014. Kakadu National Park: Rock art. In C. Smith (ed.), *Encyclopedia of global archaeology*, pp. 4235–4240. Springer, New York. doi.org/10.1007/978-1-4419-0465-2_2241.

May, S.K., P.S.C. Taçon, D. Wesley and M. Travers 2010. Painting history: Indigenous observations and depictions of the 'other' in northwestern Arnhem Land, Australia. *Australian Archaeology* 71:57–65. doi.org/10.1080/03122417.2010.11689384.

May, S.K., P.S.C. Taçon, D. Wright and M. Marshall 2015. The rock art of Kakadu: Past, present and future research, conservation and management. In S. Winderlich (ed.), *Kakadu National Park symposia series. Symposium 6: Walk the talk: Cultural heritage management in Kakadu National Park, 19–20 May 2011, Jabiru Youth Centre*, pp. 36–44. Internal Report 625. Supervising Scientists, Australian Government, Darwin.

May, S.K., J. Maralngurra, I.G. Johnston, J. Golhahn, G. Lee, G. O'Loughlin, K. May, C. Nabobbob, M. Garde and P.S.C. Taçon 2019. 'This is my father's painting': A first-hand account of the creation of the most famous rock art in Kakadu National Park. *Rock Art Research* 36(2):199–213.

May, S.K., J. Huntley, M. Marshall, E. Miller, J. Hayward, A. Jalandoni, J. Goldhahn, I. Johnston, J. Lee, G. O'Loughlin, K. May, I. Domingo Sanzand P.S.C. Taçon 2020. New insights into the rock art of Anbangbang Gallery, Kakadu National Park. *Journal of Field Archaeology* 45(2):120–134. doi.org/10.1080/00934690.2019.1698883.

May, S.K., L. Taylor, C. Frieman, P.S.C. Taçon, D. Wesley, T. Jones, J. Goldhahn and C. Mungulda 2020. Survival, social cohesion and rock art: The Painted Hands of western Arnhem Land, Australia. *Cambridge Archaeological Journal* 30(3):491–510. doi.org/10.1017/S0959774320000104.

Mountford, Charles P. 1956. *Records of the American–Australian expedition to Arnhem Land. Volume 1: Art, myth and symbolism*. Melbourne University Press, Melbourne.

Mulvaney, J. 2004. *Paddy Cahill of Oenpelli*. Aboriginal Studies Press, Canberra.

Nelson, D.E. (ed.) 2000. *The beeswax art of northern Australia*. Simon Fraser University, Burnaby.

Nelson, D.E., G. Chaloupka, C. Chippindale, M.S. Alderson and J.R. Southon 1995. Radiocarbon dates for beeswax figures in the prehistoric rock art of northern Australia. *Archaeometry* 37:151–156. doi.org/10.1111/j.1475-4754.1995.tb00733.x.

Novotny, S. 1975. Rock paintings of the Gumardir River, Arnhem Land, Australia. *Annals of the Naprstek Museum* 8:63–110.

Poignant, R. 1995. *Lost conversations, recovered archives*. Occasional Paper No. 49. Northern Territory Government, Darwin Available at: dtc.nt.gov.au/__data/assets/pdf_file/0020/241904/occpaper49_ ej10.pdf (accessed 30 October 2019; site discontinued).

Rose, F. 1942. Paintings of the Groote Eylandt Aborigines. *Oceania* 13:170–176. doi.org/10.1002/j.1834-4461.1942.tb00376.x.

Simpson, C. 1951. *Adam in ochre: Inside Aboriginal Australia*. Angus and Robertson, Sydney.

Spencer, W.B. 1914. *The native tribes of the Northern Territory of Australia*. Macmillan, London.

Spencer, W.B. 1928. *Wanderings in wild Australia*. Macmillan, London. doi.org/10.5962/bhl.title.144674.

Stewart, A. 1969a. *Green eyes are buffalo*. Lansdowne Press, Melbourne.

Stewart, A. 1969b. Rahs and runes of Aboriginals' art in Top End. *The Northern Territory News*, 7 March 1969:8.

Stockdale, H. 1891. Letter to T. Worsnop. South Australia Archives: 790 and 791.

Taçon, P.S.C. 1989. From Rainbow Snakes to 'x-ray' fish: the nature of the recent rock painting tradition of western Arnhem Land, Australia. Unpublished PhD thesis, The Australian National University, Canberra.

Taçon, P.S.C. 2001. Australia. In D. Whitley (ed.), *Handbook of rock art research*, pp. 530–375. AltaMira Press, Walnut Creek.

Taçon, P.S.C. 2019. Connecting to the Ancestors: Why rock art is important for Indigenous Australians and their well-being. *Rock Art Research* 36(1):5–14.

Taçon, P.S.C. and S. Brockwell 1995. Arnhem Land prehistory in landscape, stone and paint. *Antiquity* 69(259):676–695. doi.org/10.1017/S0003598X00082272.

Taçon, P.S.C. and C. Chippindale 1994. Australia's ancient warriors: Changing depictions of fighting in the rock art of Arnhem Land, N.T. *Cambridge Archaeological Journal* 4:211–248. doi.org/10.1017/ S0959774300001086.

Taçon, P.S.C. and C. Chippindale 2008. Changing places: Ten thousand years of north Australian rock-art transformation. In D. Papagianni, H. Maschner and R. Layton (eds), *Time and change: Archaeological and anthropological perspectives on the long-term in hunter-gatherer societies*, pp. 73–94. Oxbow Books, Oxford.

Taçon, P.S.C., E. Nelson, C. Chippindale and G. Chaloupka 2004. The beeswax rock art of the Northern Territory: Direct dating results and a 'book of record'. *Rock Art Research* 21(2):155–160.

Taçon, P.S.C., M. Langley, S.K. May, R. Lamilami, W. Brennan and D. Guse 2010. Ancient bird stencils discovered in Arnhem Land, Northern Territory, Australia. *Antiquity* 84(324):416–427. doi.org/ 10.1017/S0003598X00066679.

Taçon, P.S.C., S.K. May, S.J. Fallon, M. Travers, D. Wesley and R Lamilami 2010. A minimum age for early depictions of Southeast Asian praus in the rock art of Arnhem Land, Northern Territory. *Australian Archaeology* 71:1–10. doi.org/10.1080/03122417.2010.11689379.

Taçon, P.S.C., S.K. May, R. Lamilami, F. McKeague, I. Johnston, J. Jalandoni, D. Wesley, I. Domingo, L. Brady, D. Wright and J. Goldhahn 2020. Maliwawa Figures – A previously undescribed Arnhem Land rock art style. *Australian Archaeology* 86(3):208–225. doi.org/10.1080/03122417.2020.1818361.

Taylor, L. 2016. Recent art history in rock country. In L. Brady and P.S.C. Taçon (eds), *Relating to rock art in the contemporary world: Navigating symbolism, meaning and significance*, pp. 245–274. University Press of Colorado, Boulder.

Thomas, M. and M. Neale (eds) 2011. *Exploring the legacy of the 1948 Arnhem Land Expedition.* ANU Press, Canberra. doi.org/10.22459/ELALE.06.2011.

Tindale, N.B. 1925–26. Natives of Groote Eylandt and of the West Coast of the Gulf of Carpentaria, Parts 1 and 2. *Records of the South Australian Museum* 111:61–134.

Tindale, N.B. 1928. Native rock shelters at Oenpelli, Van Diemen Gulf, North Australia. *South Australian Naturalist* 9(2):35–36.

Turner, D.H. 1973. The rock art of Bickerton Island in comparative perspective. *Oceania* 43(4):286–325. doi.org/10.1002/j.1834-4461.1973.tb01225.x.

UNESCO (ed.) 1954. *Australia: Aboriginal paintings – Arnhem Land.* The New York Graphic Society, Milan.

Warburton, C. 1934. *Buffaloes: Life and adventure in Arnhem Land.* Angus and Robertson Ltd., Sydney.

Watchman, A.L. 1987. Preliminary determinations of the age and composition on mineral salts on rock art surfaces in the Kakadu National Park. In W.R. Ambrose and J.M.J. Mummery (eds), *Archaeometry: Further Australasian studies*, pp. 36-42. The Australian National University, Canberra.

Wesley, D. 2014. Bayini, Macassans, Balanda, and Bininj: Defining the Indigenous past of Arnhem Land through culture contact. Unpublished PhD thesis, The Australian National University, Canberra.

Worsnop, T. 1895. The prehistoric arts of the Aboriginal Australians. *Australasian Association for the Advancement of Science Reports* 6:135–148.

Worsnop, T. 1897. *The prehistoric arts, manufacturers, works, weapons, etc. of the Aborigines of Australia.* C.E. Bristow, Government Printer, Adelaide.

12

Preserving the rock art of Kakadu: Formative conservation trials during the 1980s

Melissa Marshall, Jeffrey Lee, Gabrielle O'Loughlin, Kadeem May and Jillian Huntley

Introduction

Human interactions with the world and each other across time are most clearly represented in one of the most enduring legacies of humanity – rock art. Found around the world, the creativity and complex cultural interactions and associations of First Nations peoples are illustrated in these paintings, engravings and other media, conveying inherent understandings of relationships with Country, culture and kin. Here in Australia, this creative practice is shared by Aboriginal and Torres Strait Islander people in cultural landscapes stretching across the country from the remote tropical north of Western Australia to the cold landscapes of Tasmania.

Challenges to celebrate, protect, preserve and manage rock art in a changing world have been increasing exponentially, particularly since the mining and infrastructure development booms that followed World War II introduced many outsiders to remote areas of Australia. By the late 1960s, impacts to rock art sites from complex development pressures were being identified and described (Marshall 2020:122). At places such as Murujuga in Dampier, on the West Australian coast (Bednarik 2006), the Quinkan reserves on the Cape York Peninsula (Trezise 1971) and the Arnhem Land Plateau (Chaloupka 1974), such issues were brought to the attention of the Australian public, whereby advocates sought to support Indigenous communities in the face of these previously unidentified problems.

For the Arnhem Land Plateau, recognition of the significance, value and importance of Aboriginal heritage during the twentieth century culminated in the establishment of Kakadu National Park in the 1970s and 1980s (hereafter 'Kakadu' or 'the Park'). Kakadu was created to protect not only environmental landscapes, but also the living cultural heritage of the 13 clan groups in the area. With the increasing footprint of mining and industry in close proximity, the need to protect and preserve the plethora of rock art found here was vital. With 5000 known sites recorded in Kakadu alone and a further 10,000–15,000 expected, the full extent of the rock art of this northern region may never be fully quantified. Nonetheless, endeavours to scientifically protect and preserve the sites here were among the earliest attempts at rock art conservation in Australia.

Rock art conservation in Australia emerged during the 1970s (Chaloupka 1974; Clarke 1976; Pearson 1978; Pearson and Pretty 1976; Rosenfeld 1978) and often correlated with specific (or anticipated or potential) impacts in the wake of increasing mining and development. The establishment of Kakadu National Park was no exception and, following the work of the Alligator Rivers Fact-Finding Study (Chaloupka 1975; Christian and Aldrick 1973; Edwards 1974a; Kamminga and Allen 1973; McAlpine 1973; Midgley 1973; Needham et al. 1973), this culminated in international recognition of the region through its inclusion on the World Heritage List. The need to protect and preserve this wealth of rock art was of utmost importance to Traditional Owners and rock art researchers alike. Early innovative conservation techniques were trialled, with documentation of including photogrammetric recordings, as well as the investigation of specific environmental impacts threatening the fabric of sites (Gillespie 1983a, 1983b, 1983c; Naumann 1983; Rivett 1983; Watchman 1985a).

Of particular importance were two formative investigations conducted within Kakadu to inform conservation practice nationally, both overseen at the time by Kakadu staff members Ivan Haskovec and Hillary Sullivan. These were the CORLAB trials (CORLAB 1986, 1987 and 1988), led by esteemed rock art conservators John Clarke and Neale North through The Australian National University, and the subsequent Nourlangie Restoration Project (1989) at what is now known as the Anbangbang Gallery within the Burrungkuy rock art complex. This again involved Clarke and North but also emerging conservators who have contributed greatly to the discipline since this trial, including Andrew Thorn, Bruce Ford and Philip Haydock.

The CORLAB trials were implemented across three phases and built on previous studies conducted within the Park during its formative years, which included those described in Gillespie (1983a). The conservation program included an assessment of physical and chemical properties of both ochres and natural fixatives at more than 20 rock art sites across the Park (Phase 1) (CORLAB 1986); implementation of the investigative program through the establishment of control sites (including the Koongarra Trial Site) and application of intervention trials at five of the previously examined locations on eight panels containing rock art (Phase 2) (CORLAB 1987); and an evaluation of the durability of the eight intervened panels 13 months later (Phase 3) (CORLAB 1988). This was the first and only time in Australia an intervention trial would be implemented at such a scale.

Following on from the CORLAB trials, a scientific restoration project known as the Nourlangie Restoration Project was undertaken under the direction of Kakadu Park staff and supported by consulted Traditional Owners from the Djok, Murrumburr and Mirarr clan groups (CORLAB 1989). Consideration of this process was initiated and informed by the previous investigations from which the understanding was:

> One complication of rock art conservation management in Australia occurs when re-painting of the sites, as has been the tradition over countless millennia, results in apparent rapid deterioration of the images. In one instance Calcimine, a modern manufactured white pigment, was used in conjunction with traditional ochres in the Kakadu National Park. The problems of stabilizing the flaking images demonstrate the complexities of the deterioration processes and the effective use of modern synthetic resins to stabilize the same. (CORLAB 1989:1–21, in MacLeod 2000:41)

As described in Marshall (2020:137), following discussion about the proposed methods with Traditional Owners (which will be revisited in later sections of this paper), CORLAB (1989) undertook a series of mineralogical, geochemical and microbiological studies to understand the processes active in the shelter to inform the conservation interventions. This was followed by the rock art conservation workshop under the direction of Italian conservator Isabel Dangas, from the International Centre for the Preservation and Restoration of Cultural Property. The workshop involved 12 emerging Australian rock art conservators (including Andrew Thorn, Bruce Ford, Alan Byrne and Phillip Haydock) who were trained in restoration by Dangas on sections of the 'Inclined Gallery' frieze at the main shelter at Anbangbang (CORLAB 1989:31–45).

Forming the backbone of rock art conservation interventions possible at the time, particularly in the tropical north of Australia, these two projects and their subsequent durability are the subject of this chapter. Prior to this, however, it is important to contextualise these trials within the emerging conservation frameworks in Australia at that time, illustrating the sociopolitical environment within which these investigations were formed and implemented.

Background

Rock art conservation in Australia is a younger discipline than elsewhere around the world, although apart for a handful of countries, rock art conservation remains poorly developed almost everywhere. For the Palaeolithic caves identified in Europe at the end of the 1800s, certain conservation practices were trialled soon after. In Australia, the influence of colonial settlement has had a massive negative impact on the c. 60,000-year practice (Clarkson et al. 2017) of traditional forms of rock art production, which had involved a broad range of mechanisms associated with creation, refreshing, repainting and renewal as central to cultural maintenance and survival. While cultural practices continued, particularly in the northern areas of Australia (Blundell and Woolagoodja 2005; Mowaljarlai and Malnic 2001; Mowaljarlai and Watchman 1989), colonial impacts were overwhelming for Aboriginal communities in many other locations. With the advancement of the mining and development industry booms into the 1960s and 1970s in Australia, some of the larger rock art provinces came under threat and there was an increasing need for alternative methods to be considered that looked at so-called 'natural' impacts as well as more obviously human-made ones.

The response to these impacts from Traditional Owners, archaeologists, rock art specialists and conservation practitioners during this period was diverse, and concern for the preservation of rock art particularly the subject of national interest as early as 1972 (Edwards 1975). While all were advocating for improvements in statutory protection (which resulted in the introduction of heritage legislation, such as the *Aboriginal Heritage Act 1972* in WA), grassroots initiatives from remote Aboriginal communities were also being implemented (Wright 1978; Yu pers. comm., in Marshall 2020:123). During this period, conservation specialists began meeting in earnest as part of a broader discussion on the conservation of cultural materials in 1973 (Pearson and Pretty 1976), and then in 1977 to specifically identify and reflect on scientific mechanisms to mitigate the full plethora of concerns relating to the ongoing protection and preservation of rock art (Pearson 1978). This was in itself contextualised by global efforts, such as those of the International Institute for Conservation of Historic and Artistic Works, which held a conference in Sweden in 1975 (see Smits 1975; Taylor et al. 1975; for further information on the broad development of conservation practice in Australia from both cultural and scientific perspectives, see Marshall 2020:121–134).

As specialists from around the nation came together for these workshops, consideration was given to addressing the causes of greatest concern through scientific processes that were underpinned by established practices and involved comprehensively examining the management of rock art nationally (Dix 1978:3–5) and within individual states (Wright 1978:6). These included the various methods of recording rock art and creating baseline records prior to intervention (Rosenfeld 1978:9–14), incorporating the early use of photogrammetry (Rivett 1978:15-21) and stereophotography (Clegg 1978:22–26); specifics relating to deterioration of rock art in relation to ochres (Wainwright and Taylor 1978:29–31)), silica skins (Dolanski 1978:32–35) and the natural weathering of sandstone (Hughes 1978:36–42); suggested techniques for determining deterioration rates observed through a micro-erosion meter (Smith 1978:44–53) and methods to analyse deterioration rates (Clarke 1978a:54–64); concluding with case studies of conservation and restoration projects both internationally (Avery 1978:66–68; Misra 1978:69–70) and nationally (Sullivan 1978:71–74; Chaloupka 1978:75–78; Clarke 1978b:79–84; Florian 1978:9598; Smits 1978:99102). The latter workshop was also where the Australian Institute for the Conservation of Cultural Materials was developed and presentations from attending specialists went on to inform and frame conservation practices across the country. There were several notable contributions to the field that emerged from this event: Rosenfeld (1985) wrote the first dedicated book on rock art conservation in Australia; Pearson, who drove initial conservation efforts for rock art as well as material culture more broadly, has been the subject of recent reflections (Cook 2018; MacLeod 2000; Pearson et al 2011; Scott 2018); Chaloupka (1974) and Rivett (1983), both focused on the geographic area of what was to become Kakadu and who were foundational in efforts developed to document rock art; along with Clarke, who went on to develop the intervention trials that are discussed in this chapter.

An outcome of these initiatives was that Kakadu was one of the earliest locations in Australia where conservation practices were implemented. When Kakadu National Park was first established, there was great interest from non-Aboriginal people in the analysis, conservation and preservation of the rock art. In the 1970s, Edwards (1974a, 1974b, 1975) was the first to raise issues in what was to become Kakadu, that water, wasps, termites, vegetation, wind and dust were contributing factors to the deterioration of rock art. Gillespie (1979) followed soon after with his informative research into water management, which involved camping at a site for two weeks during the wet season to watch the water action within the site. This information was then fed into the 'beginnings of a conservation management plan for Ubirr', which the Park, in collaboration with academic institutions and Traditional Owners from the Manilikarr and Bunitj clans and their representative Njanjma Aboriginal Corporation, is looking to update in 2022.

Building on these initial research endeavours, by the early 1980s the Australian National Parks and Wildlife Service (ANPWS) had compiled similar studies into a book entitled *The rock art sites of Kakadu National Park – Some preliminary research findings for their conservation and management* (Gillespie 1983a). Described in the Foreword as an opportunity to share experiences gained in the first four years since the Park's declaration, Professor J.D. Ovington (former director ANPWS: i) noted:

> There is no miracle cure or inexpensive panacea in these pages for the great variety of rock art conservation problems. What is offered is a straightforward documentation of the results of both intense scientific scrutiny of some of the problems as well as the successes and failures of relatively mundane conservation strategies. There is also discussion of the close consultation which continues between Service officers and the Aboriginal people who own or have responsibility for the rock art sites of Kakadu.

Framed by an examination of Kakadu's cultural, historic and prehistoric significance (Chaloupka 1983:1–33), the Foreword was followed by Gillespie's considerations of the challenges facing the early non-Indigenous managers, as he was given responsibility for providing advice and implementing conservation policies (1983b:34–35). Within this role, he had encouraged the engagement of four specialists to assist with specific tasks, and their investigations were presented in subsequent chapters. Hughes and Watchman (1983:37–86) examined the impacts causing deterioration and requiring conservation and management; Rivett (1983:87–126) discussed the photogrammetric techniques and subsequent records produced for a number of key sites; and Naumann (1983:127–190) investigated the biology of mud wasps and their nests. The final chapter brought together the knowledge shared by the specialists and implications for the developing conservation program (Gillespie 1983c:191–213). While providing insightful considerations on the application of artificial silicon driplines (including causes of failure) and the removal of mud wasp nests, Gillespie also considered the pros and cons of the installation of visitor infrastructure and the cultural impacts this may have:

> I have argued elsewhere [1983c] that the greatest danger from cultural tourism at sites such as those of Kakadu is that the process of developing or curating a site and interpreting it for the visiting public may lead to the site being misappropriated – to it becoming part of the European cultural baggage and lost to Aboriginal people as a viable living component of their culture. The very steps that site protectors may take to protect a site and to use it as a means of raising visitor appreciation of Aboriginal culture may be arrows for the culture's heart. Aboriginal people may find themselves in a position of helplessness – unable to exert control over the site or to carry out the responsibilities of site ownership – shut out by European infrastructure. (Gillespie 1983b:34)

The early foundational conservation work produced in those initial years established the principles and practices that would be implemented in the years that followed. Since this time there has been a plethora of research undertaken in archaeology and cultural heritage in the Country of the 13 clan groups. With this focus on conservation and visitor management, the priority of the Park management was to preserve and protect the tangible fabric of sites (Director of National Parks 2014). Conservation efforts were dedicated to understanding impacts including the behaviour of salts (Watchman 1985a, 1987; Thorn 1993a) and silica skins (Watchman 1985b, 1989); the influence of mud wasps and termites in pigment deterioration (Madycki 2006), as well as weathering (Watchman 1990); with water damage and its subsequent management also playing a key role in the research (Thorn 1993b; Lambert 1997). Examination of these types of physical impacts and documentation of rock art within the Park were emphasised during its early years (1970s and 1980s), prior to a shift to the conservation of intangible heritage and language (including cultural narrative and oral histories) from the 1990s to the 2000s. While the Park continued to maintain the public rock art sites during this time, no research or work was done further afield (see Marshall 2020:505-514). In the last decade, the focus has again shifted to a more holistic approach to incorporate all elements of the tangible and intangible cultural landscapes to look after the Country of Kakadu (Marshall et al. 2020). While all of this research has been foundational in the development of current management strategies, the two groundbreaking trials involving CORLAB and the restoration of the Anbangbang Gallery (Figure 12.1) in the mid to late 1980s have informed rock art conservation practice across Australia since.

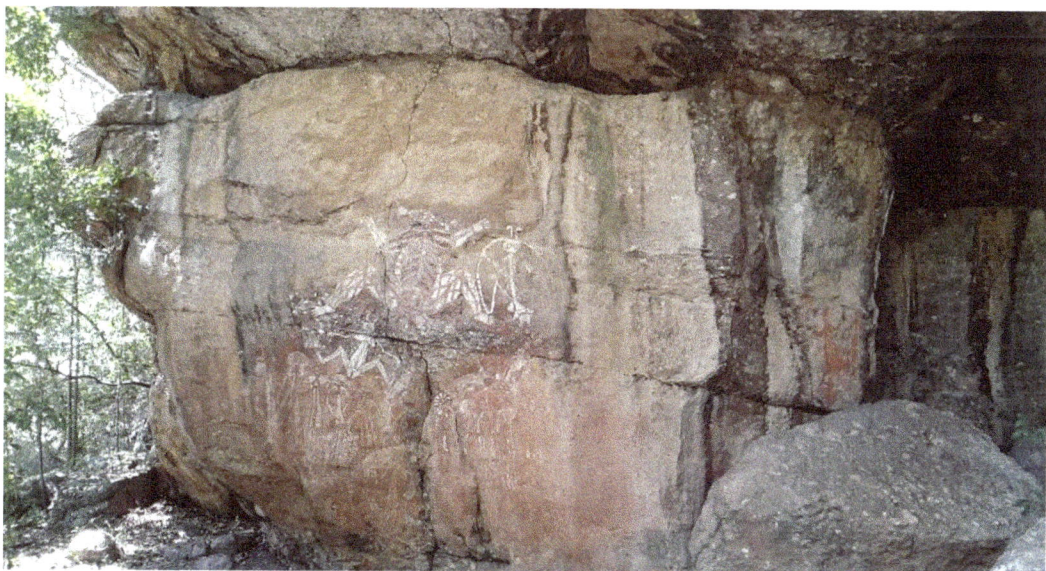

Figure 12.1: Anbangbang (Nourlangie) in 2019.
Source: Kadeem May.

CORLAB intervention trials

Throughout the formation of conservation practice in Australia, interest had also been generated in the possibility of developing silica products that could be sprayed over paintings in order to replicate the protective elements of natural silica skins and thereby improve rock art longevity (Marshall 2020:509-511). Commencing in 1986, conservators John Clarke and Neale North were engaged through a company linked to The Australian National University, known as 'CORLAB', to develop a trial program across a number of sites in Kakadu. The initiative was instigated to assess the suitability of application of various artificial silica sprays designed to withstand the destructive nature of water, dust and naturally deteriorating pigment. The process involved using a range of products in an attempt to improve the longevity of the preservation of rock art present. They applied three different types of artificial silica sprays to trial long-term responses to environmental impacts from water, salt and dust deposition. These silica sprays included three different types of material – water repellents, envelope coatings and consolidants (products such as silicone-modified vinyl acrylics, polyvinyl butyral (PVBs) and polyurethane). Treatments were applied to unpainted and painted stone surfaces, and observations were made on their effectiveness. At the outset, they cautioned that:

> a critical element in assessing a conservation treatment is not so much how long it will remain effective, but rather how will it fail? A treatment may work extremely well but its mode of failure may result in even greater damage than the natural deterioration processes. (CORLAB 1988:8)

Although one of the most recognised conservation principles is that all treatments need to be reversible, all products used in the Kakadu trials were knowingly regarded as irreversible and intentionally applied in an effort to advance knowledge within the conservation discipline (CORLAB 1988:8). The research was undertaken across three years as part of a three-part process and included the establishment of a dedicated control site at Koongarra (in the Headquarters District of the Park in the same geological formation as Burrungkuy/Nourlangie) to test and observe each of the treatments applied. The initial year, Phase 1 (CORLAB 1986), involved scientific investigation of pigment identification and the presence of alteration products in the environment including gypsum, whewellite and Obiri salt. Samples were examined from across the Park including at the Nourlangie and Ubirr site complexes, Cannon Hill, East Alligator area, Naranch (Ngarradj Warde Djobkeng), Namarrgon, Deaf Adder and Christmas Creek. Results were produced using a variety of techniques including optical microscopy, scanning electron microscopy including with energy dispersive x-ray analysis, x-ray diffraction, chemical analysis and infra-red spectroscopy (CORLAB 1986). Following this study, the analysis of the behaviours of the salts and the ability to mitigate particularly this and deterioration from water, the conservation treatment proposed was as follows:

> The study has shown that the post-estuarine period art in Kakadu is in a most precarious state because of the large salt accumulations. While careful site management can assist the preservation of the paintings through procedures such as drip lines to keep all water away, it is clear that some form of treatment will be needed to ensure that some of the more vulnerable sites survive … In most cases where salt is a problem, treatment is aimed at removal of the salts and preventing their reintroduction. This approach will not be possible at Kakadu as the salts are intimately mixed with the pigment on the surface of the rock.

> Treatment of the pigment and rock surface with a chemical consolidant may provide a solution, at least in part, to the problem. Normally in rock surface treatment it is desirable to use a permeable consolidant, such as a Silicone. This is done so that moisture within the rock can still escape through the surface. If an impermeable consolidant, such as an organic Silicate, is used there is a risk that moisture trapped below the surface will cause the surface layer to exfoliate. However, the permeable consolidants, whilst they would greatly

improve the bonding between the pigment particles, the salt and the rock surface, would not protect the pigment from further reaction with atmospheric gases, nor would they prevent mobilisation of the salts under moist conditions. The impermeable consolidants would totally encapsulate the remaining pigment and the salts, and greatly inhibit further reaction with gases or the movement of moisture in the pigment layer. It is believed that the reactions between the atmosphere and pigments that form the salts require water or at least moisture to proceed and so any treatment that prevents or lowers the amount of moisture in the pigment layer would assist the preservation of the paintings. (CORLAB 1986:21-22)

A number of issues were identified that were crucial to determining appropriate materials to trial, including the inclusion of as many products with desirable characteristics as possible (such as resistance to breakdown by ultra-violet light, and low viscosity to allow good penetration into the pigment and rock surface); attention to application procedures such as the use of different solvent mixtures and partial polymerisation; and inclusion of 'real' sites (on the basis of their representativeness and acceptability to Traditional Owners), as well as specially prepared experimental ones, to determine whether the examination of the treatment of salts and alteration products present could be replicated in trials. It was vital that the trials commence immediately, as it would take a number of years for the effectiveness or otherwise of treatments to be adequately assessed. The reassessment of an earlier trial of a silicone consolidant by the Northern Territory Museum and Art Gallery and Traditional Owners from 1978, both for the effectiveness of the treatment and assessment of the effects of salt accumulation following the treatment, was also considered vital. (The archival reports on the earlier 1978 efforts have not been found to date.)

Conservation treatments were subsequently developed and implemented, and trial results duly reported (CORLAB 1986:21-22). The results then informed the theoretical understanding of the indicators of deterioration impacts identified at the selected study sites, and Phase 2 was initiated. This involved further:

> trials to examine the mechanism of salt accumulation in the rock art shelters; to establish a number of trials to test a range of synthetic consolidants and surface treatments that could form the basis for conservation procedure for paintings in the Park; and to undertake further studies aimed at characterising the unidentified salt referred to as 'Obiri salt', responsible for rock weathering at a number of rock art sites. (CORLAB 1987:1)

Subsequently, as part of Phase 2 the following year, three control sites were established and treatment trials applied at some of the initial study sites, geographically dispersed across the Park (CORLAB 1987:4). This included examination of salt accumulation and the impact this may have had on the preservation of pigments within this environment. The challenges identified were addressed through a targeted study:

> the two main salts accumulating on and within the pigment layer were Gypsum (Calcium Sulphate Dihydrate) and Whewellite (Calcium Oxalate Dihydrate). Where there were pigments containing Calcium Carbonate (such as Huntite, Dolomite or Calcite) they showed considerable direct alteration of pigment particles to Gypsum while in non-carbonate pigments (such as the clays) Gypsum and Whewellite had accumulated within and on the pigment layer.

> These observations imply that Sulphur compounds are present in a gaseous form at least in some stage of the salt formation process. There are two sulphur compounds that could be responsible, Sulphur Dioxide and Hydrogen Sulphide. To differentiate between these two gases and make an assessment of the rate of salt formation, separate Petri dishes containing Lead Carbonate and Manganese Dioxide were placed at selected sites. Five dishes of each chemical were placed at each site along with at least one empty dish as a control. The dishes were placed on horizontal surfaces, with silicone resin being used to attach them to the rock surface. They were covered with plastic flywire 'hats' intended to lessen the risk of animal disturbance, wind effects and the addition of extraneous matter. (CORLAB 1987:2)

Dishes were placed at Canon Hill, Ubirr, Ngarradj Warde Djobkeng, Christmas Creek, Namargon and Anbangbang. The contents of these dishes are yet to be analysed and remain at the original six locations today, with only the one within the Ubirr rock art complex re-found. An evaluation of the resulting data collected during this 30-year period will be part of forthcoming research as part of Marshall's postdoctoral fellowship (2022–2024).

In addition to the salt accumulation studies and results from Phase 1, which informed the trial of the application of synthetic consolidants, three control sites were established at Koongarra, Cannon Hill and Namargon to specifically test the adhesives. The Koongarra trial (CORLAB 1987:4–5) focused on testing the preservation of three recently applied ochre lines in red, yellow and white against 18 different artificial consolidant sprays (six each of silicone-modified vinyl acrylics, PVBs and polyurethane as represented in Figure 12.2); the two Cannon Hill trials (CORLAB 1987:5-6) involved application of six different artificial sprays on rock art at the site; while the Namargon trial (CORLAB 1987:7) was conducted on the ceiling of a shelter and again involved the application of 10 different artificial sprays. Once these control sites were established, individual motifs were also treated at these sites, as well as two sites at Ngarradj Warde Djobkeng, Anbangbang and Nanguluwurr. Treatment of two motifs ascribed to Nanguluwurr have since been relocated not at this site, but near the Barrk Walk between Nanguluwurr and Anbangbang. Notably all of the trials involved the conservation specialists working alongside 10 Traditional Owners for these sites. Each trial was examined the day after application, with concern given to application success, penetration, pigment effects/preservation and surface finish/appearance.

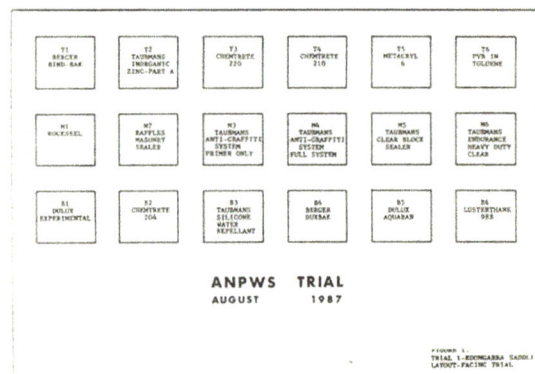

Figure 12.2: Photograph (a) and diagram (b) of materials used in Koongarra trial.
Source: CORLAB 1987 (courtesy of Kakadu National Park).

Details of the interventions were thus reported, with the final phase of the project being an evaluation of the intervention trials 13 months later (CORLAB 1988). Each trial was assessed for robustness of the intervention applied and to identify the durability of substances in this extreme environment. This time pigment effects/preservation and surface finish/appearance were again assessed, along with water repellence and overall performance. Key findings described by CORLAB (1988:13–15) recommended the use of two conservation treatments for rock art sites – silicone treatments where there is no need to consolidate the paint layers, and PVB treatments for sites with loose friable pigments and where paint layers are delaminating or very thick. They also advocated that no conservation treatments should be applied prior to consultation with and approval from Traditional Owners, the detailed recording of the imagery, as well as a comprehensive assessment of the condition of the site. Condition assessments should include:

- Pigments – factors to be taken into account are composition, condition and alteration of pigments;
- Paint structure – number of paint layers and degree of adhesion between layers;
- Permeability – of both the paint and the rock substrate should be established;
- Exposure to ultra-violet light – the amount of direct sunlight incident on the rock painting should be assessed;
- Water – the likelihood of rain or runoff contacting the painting as well as the possibility of condensation or groundwater seepage must be established;
- Soluble salts – the level of soluble salts in the rock and paintings should be assessed; and
- Extraneous materials – the presence of extraneous materials such as mud nests, termite tracks, buffalo rubbings, human graffiti etc. should be assessed and appropriate action taken (CORLAB 1988:13).

Overall, the conservators identified that:

> The assessment of rock art conservation treatment is difficult in that the ultimate success or otherwise of the treatment will not be known, in some cases, for hundreds of years. In the case of the Post-Estuarine Period Rock Art of Kakadu National Park deterioration rates can be very rapid and decisions on conservation treatment will need to be made for some of these sites within the next few years if they are to survive at all. While the trials reported on here have only been running for one year some of the materials used have been used on rock art sites elsewhere and up to 14 years observations are available on these sites … Rather than adopting the unattainable reversibility we have endeavoured to recommend treatments that will not unduly inhibit future conservation treatment and that will not result in catastrophic failure when the treatment eventually breaks down. (CORLAB 1988:8)

Despite the conservation practitioners' advocation for long-term monitoring and evaluation programs for these trials to be implemented, this recommendation is yet to be fully realised (Marshall 2016). A preliminary program has been instigated recently, whereby imagery at Nanguluwurr treated as part of the CORLAB trial has been subsequently assessed (Marshall 2020) and is now being monitored as part of Kakadu's 'Annual Rock Art Monitoring and Maintenance Program' aligned with the Park's '*Bim* [Rock Art] Strategy', which actions the Kakadu Plan of Management (Director of National Parks 2020). The results of these endeavours are now forming the basis for continuing research programs. Importantly, however, the results from these CORLAB trials were then used to inform the consequential trial of interest, the Nourlangie Restoration Project.

Nourlangie Restoration Project

By March 1989, preparations were underway to restore motifs on one of the best-known rock art sites within Kakadu, the Anbangbang Gallery at Burrungkuy (then known as Nourlangie). Many of the images in question had been painted as recently as the 1960s by revered rock artists Nayombolmi and Djimongurr (May et al. 2019). Under the direction of Haskovec, CORLAB were involved once again with conservation efforts in Kakadu, this time with the support and supervision of the French conservator of Italian paintings Isabelle Dangas through the International Centre for the Preservation and Restoration of Cultural Property (ICCROM). Building on the findings of the previous investigations (CORLAB 1986, 1987, 1988), which included findings from their analysis of the pigments used in the recent art, this discrete initiative focused on a single site (CORLAB 1989:1) and required conservators to:

1. Inspect the Anbangbang rock art site at Nourlangie Rock to determine what restoration work is needed.

2. Develop a methodology for the restoration of the art works for consideration by the Traditional Owners.

3. Demonstrate and carry out to the fullest extent possible within the limit of field investigations:

    a. repositioning of peeled paint back onto the original substrate, and

    b. other restoration and conservation procedures as deemed necessary at the site.

4. Demonstrate and carry out to the fullest extent possible within the limit of field investigations cleaning of embedded dust from the art surfaces at the site.

5. Provide detailed documentation of the restoration techniques used.

6. Conduct a workshop to demonstrate rock art conservation techniques for selected Australian conservators and restorers.

7. Provide recommendations for the future preservation of Nourlangie rock art sites (CORLAB 1989:1).

Crucially, this initiative was built around earlier findings that had determined through samples analysed with a scanning electron microscope that many of the white pigments used at Anbangbang included a dolorite/montmorillonite mixture, with trace amounts also found in red, yellow and brown pigments (CORLAB 1986:9-10). With the white pigments exhibiting the most serious deterioration, further examination of clay-based montmorillonite was conducted. It was found that montmorillonite was used (and continues to be today) to assist in increasing the viscosity of water-based suspensions, such as in the house paints known as 'Calcimine' used in the prewar years, or alternatively a proprietary whitewash to improve the suspension of lime within the pigment (CORLAB 1986:10). The conservators determined that the montmorillonite was present due to the inclusion of manufactured paints mixed with the locally sourced clays, which, when applied, resulted in a lumpy texture (CORLAB 1989:5). The conclusion that the pigments used were not 'traditional' but integrated with commercial products informed Traditional Owner decision-making around the restoration project and their approval of the methods applied (CORLAB 1989:18-19), and likewise informed the public as part of a Kakadu Park note (Director of National Parks 1989; Figure 12.3a). Recent studies have refuted this finding (May et al. 2020), and Traditional Owners are now reconsidering methods for continuing preservation efforts at the site.

Preparations for the emerging conservators' workshop as part of the Nourlangie Restoration Project displayed the same intensity and thoroughness as the initial studies, and CORLAB once again completed a detailed examination of various impacts affecting the site. Consideration was given to archival material (Attenborough 1963; Chaloupka 1982; Edwards 1975, 1979; Haskovec and Sullivan 1989) alongside an earlier condition assessment by Hughes (1979), Park records and a previous management plan for the area (CORLAB 1989:2). The ensuing condition assessment involved the detailed inspection and documentation of the painted panel. This process was divided into three main areas, these being the support or (rock) substrate, the paintings themselves and the surface accumulations that had developed subsequent to the paintings (CORLAB 1989:5–15). Their findings from this indicated that:

> The rock art of Anbangbang gallery occurs as a series of different layers with individual motifs or compositions being indiscriminately painted over previous art work. In the case of the main panel the most recent paintings are considered to be of most value because of their significance to Aboriginal people and their visual attraction to Park visitors.

The state of preservation of the underlying paint layers is difficult to assess and can only deduced from exposed edges or clearly superimposed sections. Generally the preservation status is not good and lack of cohesion is observed in a number of pigment types.

The state of preservation of the Najombolmi painting is of major concern. It exhibits a wide range of deterioration types and significant areas are at major risk of loss. It was therefore agreed that emergency intervention was required. The ANPWS and Aboriginal custodians had already decided that no repainting or additional pigment was to be added during the restoration process. (CORLAB 1989:16)

A further treatment and restoration strategy was thus devised, complete with trials, replacement of paint flakes, cleaning procedures, use of consolidation and treatment of exfoliation (CORLAB 1989:16–17, 20–22). This information was used as the basis of the key component to the Nourlangie Restoration Project, that being the inclusion of the emerging rock art conservator workshop. Involving interested conservators from around Australia, the focus of the workshop was to experiment with interventions and conservation techniques to restore the physical fabric of the site (Figure 12.3b). This initiative was in response to an increasing problem identified by the rock art conservation profession, which had ascertained that there were not enough people trained in scientific techniques to adequately preserve the rock imagery found across the country. The rock art conservation workshop was an attempt to address that imbalance, and while 12 potential conservators were trained, only two have continued to work as professionals in this field – Andrew Thorn and Bruce Ford. A limited success in advancing the number of conservators in Australia, the project provided a crucial endeavour to understand and advance restoration practices at open-air rock art sites in Australia.

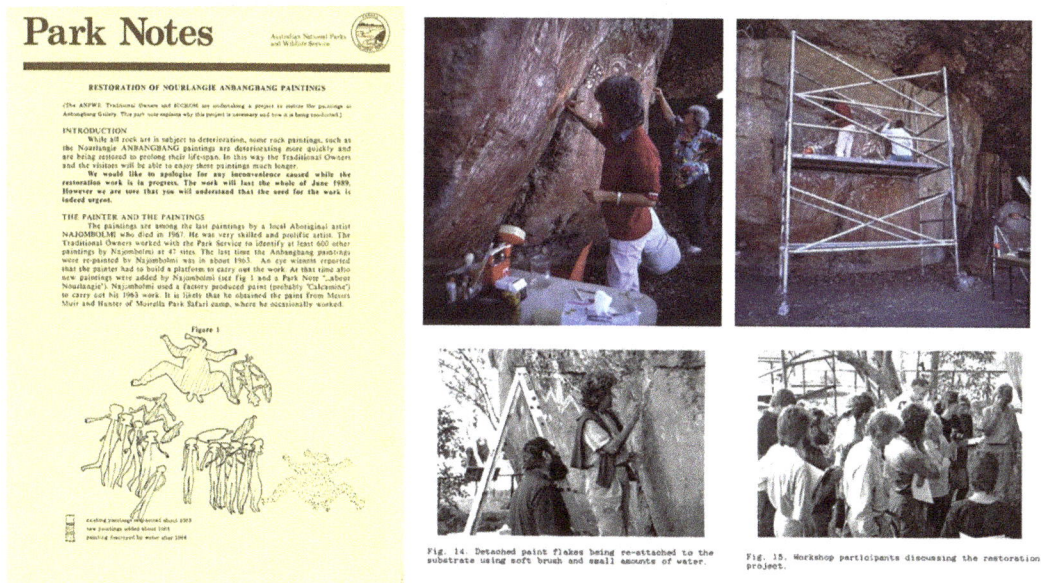

Figure 12.3: Nourlangie Restoration Project in 1989: (a) The Park note provided to visitors at the time and (b) Conservators at work during the project.

Source: Kakadu National Park and CORLAB 1989 (courtesy of Kakadu National Park).

To ensure that best practice and the most recent advancements were applied, a detailed photographic recording of the Nourlangie panel and the various features being examined was combined with overlays plotted onto photogrammetrically controlled base elevations previously prepared for the former Commonwealth department responsible for Kakadu, the ANPWS. Additional written descriptions were prepared to complement the overlays or describe features that could not be plotted. Divided into groups of three, restoration activities and techniques varied and involved the re-adhesion of pigments, cleaning of dust and removal of microbiological growth. Four specific rock art motifs were restored during this process:

- Crocodile – pigment testing, cleaning of wasp nests and pigment fixing through application of consolidant.

- Dancing woman and lizard – removal of wasp nests, dust and debris; dry brushing of algal growth; application of consolidant.

- Namargon – cleaning (general removal of algae, overall dust removal, insect remains – wasp nests and termite trails, black gypsum-staining, attention to smudging on painting); consolidation of pigments with poultices; stabilisation of botryoidal accretions; stabilisation of fissures if necessary; placement of artificial silicon drip lines (CORLAB 1989:App1. 5–15).

Considered a success overall by those involved, they noted that:

> The restoration project undertaken at Anbangbang should be regarded as an emergency operation to halt the more obvious deterioration that was occurring. The site's long term conservation will require considerable additional monitoring and research. Further intervention based on the results of this monitoring and research will be required. The areas that require further study include: 1. The Paint Layer; 2. Site climatology; and 3. Site hydrology. (CORLAB 1989:26–28)

The Nourlangie Restoration Project was the first of its kind in Australia and, to date, conservation efforts of this scale have not been repeated elsewhere. While groundbreaking in its endeavours, both the Nourlangie Restoration Project and preceding CORLAB trials advocated for the monitoring, periodic review and evaluation of these rock art restoration interventions on a semi-regular basis. This would take more than 20 years to realise.

Evaluating the CORLAB trials and Nourlangie Restoration Project

During the first 10–15 years of the establishment of Kakadu National Park and its addition to the World Heritage List, there was a plethora of research in many areas of 'natural' and cultural management, including archaeology (see Jones 1985). With the knowledge of the complexity and density of rock art in Kakadu, intensive programs were established to locate and document sites, in addition to determining the range of issues impacting the long-term protection and preservation of the paintings. By the mid-1990s, however, this emphasis had shifted to the maintenance of culture and language, oral histories and connections. The earlier work was placed to one side as Bininj (Traditional Owners in the northern clan groups in Kakadu) and Munggay (Traditional Owners from the southern clan groups) expressed concerns at the loss of knowledge as old people passed away. As noted above, while maintenance of the tangible fabric of the rock art (removing wasp nests, maintenance of infrastructure, signage) did continue at the public art sites, from the mid to late 1990s efforts moved to the documentation and maintenance of this intangible heritage, which thereby limited opportunities to adhere to the advice of the conservators with regards to monitoring and evaluation. Furthermore, greater attention was also placed on a range of cultural activities that concerned the broader landscape in which the art sites were located, such as the maintenance and community education relating to cultural burning.

Figure 12.4: CORLAB trial at Nanguluwurr in (a) 1987 and (b) 2017, highlighting further deterioration despite treatment.

Source: CORLAB 1987 (courtesy of Kakadu National Park); and Melissa Marshall.

In 2009, renewed interest in rock art conservation was articulated by Bininj and Munggay to Park management. A one-off workshop (May et al. 2009) was held, and from this grew the doctoral research of Marshall (2020). As the site of Nanguluwurr was selected for the doctoral program, the location of the earlier trial conducted there was re-identified and investigated, with observational assessments of the treated areas documented (Marshall 2020:586–588). The old reports from CORLAB were obtained from the archives, and examination of the contents of these documents subsequently raised further questions, such as the effective durability of interventions (Figure 12.4). Marshall's doctoral research has been formative in commencing the evaluative investigations of the CORLAB trials and other conservation and related programs across Kakadu and nearby areas of Arnhem Land, adhering to the advocacy of previous conservators. This has since led to non-invasive investigations in 2016 and 2019, examining individual trial sites with portable x-ray fluorescence (pXRF), results of which are in progress.

Evaluation of conservation treatments applied through the CORLAB trials

Eight sites were investigated as part of a 2016 trial conducted to determine the capability of pXRF instruments to identify applied materials remaining from previous conservation treatment programs. The initial results proved promising, with final analyses of these data forthcoming. Early results indicate (as was partially expected) that the geochemical compounds were diagnostic with the investigative tools used, whereas the sources of inorganic accretions were more difficult to identify. The primary objective was to assess the ability of so-called 'non-invasive' (i.e. relatively non-destructive) methods such as pXRF to quantify the remnants (and potential durability) of previous trials through trace chemical signatures. Some consolidants trialled, especially the 'silica sprays', contained the element ruthenium, which was initially targeted as diagnostic of the conservation interventions. However, the K α peak of ruthenium is measured at an overlapping fluorescent photon energy as the broad Compton Scatter generated by the rhodium target within the instrument used (Bezur et al. 2020). Therefore, further analysis is underway to evaluate initial findings, and to determine additional investigative tools that may better enable the desired analytical questions to be 'fully' addressed.

Evaluation of the Nourlangie Restoration Project

To further interrogate the initial pXRF study and build on the recent research, a subsequent pXRF investigation was implemented through the Pathways, People and Landscape Project with Djok people, one of the central clan groups in Kakadu. This has enabled research trials to focus on evaluating results from the broader Burrungkuy cultural landscape, including both the previous restoration project and the CORLAB trial at Koongarra. At the Anbangbang Gallery, four of the five specific images treated as part of the conservation intervention were examined, in addition to the important image of Barginj that has sustained increased damage in recent years. Results are still pending relating to the treated panels. What was questioned, however, was the hypothesis that acrylics were used in the recent paintings, and the influence the subsequent answer may have to decision-making processes for Bininj and Munggay.

Made by acclaimed rock artist Nayombolmi in the 1960s, the painting of Barginj (wife of Namarrgon, the Lightning Man, whom she is depicted next to) is painted across conglomerate bands of the bedrock that, along with the use of a thicker application of pigment, appear to have contributed to the deterioration of the image (as the conglomerate is more permeable and allows greater flow of water through the rock face in this part of the bedrock). In conjunction with the previous assertion of the use of pigments containing manufactured montmorillonite, this raised further questions as to any influence this may have also had on the preservation of the rock imagery in question. Examining the extant material compounds, recent studies have determined that the montmorillonite might in fact be local in origin (May et al. 2020:128). Therefore, the condition of Barginj is unlikely to be solely related to the accelerated deterioration of an acrylic-based painting in this environment. The question remains as to whether the incorporation of commercial, artificial compounds may or may not be contributing to accelerated deterioration for other paintings, or, alternatively, whether the presence or higher quantities of montmorillonite (from natural or commercial sources) was a contributing factor. While Welch (2015) laid blame on the poor management of wasp nests, deterioration from the nests alone has not had the same impact on the remaining paintings. This indicates that, while the nest in question may have been responsible for the ultimate deterioration, there are additional factors, such as those described here, to consider.

A final element of the current research into the trials was to review the condition of the site as initially reported by Hughes (1979) and later CORLAB (1989). Forty years on from the initial investigation, the condition of the site was again assessed in 2018, producing a comparative record. While investigations into the resilience, success or failure of the interventions performed during the restoration project are ongoing, there appears to have been minimal changes to the image since then. Key impacts continue to be water (including the deposition of evaporite minerals such as salts) and insects, alongside those from atmospheric contamination (including dust), and the microclimate (which can facilitate the growth of microorganisms including lichen).

Visitor management is likewise a key consideration given the thousands of tourists who visit the site annually. To minimise visitor impacts, infrastructure includes a viewing platform, interpretative signage and daily talks from seasonal Parks rangers (during the dry season).

Site hydrology (particularly water-wash from rain) continues to influence the preservation of the imagery. Deterioration has been identified since the 1980s CORLAB assessment and impacts remain, specifically at the peripheries of the main panel that includes Namarrgon and the group of women painted in the main part of the site. The analysis and outcomes of the condition assessment, along with the targeted evaluation of the restoration project, will soon contribute to the development of a Cultural Conservation Management Plan for the Burrungkay area. This will provide a long-term framework to support the ongoing monitoring, maintenance and management of the site for the protection and preservation of these important images.

Evaluating the control site for the Koongarra trial

Potentially one of the most important pieces of the puzzle for the CORLAB trial review was the 1987 control site at Koongarra, which was established on exposed rock devoid of other paintings. With three lines of pigment applied in red, white and brown, this trial was designed to assess the performance of the aforementioned selected treatments (products such as silicone-modified vinyl acrylics, PVBs and polyurethane) prior to their use on experimental pseudo rock art sites (CORLAB 1987:4–5). The conservators noted that:

> the exposed nature of this site will result in the treatments receiving much higher UV light levels, higher temperature variations and higher rainfall effects than will occur in typical rock shelters. The site will therefore provide useful data on the long term stability of the various treatments and their durability under exposed conditions … It is recommended that the site be assessed at six monthly intervals. (CORLAB 1987:5)

While a review of the site was conducted 13 months later (CORLAB 1988:4–5), its location was lost in subsequent years until we re-located it in 2018. In 2019, investigation of the residuals remaining 30 years on were examined (Figure 12.5). A pXRF instrument was used for its non-invasive analytical capabilities as Bininj and Munggay did not want samples taken from images at this time. The data collected are in the process of being analysed and evaluated prior to further consideration of alternative investigative methods such as Raman spectroscopy and scanning electron microscopy. What can be stated in the interim, however, is that of the 18 consolidants trialled at that time, one of those ranked amongst the worst performers the day after application and then 13 months later when reassessed, is the only treated area 30 years on that has all three ochre lines still visible.

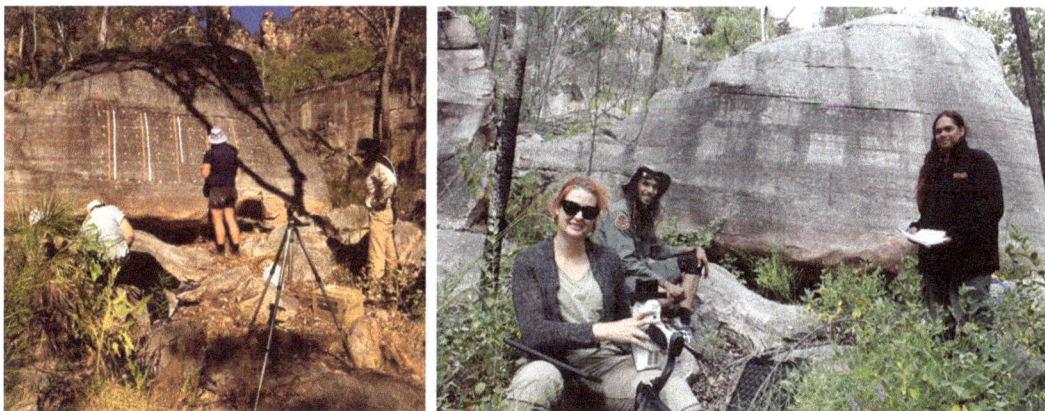

Figure 12.5: Koongarra trial in (a) 1988 evaluation and (b) 2019 evaluation.
Source: CORLAB 1988 (courtesy of Kakadu National Park); and Melissa Marshall.

Within the same complex as the Koongarra trial, a previous informal trial was established by Parks staff in the early 1980s to examine natural organic binders and two conservation treatments (CORLAB 1987:5). This reference from CORLAB is the only currently known documentation relating to this formative trial, and a search of the Park archives continues for relevant control data. Evaluation of the trials at this site will assist further in understanding the durability of the interventions applied, their success or subsequent failures. However, to do so, archival material or evidence is required to complete the evaluation, as various factors such as variation in the pigments used and whether some or all of the motifs were treated in exactly the same way will influence results.

Reinvigorating ongoing monitoring and evaluation programs

The evaluative research underway to investigate the effectiveness and durability of the earlier trials is now being used to support management of the sites themselves and associated conservation treatments. Ongoing monitoring and maintenance of rock art across Kakadu has been reinvigorated through a targeted annual program since 2014 (Marshall 2014). Priorities for the program are determined by Bininj, Munggay and djungayya (site custodians) and often target publicly accessible sites. Working together, these cultural sites are regularly maintained, resulting in benefits for the cultural values of the art and visitors alike. Non-public sites, which number in the thousands and include particularly culturally sensitive areas, are prioritised for maintenance activities at the request and in the company of Traditional Owners. The annual monitoring and maintenance program is worked out via consultation with appropriate Traditional Owners for a given site and area, to indicate which sites are targeted and the frequency of maintenance visits. Maintenance activities involve vegetation, fire and insect management, alongside checking previous interventions such as whether artificial silicon driplines installed over the past 30–40 years remain effective and secure. Vitally, the annual program is one that gives primacy to cultural authority, protocols and practices as the central drivers of conservation and management. This program was developed to support the next generation of Bininj and Munggay to remain connected to culture and Country while simultaneously developing knowledge and skills associated with scientific interventions. This twofold approach will thus assist with informed culturally based decision-making about the application and installation of future mitigation and management strategies.

Cultural responsibility

Of primary importance to Traditional Owners across Kakadu is for everyone to understand that people are still living there, telling stories and keeping culture strong. As articulated by Jeffrey Lee at the 2019 Histories of Rock Art Workshop presentation, on which this chapter is based, he and his ancestors have worked with researchers for over 40 years to find the best ways to look after Country. Both the CORLAB trial and Nourlangie Restoration Project have been instrumental in shaping rock art conservation practice in Australia. Projects such as this have assisted in the vital role of looking after Country not only now or when the Park started, but always:

> There are stories in the rock art. There are pictures of my creation ancestors, extinct animals, food, hand prints and other stories that we can't talk about because they are sacred sites.
>
> We teach our kids using the stories in the rock art, they are the next generation and they need to know the stories so that they continue into the future. We have tourists that come to our country and we need to teach them to respect our culture and to listen to our stories. We look after our rock art and visit sites to clean them up and make sure that they are protected. (Jeffrey Lee, Histories of Rock Art Workshop)

Conclusion

Evaluation of the CORLAB trials and Nourlangie Restoration Project continues in Kakadu, integrated with current research and the Park's annual monitoring program. Findings of these analyses feed directly into assisting with managing the rock art of the World Heritage Area. With the establishment of Kakadu there was a big push to look after paintings using scientific interventions in consultation with Traditional Owners. Whether the interventions themselves have worked or not still needs to be fully assessed and understood. However, what can be stated unequivocally is that no further intervention will happen without Traditional Owners driving the process, either through customary cultural methods of retouching or largely Western 'scientific' programs alike. It is up to the Traditional Owners.

References

Attenborough, D. 1963. *Quest under Capricorn*. Lutterworth Press, Cambridge.

Avery, G. 1978. Rock art conservation in South Africa. In C. Pearson (ed.), *Conservation of rock art*: *Proceedings of the International Workshop on the Conservation of Rock Art, Perth, September 1977*, pp. 66–68. The Institute for the Conservation of Cultural Material, Perth.

Bednarik, R. 2006. *Australian apocalypse: The story of Australia's greatest cultural monument*. Occasional Publication 14. Archaeological Publications, Melbourne.

Bezur, A., L. Lee, M. Loubser and K. Trentelman 2020. *Handheld XRF in cultural heritage*: *A practical workbook for conservators*. J. Paul Getty Trust and Yale University, Los Angeles.

Blundell, V. and D. Woolagoodja 2005. *Keeping the Wanjinas fresh: Sam Woolagoodja and the enduring power of Lalai*. Fremantle Arts Centre Press, Fremantle.

Chaloupka, G. 1974. *Report on the causes of damage and suggested conservation measures at the main gallery of the Deaf Adder Creek Valley*. Report to Northern Territory Government, Darwin.

Chaloupka, G. 1975. Report on Aboriginal traditional land ownership of the Alligator Rivers Region Part II: The land-owning groups (clans) and their traditional territories. Unpublished Report for the Northern Land Council, Darwin.

Chaloupka, G. 1978. Rock art deterioration and conservation in the 'Top End' of the Northern Territory. In C. Pearson (ed.), *Conservation of rock art*: *Proceedings of the International Workshop on the Conservation of Rock Art, Perth, September 1977*, pp. 75–88. The Institute for the Conservation of Cultural Material, Perth.

Chaloupka, G. 1982. *Burrunguy: Nourlangie Rock*. Northart, Darwin.

Chaloupka, G. 1983. Kakadu rock art: Its cultural, historic and prehistoric significance. In D. Gillespie (ed.), *The rock art sites of Kakadu National Park: Some preliminary research findings for their conservation and management*, pp. 1–33. Special Publication 10. Australian National Parks and Wildlife Service, Canberra.

Christian, C.S. and J.M. Aldrick 1973. *Alligator Rivers study: A review report of the Alligator Rivers Region Environmental Fact-Finding Study*. Department of the Northern Territory, Darwin.

Clarke, J. 1976. Two Aboriginal rock pigments from Western Australia, their properties, use and durability. *Studies in Conservation* 21:134–142. doi.org/10.1179/sic.1976.023.

Clarke, J. 1978a. Deterioration analysis of rock art sites. In C. Pearson (ed.), *Conservation of rock art: Proceedings of the International Workshop on the Conservation of Rock Art, Perth, September 1977*, pp. 54–63. The Institute for the Conservation of Cultural Material, Perth.

Clarke, J. 1978b. Conservation and restoration of painting and engraving sites in Western Australia. In C. Pearson (ed.), *Conservation of rock art: Proceedings of the International Workshop on the Conservation of Rock Art, Perth, September 1977*, pp. 89–94. The Institute for the Conservation of Cultural Material, Perth.

Clarkson, C., Z. Jacobs, B. Marwick, R. Fullagar, L. Wallis, M. Smith, R.G. Roberts, E. Hayes, K. Lowe, X. Carah, S.A. Florin, J. McNeil, D. Cox, L.J. Arnold, Q. Hua, J. Huntley, H.E.A. Brand1, T. Manne, A. Fairbairn, J. Shulmeister, L. Lyle, M. Salinas, M. Page, K. Connell, G. Park, K. Norman, T. Murphy and C. Pardoe 2017. Human occupation of northern Australia by 65,000 years ago. *Nature* 547:306–310. doi.org/10.1038/nature22968.

Clegg, J. 1978. Simple field techniques for recording engravings by casting and stereophotography. In C. Pearson (ed.), *Conservation of rock art: Proceedings of the International Workshop on the Conservation of Rock Art, Perth, September 1977*, pp. 22–26. The Institute for the Conservation of Cultural Material, Perth.

Cook, I. 2018. Pioneering collections conservation in the Asia-Pacific 1978–1998 A job well done, *AICCM Bulletin* 39(1):35–41. doi.org/10.1080/10344233.2018.1544877.

CORLAB 1986. *Conservation of post-estuarine period rock art in Kakadu National Park: Report on Phase 1 study: Pigment identification.* Australian Nature Conservation Agency, Wilson.

CORLAB 1987. *Conservation of post-estuarine period rock art in Kakadu National Park: Final report on Phase 2 study: Conservation treatment trials.* Australian Nature Conservation Agency, Wilson.

CORLAB 1988. *Conservation of post-estuarine period rock art in Kakadu National Park: Final report on Phase 3 study: Conservation treatment trials.* Australian Nature Conservation Agency, Wilson.

CORLAB 1989. *Conservation of post-estuarine rock art in Kakadu National Park: Nourlangie Gallery rock art restoration project.* The International Centre for the Preservation and Restoration of Cultural Property and CORLAB Pty Ltd, Canberra.

Director of National Parks 1989. *Park note: Nourlangie Restoration Project, Kakadu National Park.* Australian National Parks and Wildlife Service, Canberra.

Director of National Parks 2014. Looking after Bim: The Kakadu National Park rock art monitoring and maintenance draft manual. Unpublished manual prepared by M. Marshall for Kakadu National Park, Jabiru.

Director of National Parks 2020. *Bim (Rock Art) Strategy, Kakadu National Park 2020–2025.* Parks Australia, Jabiru.

Dix, W. 1978. The role of the Australian Institute of Aboriginal Studies. In C. Pearson (ed.), *Conservation of rock art: Proceedings of the International Workshop on the Conservation of Rock Art, Perth, September 1977*, pp. 3–5. The Institute for the Conservation of Cultural Material, Perth.

Dolanski, J. 1978. Silcrete skins – Their significance in rock art weathering. In C. Pearson (ed.), *Conservation of rock art: Proceedings of the International Workshop on the Conservation of Rock Art, Perth, September 1977*, pp. 32–35. The Institute for the Conservation of Cultural Material, Perth.

Edwards, R. 1974a. *The art of the Alligator Rivers Region: Alligator Rivers Region Environmental Fact-Finding Study.* Australian Institute of Aboriginal Studies, Canberra.

Edwards, R. 1974b. *Aboriginal rock paintings: Considerations for their future.* Australian Museum, Sydney.

Edwards, R. 1975. *The preservation of Australia's Aboriginal heritage: Report of National Seminar on Aboriginal Antiquities in Australia, May 1972*. Australian Aboriginal Studies, Canberra.

Edwards, R. 1979. *Australian Aboriginal art: The art of the Alligator Rivers region, Northern Territory*. Australian Institute of Aboriginal Studies 15 (new series). Australian Institute of Aboriginal Studies, Canberra.

Florian, M.L.E. 1978. A review: The lichen role in rock art – Dating, deterioration and control. In C. Pearson (ed.), *Conservation of rock art: Proceedings of the International Workshop on the Conservation of Rock Art, Perth, September 1977*, pp. 95–98. The Institute for the Conservation of Cultural Material, Perth.

Gillespie, D. 1979. The rock art and archaeological sites of Ubirr, Kakadu National Park N.T: The beginning of a management strategy. Unpublished report to Australian National Parks and Wildlife Service, Canberra.

Gillespie, D. (ed.) 1983a. *The rock art sites of Kakadu National Park – Some preliminary research findings for their conservation and management*. Special Publication 10. Australian National Parks and Wildlife Service, Canberra.

Gillespie, D. 1983b. The beginnings of a conservation strategy. In D. Gillespie (ed.), *The rock art sites of Kakadu National Park – Some preliminary research findings for their conservation and management*, pp. 34–36. Special Publication 10. Australian National Parks and Wildlife Service, Canberra.

Gillespie, D. 1983c. The practice of rock art conservation and site management in Kakadu National Park. In D. Gillespie (ed.), *The rock art sites of Kakadu National Park – Some preliminary research findings for their conservation and management*, pp. 191–213. Special Publication 10. Australian National Parks and Wildlife Service, Canberra.

Haskovec, I. and H. Sullivan 1989. Reflections and rejections of an Aboriginal artist. In H. Morphy (ed.), *Animals into art*, pp. 57–74. Unwin Hyman, London.

Hughes, P.J. 1978. Weathering in sandstone shelters in the Sydney Basin and the survival of rock art. In C. Pearson (ed.), *Conservation of rock art: Proceedings of the International Workshop on the Conservation of Rock Art, Perth, September 1977*, pp. 36–41. The Institute for the Conservation of Cultural Material, Perth.

Hughes, P.J. 1979. *The deterioration, conservation and management of rock art sites in the Kakadu National Park, NT*. The Australian National University, Canberra.

Hughes, P.J. and A.L. Watchman 1983. The deterioration, conservation and management of rock art sites in Kakadu National Park. In D. Gillespie (ed.), *The rock art sites of Kakadu National Park – Some preliminary research findings for their conservation and management*, pp. 37–86. Special Publication 10. Australian National Parks and Wildlife Service, Canberra.

Jones, R. (ed.) 1985. *Archaeological research in Kakadu National Park*. Special Publication 13. Australian National Parks and Wildlife Service, Canberra.

Kamminga, J. and H. Allen 1973. *Report of the archaeological survey: Alligator Rivers Environmental Fact-Finding Study*. Department of the Northern Territory, Darwin.

Lambert, D. 1997. Rock art conservation. Kakadu National Park: Final report on first field visit April/May 1997. Unpublished report from NSW National Parks and Wildlife Service to Australian Parks and Wildlife Service, Sydney.

MacLeod, I. 2000. Rock art conservation and management: The past, present and future options. *Studies in Conservation* 45(Supp. 3):32–45. doi.org/10.1179/sic.2000.45.s3.005.

Madycki, Z. 2006. Termite treatment at rock art sites. Unpublished report to Kakadu National Park, Jabiru.

Marshall, M. 2014. Kakadu National Park's rock art monitoring and maintenance program: Pilot evaluation report. Unpublished report for Kakadu National Park.

Marshall, M. 2016. Kakadu National Park's rock art monitoring and maintenance program: Year 3 evaluation report. Unpublished report for Department of Environment and Energy.

Marshall, M. 2020. Rock art conservation and management: 21st century perspectives in Northern Australia. Unpublished PhD thesis, School of Archaeology and Anthropology, The Australian National University, Canberra. doi.org/10.25911/5f969812a2f22.

Marshall, M., K. May, R. Dann and L. Nulgit 2020. Indigenous stewardship of decolonised rock art conservation processes in Australia. *Studies in Conservation* doi.org/10.1080/00393630.2020.1778264.

May, S.K., P.S.C. Taçon and M. Johnson 2009. An introduction to rock art conservation and management: Report on the June 15–17 training course for Kakadu National Park by the Institute for Professional Practice in Heritage and the Arts. Unpublished report to the Director of National Parks. The Australian National University, Canberra.

May, S.K., J.G. Maralngurra, I.G. Johnston, J. Goldhahn, J. Lee, G. O'Loughlin, K. May, C.N. Nabobbob, M. Garde and P.S.C. Taçon 2019. 'This is my father's painting': A first-hand account of the creation of the most iconic rock art in Kakadu National Park. *Rock Art Research* 36(2):199–213.

May, S.K., J. Huntley, M. Marshall, E. Miller, J.A. Hayward, A. Jalandoni, J. Goldhahn, I.G. Johnston, J. Lee, G. O'Loughlin, K. May, I. Domingo Sanz and P.S.C. Taçon 2020. New insights into the rock art of Anbangbang Gallery, Kakadu National Park. *Journal of Field Archaeology* 45(2):120–134. doi.org/10.1080/00934690.2019.1698883.

McAlpine, J.R. 1973. *Alligator Rivers Region Environmental Fact-Finding Study: Climate and water balance.* Department of the Northern Territory, Darwin.

Midgley, S.H. 1973. *Alligator Rivers region Environmental Fact Finding Study: An inventory of freshwater fish, molluscs and crustaceans with associated habitat information.* Department of the Northern Territory, Darwin.

Misra, V.N. 1978. Prehistoric cave art at Bhimbetka, Central India. In C. Pearson (ed.), *Conservation of rock art: Proceedings of the International Workshop on the Conservation of Rock Art, Perth, September 1977,* pp. 69–70. The Institute for the Conservation of Cultural Material, Perth.

Mowaljarlai, D. and J. Malnic 2001. *Yorro Yorro: Everything standing up alive. Rock art and stories from the Australian Kimberley.* Magabala Books, Broome.

Mowaljarlai, D. and A. Watchman 1989. An Aboriginal view of rock art management. *Rock Art Research* 6(2):151–153.

Naumann, I. 1983. The biology of mud nesting Hymenoptera (and their associates) and Isoptera in rock shelters in the Kakadu region. In D. Gillespie (ed.), *The rock art sites of Kakadu National Park: Some preliminary research findings for the conservation and management,* pp. 127–190. Special Publication 10. Australian National Parks and Wildlife Service, Canberra.

Needham, R.S., P.G. Wilkes, P.G. Smart and A.L. Watchman 1973. *Alligator Rivers Region Environmental Fact-Finding Study: Geological and geophysical reports.* Department of Minerals and Energy; Bureau of Mineral Resources, Geology and Geophysics, Darwin.

Pearson, C. (ed.) 1978. *Conservation of rock art: Proceedings of the International Workshop on the Conservation of Rock Art, Perth, September 1977.* Institute for the Conservation of Cultural Material, Perth.

Pearson, C. and G.L. Pretty (eds) 1976. *Proceedings of the National Seminar on the Conservation of Cultural Material, Perth 1973.* The Institute for the Conservation of Cultural Material, Perth.

Pearson, C., J. Lyall, R. Sloggett and I. Cook 2011. Preserving the past: How to ensure the development of the conservation profession in Australia is preserved for the future. Paper presented at the AICCM National Conference 2011. Available at: aiccm.org.au/wp-content/uploads/2019/11/PEARSON_NatConf2011.pdf (accessed 18 April 2022).

Rivett, L.J. 1978. Photogrammetry – Its potential application to problems in Australian Archaeology. In C. Pearson (ed.), *Conservation of rock art: Proceedings of the International Workshop on the Conservation of Rock Art, Perth, September 1977*, pp. 15–21. The Institute for the Conservation of Cultural Material, Perth.

Rivett, L.J. 1983. The application of photogrammetry to the recording of rock art and archaeological sites in Kakadu National Park. In D. Gillespie (ed.), *The rock art sites of Kakadu National Park – Some preliminary research findings for their conservation and management.* Special Publication 10. Australian National Parks and Wildlife Service, Canberra.

Rosenfeld, A. 1978. Recording rock art: A conflict of purpose? In C. Pearson (ed.), *Conservation of rock art: Proceedings of the International Workshop on the Conservation of Rock Art, Perth, September 1977*, pp. 9–14. The Institute for the Conservation of Cultural Material, Perth.

Rosenfeld, A. 1985. *Rock art conservation in Australia.* Australian Government Publishing Service, Canberra.

Scott, M. 2018. Professor Colin Pearson: 'One of the most versatile and capable conservators of his generation'. *AICCM Bulletin* 39(1):4–9. doi.org/10.1080/10344233.2018.1489456.

Smith, D.I. 1978. The micro erosion meter: Its application to the weathering of rock surfaces. In C. Pearson (ed.), *Conservation of rock art: Proceedings of the International Workshop on the Conservation of Rock Art, Perth, September 1977*, pp. 44–53. The Institute for the Conservation of Cultural Material, Perth.

Smits, L.G.A. 1975. Preservation and protection of rock art in Lesotho. In International Institute for Conservation of Historic and Artistic Works (eds), *Conservation in archaeology and the applied arts,* pp. 75–77. Preprints of the contributions to the Stockholm Congress, 2–6 June 1975, Stockholm. doi.org/10.1179/sic.1975.s1.013.

Smits, L.G.A. 1978. Rock art: Protection and development. In C. Pearson (ed.), *Conservation of rock art: Proceedings of the International Workshop on the Conservation of Rock Art, Perth, September 1977*, pp. 99–102. The Institute for the Conservation of Cultural Material, Perth.

Sullivan, S. 1978. Conservation of Aboriginal rock art in New South Wales. In C. Pearson (ed.), *Conservation of rock art: Proceedings of the International Workshop on the Conservation of Rock Art, Perth, September 1977*, pp. 71–74. The Institute for the Conservation of Cultural Material, Perth.

Taylor, J.M., R.M. Myers and I.N.M. Wainwright 1975. An investigation of the natural deterioration of rock paintings in Canada. In International Institute for Conservation of Historic and Artistic Works (eds), *Conservation in archaeology and the applied arts,* pp. 87–91. Preprints of the contributions to the Stockholm Congress, 2–6 June 1975, Stockholm. doi.org/10.1179/sic.1975.s1.015.

Thorn, A. 1993a. The control of salts damaging to rock art. Unpublished report for The Australian Institute of Aboriginal and Torres Strait Islander Studies, Hawthorn.

Thorn, A. 1993b. Condition survey of four rock art sites in Kakadu National Park. Unpublished report to the Director of National Parks, Hawthorn.

Trezise, P. 1971. *Rock art of south-east Cape York Peninsula.* Australian Institute of Aboriginal Studies, Canberra.

Wainwright, I.N.M. and J.M. Taylor 1978. On the occurrence of a parallel pigment layer phenomenon in the cross-sectional structures of samples from two rock art painting sites in Canada. In C. Pearson (ed.), *Conservation of Rock Art: Proceedings of the International Workshop on the Conservation of Rock Art, Perth, September 1977*, pp. 29–31. The Institute for the Conservation of Cultural Material, Perth.

Watchman, A. 1985a. *Geological investigations into the formation of salts at Aboriginal rock art sites in Kakadu National Park, Northern Territory.* ANUTECH Pty Ltd, Canberra.

Watchman, A. 1985b. Mineralogical analysis of silica skins covering rock art. In R. Jones (ed.), *Archaeological research in Kakadu National* Park, pp. 281–290. Special Publication 13. Australian National Parks and Wildlife Service, Canberra.

Watchman, A. 1987. Preliminary determinations of the age and composition on mineral salts on rock art surfaces in the Kakadu National Park. In W.R. Ambrose and J.M.J. Mummery (eds) *Archaeometry: Further Australasian studies,* pp. 36–42. Department of Prehistory, Research School of Pacific Studies, The Australian National University, Canberra.

Watchman, A. 1989. *Silica skins: Their composition, formation and role in conserving Aboriginal rock art.* Australian Institute of Aboriginal Studies, Canberra.

Watchman, A. 1990. *The weathering of Australian rock paintings.* 50 Ans Apres Decouverte De Lascaux: Journees Internationales D'etude sur la Conservation de L'art Rupestre, 20–23 August 1990, Dordogne – Perigord (France).

Welch, D.M. 2015. *Aboriginal paintings at Ubirr and Nourlangie: Kakadu National Park, Northern Australia.* David M. Welch Publications, Coolalinga.

Wright, B.J. 1978. The Aboriginal sites department, Western Australian Museum. In C. Pearson (ed.), *Conservation of rock art: Proceedings of the International Workshop on the Conservation of Rock Art, Perth, September 1977*, p. 6. The Institute for the Conservation of Cultural Material, Perth.

13

Aboriginal rock art of the Laura valleys: One landscape, many Stories

Noelene Cole

Introduction

The Laura and Little Laura rivers in south-eastern Cape York Peninsula, Queensland (Figure 13.1), have similar environments, shared timelines of Aboriginal history and rock art practice, and parallel trajectories of archaeological research. Like other rivers of inland Cape York Peninsula (henceforth CYP), these were focal areas for Aboriginal settlement and corridors of customary travel, facilitating the exchange of ideas, information and materials across a regional network (Chase and Sutton 1987; Cole 2016; Land Tribunal 1996). However, from the onset of the Palmer River goldrush (1873) these valleys were appropriated for colonial transport routes, settlements and cattle runs. They also were the scene of a brutal war that transformed, but did not destroy, Aboriginal society and land use.

Today these precincts lie in the heartland of the National Heritage Listed area Quinkan Country, inscribed for the richness, size, diversity and density of its rock art and its qualities as a 'dynamic cultural landscape' where the 'ongoing collaboration between traditional owners and researchers continues to provide insights into patterns of human occupation in Australia' (Australian Government Department of Agriculture, Water and the Environment 2021). The inscription notes the associations of Quinkan Country with the lives and works of Tommy George (1929–2016), George Musgrave (1921–2006), Percy Trezise (1923–2005) and Dick Roughsey (1920–1985).

This discussion is prompted by the weight of research and Aboriginal knowledge that has brought the values of the Laura valleys to light, the long trajectory of rock art research in the Laura Basin and my own research journey. I am also mindful of ongoing threats to the cultural landscape by road upgrades, agriculture, increased tourism, mining proposals and mineral exploration permits (Cole and Buhrich 2012). Previous rock art research in the valleys has tended to focus on major sites such as Giant Horse, Mushroom Rock, Split Rock, Sandy Creek and Yam Camp (Morwood and Hobbs 1995a; Trezise 1971; Watchman and Cole 1993; Wright 1971). This account takes a landscape approach to compare rock art across two significant precincts that, although separated to the south-west by a dissected plateau incised by the Mosman River, are also connected by a lowland travel route that skirts the plateaux via Sandy Creek. Given the latter connection, it is cogent to explore how the recognised spatial continuity of Quinkan rock art style (Cole 2016) applies (or does not apply) across these landscapes, and how figurative (primarily late Holocene) rock art might reflect documented models of Aboriginal cultural organisation.

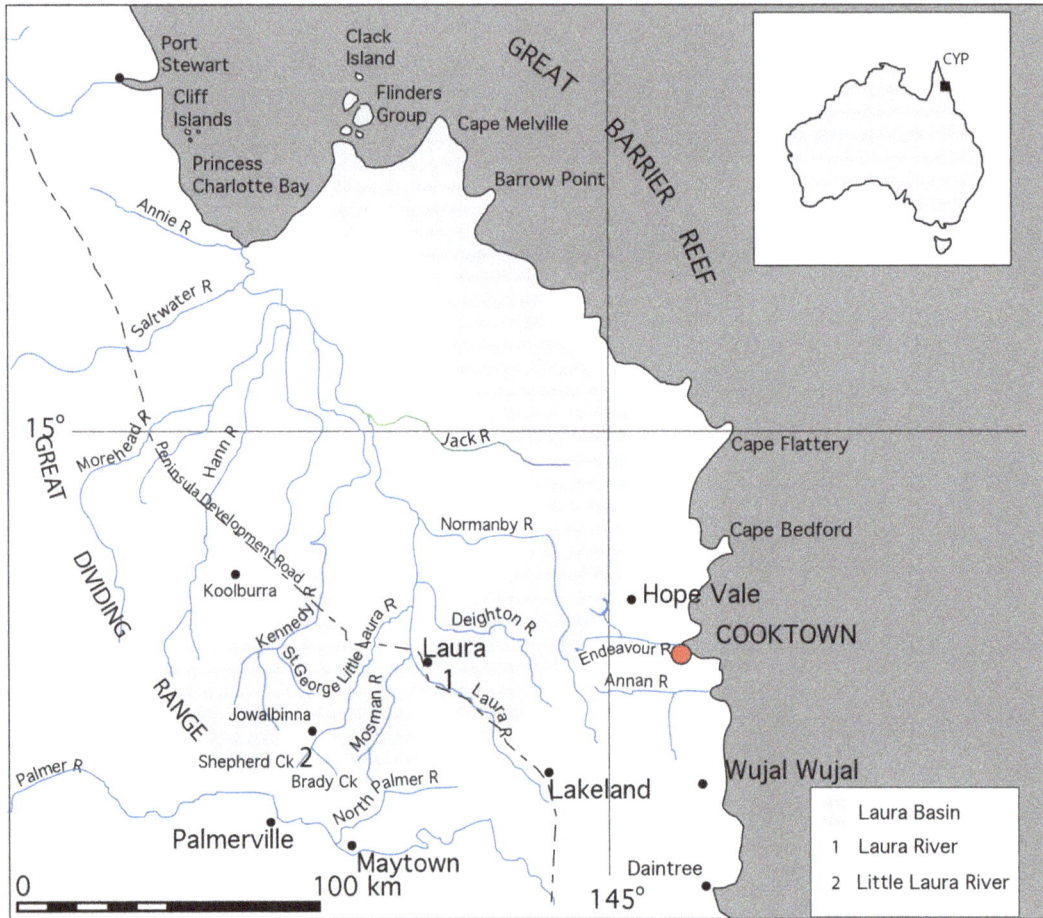

Figure 13.1: The Laura Sandstone Basin showing Laura River and Little Laura River precincts (1 and 2).

Source: Map by N. Cole.

To begin, I summarise key research and environmental and historical contexts. I then analyse and discuss landscape patterning and motif variability with reference to evidence of Aboriginal land use and social and territorial organisation. Although the Laura valleys are relatively well studied, there is always potential to refine the research. As noted by Horton (2004:180):

> The beauty of landscape methodology is that it allows for a continual accretion of meaning, as the stratigraphy of physical and symbolic landscapes grows with each new layer of documentation, analysis evaluation, and design.

Key research

In 1960, Cairns airline pilot Percy Trezise was among the first to make the long, dusty road trip to Laura to investigate the reported 'discovery' by a roadworker of a rock art site (now known as Split Rock). Over the next few decades, Trezise, his friend, Lardil artist Dick Roughsey from Mornington Island, and other colleagues located and recorded rock art across the southern Laura Basin (see Roughsey 1971; Trezise 1969, 1971, 1973, 1993). Early on, with Dick Roughsey acting as intermediary, Trezise gained the trust of senior Aboriginal men whose cultural knowledge became central to his research (see Cole 2011 for an outline and assessment of Trezise's ethnographic and ethnohistoric research). Importantly, in documenting their oral histories, Trezise broke the silence on CYP's violent colonial war. Willy Long, an Olkola Elder, told of his parents surviving a savage attack by the Musgrave Native Mounted Police (Trezise 1969:102). Harry Mole, a retired police tracker who spoke Ogo Aragu, Sugarbag Bee #2 language (Rigsby 2002, 2003) recalled being captured as a child by the police during their violent attacks on his people, the 'Gugu Warra' – that is, Koko Warra (Trezise 1969:51). Caesar Lee Cheu, who spoke his father's language, Ogo Ikarraŋgal or Freshwater Prawn language (Rigsby 2003; and see Land Tribunal 1996:114), told how he evaded the police with his family for years before they 'came in' to work on cattle stations (Trezise 1993:153).

Archaeologists were drawn to Laura, beginning with Richard Wright (1971) who excavated Laura 1, now known as Mushroom Rock (Figure 13.2). Percy Trezise persuaded Andrée Rosenfeld to excavate a rock-shelter (which came to be known in the literature as 'Early Man Rockshelter') on the Laura plateau, a seminal project that produced securely dated evidence of Late Pleistocene occupation and art practice (Rosenfeld et al. 1981). Later, Mike Morwood (1995b:1), motivated by the 'large number of rock art sites' and the 'established platform' of previous work embarked on collaborative research (the Quinkan Prehistory Project) that was facilitated by the Laura Aboriginal community and rangers led by senior men, Tommy George and George Musgrave (Figure 13.2). The project began with an excavation at Rainbow Serpent rock-shelter, where Trezise had dug in 1969 (see Morwood and Trezise 1989). At this point Rainbow Serpent rock-shelter became known as Sandy Creek 1.

Excavations at Mushroom Rock, Sandy Creek 1 and 2, Red Bluff, Yam Camp and Giant Horse revealed a long sequence of Aboriginal occupation in the Laura and Little Laura valleys (Morwood and Hobbs 1995a). Corresponding sequences of utilised ochres revealed that the first occupants were artists, and that art practice continued from c. 31,500 BP at Sandy Creek 1 into post-invasion times.

Figure 13.2: Dr George Musgrave (left) and Dr Tommy George (right) at Mushroom Rock c. 1995.

Source: Photograph by N. Cole.

The Quinkan Prehistory Project provided important chronological context for rock art, particularly in identifying mid to late Holocene changes in land use, social restructuring associated with development of 'territorial estates and local residence groups' and a 'trend towards increased linguistic and artistic diversity' (Morwood and Hobbs 1995b:180). Previously, Flood and Horsfall (1986) and Flood (1987) identified similar mid to late Holocene trends at the Koolburra plateau, west of the study area (see Figure 13.1), and David and Watchman (1991) modelled late Holocene regionalisation of rock art and social formations across an area extending from Princess Charlotte Bay to around Chillagoe, south of the Palmer River. Alan Watchman's 'direct dating' research, including in the Laura and Little Laura valleys, complemented regional research by refining the chronology of Holocene rock art (e.g. Cole et al. 1995; Cole and Watchman 2005).

Having participated in some of these projects, I was fortunate to continue fieldwork in the area with Traditional Owners. Although rock art is the key cultural feature in the landscape, Laura people also wish to record their knowledge and connections to their Old People. For example at Giant Horse, Tommy George identified a 'tracker' (Native Mounted Police) painting and spoke of how Aboriginal people fled to remote rock-shelters to escape the police; at Sandy Creek, George Musgrave demonstrated the old way to make a paintbrush from the woody stem of a cotton tree; near the Little Laura crossing of the Maytown track, the late Laura Banjo George showed me her birthplace and spoke of seeing Stories (engravings) on the rocks when walking along the river with her family as a child. Such testimonies define a 'cultural landscape perspective', one that 'recognises the continuity between the past and with people living and working on the land today' (Mitchell and Buggey 2001:45, cited by Brown 2007).

Land/people relationships

In terms of the cultural record, CYP is the most richly documented large-scale 'set of classical and historical Aboriginal landscapes' in Australia (Sutton 2011:2). This is mainly due to long-term collaborations of Aboriginal people with successive anthropologists and linguists (Verstraete and Hafner 2016). Bruce Rigsby (e.g. 1980, 1999; Sutton and Rigsby 1979; and see Verstraete and Hafner 2016) refined this research to develop a model of social and territorial organisation for the coast and hinterland of Princess Charlotte Bay based on 'native categories'. The model is key to this discussion, particularly in its distinction between land-owning descent groups (patriclans) and the land-using groups. Land owners, the patriclans, had their own distinctive languages that were named from a certain Country, principal Story or totem. Each clan estate comprised the sum of Countries or sites over which the clan had primary rights to live on, use and speak for. Importantly, Countries may be contiguous or non-contiguous tracts of land or specific sites and may also be jointly owned.

A map of clan Countries does not reflect the way people lived 'on the ground' in smaller land-using groups who, having primary rights over their own clan Countries and secondary rights through relatives to use Countries of other clans (Sutton and Rigsby 1982), had options of land use. Groups assembled periodically for ritual and secular activities and interacted as social networks or speech communities (Sutton and Rigsby 1979). Such interactions, although culturally inherited and prescribed, were strongly influenced by seasonal factors (Morwood 1995a; Thomson 1939).

As clan Countries or sites can be discontinuous, mapping them may show a mosaic distribution (Sutton and Rigsby 1982). Mapping is also complicated by constantly changing social configurations of land users and the fact that people were multilingual (Rigsby 1980). The model rejects Tindale's (1974) tribal map as an accurate representation of demography (see also Sutton 1995). Sutton and Rigsby (1979:714) do, however, identify 'culture areas' as 'the widest meaningful social networks operating in CYP'. Such networks contribute to a degree of coherence of rock art in the southern Laura Basin (Cole 2016).

Clans also owned ceremonial items such as totems, Story places, dances, songs, painted designs and narratives, all of which signified rights to land. Clan totems reflect the environment and economic interest and symbolise clan unity (Sutton 2011) and are usually complementary, indicating the social and economic interdependence between the clans. Clan ancestors are responsible for the origin of totems, as expressed in cultural narratives, names of Countries and languages, and rock art (Trezise 1971, 1993). A defining, fundamental dimension of Country is that the Ancestral Beings gave the clans their languages, dances, songs, designs and laws – and Country – during the formative era at the beginning of time, known in CYP as 'the Storytime' and elsewhere in Australia as 'the Dreaming'. As they are Stories in the landscape (Cole 2011), rock paintings and other types of rock art are deeply embedded in the cosmology, concepts and materiality of Country.

The Laura valleys

The Laura River bisects the south Laura Basin, and, with its main tributary the Little Laura River, flows north to join the Normanby River (Figure 13.1). Aboriginal land use in these stream precincts was much influenced by the rainfall regime of the tropical monsoonal climate and its impact on hydrology. River flow is at its highest between December and March, when >90 per cent of annual rainfall occurs, inundating the alluvial plains. In the dry season, the rivers are reduced to intermittent waterholes and stretches of sand and bedrock. Many creeks dry out entirely, although headwaters Brady and Shepherd creeks maintain their base flows fed by springs and perched swamps on the plateau scarps (Morgan et al. 1995), a feature that has led to their listing on the Directory of Important Wetlands of Australia (Queensland Government Department of Environment and Science 2021). The Laura and Little Laura rivers are flanked in parts by steep, eroding escarpments that contain the rock-shelters essential to the region's rock art tradition.

Aboriginal land use of the study area was based on economic and ideological systems that were 'attuned to the irregularities of the local environment' including seasonal climatic factors and availability of natural resources (Morwood 1995a:37). For example, during the wet season, the local groups moved to the elevated sand ridge country, to adopt more sedentary lifestyles, camping in rock-shelters where water can be collected from driplines, rock hollows and springs. As the land dried out, people moved back to the more biodiverse waterfront estates, congregating periodically for social and ceremonial purposes near permanent waterholes, as at the 'old bora ground' beside the Laura River that is now the site of the biennial Laura Dance and Cultural Festival (T. George, pers. comm. 2000). Although travel across the Laura and Little Laura valleys for such gatherings might involve long journeys, the distances would be well within the customary range of Aboriginal people in such settings (see Mulvaney 1976:78).

The post-invasion period

From 1873, the clan estates were invaded by hordes of miners heading to the Palmer River via the newly surveyed Palmerville and Douglas (Hell's Gate) tracks. To crush Aboriginal resistance, a Native Mounted Police camp was set up at the lower Laura River (Cole 2004). From 1877, coaches plied the Maytown track, transporting people and goods to the Palmer via the Little Laura valley. Before long, pastoralism overtook mining as the main colonial industry, entrenching the impacts on Aboriginal people and their riverside estates. In the war and its aftermath, some Aboriginal clans were obliterated and some of those who survived regrouped in the remote uplands. When independent lifestyles became unsustainable, they 'came in' to cattle stations, fringe camps near Laura and other colonial outposts as a way of staying on Country (Cole 2004). Aboriginal people continued rock art practice throughout the frontier period and evidently into the twentieth century (Trezise 1971).

Rock art sites

The rock art analysis summarised here is based on my regional records, including those for 121 sites of the Laura and Little Laura River valleys (see Table 13.1). As indicated, the study area is divided into localities based on topography (streams, escarpments and sand plains).

Table 13.1: Localities, including their acronyms used in Table 13.2, numbers of sites and figurative motifs recorded in each locality discussed in text.

Locality	# Sites	# Motifs
Laura River eastern escarpment (L1)	25	630
Laura River western escarpment (L2)	24	318
Laura River sand plain (L3)	4	130
Little Laura River escarpments (LL1)	16	226
Little Laura River (Brady and Shepherd creeks, LL2)	39	948
Little Laura sand plain (Sandy Creek, LL3)	13	226
Total	121	2478

Source: Author's data.

Site distribution, in its diverse geography, reflects the economic and ideological systems that incorporated flexible patterns of land use and access to seasonal natural resources (Morwood 1995a; Rigsby1980). Hence rock art sites are on uplands and high escarpments, alluvial terraces, sand plains, river banks and river beds, all of which were occupied by land-using groups at various times of the year. Almost invariably, sites have water at hand (sometimes seasonally), as well as suitable living and/or working spaces and smooth rock surfaces for art. Site densities are high in many places, reflecting the favourable environments of the valleys.

The typical rock art site is a rock-shelter fronting a steep slope and/or a spring-fed gully. Some sites, for example Giant Horse and the Quinkans on the eastern escarpment of the Laura River and the Sandy Creek sites on the Little Laura sand plain, occur in complexes with overhangs of different sizes, providing variable options of living spaces and seclusion. Solitary sites occur rarely, usually marking exceptional rock formations.

The Laura and Little Laura rivers each have alluvial plains and terraces ascending to escarpments of about 200 m in elevation. Sites on terraced sides of escarpments include Split Rock overlooking the Laura River and Death Adder overlooking Brady Creek. Stone artefact scatters and culturally modified trees are common features of terraces, reflecting everyday activities of people camped nearby (Pearson 1989).

The alluvial plains surrounding Mushroom Rock and Sandy Creek were formed by colluvial deposits eroding from adjacent escarpments and plateaux (Morwood et al. 1995a, 1995b). The long, winding rock formation emerging from the sand plain at Sandy Creek made a deep impression on Percy Trezise and Dick Roughsey in 1967: 'It looked like a giant snake emerging from a hole in the base of the hill. Near its middle large slabs had broken away from underneath it providing an excellent shelter – right in the guts of old Goorialla, the Rainbow serpent' (Trezise 1973:178).

Cultural features of the riverine localities include engravings and grinding marks on rocks and scatters of culturally modified Cooktown ironwood trees (*Erythrophleum chlorostachys*), reflecting dry season land use on the alluvial plains. Near Laura, the Peninsula Developmental Road crosses the river via a causeway that cuts through bedrock covered in figurative engravings (see Woolston and Trezise 1969). During fieldwork to rerecord the site, George Musgrave explained how, around 1960, roadbuilders dynamited the rocks, causing immense distress to Aboriginal people who heard the explosion tearing apart their Story Place. In a visit to monitor a more recent road upgrade, Tommy George brushed away sand and gravel to expose more engravings. In response to objections from Tommy George and his son the late Thomas George, the road authorities temporarily paused the planned upgrade. Downstream beside a permanent waterhole on Olive Vale station is another Story Place, a low rock-shelter with weathered paintings, engravings and multiple grinding marks nearby. The station advertises this place to tourists as a fishing attraction.

Living with rock art

During their seasonal round, Aboriginal people lived among (and refreshed) rock art that spans many generations and ways of marking the rocks. While living in the valleys they painted, stencilled and/or engraved rock surfaces, occasionally made hand prints or drew with ochre crayons on rock-shelter walls, and, in at least one site (at Brady Creek), infilled a panel of engravings with red paint (Cole and Musgrave 2006). The Laura River crossing and Amphitheatre sites show the overlap between the Quinkan painting and figurative engraving styles (Cole and Trezise 1992; Woolston and Trezise 1969). Open-air sites are usually engraving sites, possibly because any paintings created there would be unlikely to survive. Such sites are almost certainly under-recorded due to difficulties of distinguishing between shallow, weathered engravings and surrounding rock surfaces.

Importantly for this study, most rock paintings appear to date from the late Holocene (see Cole et al. 1995), and the presence of the dingo motif throughout the sequence may anchor the origins of this style of Quinkan art in the mid-to-late Holocene (Rosenfeld et al. 1981). Several directly dated figurative paintings (at Yam Camp and the Quinkans) are c. 600 to 700 years old, and paint recipes that include materials from in situ termite mounds indicate even more recent origins (Watchman and Cole 1993; Watchman et al. 1993). Paintings of horses, pig, policemen and a stencilled steel axe indicate the continuity of art after the region was colonised from 1873.

However, rock art of great antiquity is also part of the fabric of many sites, and although meanings of figures may have changed over time, their ancestral values remain. At Split Rock and the Quinkans near the Laura River, and Yam Camp and Death Adder near Brady Creek, colourful paintings sit alongside deeply incised mineral-encrusted engravings. Archaeologists often classify such curvilinear designs, pits etc. as 'nonfigurative', indicating that they do not appear to resemble the shape of anything identifiable. However, for George Musgrave, a Kuku Thaypan speaker and Laura Elder, these engravings are 'maps' (G. Musgrave, pers. comm. 2000). This accords with Trezise's (1971:53) record of engravings at Quinkans site B5:

> Apart from the emu tracks, the other intaglio designs present no recogniseable shapes. However they do call to mind the patterns drawn on the ground by the old men when relating the travels of the culture heroes, particularly the Rainbow Serpent.

Subjects in rock art

Trezise's (1971) major publication, *Rock art of south-east Cape York Peninsula*, provides a reference point for classifying Quinkan figurative rock art. The monograph contains reproductions ('plates') of scaled field drawings of rock art assemblages in 10 areas of the sandstone region, including the Laura and Little Laura valleys. Motifs illustrated in each plate are identified in annotated lists that accompany each plate. The lists include generic and specific labels, such as bird, crocodile, echidna or sawfish. However, without clear definitions, inconsistencies arise: for example, the 'catfish' (Trezise 1971) is also labelled 'eel' (Trezise 1993). Furthermore, as has been long pointed out by rock art specialists and social anthropologists, the deeper cosmological significance of each taxon and its shape is essentially esoteric. Here I distinguish between catfish and eel by the presence/absence of barbels (whisker-like sensory organs at the mouth), but more detailed study of this motif is underway.

At least some of Trezise's categories were directly informed by Aboriginal consultants. For example Caesar Lee Cheu, an Elder and artist of a 'Gugu Warra' (Koko Warra) clan, identified 'eels', 'rock wallabies', 'fish', 'brolgas or emus', 'butcher bird' and 'Anurra' spirits (Trezise 1969:138, 139). To identify paintings in the Quinkans complex near Laura, Trezise consulted widely:

> I got Willy [Willy Long, an initiated Olkola man] and Dick [Roughsey] to view and discuss the galleries, and Willy questioned … old Sandy and Barney, and had information from an old Gugu-Minni man at Hopevale Mission. (Trezise 1993:98)

Armed with this knowledge, Trezise (1993:98–101) went on to name and describe the subject matter. For example, the contents of the easternmost shelter include Ancestral Beings (anthropomorphs depicted with headdresses and legs raised to symbolise the dingo dance performed in initiation ceremonies), various types of fauna and artefacts and two species of yam.

Table 13.2 quantifies figurative motifs by locality; it excludes hand stencils and indeterminate motifs. The table indicates that subject matter across the valleys is basically homogenous and follows the usual range of figurative subject matter recorded in the wider region (Cole 2016; Trezise 1971). Figure 13.3 charts relative frequencies of these motif types and shows that, while many occur in similar proportions across each valley, the proportions of other motifs are more variable, as discussed below. Escarpment localities include sites on terraces and tend to have the most extensive motif range of depicted taxa in the art, possibly because they contain large rock-shelter complexes with massive overhangs and abundant space for camping and for art. Elders have said that such sites on the escarpments were mainly used in the wet season but visited and used all year (George et al. 1995:10; see also Trezise 1971:7).

Table 13.2: Figurative motifs in each locality and number of localities in which each type occurs.

Motif	L1	L2	L3	LL1	LL2	LL3	# Localities
Artefact*	4	5	0	1	4	0	4
Bark cylinder	2	1	0	0	0	0	2
Barramundi	2	0	0	0	0	0	1
Beehive	0	2	0	0	11	0	2
Bird	13	7	0	4	19	11	5
Boomerang*	10	13	1	1	11	1	6
Composite being	5	1	1	1	3	2	6
Crescent (grub)	2	0	3	0	3	6	4
Crocodile	7	3	2	4	10	7	6
Dillybag*	6	2	6	0	3	0	4
Dingo*	2	2	0	6	30	10	5
Echidna	9	3	1	0	9	5	5
Eel	36	14	6	15	36	14	6
Eel-tailed catfish	4	4	0	0	10	1	4
Egg clusters	3	0	0	0	1	0	2
Emu*	20	1	4	0	4	1	5
Fish	18	1	0	2	16	10	5
Flying fox	33	13	9	1	67	5	6
Fork-tailed catfish	4	0	3	0	9	1	4
Horse	3	0	0	0	1	0	2

Motif	L1	L2	L3	LL1	LL2	LL3	# Localities
Human (female)*	46	31	11	30	107	19	6
Human (male)*	94	41	4	39	144	22	6
Human*	138	90	14	74	283	55	6
Ibis	1	1	0	0	0	0	2
Jabiru	0	1	0	0	0	0	1
Lizard/Goanna	1	1	0	3	1	2	5
Long tom	3	1	0	0	7	6	4
Macropod	25	13	0	4	19	10	5
Plant	4	1	0	0	1	0	3
Possum	2	0	0	0	0	3	2
Quinkan spirit	9	8	3	5	16	6	6
Sawfish	3	4	1	0	0	0	3
Scrub turkey	13	1	1	0	1	0	4
Snake	13	3	2	2	10	4	6
Steel axe*	0	0	1	0	0	0	1
Stingray	3	0	0	0	0	0	1
Stone axe*	2	2	5	0	5	0	4
Track*	1	5	2	0	1	0	4
Track, bird *	3	3	8	21	1	1	6
Track, human*	2	9	16	1	4	1	6
Track, macropod*	9	12	19	0	18	0	4
Turtle	24	5	1	5	18	9	6
Unidentified animal	33	8	2	0	19	8	5
Woomera*	0	2	3	3	3	0	4
Yam	18	4	1	4	43	6	6
Total	**630**	**318**	**130**	**226**	**948**	**226**	**–**

Rare types are generally included in generic categories; * = motif may be painted and/or stencilled and/or engraved; L1 etc. are abbreviations for localities named in Table 13.1.

Source: Author's data.

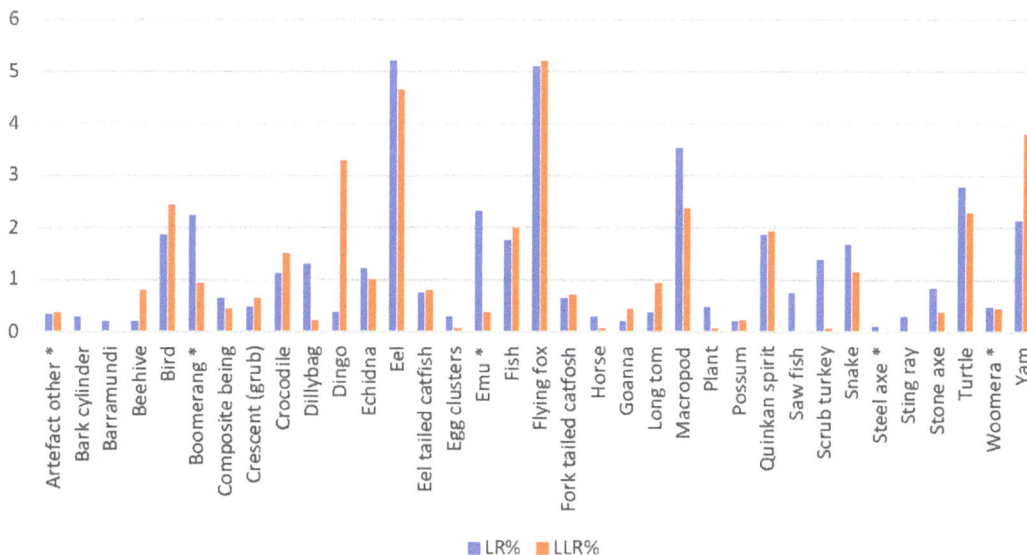

Figure 13.3: Chart indicating selectivity of figurative motifs in Laura valleys (LR=Laura River; LLR=Little Laura River); excludes human and track motifs and hand stencils.

Source: Author's data (see Table 13.2).

Supernatural figures

The large number of human motifs (c. 40–60 per cent of total motifs in most localities) cover a wide range of 'naturalistic' and 'supernatural' forms. Here I focus on the latter, as some reflect broad-scale cultural differentiation, such as Quinkans in the south Laura Basin, Echidna People at Koolburra and crescent-headed figures at Princess Charlotte Bay (Cole 2016).

Trezise's Aboriginal consultants, regardless of their clan and language affiliations, perceived Quinkans to be a pervasive and unsettling presence, lurking behind rocks and trees and hiding in crevices. Aboriginal people named Quinkans 'Anurra' (sometimes written as 'Ang-Gnarra') if short and fat (see Figure 13.4) and 'Timara' if exceptionally tall and thin (George et al. 1995:26). Anurra are painted across the study area and beyond, as are various attenuated figures possibly linked to Timara (see Huchet 1993). Evidently, Timara figures are not always confined to secluded sites, as an example is painted in the main overhang at Giant Horse rock-shelter. (George et al. 1995:35). Willy Long was in awe of Timara figures, claiming they were all-powerful (Trezise 1971). Tommy George, a Kuku Thaypan speaker and senior Ang-Gnarra Ranger, shed further light on Timara:

> He [Timara] showed the ancestors how to get food and gave them that sugar bag from the bush bee ... You can see where the ancestors took that sugar bag. That red bloodwood is just right for that Timara to hide behind. (Ang-Gnarra Aboriginal Corporation 1996:13).

Figure 13.4: Rock painting of Anurra Quinkan at Sandy Creek.

Source: Photograph by N. Cole.

As noted above, at 'the Quinkans' sites, Aboriginal men identified various Ancestral Beings by their ceremonial headdresses (see also Trezise 1971:14) including cockatoo feather headdresses of the type widely used in ceremonies by Aboriginal people across North Queensland (Roth 1910:8). In the rock art, a rayed form (Figure 13.5c) depicts a cockatoo feather headdress made from feathers of white or black cockatoos, depending on the wearer's moiety (Trezise 1993:98). A branch-like form (Figure 13.5a) represents the sugarbag tree, the home of native bees, a relationship that may explain why branch headdress figures are painted beside a Timara figure at the Quinkans complex (Ang-Gnarra Aboriginal Corporation 1996; Trezise 1971:Plate 8). However, with so many types of headdresses and head forms depicted in the rock art (e.g. see Cole 1992:Figures 4–7; Flood 1987:Figures 6 and 7; Huchet 1993:Figure 5; Trezise 1971:Figures 6 and 7), detailed study of these motif attributes is required to investigate their cultural relationships.

a)

b)

c)

d)

e)

f)

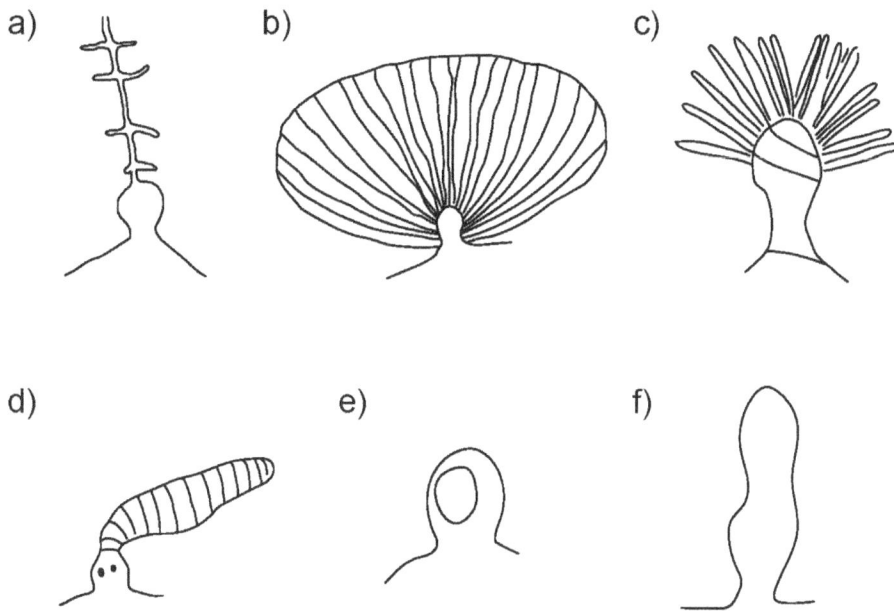

Figure 13.5: Examples of headdresses and head forms painted in the study area.
Source: Author's data.

Suffice to say, two culturally identified types of ancestral headdresses are continuous across the study area. The sugarbag headdress in rock art may link with clan identities, as linguists (Alpher 2016; Rigsby 2002, 2003) have identified Agu Aloja, Sugarbag Bee (A and B) as languages for around Laura. Although paintings of beehives (sugarbag) are less common in Laura River localities than around the Little Laura River (see Figure 13.3), they are generally abundant in Quinkan rock art (George et al. 1995:32). As sugarbag is associated with the Ancestral Being Timara (George et al. 1995:32), it is possible that spectacular, giant-sized sugarbag motifs recorded by Trezise and Roughsey on the plateau east of the Laura River (see Trezise 1993:118) have a specialised, possibly totemic, function. Sugarbag is, and was, highly prized by Aboriginal people across CYP (Cole et al. 2020; Morrison and Shepard 2013).

Fauna and totemic ancestors

Following general trends in the selectivity of subject matter across the Laura–Cooktown (Quinkan) region (Cole 1995), around one-third of figurative motifs in the Laura and Little Laura valleys are types of fauna, the most widely depicted (in 4–6 localities, see Table 13.2) being animals that were both economically important and named in Stories (see Roth 1903; Trezise 1969, 1973, 1993). These faunal motifs include those listed by George et al. (1995:21) as important 'totemic' animals in the rock art. For example, at the Quinkans sites, George et al. (1995:21) identified a kangaroo as a 'totemic ancestor' by a line painted across its body depicting a waist belt similar to those worn by Ancestral Beings painted nearby (see Trezise 1971:Plate 7, 1993:99).

The most frequently depicted faunal motif is the eel, a category that, like macropod and crocodile motifs (Rosenfeld 1982; Trezise 1977) and possibly scrub turkey/emu (Figure 13.6a), can have an ambiguous shape. Rosenfeld (1982:217) identified 'ambiguous content' as an integral, possibly unfathomable feature of the Laura art system, and concluded, by analogy with contemporary Aboriginal art practice, that 'extraneous cultural information' may be required to aid image recognition. As noted above, cultural meaning in Aboriginal art systems is cosmological in origin, hence esoteric. For example, in Yolngu art of eastern Arnhem Land, cultural meaning 'is not (if it ever is) internal to the painting', being dependent upon its context and the interpreter's identity and knowledge of 'the code' (Morphy 1991:151). Such features complicate this analysis.

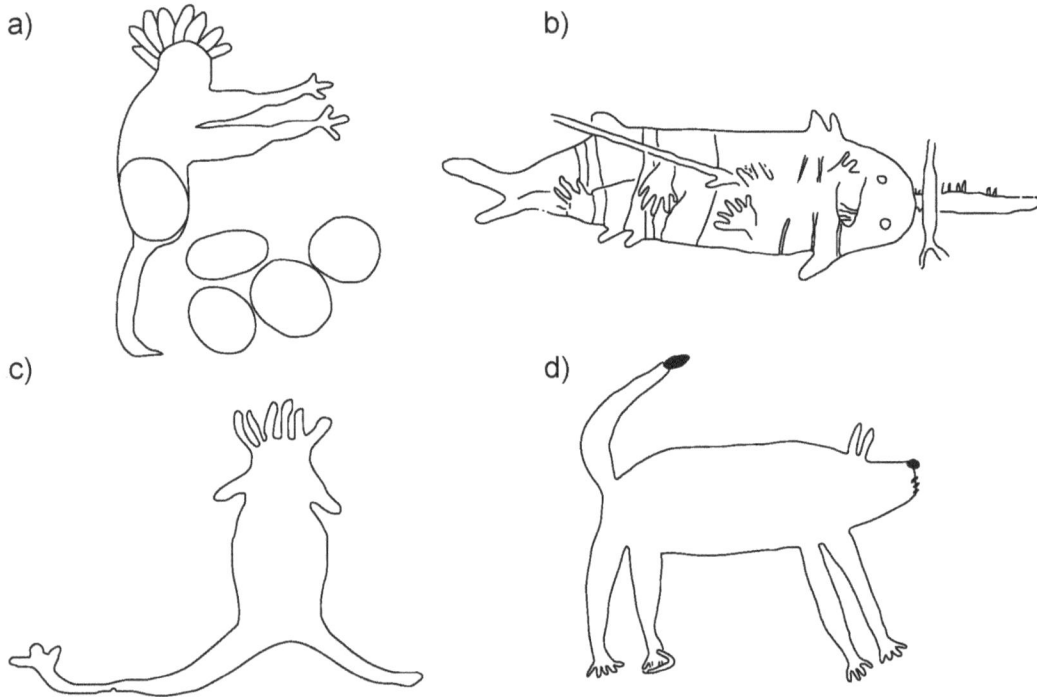

Figure 13.6: Scrub turkey (a), composite beings (b and c) and dingo (d) motifs.
Source: Author's data.

Ambiguous figures include composite beings (Table 13.2; for elsewhere, see e.g. Morphy 1989:5) that reference more than one faunal species, such as fork-tailed catfish and sawfish (Figure 13.6b), or a faunal species, such as echidna/yam/catfish, and a human being (e.g. Figure 13.6c). Each valley has examples of such composites, including 'Echidna People' like those recorded by Flood (1987, 1989) in large numbers around Koolburra. However, the examples recorded near the Laura River and Brady Creek appear to be far more weathered and possibly older than Echidna People at Koolburra. Flood (1987:118) interpreted such figures as 'ancestral mythic Echidna Beings', possibly associated with a localised totemic 'echidna cult'. However, the extended range noted here suggests complex synchronic and/or diachronic relationships for these figures. Without absolute dates for paintings of Echidna People, it is difficult to investigate this graduated distribution.

Motifs labelled as 'fish' or species of fish are distributed across the localities. However, high frequencies around Brady and Shepherd creeks (e.g. Figure 13.7) do not correspond with the typically low natural populations of fish in upstream habitats (Midgley 1990; and see Taçon 1993 for similar environmental patterns in western Arnhem Land). If the natural distribution of bioresources was the main or single factor motivating rock art, which it clearly is not (see also David 2004), numbers of fish motifs around the Laura River would exceed those around the Little Laura and its headwaters.

Figure 13.7: Rock-shelter at Brady Creek with rock paintings of fish.
Source: Photograph by N. Cole.

The dingo was an important Story figure in CYP and the Gulf of Carpentaria (Trezise 1993). It was also Harry Mole's 'bora story', telling of the ancestral journey, death and rebirth of the 'giant devil-dog', the dingo (Trezise 1993:28–29). In Harry Mole's version, the dingo travelled with his boss, the grasshopper woman, and was speared by the butcher bird boys who cut off the tip of the dog's tail that held his spirit. The remains of the ancestor transformed into the dingo we know today. There appear to be many references to this Story in rock art, for example in recurring compositions of a woman and dingo (in Little Laura, Laura and Deighton rivers localities), a depiction of the dingo dance initiation ceremony near the Laura River (Trezise 1993) and, around the Little Laura, dingo motifs with a small white ring painted at the tip of their tails (Figure 13.6d). The Little Laura assemblage of dingo paintings is particularly large (see Table 13.2 and Figure 13.3), and unusual in that it includes a finely engraved dingo (Cole and Trezise 1992). The language name for a local landmark, Red Bluff, is 'Jerrabina', meaning 'dingo ear' (Laura George, pers. comm. 1999).[1]

In a faunal survey around the Laura and Little Laura rivers, Morgan et al. (1995:Table 1.4) found the dingo (*Canis familiaris*) to be 'common' in all habitats (sandstone plateau, escarpment, plains and headwaters). Given these data and disparities in distribution of fish motifs relative to natural populations noted above, it is unlikely that the marked abundance of dingo motifs in the former area is primarily associated with bioresource patterns.

Flood (1987), citing Sharp's (1939) account of totemic ceremonies, proposed that totemic figures in rock art may be linked with local ceremonies to maintain the supply of totems. Although ethnographic information is lacking to support this directly, Trezise (1971) referred to paintings in a small, secluded Laura River site as evidence of a 'scrub turkey totemic centre'. Typically, totemic centres of the Wik Munkan people of western CYP were located where the species was abundant, 'on the hunting grounds of the clan to which they [the totems] belong' (McConnel

---

1   Percy Trezise named his leasehold property as 'Jowalbinna'.

1930:187). For example, the freshwater stingray (*min umpura*) totemic centre is near deep waterholes of a river where big fish are abundant (McConnel 1930: 193). However, it seems unlikely that distinctive paintings of stingray, freshwater prawn and sawfish in large, generalised art assemblages at Giant Horse, the Quinkans and Split Rock (Trezise 1971) were associated with secret rituals. On the other hand, the finely drawn freshwater prawn may reflect totemic values, as 'Freshwater Prawn language' was a Koko Warra language variety spoken around Laura (Rigsby 2003), and 'freshwater shrimp' was the totem of a Koko Warra speaker who informed Trezise (1993:51).

As Aboriginal consultants advised that names of particular artefacts could be used as personal totems and clan and language names (e.g. the Tomahawk language of a Hann River clan), Trezise (1971:14) proposed that some depictions of artefacts including boomerangs (see also Roughsey 1971:61) might have totemic associations. Of the various types of painted, stencilled and engraved artefacts (Table 13.2), the boomerang is the most frequently depicted, especially around the Laura River (see Figure 13.3). Unlike woomera, axe and dillybag motifs, boomerang motifs are usually very weathered and located in lower superimposition layers, an indication of relative age that corresponds with the documented absence of boomerangs from Laura material culture during ethnohistoric times (Rosenfeld 1981). Weathered depictions of boomerangs also contrast with the fresh-looking appearance of paintings of dillybags, a standard item of material culture across CYP (Roth 1904:53). Although numbers of dillybag paintings are fewer around the Little Laura River than the Laura River (see Figure 13.3), spatial distribution of the dillybag motif, like most of the motif range including boomerang, dingo and beehive motifs, continues across the study area but peaks in one or other of the valleys (see Figure 13.3).

Post-invasion art

Post-invasion motifs reflect concurrent impacts of colonisation on Aboriginal riverfront estates. The stencilled steel axe at Mushroom Rock records the rapid uptake of steel axes by Aboriginal people of this region (Cole et al. 2020; and see Sharp 1952 for the Gulf country). It may also represent one of the first exotic motifs to enter the art system, given that this accessible site was probably abandoned early in the invasion. The remarkable horse and Native Mounted Police paintings near the Laura River and Shepherd Creek reflect Aboriginal agency and land use in the war (Cole 2010).

Conclusions: A continuing cultural landscape

The Laura Basin was structured into multiple clan Countries (often referred to as 'estates' by anthropologists and archaeologists) during the ethnohistoric period. Owners lived in social units (land-using groups), and travelled and interacted widely, as reflected in strands of stylistic homogeneity of rock art of Laura/Quinkan area of the southern Laura Basin (Cole 2016). Results of this more localised study reflect some of this coherence, but also point to the complexities of unravelling finely tuned relationships between rock art, land use, social and linguistic units, and cultural values.

The presence of unique, rare, idiosyncratic/innovative, ambiguous or 'lost' motifs further complicates analysis, as it is difficult to gauge their significance and relationships, particularly if temporal factors are involved. Traces of the faded, enigmatic Echidna People outside Koolburra invite further study, given that such figures may reflect 'a cultural reality more revealing than natural species' (Morphy 1989:5). Rock art of the study area also records the strange disappearance of the boomerang, a disconnect that warrants extending Rosenfeld's (1981) more general study by investigating the spatial and temporal contexts of the boomerang in Laura Basin rock art.

Understanding the mechanisms and factors associated with such changes in the cultural record suggests the need for finer chronological resolution than currently exists for figurative rock art in CYP.

The distribution of rock art across the valleys of the Laura and Little Laura rivers is associated with the social structures, cosmological relationships and customary patterns of land and bioresource use of Aboriginal people prior to the invasion, and their restricted land use thereafter. Story Places in or near riverbeds where groups of people used to camp in the dry season (George et al. 1995) are unequivocal evidence of this type of seasonal land use. Large clusters or series of rock-shelters with multiple, intensively painted overhangs such as the Giant Horse, Quinkans, Split Rock, Sandy Creek, Yam Camp and Shepherd Creek Terrace complexes, were evidently focal, frequently used places in a well-travelled landscape. However, inter-site variations identified at Giant Horse, Sandy Creek and Yam Camp, such as the timing of initial occupation and subsequent social and technological change are considerable (see Morwood and Hobbs 1995b), possibly with implications for the art tradition. Obviously rock art in these and other sites of the study area may have had different contexts and functions over time (Morwood and Hobbs 1995b, 1995c).

Features of land and social organisation are key to interpreting patterns of motif selectivity, as rock art was embedded in these structures, but, as indicated, precise cultural mapping is not straightforward. Although we know that in the recent past, members of land-using groups had tiers of rights to visit and use clan sites and Countries, we do not know how these translate to rights to paint in the study area. In Yanyuwa Country on the Sir Edward Pellew Islands of the Gulf of Carpentaria, west of the Laura Basin, Brady and Bradley (2014) found that rights to paint can be regulated by the local groups directly related to those beings. Brady and Bradley (2014:171) also found that 'not all ceremonial designs belonging to a specific clan are restricted to their country'. Similarly flexible if complex spatial conventions of making rock art across more than one clan Country may apply in the Laura and Little Laura valleys, where trends in motif variability are usually quantitative rather than qualitative. The widespread presence of Anurra and Timara figures reflects their cultural significance in the heart of the southern Laura Basin (see George et al. 1995), if not their undifferentiated cultural meanings across sites and localities. Similarly, even though certain local concentrations of beehive, dingo and dillybag motifs may signify clan Countries and land tenure, the wider distribution of this imagery beyond the study area is unsurprising given that Stories often cross clan and language groups, although details can vary according to the cultural identity of the narrator (Trezise 1993). Evidently, land users occupying sites over which they had cultural rights of the types documented in recent times made rock art in accordance with intricate relationships to the Story Time, Country, their fellow land users and customary movements across the land.

References

Alpher, B. 2016. Connecting Thaypanic. In J.-C. Verstraete and D. Hafner (eds), *Land and language in Cape York Peninsula and the Gulf Country*, pp. 39–60. Benjamins Publishing Company, Amsterdam/ Philadelphia. doi.org/10.1075/clu.18.03alp.

Ang-Gnarra Aboriginal Corporation 1996. *Quinkan rock art: Images on rock from the Laura Area.* Ang-Gnarra Aboriginal Corporation, Laura.

Australian Government Department of Agriculture, Water and the Environment 2021. *Quinkan Country.* Available at: environment.gov.au/heritage/places/national/quinkan-country (accessed 10 April 2021).

Brady, L.M. and J.J. Bradley 2014. Images of relatedness: Patterning and cultural contexts in Yanuwa rock art, Sir Edward Pellew Islands, sw Gulf of Carpentaria, northern Australia. *Rock Art Research* 31(2):157–176.

Brown, S. 2007. Landscaping heritage: Toward an operational cultural landscape approach for protected areas in New South Wales. *Australasian Historical Archaeology* 25:33–42.

Chase, A. and P. Sutton 1987. Australian Aborigines in a rich environment. In W.H. Edwards (ed.), *Traditional Aboriginal society: A reader,* pp. 68–95. Macmillan, South Melbourne.

Cole, N. 1992. Human figures in the rock art of Jowalbinna. In J. McDonald and I. Haskovic (eds), *State of the art: Regional rock art studies in Australia and Melanesia*n, pp. 164–173. Australian Rock Art Research Association, Melbourne.

Cole, N. 1995. Rock art in the Laura-Cooktown region, S.E. Cape York Peninsula. In M.J. Morwood and D.R. Hobbs (eds), *Quinkan prehistory: The archaeology of Aboriginal art in S.E. Cape York Peninsula,* pp. 51–70. Tempus 3. Anthropology Museum, University of Queensland, St Lucia.

Cole, N. 2004. Battle Camp to Boralga: A local study of colonial war on Cape York Peninsula 1873–1894. *Aboriginal History* 28:156–189. doi.org/10.22459/AH.28.2011.07.

Cole, N. 2010. Painting the police: Aboriginal visual culture and identity in colonial Cape York Peninsula. *Australian Archaeology* 71:17–28. doi.org/10.1080/03122417.2010.11689381.

Cole, N. 2011. 'Rock paintings are Stories' – Rock art and ethnography in the Laura (Quinkan) Region, Cape York Peninsula. *Rock Art Research* 28(1):107–116.

Cole, N. 2016. Regions without borders: Related rock art landscapes of the Laura Basin, Cape York Peninsula. In J.-C. Verstraete and D. Hafner (eds), *Land and language in Cape York Peninsula and the Gulf Country,* pp. 61–84. Benjamins Publishing Company, Amsterdam/Philadelphia. doi.org/10.1075/clu.18.04col.

Cole, N. and A. Buhrich 2012. Endangered rock art: 40 years of cultural heritage management in the Quinkan region, Cape York Peninsula. *Australian Archaeology* 75:66–77. doi.org/10.1080/03122417.2012.11681951.

Cole, N. with G. Musgrave 2006. Colouring stone: Examining categories in rock art. *Rock Art Research* 23(1):51–58.

Cole, N. and P. Trezise 1992. Laura engravings: A preliminary report on the Amphitheatre site. In J. McDonald and I. Haskovic (eds), *State of the art: Regional rock art studies in Australia and Melanesian,* pp. 83–88. Australian Rock Art Research Association, Melbourne.

Cole, N. and A. Watchman 2005. AMS dating of Aboriginal rock art in the Laura region, Cape York Peninsula: Protocols and results of recent research. *Antiquity* 79:661–678. doi.org/10.1017/S0003598X00114590.

Cole, N., A. Watchman and M.J. Morwood 1995. Chronology of Laura rock art. In M.J. Morwood and D.R. Hobbs (eds), *Quinkan prehistory: The archaeology of Aboriginal art in S.E. Cape York Peninsula,* pp. 147–160. Tempus 3. Anthropology Museum, University of Queensland, St Lucia.

Cole, N., L.A. Wallis, H. Burke, B. Barker and Rinyirru Aboriginal Corporation 2020. On the brink of a fever-stricken swamp – culturally modified trees and land–people relationships at Lower Laura (Boralga) Native Mounted Police Camp, Cape York Peninsula. *Australian Archaeology* 86(1):21–36. doi.org/10.1080/03122417.2020.1749371.

David, B. 2004. Rock-art and the experienced landscape: The emergence of late Holocene symbolism in north-east Australia. In C. Chippindale and G. Nash (eds), *The figured landscapes of rock-art: Looking at pictures in place,* pp. 153–181. Cambridge University Press, Cambridge.

David, B. and A. Watchman 1991. Fern Cave, rock art and social formations: Rock art regionalisation and demographic models in Southeastern Cape York Peninsula. *Archaeology in Oceania* 26(2):41–57. doi.org/10.1002/j.1834-4453.1991.tb00263.x.

Flood, J. 1987. Rock art of the Koolburra Plateau, North Queensland. *Rock Art Research* 4(2):91–120.

Flood, J. 1989. Animals and zoomorphs in rock art of the Koolburra region, North Queensland. In H. Morphy (ed.), *Animals into art*, pp. 287–300. Unwin Hyman, London.

Flood, J. and N. Horsfall 1986. Excavation of Green Ant and Echidna Shelters. *Queensland Archaeological Research* 3:4–64.

George. T, G. Musgrave and Ang-Gnarra Rangers 1995. *Our country our art our Quinkans.* Ang-Gnarra Aboriginal Corporation, Laura. doi.org/10.25120/qar.3.1986.181.

Horton, D. 2004. Reading the cultural landscape at Dyea, Alaska, in D. Harmon, B.M. Kilgore and G.E. Vietzke (eds), *Protecting our diverse heritage: The role of parks, protected areas, and cultural sites, Proceedings of the 2003 George Wright Society/National Park Service Joint Conference,* pp. 177–181. The George Wright Society, Hancock, Michigan.

Huchet, B. 1993. A Spatial analysis of rock art motifs of the Laura area, Australia. In J. Steinbring, A. Watchman, P. Faulstich and P. Tacon (eds), *Time and space: Dating and spatial considerations in rock art research*, pp. 92–100. Australian Rock Art Research Association, Melbourne.

Land Tribunal (Queensland) 1996. *Aboriginal land claim to Lakefield National Park 1996: Report of the Land Tribunal established under the* Aboriginal Land Act 1991. Land Tribunal, Brisbane.

McConnel, U. 1930. The Wik-Munkan tribe: Part II. Totemism. *Oceania* 1(2):97–125, 181–205. doi.org/10.1002/j.1834-4461.1930.tb01644.x.

Midgley, H. 1990. Shepherd Creek and a major tributary, Brady Creek, part of the Little Laura River Catchment of the Normanby River system Cape York Peninsula. A brief bio-resource study of some aquatic fauna and water characters. Unpublished report to N. Cole.

Mitchell, N. and S. Buggey 2001. Category V protected landscapes in relation to World Heritage cultural landscapes: Taking advantages of diverse approaches. *Landscape conservation: An international working session on the stewardship of protected areas.* Conservation and Stewardship Publication No. 1. IUCN – The World Conservation Union and QLF/Atlantic Centre for the Environment, Woodstock, Vermont.

Morgan, G., J. Terrey, T. Bean and M. Abel 1995. The biophysical environment. In M.J. Morwood and D.R. Hobbs (eds), *Quinkan prehistory: The archaeology of Aboriginal rock art in S.E Cape York Peninsula Australia*, pp. 5–14. Tempus 3. Anthropology Museum, University of Queensland, St. Lucia.

Morphy, H. 1989. Introduction. In H. Morphy (ed.), *Animals into art*, pp. 1–20. Unwin Hyman, London.

Morphy, H. 1991. *Ancestral connections: Art and an Aboriginal system of knowledge.* University of Chicago Press, Chicago.

Morrison, M. and E. Shepard 2013. The archaeology of culturally modified trees: Indigenous economic diversification within colonial intercultural settings in Cape York Peninsula. *Journal of Field Archaeology* 38(2):143–160. doi.org/10.1179/0093469013Z.00000000044.

Morwood, M. 1995a. Aboriginal ethnography, S.E. Cape York Peninsula. In M.J. Morwood and D.R. Hobbs (eds), *Quinkan prehistory: The archaeology of Aboriginal rock art in S.E Cape York Peninsula Australia*, pp. 33–39. Tempus 3. Anthropology Museum, University of Queensland, St. Lucia.

Morwood, M. 1995b. Introduction: The archaeology of Quinkan rock art. In M.J. Morwood and D.R. Hobbs (eds), *Quinkan Prehistory: The archaeology of Aboriginal rock art in S.E Cape York Peninsula Australia*, pp. 1–4. Tempus 3. Anthropology Museum, University of Queensland, St. Lucia.

Morwood, M.J and D.R. Hobbs 1995a. *Quinkan prehistory: The archaeology of Aboriginal rock art in S.E Cape York Peninsula Australia.* Tempus 3. Anthropology Museum, University of Queensland, St. Lucia.

Morwood, M.J. and D.R. Hobbs 1995b. Conclusions. In M.J. Morwood and D.R. Hobbs (eds), *Quinkan Prehistory: The archaeology of Aboriginal rock art in S.E Cape York Peninsula Australia*, pp. 178–185. Tempus 3. Anthropology Museum, University of Queensland, St. Lucia.

Morwood, M.J. and D.R. Hobbs 1995c. Themes in the prehistory of tropical Australia. In J. Allen and F.O. O'Connell (eds), *Transitions: Pleistocene to Holocene in Australia and Papua New* Guinea, pp. 747–768. Antiquity 69, Special Number 265. Antiquity Publications, Ann Arbor, Michigan. doi.org/10.1017/S0003598X00082314.

Morwood, M. and P. Trezise 1989. Edge-ground axes in Pleistocene Australia: New evidence from S.E. Cape York Peninsula. *Queensland Archaeological Research* 6:77–90. doi.org/10.25120/qar.6.1989.138.

Morwood, M.J., D.R. Hobbs and D. Price 1995a. Excavations at Sandy Creek 1 and 2. In M.J. Morwood and D.R. Hobbs (eds), *Quinkan prehistory: The archaeology of Aboriginal rock art in S.E Cape York Peninsula Australia*, pp. 71–92. Tempus 3. Anthropology Museum, University of Queensland, St. Lucia.

Morwood, M., S. L'Oste-Brown and D. Price 1995b. Excavations at Mushroom Rock. In M.J. Morwood and D.R. Hobbs (eds), *Quinkan prehistory: The archaeology of Aboriginal rock art in S.E Cape York Peninsula Australia*, pp. 133–146. Tempus 3. Anthropology Museum, University of Queensland, St. Lucia.

Mulvaney, D.J. 1976. Chains of connection. In N. Peterson (ed.), *Tribes and boundaries in Australia*, pp. 79–94. Australian Institute of Aboriginal Studies, Canberra.

Pearson, W. 1989. A technological analysis of stone artefacts from Yam Camp surface scatter and rockshelter. *Queensland Archaeological Research* 6:91–102. doi.org/10.25120/qar.6.1989.139.

Queensland Government Department of Environment and Science 2021. Laura Sandstone DIWA nationally important wetland – facts and maps. *WetlandInfo*. Available at: wetlandinfo.des.qld.gov.au/wetlands/facts-maps/diwa-wetland-laura-sandstone/ (accessed 10 April 2021).

Rigsby, B. 1980. Land, language and people in the Princess Charlotte Bay area. In N.C. Stevens and A. Bailey (eds), *Contemporary Cape York Peninsula*, pp. 89–94. Royal Society of Queensland, St Lucia.

Rigsby, B. 1999. Aboriginal people, spirituality and the traditional ownership of land. *International Journal of Social Economics* 26:963–972. doi.org/10.1108/03068299910245741.

Rigsby, B. 2002. Introduction to Kuku Thaypan. Draft MS provided to the author.

Rigsby, B. 2003. The languages of the Quinkan and neighbouring regions. Unpublished report to the Quinkan and Regional Cultural Centre, Laura.

Rosenfeld, A. 1981. Boomerangs north of the Palmer River. *Australian Archaeology* 13(1):80–94. doi.org/10.1080/03122417.1981.12092825.

Rosenfeld, A. 1982. Style and meaning in Laura art: A case study in the formal analysis of style in prehistoric art. *Mankind* 3(3):199–217. doi.org/10.1111/j.1835-9310.1982.tb01231.x.

Rosenfeld, A., D. Horton and J. Winter 1981. *Early man in North Queensland*. The Australian National University, Canberra.

Roth, W. 1903. *Superstition, magic and medicine*. North Queensland Ethnography, Bulletin 5. Government Printer, Brisbane.

Roth, W. 1904. *Domestic implements: Arts and manufacture*. North Queensland Ethnography, Bulletin 7. Government Printer, Brisbane.

Roth. W. 1910. *Decoration, deformation, clothing*. North Queensland Ethnography, Bulletin 15. Government Printer, Brisbane.

Roughsey, D. 1971. *Moon and rainbow: The autobiography of an Aboriginal.* A.H and A.W. Reed, Sydney.

Sharp, L. 1939. Tribes and totemism in north-east Australia. *Oceania* 9(3):254–275. doi. org/10.1002/j.1834-4461.1939.tb00232.x.

Sharp, L. 1952. Steel axes for Stone Age Australians. In E.H. Spicer (ed.), *Human problems in technological change: A casebook*, pp. 69–90. Russell Sage Foundation, New York.

Sutton, P. 1995. *Country: Aboriginal boundaries and land ownership in Australia.* Aboriginal History, Canberra.

Sutton, P. 2011. Cape York Peninsula Indigenous cultural story: Preliminary outline. Unpublished report to Commonwealth Department of the Environment. World Heritage Workshop, Cairns.

Sutton, P. and B. Rigsby 1979. Speech communities and social networks on Cape York Peninsula. In S. Wurm (ed.), *Australian linguistic studies*, pp. 713–732. Pacific Linguistics, Canberra.

Sutton, P. and B. Rigsby 1982. People with 'politicks': Management of land and personnel on Australia's Cape York Peninsula. In N. Williams and E. Hunn (eds), *Resource managers: North American and Australian hunter-gatherers*, pp. 155–171. American Associates for the Advancement of Science, Washington DC. doi.org/10.4324/9780429304569-8.

Taçon, P. 1993. Regionalism in the recent rock art of western Arnhem Land, Northern Territory. *Archaeology in Oceania* 28(3):112–120. doi.org/10.1002/j.1834-4453.1993.tb00302.x.

Thomson, D. 1939. The seasonal factor in human culture. *Proceedings of the Prehistoric Society* 5:209–221. doi.org/10.1017/S0079497X00020545.

Tindale, N. 1974. *Aboriginal tribes of Australia.* University of California Press, Berkeley.

Trezise, P. 1969. *Quinkan Country: Adventures in search of Aboriginal paintings in Cape York.* A.H. and A.W. Reed, Sydney.

Trezise, P. 1971. *Rock art of south-east Cape York Peninsula.* Australian Institute of Aboriginal Studies, Canberra.

Trezise, P. 1973. *Last days of a wilderness.* Collins, Sydney.

Trezise, P. 1977. Representations of crocodiles in Laura art. In P. Ucko (ed.), *Exploring the visual art of Oceania: Schematisation in the art of Aboriginal Australia and prehistoric Europe*, pp. 325–333. Australian Institute of Aboriginal Studies, Canberra.

Trezise, P. 1993. *Dream road: A journey of discovery.* Allen and Unwin, St Leonards.

Verstraete, J.-C. and D. Hafner (eds) 2016. *Land and language in Cape York Peninsula and the Gulf Country.* Benjamins Publishing Company, Amsterdam/Philadelphia. doi.org/10.1075/clu.18.

Watchman, A. and N. Cole 1993. Accelerator radiocarbon dating of plant-fibre binders in rock paintings from northeastern Australia. *Antiquity* 67:355–358. doi.org/10.1017/S0003598X00045415.

Watchman, A., J. Sirois and N. Cole 1993. Mineralogical examination of rock painting pigments near Laura, North Queensland. In B.L. Fankhauser and J.R. Bird (eds), *Archaeometry: Current Australasian research*, pp. 141–149. The Australian National University, Canberra.

Woolston, G. and P. Trezise 1969. Petroglyphs of Cape York Peninsula. *Mankind* 7(2):120–127. doi.org/ 10.1017/S0003598X00045415.

Wright, R. 1971. Prehistory in the Cape York Peninsula. In D.J. Mulvaney and J. Golson (eds), *Aboriginal man and environment in Australia*, pp. 133–140. The Australian National University, Canberra.

14

Australia-affiliated rock art research in Southeast Asia and Micronesia

Andrea Jalandoni

Introduction

It has long been suspected that Australia-affiliated researchers have dominated Southeast Asian and Micronesian rock art studies, but the extent and implications were unknown. For this project, a systematic quantitative literature review was used to update previous work (Jalandoni et al. 2019) that investigated the distribution of rock art publications, the methods employed and the author affiliations of rock art research in the region. The results highlighted research trends and quantitatively verified the dominance of Australia-affiliated authors. As a consequence, further investigation into the proportion of Australian involvement in research outputs per geographic location, the institutional affiliations, the productivity of authors, the types of collaboration and the distribution of the first authorship when publishing with locals was undertaken.

The purpose of this paper is to open a conversation around the ways in which ethical collaboration can be envisaged and designed to ensure an inclusive and diversified approach in archaeological research. Emerging trends indicate that, while there has been a surge of interest in archaeological research in Southeast Asian and Micronesian rock art, there has also been an increasing need to question the modes of research design and collaboration implemented by researchers. This conversation is particularly relevant in an academic environment and in the wider sociopolitical context as a principal aspect of decolonising academic work, embedded in ensuring that Indigenous and non-Western voices challenge the Western trajectories of research methodologies and representation.

In 2019, Jalandoni et al. published a systematic quantitative literature review (SQLR) of Southeast Asian and Micronesian scholarship collected in mid-2017 and derived from Jalandoni's (2018) PhD thesis. The purpose of the 2017 SQLR was to understand the context of Philippine rock art and rock art narratives in the wider region of Southeast Asia and Micronesia by investigating what had been published. The results revealed that Australia-affiliated researchers, based on institution, dominated the region. Out of a total of 126 research outputs, 47 were authored by researchers affiliated with an Australian institution. By presenting the data quantitatively, this observation is no longer anecdotal.

As a follow-up to this research project, in February 2020 the SQLR data were updated, and 53 research outputs were added to understand the present situation of scholarship in the region. In this paper, graphs from Jalandoni et al. (2019) were updated to show the distribution of research outputs by year, geographic distribution, methods used and author affiliation. A subset of 65 publications with Australia-affiliated authors was used to examine questions of published research proportion in each location, funding sources, author productivity and collaboration style.

The SQLR has many shortcomings and biases, which are explored in the method and discussion sections. It is contentious to look at data purely quantitatively, but the SQLR still has merit as a way of presenting data and identifying gaps in the research. It may expose patterns but requires further qualitative studies to explain the cause. This paper describes Australia-affiliated research in Southeast Asia and Micronesia as presented by publications; it does not provide an explanation for the results. The paper makes no conclusions but begs reflection throughout.

In the interest of ethical transparency, it should be noted that I am an early career researcher of Southeast Asian heritage, funded by the Australian Research Council and Griffith University, an Australia-affiliated institution.

Method

The primary data used for this article were produced through an SQLR. The data were collected in a form that makes them quantifiable and, as a result, easily analysed. The method for updating the SQLR followed the same data gathering and tabulation described in Jalandoni et al. (2019). The search date range was set from 2017 until 2020 to update results from the previous SQLR. For a detailed methodology on conducting an SQLR, see Jalandoni et al. (2019), Pickering and Byrne (2013), and Petticrew and Roberts (2006).

During the 2017 data gathering, a range of (English language–based) library data sources were searched. It was found that Google Scholar located everything that was on the other databases except for some doctoral theses. As a consequence, for the current updated study, only Google Scholar was used as a search engine. It would seem that the Google Scholar algorithms have changed since 2017 and doctoral theses are now included in the results. Every geographic location (Southeast Asia generally, Indonesia, Malaysia, the Philippines, Thailand, Vietnam, Cambodia, Laos, Brunei, Myanmar, and East Timor/Timor-Leste, Taiwan, Hong Kong, Marianas/Mariana Islands, Guam, Saipan, Tinian, Rota, Palau, Federated States of Micronesia/FSM, Yap, Pohnpei, Chuk/Truk/Chuuk, Kosrae, Marshall Islands and Kiribati) was Boolean-searched using the following rock art terminologies: rock art, rock-art, cave art, painted site, pictograph, pictogram, stencil, engravings and petroglyph.

For compiling the SQLR, every record identified by the Google Scholar search engine was added to a spreadsheet and duplicated records were removed. Each record was then screened for access and language and the resulting abstracts, books, book chapters, theses and journal articles were analysed; entries that were geographically out of scope or not about rock art were excluded. The remaining eligible entries were tabulated in an Excel spreadsheet based on author location affiliation, year of publication, journal title (if applicable), geographic region, kind of rock art, artist, sites discussed and study methods used. Figure 14.1 is a flowchart of the method adapted from Moher et al. (2009) for systematic reviews.

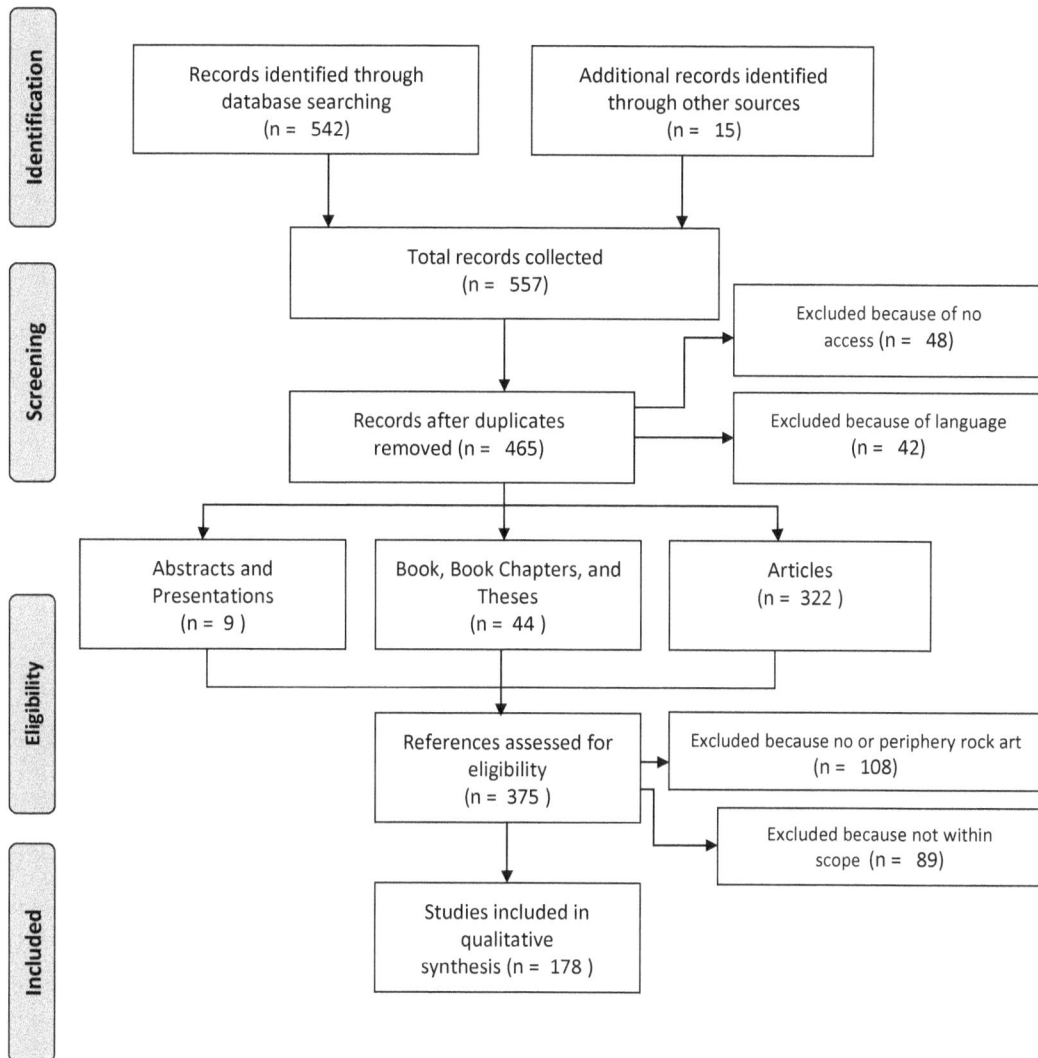

Figure 14.1: Flowchart using PRISMA (preferred reporting items for systematic reviews and meta-analyses) statement for the systematic review.
Source: Adapted from Moher et al. 2009.

The most conspicuous limitation of this method for the study area is that only publications in English are included. There are several Southeast Asian countries that publish in their native language(s) and those publications were excluded, which may have altered the patterns observed in this study. Fortunately, the method allowed for this and other exclusions as long as the exclusions were made explicit. Museum papers were excluded owing to access constraints. Unfortunately, these exclusions limit the scope of the study, but they were necessary because a comprehensive list of all the literature available on the rock art of Southeast Asia and Micronesia would have required physically visiting museums and historic preservation offices across the region (Jalandoni et al. 2019), clearly beyond the scope of current research. Furthermore, if museum papers were included, they would bias the counts in favour of areas where I have worked extensively, such as the Philippines, Palau, Guam and Saipan.

Some grey literature was also omitted using this method, largely because such literature is often of restricted access; permissions for access to such literature could take years to obtain and, in some cases, never be received. Even if some access were granted, the literature would have required translation from, for example, Bahasa Indonesian, Bahasa Malayan, Thai, Vietnamese, Khmer and Mandarin languages into English.

Finally, it was deemed necessary for this current study to use the same methodology, with the same limitations, as was used in Jalandoni et al. (2019) to provide a basis to compare the June 2017 data with the updated February 2020 data.

For the second part of the research presented in this paper, a subset of the data was created that only included works where there was at least one Australia-affiliated author. This subset of 65 publications was less prone to have been impacted by the limitations of the SQLR because Australia-affiliated researchers do not often author non-English publications and local grey literature.

Results

Updating from June 2017 to February 2020

The updated search revealed 157 new entries collected from June 2017 until February 2020. When the records of 2017 and other sources were added there was a total of 558 entries. After duplicates were removed and the entries screened for language and access, 466 references remained. Those references were further analysed, and 197 were excluded because they were not related to rock art, they only peripherally mentioned it or their topics were not within our scope. A total of 179 references were included in the February 2020 systematic review, up from 126 in June 2017, which equates to a 42 per cent increase in scholarship in less than three years.

Distribution of publications by year and location

There was a gradual rise in Southeast Asia and Micronesia rock art scholarship, with a peak in 2018 (Figure 14.2). The high count in 2018 was partially explained by the O'Connor et al. (2018) edited book on Sulawesi, which presented several chapters of rock art research. Up to 2017, Thailand and Peninsular Malaysia and Malaysian Borneo, in that order, had the most research outputs for the region (Table 14.1). By 2020, there was an overall increase in research across the region, but Sulawesi had more than doubled its output, placing it with the most outputs, followed by Thailand, and Peninsular Malaysia tied with East Timor (Table 14.1, Figure 14.3). Aubert et al. (2014) triggered global interest in the oldest figurative and stencil rock art in Sulawesi, which has had a ripple effect on research, with researchers responding and more research being conducted on the island.

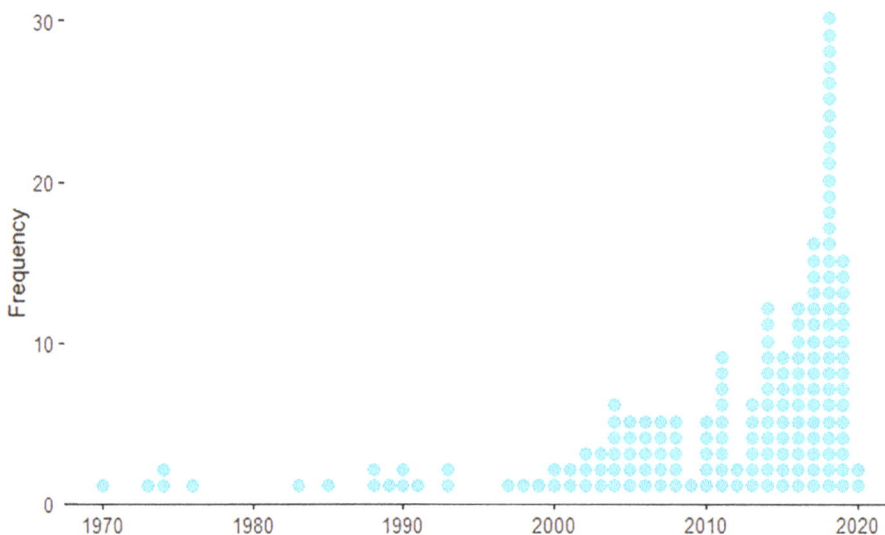

Figure 14.2: Distribution of rock art research output by year. Each dot is one output.
Source: Author's summary.

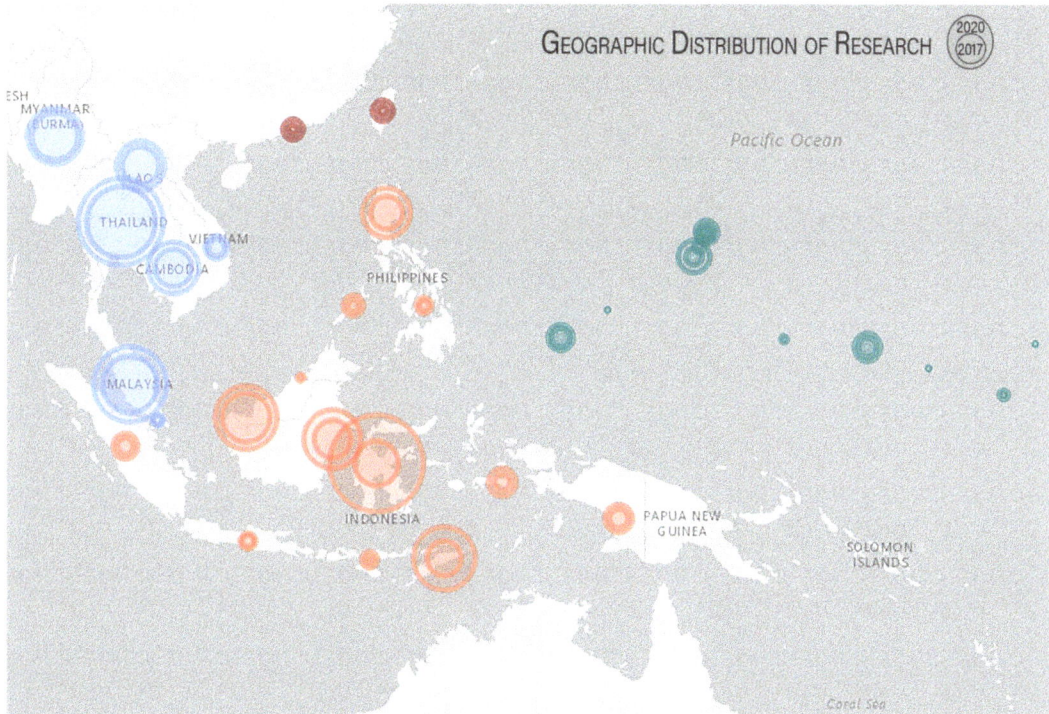

Figure 14.3: Geographical distribution of rock art research by 2017 (inner circle) and 2020 (outer circle).

Source: Author's summary.

Table 14.1: Counts for four areas of most published rock art research in Southeast Asia and Micronesia pre-June 2017 and June 2017 until February 2020.

	Sulawesi	Thailand	P. Malaysia	M. Borneo	East Timor
Up to June 2017	14	22	18	16	11
June 2017 – February 2020	17	5	6	4	9
Total	**31**	**27**	**24**	**20**	**20**

Source: Author's summary of results.

Methods used in publications

Methods described in each research output were classified as recording or survey, observation, literature review, interpretation, condition assessment, dating, excavation and pigment analysis (Figure 14.4). One research output might have employed several methods and all were counted. All the methods were self-explanatory except observation, which was classified as those publications that might have been focused on some other archaeological site and mention that it was near rock art with no other information; usually it was the only method used in the publication. The drop of observations from 36 in the 2017 dataset to only six additional entries in the 2020 dataset could be an indication of rock art research no longer being treated as 'fringe' archaeology.

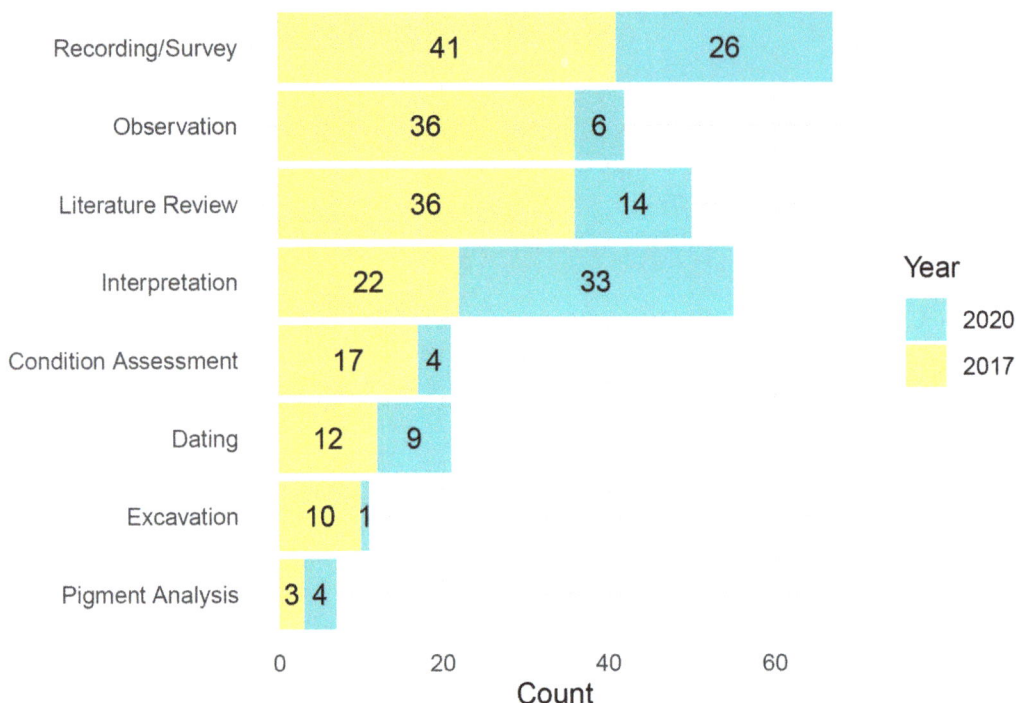

Figure 14.4: Methods used in Southeast Asian and Micronesian rock art research by 2017 and 2020.

Source: Author's summary.

The most common methods of rock art research documented in the publications were recording or survey. This was expected because surveying and recording are the foundation of rock art research. Although not represented in Figure 14.4, the survey and recording methods have become more sophisticated over recent years. Between 2017 and 2020, the publications were more recording than survey and the recordings were no longer manual recordings, but employed digital techniques, such as multispectral imaging, drones, and 3D models from photogrammetry and laser scanning (see Majid et al. 2017; Zainuddin 2019). There was also a significant increase in publications providing interpretations of the rock art. For example, researchers were making more connections between motifs and using rock art to answer questions of migration or providing some additional insight into the rock art besides recording.

There are overall very few research outputs with condition assessment, dating, excavation and pigment analysis. A possible explanation for this is that those methods can be costly or require specialist training. However, there were proportionally more papers on dating and pigment analysis in the last three years than before mid-2017.

Author affiliation

Data on author affiliation included all authors, but if more than one author was from the same country, that country was only counted once per publication, following Jalandoni et al. (2019). For example, one article may have several Australian authors and one Malaysian author but would only be counted as one for Australia and one for Malaysia. The updated 2020 data still showed Australia-affiliated authors dominated the research publications in Southeast Asia and Micronesia (Figure 14.5). East Timor ties with Malaysian Borneo for the fourth most research outputs (Table 14.1; Figure 14.5).

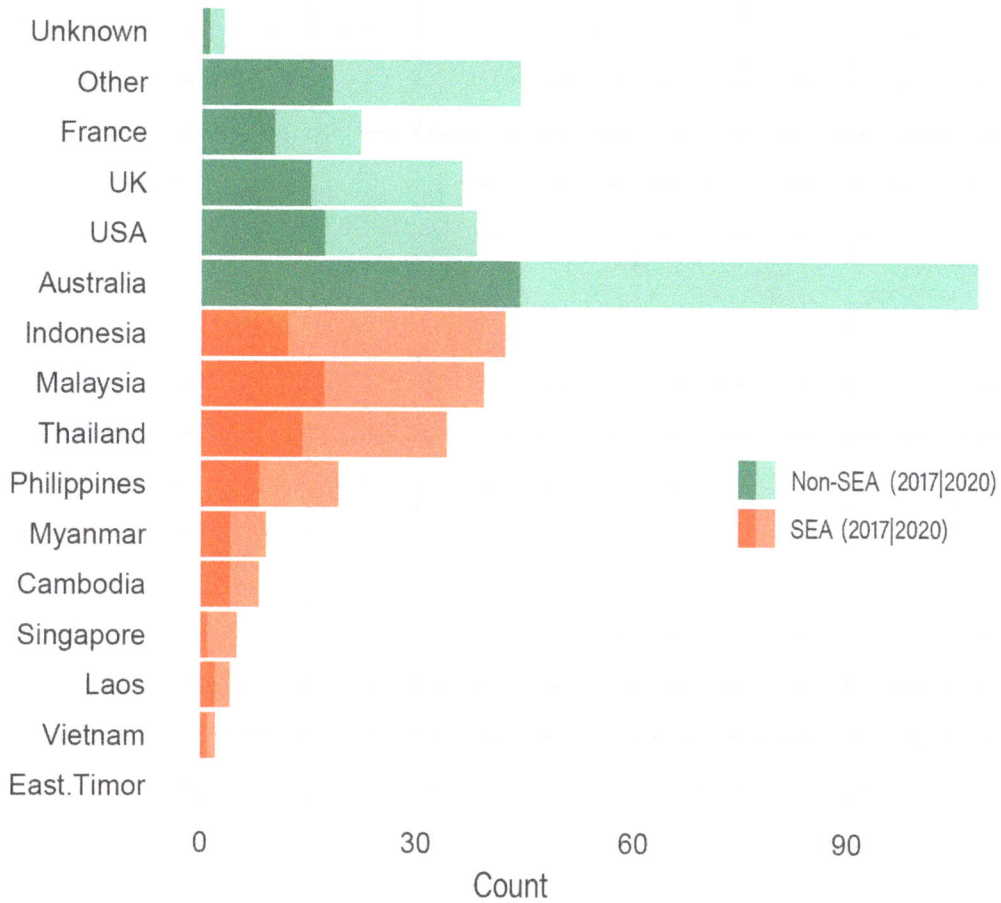

Figure 14.5: Author affiliations for rock art research done in Southeast Asia and Micronesia by 2017 and 2020.

Source: Author's summary.

Australia-affiliated researchers

After seeing the dominance of Australia-affiliated authors in the region (Figure 14.6), more analysis was necessary to understand the implications. The data used for this part of the study were a subset of 65 out of the total 179 in the SQLR that filtered for publications that had at least one Australia-affiliated author. First, the geography of the scholarship was used to determine whether the research focused on particular locations or spread out across the region. Second, authors were traced back to their affiliated institutes in Australia. Third, collaboration based on the authorship was examined to see whether Australia-affiliated researchers published with locals, as indicated by an author affiliation on the publication from the country where the rock art was located. Finally, when Australia-affiliated authors collaborated with locals, which of the two was first author was noted. The word 'local' indicates authors who are affiliated with institutions in Southeast Asia and Micronesia.

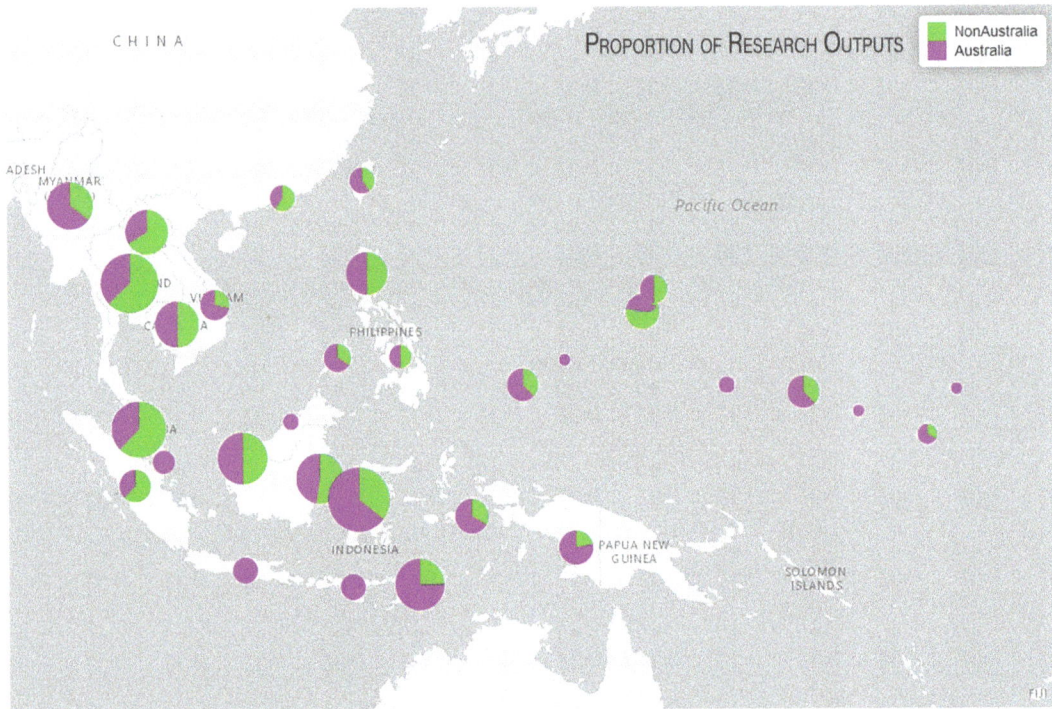

Figure 14.6: Geographic distribution of rock art research outputs in Southeast Asia and Micronesia proportioned between Australia-affiliated and not affiliated with Australia. The bigger the circle, the more research outputs mention the area.

Source: Author's summary.

Geographic proportion of Australia-affiliated research

Every publication was analysed for the location of the work and whether the publication had at least one Australia-affiliated researcher or only non-Australia-affiliated researchers. If one publication talked about several locations, all research locations were included in the calculation. Every country and island group in Southeast Asia and Micronesia has had an Australia-affiliated researcher publish about its rock art (Figure 14.6). Australia-affiliated researchers have been involved in the majority of English-language rock art publications that discuss East Timor, Sulawesi, Myanmar, West Papua, Maluku, Vietnam, Taiwan, Palau, Saipan, Pohnpei and Kiribati. All the rock art publications found in the SQLR of Java and Lesser Sunda, Indonesia, have Australia-affiliated authors. There is no known rock art in Singapore, Brunei, Yap, Chuuk, Kosrae and the Marshall Islands and this has been mentioned only by Australia-affiliated researchers.

It is interesting to note that a large proportion of the publications about Thailand and Peninsular Malaysia have no Australia-affiliated researchers, and yet they are still among the areas with the most research outputs. The publications with no Australia-affiliated researcher involved were published by locally affiliated researchers or with co-authors affiliated with institutions from the United Kingdom, the United States of America, France or elsewhere (see Jalandoni et al. 2019 for further discussion). Also, much of the research in Thailand is in Thai and therefore excluded from the SQLR, so Thai scholarship may be much higher than is represented in this paper. Sumatra, Laos, Hong Kong and Guam are also locations where most of the rock art research has been published without any affiliation with Australia.

Institutional affiliation

Australia-affiliated academics are producing many publications on the rock art found throughout Southeast Asia and Micronesia (Figure 14.6). The next step in the analysis of these publications was to trace the institutions the authors list as their affiliation (Figure 14.7). The information could be of interest to prospective students who plan to make this region their study area. The dominance of Australia-affiliated rock art researchers for the region indicates that there has been extensive funding and support from institutions and that the researchers in those institutions are successfully receiving Australian Research Council and other grants to conduct their research.

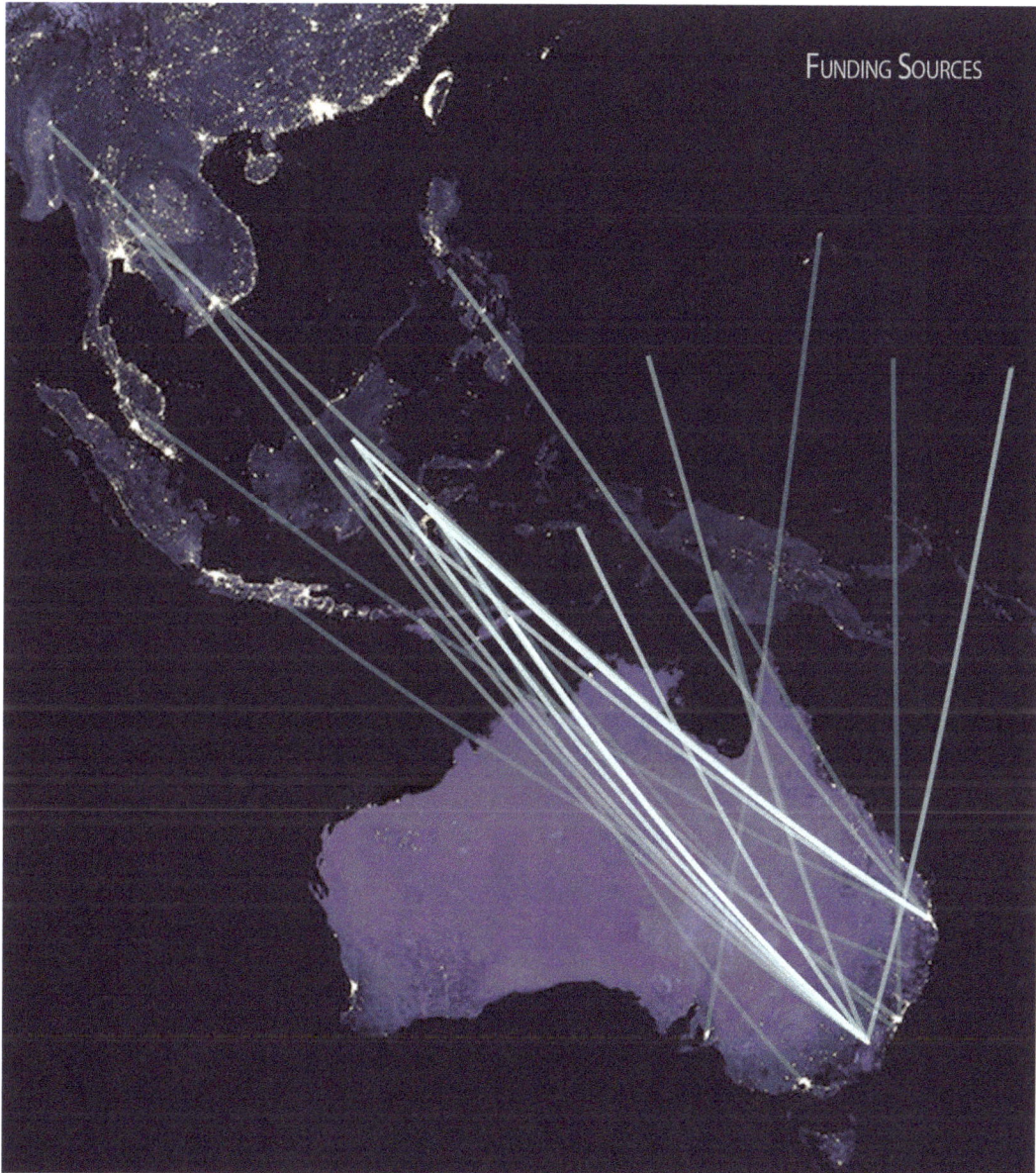

Figure 14.7: Publications from Southeast Asia and Micronesia rock art traced back to the Australia-affiliated authors' institutions.

Source: Author's summary.

The first or earliest Australian author's institution was counted for this study and if an author listed several affiliations, only the primary institution was included. Therefore, every publication involving an Australia-affiliated researcher was recorded from one location in Australia to one location in Southeast Asia or Micronesia. If the work involved all of Southeast Asia, such as a regional overview, then it was connected to one point in Southeast Asia, decided by Google to be in Borneo. Malaysian Borneo and Indonesian Kalimantan were combined into one point. The purpose of Figure 14.7 was to trace the institutional affiliations of the authors to determine which institutions in Australia are supporting particular research. However, this does not take into account the possibility that an author did the fieldwork while at one institution but wrote the paper affiliated with another institution and other scenarios.

Most of the researchers we identified are affiliated with Canberra and southeast Queensland (Figure 14.7). While The Australian National University (ANU) in Canberra has a higher total tally of 35 research outputs, in the last three years Griffith University (GU) in southeast Queensland has almost doubled its research outputs and exceeded the research output of ANU for the same period (Table 14.2). From mid-2017 to early 2020, there have been 21 Australia-affiliated research outputs: 11 GU, eight ANU, one University of Wollongong and one University of Queensland. Most of the research projects have been funded by the Australian Research Council.

Table 14.2: Distribution of author affiliation to The Australia National University, Griffith University and all other Australian institutions pre-June 2017, and June 2017 until February 2020.

Year	The Australia National University	Griffith University	Others	Total
Up to June 2017	27	12	5	**44**
June 2017 – February 2020	8	11	2	**21**
Total	**35**	**23**	**7**	**65**

Source: Author's summary.

It is important to reflect on the extent to which these research bodies, and the government perspectives and policies that guide and regulate their activities, are addressing questions of diversity, inclusion and ethical representation, while conducting research work in these areas. Part of the aim of decolonising academic imperialism is ensuring Indigenous voices are represented to challenge Western research design. These forms of collaboration, facilitated through the consideration of representation and inclusivity, often aid in decentring colonial academic practices. In this context, the policies of Western research bodies and universities call for scrutiny. Questions of intersectionality (how aspects of a person's social and political identity can expose them to overlapping forms of discrimination) must be raised when thinking about ethical collaboration and research design to counter Eurocentric approaches to archaeological research (Monton-Subias and Hernando 2018). One of the significant processes through which efforts of decolonisation can take place is through reconsidering the 'underlying logics' of writing historical narratives that are central to archaeological research (Monton-Subias and Hernando 2018).

Author productivity

The next line of investigation was on who were the most prolific authors. Again, this could interest prospective students looking for mentors. A word cloud is a good graphic for quickly visualising the frequency of authors (Figure 14.8). The data used to generate the word cloud included only Australia-affiliated authors. Therefore, if an author has another institution as their primary affiliation, they are no longer counted among Australian authors.

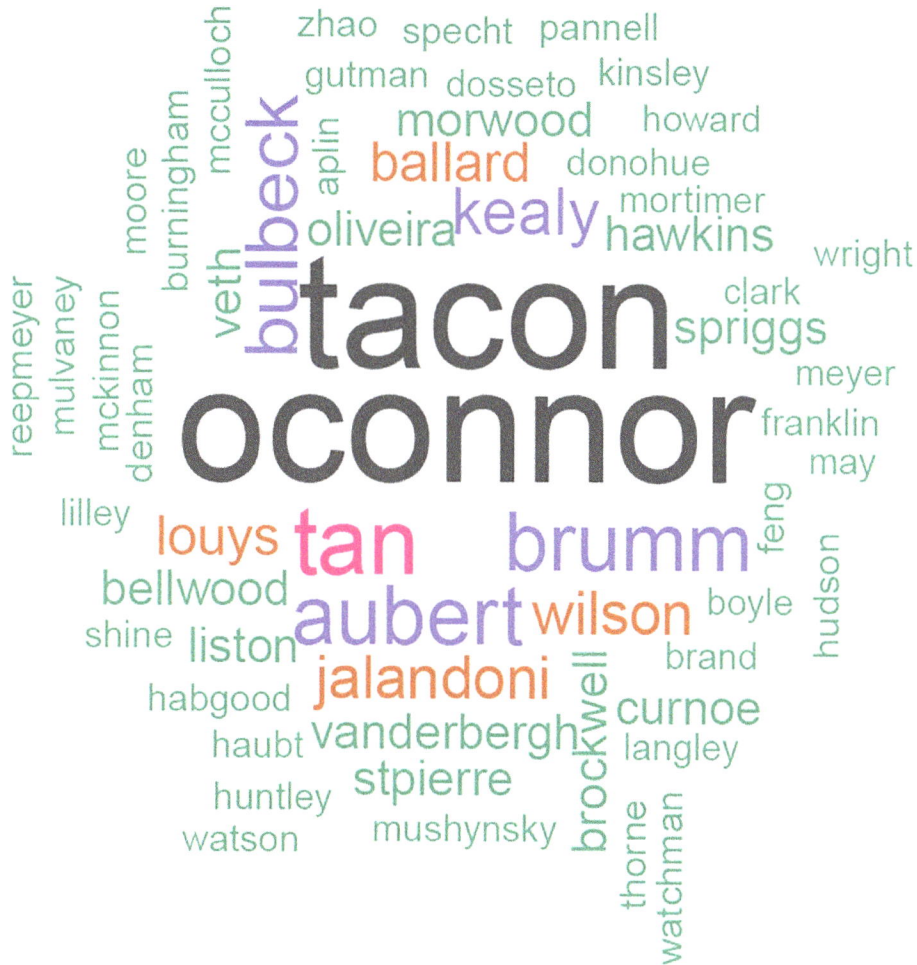

Figure 14.8: Word cloud of Australia-affiliated rock art authors. The larger the size of the name, the more outputs.

Source: Author's summary.

As of early 2020, Sue O'Connor was the most prolific Australia-affiliated rock art researcher of the Southeast Asian and Micronesian region with 19 publications, and Paul Taçon was a close second with 18 publications (Figure 14.8). Between mid-2017 and early 2020, O'Connor (ANU) and Taçon (GU) were the most prolific authors with seven outputs each, while Jalandoni (GU) and O'Connor (ANU) tie for the most first-author publications with four each. O'Connor was involved with seven and Kealy with four of the eight publications to have come out of ANU. In contrast, GU has their 11 publications spread among Taçon (seven), Brumm (five), Aubert (four) and Jalandoni (four), who sometimes published with each other.

Collaboration style

With all these Australia-affiliated researchers working in Southeast Asia and Micronesia, the type of collaboration with locals was the next line of inquiry. Five types of collaboration were identified and each publication was classified accordingly.

- Type 1: Australia-affiliated researcher collaborated with a local researcher
- Type 2: Australia-affiliated researcher published as sole author
- Type 3: Australia-affiliated researcher collaborated with other Australia-affiliated researchers
- Type 4: Australia-affiliated researcher collaborated with a non-local international researcher

- Type 5: One of the authors was Australia-affiliated in the publication but identified as Southeast Asian or Micronesian. Type 5 publications included doctoral theses from Australian institutions authored by Southeast Asians or Micronesians.

Out of 65 publications with Australia-affiliated researchers, 27 were Type 1 and 10 were Type 5, therefore 57 per cent of the publications had local-affiliated authors involved (Figure 14.9). Up to mid-2017, there were 23 instances of Types 1 and 5 publications out of 44 in total, making 53 per cent. There was an increase from mid-2017 to early 2020, as there were 14 examples of Types 1 and 5 publications out of 21, making for 67 per cent. The ratio of collaboration between Australia-affiliated and local researchers increased during this period. There has been only one additional publication each for Type 2 and Type 4 collaborations in the three-year period from 2017 to 2020. However, the number of Type 3 collaborations almost doubled in the same period (see Figure 14.9).

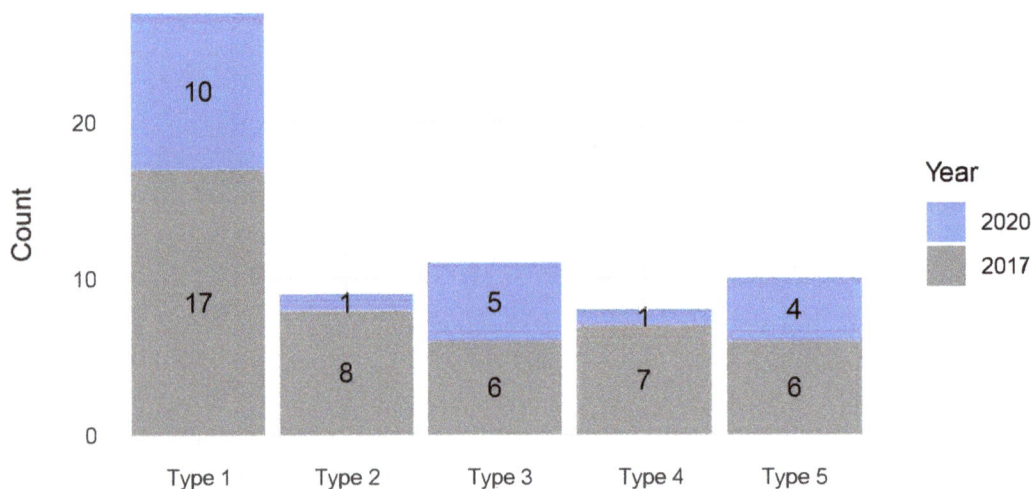

Figure 14.9: Distribution of collaboration for Australia-affiliated publications.
Source: Author's summary.

In this context, re-examining the choices made in designing ethical collaborative work is crucial (Rogers 2006). One of the major tenets to keep in mind while rethinking diversity and representation in academic work is cultural representation.

Communication scholars define cultural appropriation as 'Any instance in which a group borrows or imitates the strategies of another – even when the tactic is not intended to deconstruct or distort the other's meanings and experiences' (Shugart 1997:210–211). Although this definition is far from complete, as it ignores social and political nuances of disadvantaged or oppressed groups appropriating the culture of the majority, this concept has gained rightful relevance and significance in broader social, cultural and political contexts (Black 2002; Harold 2004).

Examining the most commonly practised modes of collaboration between researchers opens dialogue for rethinking the ways in which oppressive cultural appropriation is often facilitated and can be avoided in terms of research collaborations. The context of decolonisation becomes relevant as it is the 'anti-colonial struggle that grows out of grassroot spaces' (Zavala 2013:58). Thinking in terms of representation and inclusion, considering how research collaboration might look in non-Western spaces, can become a significant agent of change and decolonisation. While decolonisation, both as a concept and process, is gaining momentum in archaeological research (Atalay 2006; Lilley 2006), the complex way in which neoliberal ethnocentric attitudes and approaches become inherent to research design requires reflection, specifically within the context of Australia and Southeast Asia and Micronesia.

Type 1 and Type 5 publications were the ideal collaborations because they indicated a sharing of knowledge. For example, the Australia-affiliated researchers might have brought their technological and theoretical background of rock art research and the local collaborators provided local context and insight. For this reason, Type 5 can be solo-authored publications because they embody the shared knowledge in one person – a local with community knowledge that has Australian research training and support or other motivations.

Ulm et al. (2013:42) noted 'low participation rates of professionally qualified Indigenous archaeologists' after a survey of Australian archaeologists. Building capacity among locals whenever possible should be included in every project plan for ethical research. In this way the knowledge is shared, and the research can be sustainable if the locals are engaged and empowered. Further, it is important to note that while sharing knowledge is productive, it is not always ethical. Often, first authors of research outcomes are decided based on several factors such as funding bodies like universities and research centres as well as host countries. As a result of systemic hierarchies, it is usually expected that researchers from universities and researchers who are representative of the funding bodies invite local ethnic researchers for collaboration but at a cost: namely the senior partner(s) is/are to be the first author(s). This is indicative of the ways in which the hierarchical and marginalising systemic patterns, in which academic research practice often functions, creates a lack of cultural consideration for conducting research in non-Western geographical areas. An alternative way of addressing this issue could be centred around prioritising the voice of the local authors in the research that emerges out of these areas. Admittedly, publication authorship concerns are a Western concept and may not even be an aspiration for local collaborators; this is still a discussion that needs to be made.

First author affiliation

The increase in Type 1 and Type 5 collaboration between researchers from Australia and Southeast Asia and Micronesia was reassuring. It prompted the next inquiry into the distribution of first authorship when Australia-affiliated researchers collaborated with locals and vice-versa. The data collected up to 2017 showed that locals had more first authorships than Australia-affiliated researchers (Figure 14.10). From mid-2017 to early 2020, there are more Australia-affiliated authors who are first authors. However, this does not take into account that there are also many locals now publishing without any international researchers (see Fauzi et al. 2019; Idrees and Pradhan 2017; Leihitu and Permana 2018). This could signal a positive direction in which ethical and considered research patterns are gradually developing within archaeological research. While it is unproductive to pit these two emerging patterns against each other, it is also important to celebrate the gradual emergence of local voices in rock art research.

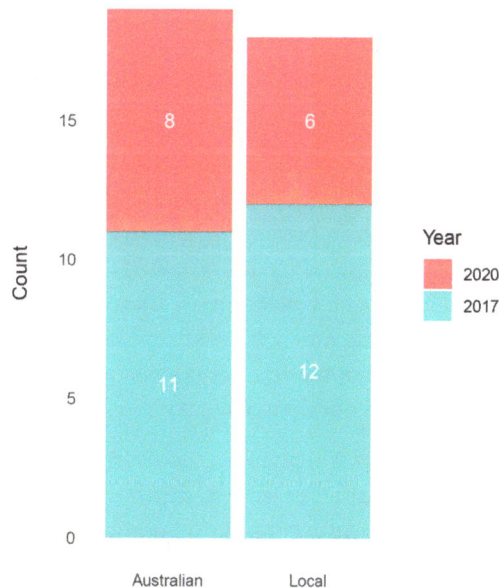

Figure 14.10: Distribution of first authorship between Australia-affiliated researchers and locals by 2017 and 2020.

Source: Author's summary.

Discussion

By updating the SQLR data of Southeast Asia and Micronesia rock art research from mid-2017 to early 2020, many of the revelations from Jalandoni et al. (2019) have been reaffirmed, notably that the number of publications by year is on a rising trend and that English publications are still dominated by Australia-affiliated researchers.

Although there is a significant rise in the rock art research from these geographical areas, the local voices that are crucial in understanding the heritage, culture and complex historical trajectories in the region are sometimes still absent. The problematics of a lack of ethical collaborations are too many to be enumerated in this paper. However, the data presented in this paper serve as a basis to reflect on collaborations and project development in archaeological research in the Southeast Asian and Micronesian region and, if needed, how they can be decolonised and made more diversified and ethical. The inequities of Australian archaeology, such as the 'glass ceiling' for women and low Indigenous participation rates, noted by Smith and Burke (2006) and Mate and Ulm (2021), respectively, should not be exported.

Australia-affiliated rock art researchers also need to reflect on whether they are unconsciously propagating 'colonial science' or 'parachute science' in Southeast Asia and Micronesia. 'Parachute science' is a term used to describe how high-income or Western countries drop in on low-income countries to conduct research without providing any benefit, such as capacity building or infrastructure, to local researchers or the community (de Vos 2020). As a critique against parachute science, researchers used a similar SQLR method on warm water coral reef biodiversity research that showed approximately 40 per cent of publications for fieldwork conducted in Indonesia and the Philippines had no local researcher involvement, but the trend was moving towards more local involvement (Stefanoudis et al. 2021). Stefanoudis et al. (2021) provided many suggestions for avoiding parachute science, such as engaging the next generation of local researchers and sharing collections. Capacity building might be measured in the future in the form of more local-led publications, as the trend has already shown.

A valid criticism against the work presented here is that systematic quantitative literature reviews are a Western methodology themselves. Therefore, this work is inadvertently colonial in itself, best evidenced by the inclusion of only English publications, as is standard for this methodology. However, this methodology was chosen to have a basis of comparison with the previous SQLR conducted by Jalandoni et al. (2019), without any social issues in mind. The issues of colonialism and collaboration became apparent from describing the subset of Australia-affiliated research using publication-related metrics. Admittedly, SQLRs are not the right tool to examine these important issues because the data are derived solely from quantitative metrics about the publication, but they may help in exposing them.

It is important that the patterns of research collaboration with locals are reflected on as they contribute to a rich and in-depth diversity of knowledge and lead to newer ways of rethinking and implementing innovative research methods. Further, dialogue between the local voices of expertise in these regions opens up more complex historical, material and cultural decolonisation of archaeological practice and research that is seminal to the growth and development of the discipline. This is an important aspect of conducting research in non-Western areas, as it often succeeds in capturing the multiple sensorial and affective cultural, social and historical layers of these rock art sites and their complex traditional perspectives.

It is important to continually critique the reasons for a dominance of Australian publications in these regions and to open a scope for critiquing Eurocentric patterns. While the SQLR may invoke questions, further data collection and other methods of analysis are necessary to answer them. The intention of this paper has been to be a starting point for discussion about ethical collaboration and academic imperialism, among other topics. While these data might seem limited to a subset of researchers of a specific region, the points of reflection extend to the general field of archaeology.

References

Atalay, S. 2006. Guest editor's remarks: Decolonizing archaeology. *American Indian Quarterly* 30(3/4):269–279. doi.org/10.1353/aiq.2006.0014.

Aubert, M., A. Brumm, M. Ramli, T. Sutikna, E.W. Saptomo, B. Hakim, M.J. Morwood, G.D. van den Bergh, L. Kinsley and A. Dosseto 2014. Pleistocene cave art from Sulawesi, Indonesia. *Nature* 514(7521):223–227. doi.org/10.1038/nature13422.

Black, J.E. 2002. The 'mascotting' of Native America: Construction, commodity, and assimilation. *American Indian Quarterly* 26(4):605–622. doi.org/10.1353/aiq.2004.0003.

de Vos, A. 2020. The problem of 'colonial science': Conservation projects in the developing world should invest in local scientific talent and infrastructure. *Scientific American* 1 July 2020. Available at: www.scientificamerican.com/article/the-problem-of-colonial-science (accessed 27 April 2021).

Fauzi, M.R., F.S. Intan, and A.S. Wibowo 2019. Newly discovered cave art sites from Bukit Bulan, Sumatra: Aligning prehistoric symbolic behavior in Indonesian prehistory. *Journal of Archaeological Science: Reports* 24:166–174. doi.org/10.1016/j.jasrep.2019.01.001.

Harold, C. 2004. Pranking rhetoric: 'Culture jamming' as media activism. *Critical Studies in Media Communication* 21(3):189–211. doi.org/10.1080/0739318042000212693.

Idrees, M.O. and B. Pradhan 2017. Characterization of macro- and micro-geomorphology of cave channel from high-resolution 3D laser scanning survey: Case study of Gomantong Cave in Sabah, Malaysia. In S. Karabulut and M.C. Cinku (eds), *Cave investigation,* pp. 1–22. InTech, London. doi.org/10.5772/intechopen.69084.

Jalandoni, A. 2018. The archaeological investigation of rock art in the Philippines. Unpublished PhD thesis, School of Humanities, Languages and Social Science, Griffith University, Gold Coast. doi.org/10.25904/1912/404.

Jalandoni, A., P. Taçon and R. Haubt 2019. A systematic quantitative literature review of Southeast Asian and Micronesian rock art. *Advances in Archaeological Practice* 7(4):423–434. doi.org/10.1017/aap.2019.10.

Leihitu, I. and R.C. Permana 2018. Looking for a trace of shamanism, in the rock art of Maros-Pangkep, South Sulawesi, Indonesia. *Kapata Arkeologi* 14(1):15–26. doi.org/10.24832/kapata.v14i1.496.

Lilley, I. 2006. Archaeology, diaspora and decolonization. *Journal of Social Archaeology* 6(1):28–47. doi.org/10.1177/1469605306060560.

Majid, Z., M. Ariff, K. Idris, A. Yusoff, A. Aspuri, M.A. Abbas, K. Zainuddin, A.R.A. Ghani and A.B. Saeman 2017. Three-dimensional mapping of an ancient cave paintings using close-range photogrammetry and terrestrial laser scanning technologies. *The International Archives of Photogrammetry, Remote Sensing and Spatial Information Sciences* 42-2/W3:453–457. doi.org/10.5194/isprs-archives-XLII-2-W3-453-2017.

Mate, G. and S. Ulm 2021. Working in archaeology in a changing world: Australian archaeology at the beginning of the COVID-19 pandemic. *Australian Archaeology* 87(3):229–250. doi.org/10.1080/03122417.2021.1986651.

Moher, D., A. Liberati, J. Tetzlaff, D.G. Altman and PRISMA Group 2009. Preferred reporting items for systematic reviews and meta-analyses: The PRISMA statement. *PLoS Medicine* 6(7):e1000097. doi.org/10.1371/journal.pmed.1000097.

Monton-Subias, S. and A. Hernando 2018. Modern colonialism, eurocentrism and historical archaeology: Some engendered thoughts. *European journal of archaeology* 21(3):455–471. doi.org/10.1017/eaa. 2017.83.

O'Connor, S., D. Bulbeck and J. Meyer 2018. *The archaeology of Sulawesi: Current research on the Pleistocene to the historic period.* Terra Australis 48. ANU Press, Canberra. doi.org/10.22459/TA48. 11.2018.

Petticrew, M. and H. Roberts 2006. *Systematic reviews in the social sciences: A practical guide.* 1st edition. Blackwell, Malden, Massachusetts. doi.org/10.1002/9780470754887.

Pickering, C. and J. Byrne 2013. The benefits of publishing systematic quantitative literature reviews for PhD candidates and other early-career researchers. *Higher Education Research & Development* 33(3):534–548. doi.org/10.1080/07294360.2013.841651.

Rogers, R.A. 2006. From cultural exchange to transculturation: A review and reconceptualization of cultural appropriation. *Communication Theory* 16(4):474–503. doi.org/10.1111/j.1468-2885.2006. 00277.x.

Shugart, H.A. 1997. Counterhegemonic acts: Appropriation as a feminist rhetorical strategy. *Quarterly Journal of Speech* 83(2):210–229. doi.org/10.1080/00335639709384181.

Smith, C. and H. Burke 2006. Glass ceilings, glass parasols and Australian academic archaeology. *Australian Archaeology* 62(1):13–25. doi.org/10.1080/03122417.2006.11681826.

Stefanoudis, P.V., W.Y. Licuanan, T.H. Morrison, S. Talma, J. Veitayaki and L. Woodall 2021. Turning the tide of parachute science. *Current Biology* 31(4):R184–R185. doi.org/10.1016/j.cub.2021.01.029.

Ulm, S., G. Mate, C. Dalley and S. Nichols 2013. A working profile: The changing face of professional archaeology in Australia. *Australian Archaeology* 76(1):34–43. doi.org/10.1080/03122417.2013.116 81963.

Zainuddin, K. 2019. 3D modelling for rock art documentation using lightweight multispectral camera. *The International Archives of the Photogrammetry, Remote Sensing and Spatial Information Sciences* 42-2/W9:787–793. doi.org/10.5194/isprs-archives-XLII-2-W9-787-2019.

Zavala, M. 2013. What do we mean by decolonizing research strategies? Lessons from decolonizing, Indigenous research projects in New Zealand and Latin America. *Decolonization: Indigeneity, Education and Society* 2(1):55–71.

Contributors

Mary Blyth

Miniaga Traditional Owner and retired from Kakadu National Park, Kakadu Hwy, Jabiru, Northern Territory, 0886, Australia. mary.blyth4@bigpond.com.

Anne Clarke

Department of Archaeology, School of Philosophical and Historical Inquiry, University of Sydney, New South Wales, 2006, Australia. annie.clarke@sydney.edu.au.

ORCID: 0000-0002-2273-510X

Noelene Cole

College of Arts, Society and Education, James Cook University, Cairns, Queensland, 4811, Australia. noelene@a-ncole.com.

ORCID: 0000-0001-7897-9974

Ursula K. Frederick

Centre for Creative and Cultural Research, University of Canberra, Australian Capital Territory, 2617, Australia. Ursula.Frederick@canberra.edu.au.

ORCID: 0000-0001-8132-0310

Joakim Goldhahn

Rock Art Australia Ian Potter Kimberley Chair, Centre for Rock Art Research + Management, University of Western Australia, Perth, Western Australia, 6009, Australia. joakim.goldhahn@uwa.edu.au.

ORCID: 0000-0003-4640-8784

Jake R. Goodes

Parks Victoria, Halls Gap, Victoria, 3381, Australia. jake.goodes@parks.vic.gov.au.

Robert G. Gunn

Independent researcher, Lake Lonsdale, Victoria, 3381, Australia. gunnb@activ8.net.au.

ORCID: 0000-0002-7565-8697

Sam Harper

Centre for Rock Art Research + Management, University of Western Australia, Perth, Western Australia, 6009, Australia. sam.harper@uwa.edu.au.

ORCID: 0000-0002-1590-2387

Jillian Huntley

Griffith Centre for Social and Cultural Research, Griffith University, Queensland, 4222, Australia. j.huntley@griffith.edu.au.

ORCID: 0000-0002-9701-9925

Andrea Jalandoni

Place, Evolution and Rock Art Heritage Unit, Griffith Centre for Social and Cultural Research and Australian Research Centre for Human Evolution, Griffith University, Queensland, 4222, Australia. a.jalandoni@griffith.edu.au.

ORCID: 0000-0002-4821-7183

Iain G. Johnston

Return of Cultural Heritage, Australian Institute of Aboriginal and Torres Strait Islander Studies, Acton, ACT, 2601, Australia. iain.johnston@aiatsis.gov.au.

ORCID: 0000-0003-3722-2128

Jeffrey Lee

Djok Traditional Owner, Kakadu National Park, Kakadu Hwy, Jabiru, Northern Territory, 0886, Australia.

Susan Lowish

School of Culture and Communication, Faculty of Arts, University of Melbourne, Melbourne, Victoria, 3010, Australia. susan.lowish@unimelb.edu.au.

ORCID: 0000-0002-8012-3718

Melissa Marshall

Nulungu Research Institute, University of Notre Dame, Broome, Western Australia, 6725, Australia. melissa.marshall@nd.edu.au. ORCID: 0000-0002-3431-9007

Kadeem May

Kakadu National Park, Kakadu Hwy, Jabiru, Northern Territory, 0886, Australia. Kadeem.May2@environment.gov.au.

Sally K. May

School of Humanities, University of Adelaide, Adelaide, South Australia, 5005, and adjunct Griffith Centre for Social and Cultural Research, Griffith University, Queensland, 4222, Australia. sally.may@adelaide.edu.au. ORCID: 0000-0003-2805-023X

Jo McDonald

Centre for Rock Art Research + Management, University of Western Australia, Perth, Western Australia, 6009, Australia. jo.mcdonald@uwa.edu.au. ORCID: 0000- 0002-2701-7406

Ken Mulvaney

Rio Tinto, PO Box 842, Karratha, 6714, Western Australia and Centre for Rock Art Research + Management, University of Western Australia, Perth, Western Australia, 6009, Australia. Ken.Mulvaney@riotinto.com. ORCID: 0000-0003-3713-4312

Gabrielle O'Loughlin

Retired from Kakadu National Park, Kakadu Hwy, Jabiru, Northern Territory, 0886, Australia. gabrielle.oloughlin@gmail.com.

Sven Ouzman

Archaeology and Centre for Rock Art Research + Management, University of Western Australia, Perth, Western Australia, 6009, Australia and Rock Art Research Institute, School of Geography, Archaeology and Environmental Studies, Origins Centre, University of the Witwatersrand, South Africa. sven.ouzman@uwa.edu.au. ORCID: 0000-0002-9379-2996

June Ross

Archaeology, Faculty of Humanities, Arts, Social Sciences and Education, University of New England, Armidale, New South Wales, 2351, Australia. jross4@une.edu.au. ORCID: 0000-0001-6552-0531

Claire Smith

College of Humanities, Arts and Social Sciences, Flinders University, Adelaide, South Australia, 5042, Australia. claire.smith@flinders.edu.au. ORCID: 0000-0001-9028-6687

Mike A. Smith

Archaeology, College of Humanities, Arts and Social Sciences, Flinders University, Adelaide, South Australia, 5042, and National Museum of Australia, Canberra, Australian Capital Territory, 2601, Australia. mike.smith@nma.gov.au. ORCID: 0000-0002-6177-8217

Paul S.C. Taçon

Place, Evolution and Rock Art Heritage Unit, Griffith Centre for Social and Cultural Research and Australian Research Centre for Human Evolution, Griffith University, Queensland, 4222, Australia. p.tacon@griffith.edu.au. ORCID: 0000-0002-0280-4366

Peter Veth

Centre for Rock Art Research + Management, University of Western Australia, Perth, Western Australia, 6009, Australia. peter.veth@uwa.edu.au. ORCID: 0000-0002-1717-6390